TRACING COMMON THEMES
Comparative Courses in the Study of Religion

SCHOLARS PRESS
Studies in the Humanities

Suicide

John Donne
William A. Clebsch, editor

Tragedy as a Critique of Virtue:
The Novel and Ethical Reflection

John D. Barbour

Lyric Apocalypse: Reconstruction
in Ancient and Modern Poetry

John W. Erwin

The Unusable Past: America's Puritan
Tradition, 1830 to 1930

Jan C. Dawson

The Visual Arts and Christianity
in America: The Colonial Period through
the Nineteenth Century

John Dillenberger

Chaos to Cosmos: Studies in Biblical
Patterns of Creation

Susan Niditch

Melville and the Gods

William Hamilton

The Character of the Euripidean Hippolytos:
An Ethno-Psychoanalytical Study

George Devereux

To See Ourselves As Others See Us:
Christians, Jews, "Others" in Late Antiquity

Jacob Neusner,
Ernest S. Frerichs, editors

Civitas: Religious Interpretations of
the City

Peter Hawkins, editor

The Riddle of Liberty:
Emerson on Alienation, Freedom, and Obedience

Lou Ann Lange

Why Persimmons and Other Poems

Stanley Romaine Hopper

Gregor Sebba: Lectures on Creativity

Helen Sebba,
Hendrikus Boers, editors

Beyond the Classics? Essays in Religious
Studies and Liberal Education

Frank E. Reynolds,
Sheryl L. Burkhalter, editors

Teaching the Introductory Course
in Religious Studies: A Sourcebook

Mark Juergensmeyer, editor

Tracing Common Themes: Comparative Courses
in the Study of Religion

John B. Carman,
Steven P. Hopkins, editors

TRACING COMMON THEMES
Comparative Courses
in the Study of Religion

edited by

John B. Carman
Steven P. Hopkins

Scholars Press
Atlanta, Georgia

TRACING COMMON THEMES
Comparative Courses
in the Study of Religions

edited by

John B. Carman
Steven P. Hopkins

BL41
T73
1991

©1991
Scholars Press

Library of Congress Cataloging in Publication Data

Tracing Common Themes : comparative courses in the study of religion /
    edited by John B. Carman, Steven P. Hopkins.
    p. cm. — (Scholars Press studies in the humanities ; no. 16)
    Includes bibliographical references.
    ISBN 1-55540-563-0 (alk. paper). — ISBN 1-5540-564-9 (pbk. :
    alk. paper)
    1. Religion—Study and teaching. I. Carman, John Braisted.
II. Hopkins, Steven P. III. Series : Scholars Press studies in the
humanities series ; no. 16.
BL41.T73 1991
291'.07—dc20
                                   91-34265
                                   CIP

Printed in the United States of America
on acid-free paper

IN MEMORIAM
Kendall Wayne Folkert
March 5, 1942 - October 29, 1985
Critical Scholar and Imaginative Teacher
Generous Colleague and Loyal Friend

THE BERKELEY-CHICAGO-HARVARD PROGRAM: RELIGIOUS STUDIES IN THE LIBERAL ARTS

This volume is a product of the Berkeley-Chicago-Harvard Program, a five-year series of institutes, workshops and related projects aimed at enlarging the role and scope of religious studies in the undergraduate liberal arts curriculum. The objective was to collect resources to assist teachers of undergraduate courses in religious studies—especially those teachers whose training has been limited to only one religious tradition—and to provide reflection on the changing nature of the liberal arts curriculum, and the role that religious studies plays within it.

These two objectives are linked. The basic courses in religion have within recent years begun to move away from the periphery of the liberal arts to which they have been banished for over a century. Increasingly they have come to occupy a more central location in the college curriculum. In many schools the "world religions" and "introduction to religion" courses serve as integrators for the humanities and the social sciences. These courses give an overview of the history of world civilization, provide a window on the cultural dimensions of global politics, and supply a way of perceiving many of the modern quests for personal meaning. This three-volume sourcebook and other projects related to the Berkeley-Chicago-Harvard Program were created to facilitate this new and expansive vision of religious studies in the liberal arts.

The Berkeley-Chicago-Harvard Program was funded by grants from the National Endowment for the Humanities and was sponsored by the Office for Programs in Comparative Religion at the Graduate Theological Union, Berkeley; the History of Religions Program in the Divinity School of the University of Chicago; and the Center for the Study of World Religions at Harvard Divinity School. The codirectors were John Carman (Harvard), Mark Juergensmeyer (Berkeley), and Frank Reynolds (Chicago).

Contents

Contributors ...vii

Acknowledgments ...ix

    I   *Thematic Comparison in Teaching the History of Religion*
        JOHN B. CARMAN AND STEVEN P. HOPKINS ...1

   II   *A Thematic Course in the Study of Religion*
        KENDALL W. FOLKERT, EDITED BY JOHN E. CORT ...19

  III   *A Mega-Theme for an Introductory Course in Religious Studies*
        FREDERICK J. STRENG ...37

  IV   *Pilgrimage as a Thematic Introduction to the Comparative Study of Religion*
        RICHARD R. NIEBUHR ...51

   V   *Pilgrimage Out West*
        JOHN STRATTON HAWLEY ...65

  VI   *'Healing' as a Theme in Teaching the Study of Religion in a Liberal Arts Setting*
        LINDA BARNES ...81

 VII   *The Strange in the Midst of the Familiar: A Thematic Seminar on Sacrifice*
        MICHAEL D. SWARTZ ...101

VIII   *The Symbol of Destruction and the Destruction of Symbol: Sacrifice as a Thematic Course Focus*
        WILLIAM R. DARROW ...113

  IX   *Mysticism: A Popular and Problematic Course*
        FREDERICK J. STRENG ...127

Contents

X   *Spiritual Practices in Historical Perspective*
CAROL ZALESKI ...139

XI   *Understanding the Self: East and West—An Interdisciplinary Study of a Theme*
FREDERICK J. STRENG ...155

XII   *Bourgeois Relativism and the Comparative Study of the Self*
LEE H. YEARLEY ...165

XIII   *Scriptures and Classics*
WILLIAM A. GRAHAM ...179

XIV   *Words, Truth, and Power*
MIRIAM LEVERING ...199

XV   *Religion and Gender: A Comparative Approach*
MIRIAM LEVERING ...219

XVI   *Women in African-American Religions: The Caribbean and South America*
KAREN MCCARTHY BROWN ...235

XVII   *Teaching Comparative Religious Ethics*
ROBIN W. LOVIN AND FRANK E. REYNOLDS ...249

XVIII   *Comparative Ethics*
MARK JUERGENSMEYER ...263

XIX   *Creativity and Art: Artists, Shamans, and Cosmology*
THOMAS V. PETERSON ...273

XX   *Better Questions: Introduction to the History of Religion and Art*
RICHARD M. CARP ...287

XXI   *Concluding Reflections: The Fulcrum of Comparison*
JOHN B. CARMAN AND STEVEN P. HOPKINS ...301

Contributors

LINDA BARNES
Ph.D. Candidate in the Study of Religion
Harvard University

KAREN MCCARTHY BROWN
Professor of Sociology
Drew University

JOHN B. CARMAN
Parkman Professor of Divinity
and Professor of Comparative Religion
Harvard Divinity School

JOHN E. CORT
Lecturer in the Study of Religion
Harvard University

RICHARD M. CARP
Vice President for Academic Affairs
Kansas City Art Institute

WILLIAM R. DARROW
Associate Professor of Religion and
History
Williams College

KENDALL W. FOLKERT
Late Professor in the Study of Religion
Central Michigan University

WILLIAM A. GRAHAM
Professor of the History of Religions and
Islamic Studies
Director, Center for Middle Eastern
Studies
Harvard University

JOHN STRATTON HAWLEY
Professor of Comparative Religion–
Hinduism and South Asian Studies
Chair, Department of Religion
Barnard College
Columbia University

STEVEN P. HOPKINS
Ph.D. Candidate in the Study of Religion
Harvard University

MARK JUERGENSMEYER
Dean of the School of Hawaiian, Asian,
and Pacific Studies
University of Hawaii at Manoa

MIRIAM LEVERING
Associate Professor in the Religions and
Philosophies of China and Japan
University of Tennessee

ROBIN W. LOVIN
Associate Professor of Ethics and Society
University of Chicago

RICHARD R. NIEBUHR
Hollis Professor of Divinity
Harvard Divinity School

THOMAS V. PETERSON
Professor of Religious Studies
Alfred University

FRANK E. REYNOLDS
Professor of History of Religion, Buddhist
Studies
University of Chicago

FREDERICK J. STRENG
Professor of History of Religion, Buddhist
Studies
Southern Methodist University

MICHAEL D. SWARTZ
Assistant Professor of Jewish Studies
University of Virginia

LEE H. YEARLEY
Professor of Christian Thought
Stanford University

CAROL ZALESKI
Assistant Professor of Religion and Biblical
Literature
Smith College

Acknowledgments

We should like to thank the many people who participated in the project behind this volume and in the preparation of the volume itself. This includes the co-directors of this project, Mark Juergensmeyer and Frank Reynolds, and the co-director of the Harvard Institute, William Graham, as well as the participants in the planning conferences, the twenty-five college teachers, the Harvard faculty, and the special lecturers who participated in the 1988 Harvard Summer Institute, and the contributors of essays in this volume. In particular, we want to thank John Cort for skillfully pulling together into one essay the various drafts of the paper Kendall Folkert was working on at the time of his death.

We are grateful to all who have given secretarial and editorial assistance: to Helen Schultz and Andrew Rasanen for the earlier stages, and to Lisa Hammer, who has carried an additional burden in completing the volume after Steven Hopkins' departure for India. We have benefited from the critical reading of our chapters by Ineke Carman, John Cort, William Graham, and Lawrence Sullivan. Dr. Sullivan also allowed us to continue to use the facilities of the Center for the Study of World Religions. We want also to acknowledge the general editorial supervision of the staff at Berkeley, George McKinley, Amelia Rudolf, and Yvonne Vowels, and the editors at Scholars Press.

Introduction: The Lens of Thematic Comparison

JOHN B. CARMAN AND STEVEN P. HOPKINS

The Development of this Project

The essays in this volume represent one of three approaches described in the common Preface to all three volumes. All are the fruit of a five-year project originally entitled, "The Study of Religion and Liberal Education: Towards a Global Perspective." The Chicago volume discusses general issues in the relation of religious studies to the liberal arts while the Berkeley volume focuses on problems in teaching the introductory course in the study of religion. The approach of this volume stands in between those of the companion volumes. Most of the essays are presentations of and reflections on specific undergraduate courses of a particular kind: the comparison of different religious traditions by focusing on a particular theme. The central issue with which all these essays deal, in very different ways, is both practical and theoretical, for thematic comparison has been championed by some as the very heart of a globally comprehensive study of religion but rejected by others as an inadequate and outmoded approach. That debate among scholars in religious studies has its parallels in both past and contemporary discussions in other academic fields on the value of comparison. In most cases the theoretical issues in this book have been approached as questions of pedagogy: what do we teach about a vast and complicated subject, and how do we teach it?

This project is the second cooperative venture joining, but not limited to, faculty members related to the Graduate Theological Union and the University of California at Berkeley, the History of Religions Department

1

in the University of Chicago Divinity School, and the Center for the Study of World Religions at Harvard University. The first project, like the present one, was supported by the National Endowment for the Humanities and also received a grant from the Henry W. Luce Foundation. That five year exploration of comparative ethics included conferences and new courses at each of the three institutions. The two essays on comparative ethics in this volume both report and reflect on some of the fruit of that project, which sought to draw together scholars in the comparative study of religion and religious ethics, as well as others in various areas of the social sciences and of theology, and to focus on a neglected interface of our work.

Planning for this second project began in Berkeley in the summer of 1985, when we divided into three sub-groups, each of which would pursue one of the three approaches. Choosing thematic comparison as the central focus of the Harvard sub-group was somewhat arbitrary, and there has continued to be a sharing of personnel and ideas between the groups.

Through its three summer institutes this second project involved twenty-five teachers each summer from a great variety of colleges and universities. Most of them had several years experience offering courses in the study of religion to undergraduates. The 1988 Institute at Harvard, directed by John Carman and William Graham, was the third and last. Like the others, it included in its six-week session lectures, presentations, and discussion among the faculty and participants; individual and small group projects whose results were presented to the whole group, and several special evening lectures. We linked the Harvard Institute to the Berkeley and Chicago Institutes by inviting as guest lecturers their directors (Mark Juergensmeyer and Frank Reynolds) and some of their faculty. We also used the *Sourcebook*, which included earlier versions of some of the essays in this volume and in the other two volumes. We deliberately chose to include college teachers with specializations in many different fields and areas of the world, even when some fell outside the academic confines of the study of religion, in order that their diverse competence would enrich our discussion of comparative themes.

In our morning plenary sessions, we involved many Harvard faculty members in the study of religion. We concentrated on two themes that have been successfully used for courses at Harvard during the past decade: Pilgrimage and Scripture. The Pilgrimage theme, which we took up first, has a number of advantages. First, it involves visible action and is often one of the more public and even dramatic aspects of religious life. Second, that action is often interpreted as a metaphor for an inward or spiritual journey, which sometimes accompanies the external pilgrimage and sometimes replaces it. Third, pilgrimage is an aspect of religion that not only can be seen by outsiders but also to some extent can be shared by them. Finally, the wide range of pilgrimage practices and metaphorical interpretations of the "path" or "way" in various religious traditions provides a good test case for considering both similarities and differences among those traditions.

The second theme, Scripture, when understood as a survey of sacred books in different religious traditions, is a staple of introductory courses, but our aim was different: to look at the different *concepts* of "scripture" and the diverse *functions* of sacred writings and utterances in people's lives. This theme is more controversial than the first, and certainly more theoretical, for it immediately raises questions, not only about the nature of "scripture," but also about the nature of "sacredness." Hard questions must also be faced about the relation between religions with scriptures and those apparently without them, and about the distinctions between texts considered sacred and those considered important but not sacred. Some participants criticized our postponement of this more theoretical topic until the second half of the Institute, arguing that we should have started out with the hard question of definition. That postponement was deliberate. Not only did we think it wiser to begin with more concrete subject matter involving ritual action, but we also hoped that the more explicit debate on theoretical issues in the second three weeks would benefit from our having become acquainted with one another in the first three weeks. Both themes were intended to challenge participants to discover the possibilities and ponder the problems of these two themes, as well as to continue personal reflection on the past or future use of other themes for comparative courses.

As a result of our experience throughout the project and especially during the Harvard Institute we have added several themes to those chosen at the first planning conference. Most of them have been treated twice, in order better to demonstrate the great variety of classroom situations and instructors' choices in developing a theme. The course on Pilgrimage described by Richard Niebuhr, for example, was taught by three faculty members at Harvard and was taken by some Divinity School students as well as a larger number of undergraduates. In contrast, Jack Hawley points out, his course on Pilgrimage was taught to undergraduates at a state university three thousand miles from Harvard. Two of the contributors to the volume, Michael Swartz and Thomas

Peterson, participated in the Harvard Summer Institute, while Richard Carp participated in the Berkeley Institute. Several contributors were part of the Chicago or Berkeley sub-groups, including William Darrow, Lee Yearley, Karen McCarthy Brown, Robin Lovin, Frank Reynolds, and Mark Juergensmeyer.

Problems in Choosing a Theme

We begin with a critique of the whole comparative enterprise, as well as a constructive proposal for a different kind of comparison, by the late Kendall Folkert, to whom this volume is dedicated. Ken Folkert had participated in our first planning session in Berkeley in June 1985 and had written some drafts of his essay just before his death in India that October. He was very concerned that our project might simply perpetuate a lot of widespread ideas in the study of religion, whereas we ought to be identifying and dealing critically with them. These ideas range from the general notion of "religions," so often present in our survey courses, and the more subtle ambiguities of a phrase like "world religions," to implicit taxonomies in our descriptions and analyses of religious traditions. He was concerned that the choice of topics for this volume represented a "hodge-podge of courses." This might reflect outdated notions of "comparative religion": religion pointing to a single goal, religions being ranked according to their expression of the same single truth, or different aspects of religion being ranked as more or less valuable. Alternatively, old conceptions might be rejected without substituting new ones, leaving the choice of theme to some personal predilection.

Ken Folkert's course proposal focuses on the human life-cycle as an example of one of two major types of thematic approach. The other one is a study of conceptual themes within a tradition, such as deity or salvific process. His approach takes up "matters of practice which may have been regularized and discerned in the tradition's literature, but which are more frequently *not* the subject of significant speculation or expressive literature." His course is one that emphasizes religious actions in rites of passage and the calendar (a structuring of time), and then goes on to relate these ritually related practices and ideas to central features of three religious traditions. The course's emphasis on psycho-physical liminality affirms that "the simple existence of oneself, as a body, as something separate from and yet necessarily related to other things, as a being thing, is a *mysterium tremendum*, a pan-human experience."

The major effort in which Folkert wanted to enlist both us and our students is a search for a "pan-human experience" not already defined by our theoretical starting point. He criticized our tendency to retain outmoded habits of thought and our failure to develop a new anthropology for comparative study. Though the essay is unfinished we believe that Ken's thoughts are crucial to our discussion of thematic comparison. Perhaps the essays that follow still exhibit the stance he criticized. Certainly they struggle with the issues he has raised.

The next essay, the first of three contributions by Frederick Streng, deals with a theme central to his teaching and writing, what he rightly calls the "mega-theme" of "Ways of Ultimate Transformation." This is so large a theme that some might regard it as synonymous with the whole of religion, and indeed, he has used the variations on this theme as a way of characterizing major types of religion. "Way" is both a common feature of all human life and the widest metaphorical meaning of pilgrimage. "Ultimate Transformation" has been called "salvation," "total liberation," and "harmonious living." We might note here that salvation has specifically religious connotations in English though its equivalent in the Germanic languages, *Heil*, also includes the connotation of the English cognates "hale," "healing," and "health." Even though "Ways of Ultimate Transformation" is a broad theme, it is only one of several possible approaches to being religious. Hindu religion, for example, can itself be divided between *dharma,* the ritual and moral norms for maintaining and enhancing both physical and spiritual well being, and *marga,* the "ways" to a goal that transcends the world in its present state, ways that aim at liberation from bondage to worldly existence. *Dharma* in this classical Hindu sense has analogies in many other forms of religion that assume the basic rightness of the world order and see religious practice as a way of keeping it so. In fact, many religious traditions emphasize in different proportions both maintaining the world order and following a path from an unsatisfactory world to a state of peace, happiness, or salvation. It is in the latter kind of religion that the theme of personal transformation is so important.

By a very different route than Ken Folkert's, Fred Streng has in this course and in his various publications raised fundamental questions about defining religion. He has brought a Buddhist conception into Western thinking about religion, for Buddhists reject the Hindu notion of a substantial order of the cosmos, understanding *dharma* both as a way (*marga*) out of suffering existence and as the truth of insubstantiality that necessitates this way. For both scholars the choice of a theme involves decisions that are practical tests of our particular conceptions of religion and reminders of our common problems in understanding religion.

Dimensions of Ritual Life

The first pair of thematic essays deal with Pilgrimage, a topic that is relatively recent in its use as an introduction to world religions, but which has a number of advantages for that purpose, as both Richard Niebuhr and Jack Hawley point out. For one thing, it is evidently present in different cultures in recognizably similar forms. This does not mean that all pilgrimages are of the same type, even within the same religious tradition. The English word we use comes from the Latin *peregrinatio*, literally a "wandering around." This refers to the penitential journeys of the Irish Christian monks, in which the emphasis was on their self-imposed exile from the familiar homeland. The content of Christian pilgrimages also included journeys to sacred places, both trips to the Holy Land emulating the Jewish "going up" to Jerusalem and visits to the tombs of Christian saints and martyrs. The hardships of the journey and the satisfaction of reaching the goal are incorporated into the rich metaphorical meanings of Christian pilgrimage.

In many religious traditions, the theme of pilgrimage includes both actual physical journeying and the idea of a spiritual journey. These are sometimes combined, but they are occasionally radically separated, as in the English Puritan repudiation of medieval Catholic pilgrimage while accepting pilgrimage, in John Bunyan's classic, as a primary metaphor for spiritual journeying to the Heavenly City. Within religious traditions there are different directions taken in generalizing about pilgrimage. At one extreme, perhaps, is the Hindu custom of replicating several mountains and rivers in other places, and in Banaras, incorporating miniature versions of other holy places within the holy city, so that one may derive the specific benefits of visiting all these places while journeying around and within Banaras. At the other extreme is the Muslim insistence on the absolute singularity of the *hajj*. This term is used only for the pilgrimage to Mecca during the appropriate month. It does not apply to visits to Mecca or Medina at other times, and another word (*dua*) is used for journeys to saints' tombs. Our use of the word pilgrimage in a broad sense should remind us that, as with so many other comparative categories, we are making Christian pilgrimage rather than the Islamic *hajj* our point of departure.

The interplay between pilgrimage and other aspects of religious life is another important advantage of this theme, especially if our aim is *introduction*, guiding students into reflection on the breadth and depth of human religious life. The physical and metaphysical journey of pilgrimage are also points of connection between the more evidently religious and apparently more secular aspects of culture. Sightseeing and mountain climbing are examples of secular pilgrimage. Yet a work like René Daumal's *Mount Analogue* consciously uses such "secular" pilgrimages as metonymies of the inner spiritual pilgrimage.

Next we have included an essay on Healing, a theme that like Pilgrimage is both act and metaphor: an elaborate ritual for physical cleansing and restoration of health and a basic metaphor for the spiritual life in many religious traditions. Linda Barnes' essay is distinctive in referring to three different courses that were offered at Harvard at about the same time; she also consulted with other scholars who have offered courses on healing.[1] Since this topic is still unusual it was somewhat accidental that these courses were taught at about the same time. At our planning meeting in 1985 we thought this was a theme that might become increasingly important in religious studies as more and more connections develop between medical anthropology, the healing professions in North America, and the growing emphasis on physical as well as spiritual healing in American religious groups from a variety of traditions. Whether or not that proves to be the case, it is worth noting that two significant volumes of essays have appeared since 1985 concerned with this theme.[2]

We certainly need not be forced by some development outside the academy to introduce a new course on a particular theme. The merits of a particular theme need to be assessed. It is certainly appropriate, however, for our teaching to be sensitive to this significant contemporary development in which the prominence of the healing professions in modern society and the popularity of counter-cultural alternatives to modern medicine are pushing religious people as well as others to re-examine our fundamental notions of health and healing.

Linda Barnes ꞏ ꞏtes Charles Long's suggestion that "healing itself . . . can serve as an analogy to the process of education." A parallel suggestion is made at the beginning of Lawrence Sullivan's Introduction to

[1] One of these was taught by Lamin O. Sanneh, then at Harvard Divinity School and now Professor of the History of Religions and World Christianity, Yale University. He makes an interesting distinction, based on present-day African usage, between "religious healing" and "faith healing." One of the remarkable features of this contrast is that from the standpoint of "faith healing," "religious healing" appears more "magical" than religious.

[2] Ronald L. Numbers and Darrel W. Amundsen, eds., *Caring and Curing: Health and Medicine in the Western Religious Traditions* (New York: Macmillan, 1986); and Lawrence E. Sullivan, ed., *Healing and Restoring: Health and Medicine in the World's Religious Traditions* (New York: Macmillan, 1989).

Healing and Restoring: "If illness is a part of the human condition, so is the questioning that accompanies it. . . . Could the peculiar way in which humans experience illness have sparked their very capacity to inquire?"[3] The two sides of the religious response to illness are the efforts to cure and the struggle to come to terms with what cannot be cured, with a human wholeness and well-being that seem irretrievably lost. It is possible to link both sides to the most elemental as well as the most profound activity of the questing and inquiring mind. Indeed, the two sides of the human response are often considered religious (and/or faithful) to the extent that extraordinary or superhuman powers are brought to bear on the illness and the perspective of the ill person is changed. Even if the modern educator keeps any thought of such traditional divine powers far away, there is often an effort to discover some hidden power within the mind that will make possible a new perspective on reality and a new capacity to deal with it. The theme of healing brings the educational process into conjunction with religion and medicine; this is surely a good reason for its use in making connections among the separated fields of the modern academy.

The approaches of all these courses on Healing seem to reverse the initial problem of a comparative course: the question of the appropriateness of a Western religious cultural category in discerning meaningful patterns in quite different religious traditions. In this case, what is no longer a religious category in the modern West, healing, is found in many non-Western cultures to be "religious" (i.e., to be similar to what in Western scholarship is considered religious). That comparison easily extends to forms of Western healing outside of the medical establishment. The frequent interplay of the physical and the spiritual in non-Western definitions of healing challenges the modern Western concept with which the comparison began; that is, it challenges the adequacy of the biomedical model for understanding the broader dimensions of healing in our own culture. This is a special illustration of the frequent "mirror effect" of comparative study. In seeking to understand the different religious meanings of others, we start to look differently at ourselves, both as modern Western intellectuals and as participants in particular religious communities.

Treating the theme of Sacrifice, as Michael Swartz remarks, is an exercise in *Verfremdung*, in Brecht's sense of "making the strange familiar and the familiar strange." Sacrifice is one of the most omnipresent of themes and conceptual categories in religion as well as in religious studies, yet it

---

[3] op cit., 1-2.

is also one of the least understood and least nuanced by scholarly inquiry. In the West we have reflected relatively little on the importance this theme has had in the creation of a Reformation religious sensibility which still, in Michael Swartz's words, "deeply informs our modern views of religion." The more we enter the rich conceptual and existential worlds of what we are calling "sacrifice," however, the more ambiguous and elusive the term becomes. The familiar becomes alien; the banal becomes intriguing, and the simple becomes multivalent. William Darrow focuses on the polyvalence of the term in his course, alerting students right away to the problem of translation: if we select terms from other traditions to denote sacrifice, i.e., a term which in its strict etymological sense means "making sacred" (from the Latin *sacrificium: sacer + facere*), then we generate an array of meanings, overlapping at some points, diverging at others. We would then create a charged semantic field that would show the problems in trying to give a simple, univocal meaning to this important category in the comparative study of religion. As Bill Darrow observes, the Indo-Iranian *yajna* yields the sense of "worship"; the semitic *qurban* emphasizes "drawing near"; the Greek *thuein* indexes the smoke of the sacrifice uniting the earthly and heavenly realms; the Chinese term *jisi* alludes to "display"; even the German word *Opfer* contains the "crucial intersection of the ideas of victim and offering."

Michael Swartz notes that the theme of sacrifice draws to itself many sub-themes, which students must grapple with, such as ritual action in general, sacred space, purity, anthropomorphism, and the links between myth and ritual. Bill Darrow speaks of the many sub-types of sacrifice itself: tribute, praise, thanksgiving, sustaining the world, supplication, catharsis, purification, communal celebration, and expiation. What at first sight seemed to be a single, clear cut issue, the one, "original" type of sacrifice, becomes a cluster of issues, a subject area without easy closure. We are certainly made aware that something called sacrifice exists, and is symbolically and viscerally a most powerful element in the religious life of many peoples; yet we are loath to limit its semantic densities, the valences of its meaning. We become accustomed to seeing a charged field of meanings as it were in one glance. Our focus becomes plural. "There is an irony here," Bill Darrow remarks, "in that the category remains, the phenomenon exists, even if it is one that has been constituted for the most parochial reasons and whose original or purest form cannot be agreed upon."

Both articles on sacrifice uncover one potential of comparison: it can reveal distinctive differences within what has been taken too naively as a single concept while at the same time it maintains the utility of the concept in different cultural settings. Sacrifice holds difference and similarity together in tension. One other great advantage of this theme, as articulated by our authors, is that students are immediately confronted with the visceral and physical elements of sacrifice. Both Swartz and Darrow recommend creative use of ethnographic films which thrust us into the arena of ritual action, indeed at times into scenes of sheer physical horror and repugnance that bridge the worlds of thought and action, theology and praxis.

Exploring the Interior Life

Mysticism is a topic that some people interpret so broadly as to be virtually synonymous with religion, while others consider mysticism as an exceptional form of all religious traditions. Even its exceptional status, moreover, can be positively viewed as evidence of great saintliness, or treated with great suspicion as a sign of heresy. There are also some scholars who see mysticism as especially characteristic of oriental religion but an aberrant development in the three Western monotheistic traditions. Yet it is a Western term going back to the Greeks that we use for this category, and the Jewish and Islamic equivalents to Christian mysticism are easier for us to identify than it is for us to know whether all or nothing of oriental religious traditions should be called "mysticism." It is with full recognition of the theoretical problem of definition that Fred Streng begins his essay. In point of fact, courses in mysticism are among the most common thematic courses that are offered, and if this turns out to be a topic that is not so universal as has been thought—or has to be reformulated to become properly cross-cultural— then surely our volume should recognize both the general problem and this particular instance.

Carol Zaleski's article on the theme of Spiritual Practices makes us aware of another very important aspect of this topic. The hard-won distinction between study within a religious community and academic study of religion may never have been as important to college students as it has been to their professors. Moreover, as she observes, the comparative study of religion has itself been greatly responsible for existential interest in the mystical traditions of the world and the "proliferation of spiritual techniques in contemporary Western society." The "quest for spiritual disciplines in our society," Carol Zaleski claims, "mirrors and runs parallel to the recent history of that spiritual quest (or quest for understanding) which we call comparative study of religion." Indeed, courses on mysticism are one place where the demand is voiced that to be faithful to the insights of all mystical traditions, meditational practice should accompany theoretical reflection. American academic practice varies widely in this regard. State institutions often differ from private colleges. Moreover, engaging in or excluding such practice from the classroom is often related to the teacher's (or department's) answer to the question of whether there are genuinely different mystical traditions or one underlying mystical path. Most of us in our teaching confront this kind of question sooner or later, even if we have never thought of offering a course on mysticism, so it is helpful to discuss a course in which that question can become explicit. Carol Zaleski directly addresses these issues of study and practice, not by presenting a theoretical concept of mysticism but by introducing students to meditation. The course focuses on what people *do* in a variety of historical and traditional contexts. What emerges is the same complex vision outlined in our discussion of that other familiar topic, sacrifice. She concludes:

> The value for comparative study of a term like "spiritual discipline" does not stand or fall on our ability to develop a fixed, univocal definition that will always be valid cross-culturally. The inherent ambiguities in our terminology give the course an open-ended and unfinished character which I find at once limiting and intellectually liberating.

Fred Streng's course on the Self is an excellent example of a course that deals with a central religious and philosophical issue. This is an issue that has been a point of fundamental distinction in South Asia between Buddhism, on the one hand, and Hinduism and Jainism, on the other. In his way of treating the question, however, it also becomes a fine cross-disciplinary study, where modern neuro-physiology and philosophy are brought into conversation with several traditional views of the self. Such a course may also prove to be a point where the objectivity of the academic approach can actually aid rather than discourage the existential decision that is posed by the question: who am I?

We shall save our discussion of Lee Yearley's course for the concluding chapter; it is important in lifting up the contemporary issue of relativism and in giving a candid self-portrait of a teacher changing his mind and redesigning a "successful" course.

Old Themes Reconsidered

Both Miriam Levering's and William Graham's essays deal with new courses that are the fruit of recent reflections on one of the oldest comparative topics: Scripture. A century ago this was not so much a separate topic as a super-topic, the assumed common structure of all the "great religions." When Max Müller succeeded in assembling an impressive array of English translations of The Sacred Books of the East, he assumed such a common category of scripture and further assumed that the most essential and exalted elements of each of these religions could clearly be discerned in its scripture.

There has been growing recognition that scripture functions quite differently for different religious communities, and there has been some treatment in phenomenological surveys of the broader category of sacred word. The NEH Seminars led by Wilfred Cantwell Smith at Harvard in 1982 and 1984, went further in giving specific attention to the concept of scripture in specific traditions and in questioning the appropriateness of scripture as a comparative category.[4]

In her course Miriam Levering combines the reflection on sacred books with the recent thinking about the function of the printed word in human culture. The course she develops demonstrates the interplay between the religious category of sacred word and the whole range of the cultural use of words, especially their fixation in writing, print, or some electronic retrieval bank. She notes the possibility of crossing a Western boundary between the sacred and secular and of reflecting on the location of that boundary in other cultures as well as in our own. The course shows promise of fulfilling one aim of all these courses: moving from some particular topic to the most fundamental questions about the nature of the religious dimension of human experience. Its very complexity, moreover, invites a collaboration of teachers, not only in different fields of religion, but also in different disciplines in the humanities and social sciences.

William Graham's course, while ostensibly a survey of the Great Books of several cultures, supplements the focus on the written word with detailed treatment of the fundamental orality of scripture, even in the most literary of cultures, and the communal or relational aspects of sacred texts. He holds—against Derrida, for instance—to the ultimate primacy of the "voice" over "writing" in sacred texts cross-culturally. He

---

[4] These topics are addressed in a volume edited by Miriam Levering, *Rethinking Scripture: Essays from a Comparative Perspective* (Albany: State University of New York Press, 1989).

includes classics as well as scriptures because Western culture makes a distinction that Western scholars have sometimes followed in their comparative work. He also thinks that it is important to focus on a culture's choice of its classics. "All truly great texts," he observes, "can be mined to some degree for what they can tell us about the religious values of the tradition that has accorded them 'classic' status."

We include two essays, one by Robin Lovin and Frank Reynolds, and the other by Mark Juergensmeyer, which discuss courses in comparative ethics. Both essays draw considerably from our earlier inter-institutional project on that subject. One represents the kind of cooperation between a historian of religion and an ethicist that that project sought to promote. The other shows the internalization of concerns coming from both fields. During that five-year project some of the historians and anthropologists pointed out that religious ethics seemed unaware of its Western character in claiming a universal validity. On the other hand, ethicists complained that historians and anthropologists were avoiding issues of values and the conflict of values and moral norms in the "real world." Some of what was learned on both sides is reflected in the publications.[5] The graduate seminars held in all three institutions may help the next generation of scholars to approach these questions from a broader perspective.

The ethics courses discussed in this volume do not seek to uncover a universal pattern of religious reason—as Ronald Green has attempted in his seminal Neo-Kantian approach—nor do they attempt to discern a single structure of practical reason. The comparative religious ethics undergirding these courses takes an empirical, descriptive approach that tries to understand various cultures' revolving hierarchies of values in their own terms. But to deny a common structure of moral reasoning does not mean, they maintain, that we can do no more than explore the variety of culturally acceptable mores, nor is it mere capitulation to the bourgeois relativism vividly evoked by Lee Yearley. When attention is drawn, not only to the many different patterns of moral choice and action among several world traditions, but also to those differing patterns even within a single tradition, we discover a charged semantic field, a

---

[5] To date these include edited works by Robin Lovin and Frank Reynolds, John Stratton Hawley, Donald Swearer and Russell Sizemore, along with the encyclopedic *A Bibliographic Guide to Comparative Religious Ethics*, written by doctoral students at Berkeley and Harvard and edited by Juergensmeyer and Carman, (Cambridge: Cambridge University Press, 1991). See the essay "Teaching Comparative Religious Ethics" by Robin Lovin and Frank Reynolds in the present volume for full bibliographic citations of these works.

diversity of moral terminologies that better reflects real intra- and inter-cultural tensions, conflicts, and ambiguities. It is only by way of such diversities of moral expression that the historian of religions, as Lovin and Reynolds claim in *Cosmogony and Ethical Order*, is able "to reproduce the complexity of a tradition and allow the identification and meaningful comparison of the most crucial elements within it."[6] Through such an empirical approach we are able to develop a broad and significantly nuanced cross-cultural vocabulary at least to *begin* the task of adjudication and critique. It is still hotly debated as to whether proceeding further with comparative evaluation requires a normative approach. We shall return to this topic in the concluding chapter.

New Directions

Gender may not be a "theme" in the sense of some of the other themes we have included, and many would prefer to emphasize that issues of gender affect all courses in the comparative study of religion. Yet gender is part and parcel of the complex field of symbolic behavior that makes up religious and cultural self-understanding. It is as inseparable from the phenomenon of religion itself as it is from our individual sensibilities and academic approaches to cross-cultural study. It is the shadow out of which we cannot leap. As Caroline Walker Bynum puts it, in her influential introduction to *Gender and Religion*, there is no such thing as a "generic *homo religiosus*," but all human beings are "gendered."[7]

As we shall argue in the concluding chapter, there is no specific list of acceptable themes that are genuinely cross-cultural or inter-religious. Not only do themes come to our minds in a primary exemplification from a particular source, but the circumstances that mark the choice of one theme above another are historically contingent. Certainly the present moment in North American cultural and specifically academic history is one in which gender is recognized as a social and religious construct. More important than the choice of a topic to serve as a comparative theme are the various decisions that have to be made about using that theme in a particular course with particular students, as Miriam Levering has illustrated. The fact that she was co-teaching this course with a male colleague with a different specialization was important, as were the specific interests of the various students who took the class. Her

---

6 See Reynolds and Lovin, eds., *Cosmogony and Ethical Order: New Studies in Comparative Ethics* (Chicago: University of Chicago Press, 1985), 30.

7 Caroline Walker Bynum, "Introduction: The Complexity of Symbols," in Caroline W. Bynum et al., eds., *Gender and Religion* (Boston: Beacon Press, 1986), 2.

essay is illuminating, not only in its description of the choices made but also in noting possible alternatives that were not followed. The course that she and Lee Humphreys taught was offered as a proseminar that would survey "new kinds of scholarship in religious studies that take gender into account" but would select the readings in such a way as to have a running comparison between some aspects of Western religion and some aspects of religion in East Asia. During the course most students became "more aware of the ways in which women and men in many cultures participate and interpret differently in religious life," and the extent to which women have had difficulty finding fulfillment in the permissible religious identities.

Karen McCarthy Brown's course was different from Levering and Humphrey's course in many ways, but perhaps most strikingly different in its focus on Caribbean and Afro-Brazilian religious traditions in which women play major leadership roles. The course is not only about women's leadership roles, but also about the characteristic features of these religions: "their non-textual form, multi-cephalic organization and tendency to blur their boundaries." In many religions women do the cooking, sewing, and singing that supports or accompanies the official ritual, and often also attend the rituals in greater numbers than the men, yet scholars, emphasizing texts and orthodox doctrines, have not recognized the importance of women's handing on of religious traditions in acts of domestic piety. Karen Brown notes the irony of including "women" in this volume. "This particular 'theme' is more like a lens which drastically changes our perspective on entire traditions as well as on our own academic disciplines." This lens of women's lives not only reinforces "the critique of religious studies. . . . It adds a significant new dimension." The cataclysmic effects of bringing Africans to the New World as slaves provoked religious responses that included a shift in gender roles. This not only brought women into positions of leadership but also generated fundamental changes in religious symbols.

Both of these courses, like most of those previously discussed, are not so much the presentations of a particular sector of human religious life as the offering of a new lens through which to look at the religious phenomena being viewed. In some cases, as in these two essays, this is also a new lens with which—to stretch the metaphor—we may view the viewer as well.

The last two essays on specific courses deal with perhaps the most ignored area of cross-cultural religious studies: Artistic Creativity. Both Thomas Peterson and Richard Carp in their essays on religion and art, along with Karen Brown in the essay just discussed and Lawrence Sullivan in his essay in the Chicago volume of this series, radically call into question the pervasive textualism of the study of religion. This text-bias is, in great measure, an "artifact," as Carp remarks, "of the Judeo-Christian, largely Protestant, roots of the academy in the United States and of the academic study of religion." Related to this fixation on the text and its authority is our persistent fretting over social scientific categories in the study of religion, to the detriment of what Peterson calls the perspective of "metaphorical truth," from which perspective "religion can be approached as a creative activity that relies on imaging the world through such art forms as poetry, music, painting and dance." Attention to such artistic, non-textual elements of religious expression as dance, architecture, music, painting, and iconography may reveal alternative construals of meaning to those housed in the orthodoxy of the texts; or, put a different way, it may reveal orthodoxies until then hidden from view. What is articulated, for instance in stained glass, may foreground, for the eye skilled in their "reading," *realia*, spiritual practices, or images of the divine suppressed in the normative, usually textual or liturgical tradition. Though these counter-images do not always index the "subjugated" elements in any given culture—they may represent an esoteric or guild elite, for instance—they certainly contain a wealth of material hardly tapped by the comparative study of religion. We are too often predisposed to see images as mere illustrations of texts; yet often, as Carp observes, it is "the other way around": texts "may be explanations of concepts originally articulated visually, kinaesthetically, or orally."

It is notable that Tom Peterson's course, like Lee Yearley's, went through a metamorphosis. In this case, Peterson says, "the religious data [as interpreted by the students in discussion] began to challenge whether 'creativity' was an appropriate category for the study of the religious traditions of non-literate people." This, in turn, led to a change in the course title, substituting "Cosmology" for "Creativity." This confirmed his conviction that "the final value of a particular theme can only be discovered in the teaching process itself." "Cosmology" or "cosmologizing" here means "the artistic process of forging meaningful worlds," a process that is not entirely individual but involves interaction with the community. The students' active participation in mask-making was the most striking way of understanding such "cosmology." Richard Carp's own answer to the lack of a prominent place for the arts in the academic study of religion focusses on its overuse of texts but even more on the metaphor of "text" to convey the process of meaning. Where this "text-bias" comes from is clear, but we should recognize that the positive evaluation of the sacred word is accompanied in many Western religious traditions by a negative evaluation of the visual image and sometimes of other artistic forms as well. The sources of that iconoclasm are complex; they are Gnostic as well as biblical, but we need to see them, not simply as prejudice, but as part of deeply held convictions informing an entire world view. Once we have incorporated the icon into the subject matter of religious studies, we shall have to return to our Western past and also deal adequately with iconoclasm.[8]

Questions of Comparison

One general question arising in all these essays is the extent to which the particular theme chosen is genuinely cross-cultural. A second is whether the theme is significant for the student's increasing understanding of what it is in human culture that may be considered religious. A third may appear to be the obverse of the second: What connections does the theme suggest between the religious and other aspects of culture? This question is related to the specific emphasis of the 1986 Chicago Institute on the place of studies of religion (especially those with a global scope) in the liberal arts and the social sciences. We believe that all the following essays deal with these three questions, though some more explicitly than others.

The cross-cultural nature of a particular theme does not necessarily mean that a teacher will choose to organize a course with materials from widely different religious traditions. That is usually the case, but each of the courses on healing, for instance, focuses on one particular cultural area. They all assume that they are dealing with a topic of general human (and specifically religious) significance, but the demonstration of the assumption is provided by the diverse materials themselves. A number of the other essays discuss the question of the range of material and the examples that ought to be included in the comparative treatment of a religious theme. Pedagogically, there are advantages to limiting the number of instances presented. This is one reason why a course may treat the same subject quite differently than a comparative monograph, which aims to be as complete as possible in organizing the number of known instances into a number of differentiated types. In fact, however, the number of book-length theoretical discussions of the topics we have included is in some cases extremely limited, so that many of these

---

[8] This is attempted by Gerardus van der Leeuw in *Sacred and Profane Beauty: The Holy in Art* (New York: Holt, Rinehart and Winston, 1963).

courses are breaking new ground theoretically as well as providing a new kind of educational experience. The difficulty of determining a cross-cultural definition of either familiar or unfamiliar themes is such that each new course must grapple afresh with the issue of the theme's definition, scope, and applicability.

We end this glance at the following essays by noting some of the comments on the nature of themes that Fred Streng proposed during our first planning session. "Themes…that use traditional religious terminology have both specific and more general meaning," he suggests, and they sometimes have multiple definitions within a particular tradition as well as both divergent and overlapping meanings in other religious traditions. A concept drawn from one tradition "to illumine key expressions in other traditions, then, is used in a self-consciously ambiguous manner." A comparative theme is a verbal construct, an abstraction from "specific subjective experience, overt behavior and concrete symbols." It provides

> a conceptual lens through which a person can see relationships (i.e. similarities and differences) between specific human experiences and behavior that are recognized as "religious" in form or function. This lens has a limitation but also a potential for expressing a category of human awareness and for indicating significant aspects of one's environment. A conceptual lens shapes what is, and what can be, seen.
>
> The verbal lenses (the themes) are chosen from one or more religious traditions to express ideal attitudes, beliefs, practices and communal responsibility. These interpretive (thematic) lenses can be derived from another discipline of study such as philosophy, anthropology or biology. Or, they can be suggestive general terms drawn from common human experience which through their generality attempt to bridge religious traditions and academic disciplines. Whatever term one uses as a comparative and interpretive theme sets conceptual parameters, evokes associations, and indicates patterns of felt significance so that some similarities and differences are given focus rather than others. That is the point of the choice of lens.

❧II❧

A Thematic Course in the Study of Religion

KENDALL W. FOLKERT, EDITED BY JOHN E. CORT

Editor's note: This unfinished essay has been compiled from several drafts and notes left by Ken Folkert. Ken was killed in October, 1985, in a traffic accident while doing fieldwork on the Shvetambar Murtipujak Jains in Gujarat. Had Ken been able to finish this essay, it would undoubtedly look very different from this version. Nonetheless, despite the unfinished nature of the essay, he has raised some very important issues. Several notes have been included in the beginning of the essay which help locate it in terms of the broader issues being discussed.

I. PRELIMINARY NOTES FROM JUNE 1985 MEETING

Why thematic courses in religion, rather than comparative?

1) We are interested in differences as well as in commonality.

2) Older usages of "comparative religion" too often implied either an ultimate sameness as unity or a hierarchy to be discovered/demonstrated via the inquiry.

3) "Comparative" courses were often over-ambitious, seeking to slot everything into a typology or taxonomy.

Our concern for terminology then reflects a vision of the course: specific and focused, and as open as possible to various outcomes.

Two major thematic approaches may be discussed:

1) conceptual/reflective (within traditions) themes: e.g., deity, salvific processes,

2) descriptive approaches: e.g., life-cycle rites, calendar.

We could have a major debate over the validity of this distinction and it would be a very interesting and valuable debate, including even the question of whether "myth" or "symbol" belong in either category.

By and large, the basis for the distinction is straightforwardly this: in the first category are items on which the tradition itself has spoken, and for which the literature of the tradition is a major (but not *the only*) source. In the second category are matters of practice which may have been regularized and discerned in the tradition's literature, but which are more frequently *not* the subject of significant speculative or expressive literature.

I see the caution signals flying—this distinction appears to perpetuate the most unfortunate dichotomy in the study of religious life: the textual historian versus the ritual/social/anthropological scholar. But it is important to recall that this distinction in approaches did not spring solely from internecine academic squabbles. The materials and their nature *are* (significantly) different.

II. PRECEDING UNSCIENTIFIC FOREWORD

What I am sharing with my team and with the workshop in general is hardly a comprehensive essay on comparative religion. At one point, in fact, I felt—even during our June meetings—that the study of religion has become so idiosyncratic that to essay general principles is truly impossible. In the end, however, I conclude that this apparent idiosyncracy springs largely from our field's frequently passive acquiescence in the perpetuation of *impedimenta* from the last century: "world religions" and "comparative religion" are the *Paradebeispiele* of such impedimenta.

A revisionist essay on that subject lies beyond me at this point, and I don't know but that it might not be just as profitable for us all to resolve to drop those terms, without debate. I would rather, in any case, make what I think to be a positive statement. The study of religion, I would aver, requires most of all a distinctive anthropology—in the generic sense of the term—and a good introductory course in religion requires this most of all. I do not propose to prescribe a particular anthropology; but I want to prescribe the development of *an* anthropology.

Therefore, what follows does not always as often defend its conceptual and methodological bases—but the whole is intended to show how a course can be constructed on the basis of an anthropology. Perhaps you will argue that what I have called *impedimenta* are also based on anthropologies. I would not argue that they were never so based; but I would also challenge you to tell me what those anthropologies were/are, to show how the run-of-the-mill introductory survey course or text-book develops them, and to say whether you wish to perpetuate them.

This most basic task seems to me to be at the forefront of any commitment to our workshop's sub-rubric: to move "towards a global approach."

In my view, the study of religion has settled into a careless contentment with its subject-matter, a contentment that it can afford because the last seventy-five or so years have seen it:

1) Come to control a very large and growing body of material that other disciplines (often by default) aren't covering; this equals shallow cosmopolitanism, and leads to the conceit that we are the only "world historians," and so we are content with that.

2) Simply accept for both study and teaching the notion of "religions," which despite some tinkering (e.g., "traditions") has a relatively unexamined structure.

Real grappling with a number of issues is still out there to be done, and "comparative" vs. "descriptive" is a focal point for grappling.

III. CONCERNS

Rather than plunge directly into a discussion and description of a particular kind of comparative course in the study of religion, I want to begin this long-distance presentation to my team and to the workshop as a whole by stating a series of concerns. There are matters that were more or less nascently present in my thoughts and comments in June, and that have become sharper and more urgent for me over the intervening months.

It is not felicitous that I should present these concerns only in writing, and not be with you to either defend or press them. But, regardless of the circumstances, I feel quite strongly that I must express them. Without further ado, here they are. I will preface them only by saying that I do not believe them to be either earth-shattering or fully-stated; my primary point is to raise them.

Impedimenta

There is, first, a simple problem of what we might as well call *impedimenta*. I will be unhappy if our workshop and institutes do not grapple— or at least open the door for grappling—with some of these.

The study of religion, particularly at the level of introductory course-work and diet-book composition, is beset by a crippling burden of re-ceived and uncritically accepted scholarly structures. My first concern is that our workshop should be identifying and dealing critically with these, rather than—wittingly or unwittingly—perpetuating them. Rush-ing in where angels fear to tread, I shall express this first concern by identifying some of the "baggage" structures that I feel were not re-flected upon in June:

A. The notion of "the world's religions," or "world religions," or the several variations in such a phrase that one encounters everywhere; and

The presence in departmental offerings of the survey course, and on bookshelves of the survey volumes, based by and large on the inher-ited "world religions" model.

B. The general presence of implicit taxonomies in description and analysis of religious traditions, taxonomies that might be necessary and valuable but which, unreflectively used, are neither.

C. Overarching all of this, a near-absolute failure to reflect upon the structure, virtue, and deliberate purpose of the introductory course in religion.

I don't expect anyone in the workshop to view this as an exhaustive list. I don't. But these are items that simply won't go away as I work through what we are doing. With (or even without) your indulgence, I should like to treat them a bit more extensively one by one.

A. "World Religions," etc.

If one scrabbles, one may find a few reflective (but now out-dated) scholarly uses of this cluster of notions. But I would rather submit, solely for argument's sake if need be, that at least two damaging states of affairs exist as concerns them. The first is that these notions are generally bereft of coherence, very nearly meaningless rubrics. If this is even possibly the case, this workshop may be in trouble, for it seeks a "global approach to the study of religion." One feels obliged to ask: can such a goal be reached so long as such notions at the very least simply hamper proper critical thinking?

The unfortunate state of affairs is this: The general notion of a set of world religions derives from the general approach to the subject that was in vogue in the first half of the nineteenth century, i.e., an utterly hybrid approach, compounded of continental idealist romanticism, linguistic and literary preoccupation, occidental historicism, and cultural superior-ity. (I need not repeat for you or urge on you Edward Said's views; he was frequently describing what ought to be evident to us.) Not only does this state of affairs hamper one's ability to think clearly about religion in world perspective; it positively poisons the well.

I would wish to argue that both perspectives/usages are present in course-conception, in teaching and textbook vocabulary, and in other loci in departments of religion. Neither is innocuous; and the basic question facing the workshop is whether a strong effort ought not be made, in the summer institutes, to work against the use of such notions in undergraduate teaching.

This is particularly so because the idea of "world religions" generates either or both of the following detrimental tendencies in introductory courses:

1) It gives a false sense of totality in terms of subject-matter and the coverage of it;

2) It opens the door to unexamined perceptions that the religions are all species of a single genus, or that they can or should be hierarchically or otherwise arranged in what are generally unhappy orderings.

The existence of both possibilities is, so far as I can see, a clear inheritance from parts of our academic and intellectual ancestry that ought to be subject to the most severe re-examination. It is the habits of mind that "world religions" represents that are the real problem. These mental habits blossom in survey courses and volumes. If "world religions" is a troubling business, then these academic *flora* are overdue for major reconsideration. At the simplest level of concern, the sampler-course or volume levels itself to the tourist approach to the study of religion; i.e., a quick, thoroughly guided trip through strange places, with refuge each night in familiar grounds. This approach to the religious life of other cultures is, moreover, not merely a shallow titillation with time for me to shop for a few exotic mental souvenirs; I would share the view that it rests more deeply in an occidental sense of intellectual "control" of the expressions of other cultures. This verges on my next subject of concern, but is not quite the same as what I shall be seeking to say shortly; rather, the sense of "control" intended here is both less ambitious and more insidious than any formalized intellectual framework.

The section or team for which I am writing is burdened with one other piece of baggage: "comparative" religion. As one of our team-members said in June, with some dismay, debates over the nature and value of comparative religion are often deadening and dreadful (or words to that effect). I didn't make that statement, but will attend to it to the extent that this discussion of thematic introductory courses in religion begins with the concrete: a specific course, developed in practice, and embodying what I wish to essay as proper goals both for an introductory course within the liberal arts/humanities and for a course that seeks a basic approach to the phenomena of human religious behavior. In June, we softened the blow of this notion largely by ducking around it and using such terms as "thematic" to describe a certain sort of introductory course. But *I'm* not happy with the result. Whether it be a single theme (pilgrimage, scripture, transmission of religion between cultures, healing, the self/mysticism), or clusters of themes (ways of salvation, patterns of religious activity, types of religious expression), *none* of this makes me really any happier about my basic concerns: the *absolute* lack of any sense of *acceptance or rejection* of taxonomic possibilities (i.e., it looks like Larry Shinn's dictionary). The subject of healing seems to me to be an example of the worst sort of approach: whatever turns you on and is momentarily relevant, with insufficient effort to *reduce* the subject (in the best sense) to essentially comparative/comparable themes.

There are two reasons I'm not happy with the result:

1) We avoided thinking about "comparative" study, except for saying that it does not involve just finding differences. This is something of an improvement on comparative religion's wellsprings, perhaps—except that I think the notion has such a mixed pedigree (see below) that it really ought to be junked. This is not fair on my part, because I'm not going to try to write an essay on the whole business of comparative studies in whatever field. I'll say only this: comparative religion can't stand outside the debate on comparative studies, and if the prospect of getting involved in it tires us in advance, we should perhaps recognize that we may not belong in it.

2) Having thought in a non-rigorous manner about comparative study, we then produced a mix of ad hoc courses that illustrate the very worst features of the present stage of the notion. "Comparative" or "thematic" is apparently so wide open to interpretation that the result is thoroughly hybrid and quite random.

Yet perhaps not absolutely so, and a way of drawing both criticisms under one roof seems to me to be this: "comparative religion" in either case represents the continuing presence in the study of religion of various taxonomic habits of mind, of two basic sorts:

1) When we don't think about it very hard (i.e., just sort of let the old category hang around), we leave some life and breath in at least one old notion: that all religions can be ranked/arranged/arrayed so as to point to a single essential goal or truth (cf. Huston Smith, *The Religions of Man*).

This too often includes the nascent sense that religions can be ranked hierarchically with respect to their expression of that truth, or that parts of religions are more worthy of thought and reflection than other parts.

2) When we do what we did in June, we don't rank religions, but we do a good deal of subjective or habitual selection of topics about which to be comparative, and these topics represent our own theological or cultural or personal biases.

IV. AN EXAMPLE

Rather than discuss the course in advance, I shall simply print it, and then take up its objectives, problematic points, and what I see to be its contributions to the critical foci of the workshop's tasks. (Note: I do teach this course at CMU, but what is given here is not a model syllabus; it is a simplified course outline as a springboard for discussion. This is a single-semester course: ca. 15 weeks of class-meeting, plus an exam-week. The course meets three times per week. I am stuck with the course-title by departmental inertia; I do regularly ask whether other individual faculty in the department should not head their syllabi "Introduction to Religions"; and my own syllabi bear the subtitle "Religiousness and 'Reality.'")

RELIGION 101: INTRODUCTION TO RELIGION

A. Patterns in religious activity. (8 weeks)
  1. The question of starting points: "religious" *versus* "religion" or "religions."
  2. Religious activity in rites of passage.
     a. The basic structure of such rites: separation, transition, incorporation; the phenomena of liminality.
     b. Specific rites and examples.
        1) Childbirth (India; U.S.)
        2) Adulthood (the Nuer, U.S.)
        3) Marriage (student-selected examples)
        4) Death-rituals (student-selected examples)
     c. Re-consideration of the elements of the structure of these rites, focusing on two matters: the role and nature of liminality, and the way in which ritual processes have power to give structure to human experience: in short, the construction of "reality." (This is open to the "social reality" critique, but for the

        stress on personal liminality.)

3.   Calendars and the structuring of time.

    a.   Calendars and time-valuation: the "reality" of time.

    b.   The basic patterns of three calendars:

        1)   Judaic.

        2)   Christian.

        3)   Hindu.

    c.   Calendars: myth, ritual, and memory.

        1)   Calendrical re-enactments.

            a)   Myths and accounts of origins and ideals.

            b)   The interaction of myth and ritual in the re-enactment of such accounts.

        2)   Calendrical and textual relationships: a discussion of the interconnection of calendar, ritual, and text/"scripture."

    d.   Recapitulation: Calendars and the structuring of time as a further dimension of the construction of "reality."

B.   Seeing general problems within a whole tradition. At this juncture, four to five weeks are given to study of particular religious traditions, but in the following manner:

    1.   Course lectures focus on one tradition, the choice of which varies from term to term.

    2.   Each student selects one other tradition, and carries out a program of reading and work-sheet assignments, which are in general parallel to the lecture topics and common readings.

    3.   The core topics involved in lectures and reading programs are:

        a.   An overall historical outline.

        b.   The basic institutional forms of the tradition.

        c.   The tradition's major activities and texts.

        d.   An inquiry into the general viewpoint of the tradition, using the following table of pairs which serve to characterize the tradition's teachings/perspectives:

1)	the world, if flawed is reparable	the world is ultimately irreparable/of no value
2)	the human being is a whole; the concept of an afterlife is not	the human being is divided into body and soul; the afterlife is given

	prominent	significant attention
3)	Concrete ritual acts are essential	One's inner/spiritual attitude is essential
4)	One is a member of the tradition by birth and upbringing	One is a member by means of a conversion act
5)	Asceticism absent	Asceticism prominent

Care is given to point out that between these pairs there is frequent tension or disagreement within a tradition; e.g., infant baptism controversies represent a Christian tension in terms of pairs 3) and 4). The pairs should represent ways of organizing and critically analyzing basic premises of a tradition, and should not become a rigid set of categories into which a tradition is to be wedged.

C. Recapitulation
The course concludes with a one-week review and synthesis, in order to draw together the specific interpretations of ritual and mythological "structuring" and the general study and characterization of whole traditions.

V. DISCUSSION

At this point, having labored over several drafts of explication, I'm tempted to leave the outline to speak altogether for itself. The course I've just outlined looks eclectic and is to some extent; but it rests on a set of specific objectives, and on some larger bases that I consider vital for the study of religion. But I expect that this outline, in its compressed statements, raises a number of questions about just what stitches together this rather eclectic approach to studying religion; and beyond that, I feel it to be important that something be said about what is not in the course.

One of my feelings of disquiet about the "comparative" team's work in June was that, in the end, we appeared to have generated a hodgepodge of courses, a collection that seemed to represent the worst sort of outcome possible from hanging on to an outdated and empty rubric, viz. "comparative religion." As a result, I feel compelled to state how the above-outlined course would not be subject to that same criticism.

I also recognize only too well that a number of the choices made in terms of approaches to the subject matter touch areas of great and protracted methodological controversy. I believe that my choices are defensible; but they cannot be altogether defended in less than a book-length piece. Therefore, I prefer to explain this course in terms of a set of more direct and programmatic statements about what it seeks to do and what it chooses not to do; to point out, only, the larger areas of debate that lie behind these points; and to say, finally, how I feel that the course satisfies my initial condition for such courses: that they be based on an anthropology.

What the course does

First of all, this course draws students into active analysis of religious phenomena, especially by using the religious and cultural settings of their own lives as part of what is studied. This objective is particularly fulfilled in the first part of the course, where rites of passage and calendars are used. In simple terms, I want them to use their eyes and personal memories and observations, and not treat religion as a distant phenomenon that belongs or belonged to other individuals and groups.

Second, I want students to be challenged to think beyond their usual perceptions about the nature and extent of "religion." This, too, is accomplished in the first part of the course, especially with the help of the study of rites of passage, which range from events typically associated with churches or religious institutions, e.g., marriage, to events whose key processes are often far removed from what they may perceive as religion, e.g., childbirth or initiation rites.

Third, I want students to learn to use a conceptual and analytical "tool kit" for thinking about religious activity, so that they can themselves begin to sniff about for things that they can analyze. This is to some extent a continuation of the previous point, but it has its own value in other areas.

The conceptual and analytical tools are simply drawn from van Gennep: the use of "separation, transition, and incorporation" to describe and analyze the structure and stages of a rite of passage, and the use of "liminality" to characterize the status of both individual and group at the time of such rites. I also use, partly as a didactic device and partly as groundwork for later analysis, a derived set of characteristics of religious activity: the involvement of a specialized class or set of persons, the use of particular kinds of clothing, the presence of an unusual or special language/vocabulary, a notable role for acts involving food/eating, and the utilization of particular spaces or places.

With these three objectives in mind, the course begins by asking students to think not about "religion" or "religions," but to look for "religiousness," and even this, I admit, I leave as undefined as possible. Instead, I ask them to try to see the world as if they were visitors from another planet, who do *not* know what religion is, know only that they are looking for certain patterns of human activity. To define these patterns, I use a derived set of characteristics: the involvement of a specialized class set of persons, the use of particular kinds of clothing, the presence of an unusual or special language/vocabulary, a notable role for acts involving food/eating, the utilization of particular spaces or places. The point, then, is to begin scanning human activity as widely as possible, looking for the occurrence of chunks of these characteristics. Again, a range of subject-matter emerges: from the eucharist to athletic events, and notably, rites of passage themselves.

Rites of passage in the life-cycle provide an effective way of carrying this beginning forward because of several of their features. Among other things, they are a set of occasions that is controllable as subject-matter, and they represent as nearly as anything a pan-human experience. They also range from events more directly associated in students' experience with formal religious institutions (e.g., marriages and funerals) to events whose major features are more outside of such institutions, e.g., childbirth. Finally, the students' own lives and the life of the community around them can serve as actual primary data for their work; here structuring this part of the course in terms of couples from both the United States and other cultures.

Yet this remains a tautology, and so the rites of passage are used as a more systematic area within which to work out the major conceptual task of the first part of the course: to see "religiousness" as the engagement of ordering and structuring the raw fact(s) of existence, and—important to note at once—the rejection/questioning of such structuring. Raising and shaping this conceptual task is accomplished particularly by adding to the "tool kit" the notion of liminality, and studying it first in terms of liminal states in rites of passage, then as a general descriptive concept. This point—that there is a major conceptual framework within which the three more straightforward objectives operate, and that it uses such a notion as liminality—is something that I want only to interleave at this juncture, and return to a bit later. (I will observe, here, that the calendar study is basically an extension of this larger conceptual task, adding other important features to it.) Before getting into that matter, I want to lay out as directly as possible what the course omits.

What the course does not do

This is, above all, not a world religions course. It does not pretend to cover all religions, nor does it, for that matter, pretend to be factually comprehensive about even one or two. The second part of the course does treat unitary religious traditions, but treats them thematically, and in a way that is related to—and an outcome of—the development of a larger conceptual framework.

The course also is not comparative in the sense in which comparative religion has frequently dealt in general conceptual comparisons: ideas of God, paths to salvation, mysticism, etc. These are, in fact, terms that I purposely try to avoid using in the course. The point here is straightforward: most such comparisons pretend to be direct, when in fact they are enormously complex translations of specific linguistically and culturally shaped terms into a generic term drawn from occidental theology. Or, as in the case of "mysticism," they rest on a generic term that does not even exist in the religious vocabulary of most traditions. I would say—even if for simple shock value—that such "comparative" study represents a particularly vicious form of reductionism.

The course is also relatively a-historical and a-textual, in terms of primary sources. This is perhaps an over-correction on my part, but it rests on a conviction that focussing on history and texts in an introductory course is too often the mere extension without reflection of the two dominant features of study of the Christian tradition into the study of all other traditions. Let me dwell on the latter for a moment, by way of illustrating my concerns.

Students in this course do not, by and large, read "primary sources" for content. The whole phenomenon of "The Sacred Books of the East" or "The World Bible" seems to me to be a classic case of "comparative religion" run amok, and reading sacred texts in translation is, I would argue, a true instance of a little bit of knowledge being a very dangerous thing. Text-scholars will frequently complain that anthropologists and sociologists are given to observing a community's behavior and saying that, whatever the community says it is doing, the real significance of the behavior is "x" or "y." The same, alas, is true of textual scholarship. Holmes Welch, in his *Taoism: the Parting of the Way*, observed that no Chinese would ever have read the Tao Te Ching without reading it through a commentary. The same statement applies to many, if not most, traditions, whether the commentary be oral or written (and it applies equally to the Christian use of the Bible, whose close association in "Bible-based" Protestantism with a preaching tradition would be overlooked at his or her peril by a careful scholar). Yet text scholars have been obsessed with original texts, degrading the value of commentaries, and being quite happy to tell other traditions that whatever they think their texts say, the texts "really" say "x" or "y."

Given this, and given that primary sources are not read in isolation by the members of traditions, I must doubt the value of reading them in isolation (and in translation) by students wholly outside the traditions, unless an entire course is set up specifically to accomplish very carefully constituted objectives with respect to the phenomenon and nature of the texts themselves. Such an introductory course is not ruled out by any means—but it would be a far cry from the usual use of scriptures in the presentation of concepts in what passes for comparative study.

With these omissions briefly and somewhat unsatisfactorily outlined, I want now to return to the more fundamental discussion of what the course does: its larger conceptual framework.

Underlying the features of the first part of the course are what I spoke of as larger bases on which the study of religion needs to rest. Principal among these is what I would call a distinctive anthropology, in the generic sense of the word. Developing and demonstrating such an anthropology is the task that underlies the study of specific phenomena in the beginning of the course.

Here I need also to insert a clarifying note. I present what follows as an illustrative anthropology, not a normative one, nor one that I am trying to foist on the workshop...yet. The point that I wish to make, autobiographically, is that an introductory course needs to rest on an anthropology.

The key item in this task is "liminality." Rites of passage and van Gennep's own use of the concept of liminal, gives a built-in opening for further work with the idea. (I do not ask students to read Victor Turner; I acknowledge to them and to you my indebtedness to his work; but I feel free to derive what follows quite freely from him, from other scholars, and from my own thinking.) In essential terms, liminality is used in this course to explicate both the social and the psycho-physical sense of "reality" or "identity" that operate in groups and individuals. This task proceeds within a framework hypothesis that shows up in comments within the course outlined above, namely, that religious activity deals at base with the ordering and structuring of the raw fact(s) of existence.

Religiousness and "Reality"

This, the subtitle of my syllabus, is the course's basic theme. I spoke a bit earlier of religiousness as the engagement in, or rejection of, ordering and structuring the raw fact(s) of existence, and the purpose of studying rites of passage and calendars is in the first instance to engage students in seeing how these simple, raw events of existence are shaped, structured, constructed into one's perceived reality. The use of the concept of liminality is of particular value in getting this study launched, and I develop it in two dimensions. The first is the more or less conventional notion of liminality as having reference especially to social identities, a liminal state being one where one's social role, status, identity, etc., are indeterminate or under stress. This is a primary and typical way of looking at what rites of passage accomplish—the securing or re-securing of an individual's and group's identity when something occurs to call it into question.

But there is a second dimension, which moves—I believe—beyond the primarily social significance of liminality. The dimension involves what I call "psycho-physical liminality." It is based on the thesis that, just as social settings, where liminal states involve threshold-situations, i.e., conditions where a person, persons, or a group are between identities or in a condition where their identities are in doubt or under stress, and which are treated by means of carefully structured behavior, so too the individual's sense of personal, emotional and physical wholeness involves liminal thresholds and highly structured treatment of them. These liminal thresholds are at the simplest level physical: they are the openings between one's body and the outside world. Acts that involve passing through or across these thresholds—e.g., the mouth, the anus, the sex organs, the nose—are all liminal in character. Defecation, urination, menstruation, ejaculation, spitting, vomiting, eating, childbirth, sexual intercourse,…all are occasions where psycho-physical liminality is present, and where humans treat it in carefully, even elaborately, structured ways, including careful and elaborate silence on the subjects.

Rites of passage make use of both these dimensions of liminality, frequently using psycho-physical liminal states—nakedness, scatological acts, food tricks, and eating—as a crucial feature.

This is a thesis that requires lengthier and more persuasive presentation than I can give here, and I recognize that it is a two-fold thesis: first, that psycho-physical liminality is a phenomenon that bears up under investigation and that gives depth to the general idea of liminality in more social interpretations; and second, that the use of both types of liminality as a lynch-pin for understanding humans in ritual processes is a proper and valuable tool for understanding human religiousness. As the latter is a key part of what I've called this course's anthropology, I must give it priority in discussion.

As I said before, liminality is used to get at an understanding of the problem of "reality" or "identity" for groups and individuals. This is done within a framework hypothesis that shows up in the comments within the course outline above. That framework hypothesis is that religious activity involves giving order and structure to the raw facts of existence. This structuring, or—important to note—the rejection of it, is the driving force in religious behavior.

I expect that, at first glance, this approach looks reductionist. I wish to argue that it is not so, on several counts. First, I would maintain that the use of psycho-physical liminality is an important counterbalance to any tendency toward reducing religious behavior to a force in the development of purely social order. I cannot argue it with the force and length that I should like to give it, but the key asseveration that I want to make is this: the simple existence of oneself, as body, as something separate from and yet necessarily related to other things, as a being thing, is a *mysterium tremendum*, and no response to that is trivial or reducible. There is, for example, nothing trivial about death, or the "fear" of it; and why anyone should think that by saying something like "religion is just the fear of death" he or she has disposed of some problems is quite beyond me.

As noted before, my point in raising all of this, with all its dangers in terms of old and endless arguments about nature *versus* nurture, etc., is not to give a course on liminality, but to point out that even the most basic and natural features of being human are in fact subject to shaping and structuring by pervasive and very powerful ritual processes, and that it is the shaped and structured versions of these natural features that comprise what most humans live in as everyday reality.

This task is extended by turning to calendars and the structuring of time. It is always interesting simply to point out to students that the bare statement of what day it is (e.g., Wednesday, September 9, 1985) is a statement that cannot be shown to have any actual physical factual content. Yet knowing "what time it is," i.e., where one is "in" time, is a crucial component of "reality." Thus in one sense, working with calendars extends the basic starting point of the course: that even the most commonplace, taken-for-granted dimensions of everyday life are the products of complex and powerful processes.

The same statements as made about the rites of passage can, by and large, be made of the next section, which deals with calendars. They present a self-limited set of occasions, are pan-human, break out of typical limits of "religion," and direct students toward their own cultural and personal experience.

But working with calendars takes the discussion of religious activity further, in several important ways. First, calendars are an occasion to discuss myth and ritual in a concrete context. As the course outline reveals, calendars involve not merely the reckoning of time, but also the re-presentation of origins and ideals as embodied in myths. This provides an occasion to enquire into the use of myth and text in religion, in a particular context: e.g., the use of the Bible in the lectionary of the Christian year.

In addition, the study of calendars and ritual processes moves beyond the dimensions of "reality" dealt with in rites of passage, and begins to have to deal with larger social and institutional structures, including the matter of "founders" of traditions, whose lives are significantly re-presented in calendrical rituals.

In terms of the course's larger conceptual task, then, the two sections—on rites of passage and on the calendar—work together to show at least some of the range of forms and the depth of force that religious activity exerts in the construction of reality at personal, social, and institutional levels; and, to my mind fully as significant: the investigation continues to use as its touchstone a set of common, universal, and basic sorts of everyday experience and behavior, matters that are at hand for students, that they live in and react to, and can investigate directly.

Turning full circle

The second half of the course is both an extension of the institutional and ritual investigations of the first half, and a counterpoint, of sorts, to the presentation of ritual processes as an enormous force in shaping perceptions of reality. In the latter sense, it is thus an important part of the anthropology that underlies the course as a whole.

When presented with the possibility that their perceptions of themselves, their identities, their realities are the products of powerful processes over which they exercise little control, students—especially contemporary, American students—exhibit considerable resistance. Whatever its basis, this resistance provides the occasion for pointing out, as hinted earlier, that religiosity also invalues, and has done so historically, the resistance, rejection, and questioning of "structured reality," and that religious traditions are in fact rife with tension on this particular point.

The exhibiting of these tensions in the context of whole traditions is the burden of the second part of the course, and comprises the immediate utility of the sets of paired opposites given in the outline.

The objectives of this course bear generally on the task of this workshop and of the comparative team in two major arenas of concern which are major foci of what I hope to contribute to our work. The first concern is that comparative courses be comparative in a particular way, a way that I feel is a defensible and distinctive way of doing comparative work. The second is that basic coursework in religions embody a perspective, within the larger framework of the liberal arts. Either of these would be grist for a book, and one has been the concern of a whole team, but I hope that a condensed statement can be persuasive and useful, and I prefer to discuss the latter arena.

The "Comparative" Issue

We all have concerns about comparative religion, and ought to have them. My own chief concern is that there be a distinction between comparison that is based on conceptual and reflective material (e.g., "Ideas of God," "ways to salvation") and comparison that is based as much as possible on observable activity. In the totality that is human experience, these two are not finally separable, nor do they exist in isolation from each other, and so I do not wish to foist some deadly version of "great/little" distinctions upon this enterprise. But I do want, in the first instance, to insure that we know which kind of comparison we are doing, and what each one's limitations are. For example, the former (more conceptual comparisons), if done with care, can be historically based; the latter tends towards the a-historical. All of this is in many ways obvious, and runs along lines that we have probably all debated, e.g., textual versus behavioral study. But, simplistic as this whole matter may seem, it is of cardinal importance for doing any sort of comparative work that it be borne at all times in mind, especially as it has distinctive practical consequences in formulating introductory courses.

I want students to understand ritual processes and their power, and I want them to explore the way that those processes shape and structure their sense of reality. But I also want to use liminality to ground the course in what I see to be the larger framework of the liberal arts and humanities. I know that the latter has been one entire team's subject, but it is interwoven with my concerns about basic coursework to such an extent that I feel compelled to address it myself, and will take it up briefly.

Religion and the Liberal Arts

The study and teaching of religion justifies its presence in the liberal arts to the extent that it presents and sustains what I want to call a distinctive anthropology in the generic sense of the term. The anthropology that underlies the study of religion also justifies its being placed, as it commonly is, among the humanities. These two statements seem especially important to make, given the nature of the course outlined above, which certainly has in it strong elements of what we usually think of as social-scientific approaches to religion.

To amplify them a bit: studying religion is—and has been—a demanding process of inquiry into the fundamental character of human being. It is necessary to recognize that this is not only an inquiry into various claims about human being, but that it also rests on an anthropology, in fact, has rested on a series or cluster of them.

Yet these several anthropologies often go untested, and study and teaching too often pass along unreflected assumptions about humans.

On that point, I wish to argue that it is crucial for the study of religion to have an anthropology that is neither reductive nor what I call "assumptive." By way of an amplification: reductionist approaches to religious behavior are not merely injurious to understanding religion, but also, ultimately, degrading of humans.

❦III❦

A Mega-theme for an Introductory Course in Religious Studies—"Ways of Ultimate Transformation"

FREDERICK J. STRENG

The goal of this course is to introduce students to a broad notion of religion: the human structuring, and living in, a context of comprehensive value. The procedure is to explore some key ideas, experiences, and social behavior of human beings in the past and present, and in the East and West, which intend to achieve superlative well-being. These efforts include symbolically constructing a world of meaning, developing a spontaneity which frees one from one's own construction, manifesting one's place in a natural rhythm of the universe, and developing selfhood through extraordinary experience. By examining some similar, and some conflicting, religious expressions, this course attempts to explore the nature of religious life.

I. Assumptions of the Course

This approach to understanding the nature and diverse expressions of religion includes two assumptions. The first is that the human situation is multidimensional in its basic nature. Human behavior and social institutions have irreducible multiple levels and kinds of meaning. They may, for example, refer to political, psychological, and philosophical contexts simultaneously. The concepts used to describe value-laden experiences and behavior are often paradoxical or ambiguous. Similarly, a person's self-awareness includes unconscious and hidden undercurrents of motivation and sensitivity. The second assumption is that human beings both create and discover moral obligations, aesthetic sensitivities, symbolic meaning, and personal identity. Personal views and social institutions are embedded in a cultural fabric which reflects specific times and places. Conversely, values, intentions, ideal images, and cultivation of certain qualities of consciousness condition and reform implicit structures of meaning and behavior.

This comparative approach suggests that religious intentionality is as important as the (often stated) social or psychological functions of religion, such as socialization, development of self-identity or implementation of life-cycle transitions. Religious intentionality can be broadly defined as the intention to achieve comprehensive well-being, which requires establishing a relationship, or an identity, with what is perceived as ultimate reality. This is experienced by religious advocates as a transformation (of one's life, community, and world)—a transformation whereby they know, embody and express that which is of superlative value because it manifests what really is. Such ultimate transformation has been called "salvation," "total liberation," and "harmonious living."

In using the mega-theme "ways of ultimate transformation" students perceive a central and deep concern found in diverse religious traditions, ideologies, and humanistic techniques for comprehensive well-being. By recognizing concrete phenomena of both traditional institutional religion and humanistic efforts for comprehensive well-being as expressions of "ways of ultimate transformation" the cultural forms are seen as moments within a dynamic process of profound personal and social change. The historical data—which include liturgies, myths, meditation practice, moral rules, psychotherapy sessions, and socio-political revolutionary appeals—are understood as ways to actualize the most significant values found in this or another life, or both.

This approach explores not only the religious significance of different religious forms, but also seeks to ask the perennial question about the "nature," or deepest character, of religious life. Such exploration is achieved by asking two questions:

(1) What is the central concern or intention of the religious experience and behavior according to the religious advocates themselves, and

(2) How do the religious advocates go about achieving this deepest intention (actively, passively, or both)?

The course begins with an effort to raise the student's self-consciousness about his or her assumptions and expectations of what counts as "religious." Then, through exposure to readings of religious advocates and sympathetic interpreters from different cultures the student extends her or his scope for understanding the ways people affirm and live out their comprehensive value(s). Primary source material (i.e., concrete religious data) and interpretive analyses of religious expressions are read and analyzed in relation to a paradigm of religious intentionality. This paradigm expresses a general definition of religion for its advocates as the "means of ultimate transformtion." It requires the student to ask five questions of any religious datum:

(1) What is the fundamental problematic in the human situation which prevents people from effecting comprehensive well-being?

(2) What is the nature of the ultimate reality (or highest fulfillment) as perceived by the advocate?

(3) What are the means by which the problematic is overcome so that the highest fulfillment is achieved?

(4) What are the characteristics of the personal expressions, and

(5) the characteristics of the social expressions of the religious transformation?

In order to heighten the students' sensitivities to the assumptions of the advocates' formulations of the general human problematic, ultimate reality and means (for attaining comprehensive well-being), two critiques of these assumptions are presented along with advocates' claims in each of the types (ways) of ultimate transformation. By focusing on these assumptions, the students are encouraged to develop sensitivities to the evaluative processes used in religious judgments. Identifying the processes of valuation in different ways of ultimate transformation, in turn, aids the students in adjudicating value choices in their personal efforts toward achieving ultimate well-being.

An important part of this introductory course is the recognition that there are significant differences in the content and forms of traditional religions and in non-traditional ways of structuring comprehensive value. We look first at the religious intention or purpose of key traditional religious expressions. The five-fold religious paradigm of religious intentionality, then, provides a basis for examining also the claims, experiences and behavior of people outside traditional religious communities that function for them as "a way of ultimate transformation." Nevertheless, despite the real historical and cultural differences among religious expressions, the root or core concern in all of them is recognized to be the transformation from some deeply problematic universal condition in existence to a state of comprehensive fulfillment, e.g., perfect enlightenment, eternal life, identity with the universal order, or fulfilling human relationships.

The course outlined below is designed as a one-semester course. The materials are organized by one-week assignments which presume three class-hours per week. The assigned readings are found in F. J. Streng, *Understanding Religious Life*, 3rd ed., (Belmont, CA: Wadsworth Publ. Co., 1985; first edition published in 1969, and abbreviated as URL), and F. Streng, C. Lloyd and J. Allen, eds., *Ways of Being Religious* (Englewood Cliffs, NJ: Prentice-Hall, 1973). The anthology *Ways of Being Religious* was developed by the editors over three years of classroom use of different mimeographed readings. During that time students were asked to evaluate each reading at the conclusion of each semester course. Only those readings that achieved a sustained high level of positive student response were included in this book of readings. Films that have been used in class are also noted in the outline below. After the first week, the materials are organized according to different "ways of ultimate transformation" (or "types" of religious life). Each traditional "way" of being religious is documented by readings from different religious traditions; each non-traditional "way" of being religious is documented by excerpts from contemporary advocates.

II. Course Outline

1st week: What is "religion"?

Students fill out a questionnaire on their experience and understanding of religious life; they share and discuss the range of their experience. Then they are introduced to an academic understanding of the nature and forms of religion in a religiously plural world. Some simple comparative religious concepts e.g. myths, initiation rituals, and spiritual practices, are discussed, and the relation of cultural-historical forms to religious intention or purpose are examined.

At the final class session of this week we discuss the possibilities and difficulties of learning another person's religious intention. We use the assigned readings to explore the students' grasp of the religious intention found there, and identify different "ways of ultimate transformation." We conclude with a discussion on the significance of apparently divergent claims to truth, reality, and well-being for the study of religion.

Readings:

"Interviews with Yasutani Roshi," from P. Kapleau, ed. *The Three Pillars of Zen*

"Periodic Worship of the Zunis," from R. Benedict, *Patterns of Culture*

"Experience of the Lord," from *The Complete Works of Saint Teresa*

"On *Li* (Rites, Propriety, Rules of Decorum)," from *Hsun Tzu: Basic Writings*, trans. B. Watson

URL, Ch. 1 "The Nature and Study of Religion," and pp. 21-24

2nd week: Introduction to Type 1: Personal Apprehension of a Holy Presence

Students read assigned readings. In class we discuss in detail the assigned data, locating the expressions of (1) the problematic, (2) the ultimate reality, (3) the means of ultimate transformation, (4) the personal expression of transformation, and (5) the social expression of transformation in each of the data.

Readings:

URL, Ch. 2 "Personal Apprehension of a Holy Presence"

"I Am Blessed but You Are Damned," from C. H. Johnson, ed., *God Struck Me Dead*

"Biblical Examples of Divine Encounter": Isaiah 6:1-8; Acts 11:1-18; Acts 9:1-19

"Experience of the Divine Mother," by Sri Ramakrishna, from C. Isherwood, *Ramakrishna and His Disciples*

Film: "Holy Ghost People"

3rd week: Type 1 continued

Students read assigned readings. In class we analyze the data from the advocates and sympathetic interpreters, focusing on the same five elements of the process of ultimate transformation as before. The readings of the critics, i.e., those who reject the assumptions of the advocates of this type of religious life, are discussed in class focusing on a comparison of the reasons given by the advocates and by the critics for their respective value judgments.

Readings:

"The Inner Ecstasy," from M. Bach, *The Inner Ecstasy*

"Importance of Prayer for Knowing God," from Nels F. S. Ferre, *Making Religion Real*

"The Awesome and Fascinating Mystery," from R. Otto, *The Idea of the Holy*

"On Men's Self-denial in the Face of the Holy as a Psychological Illness," from P. Berger, *The Sacred Canopy* (critique)

"On the Justification of Claims Based on Religious Experience," from C. B. Martin, *Religious Belief* (critique)

*4th week: Introduction to Type 2: Creation of Community
through Sacred Symbols*

Students read assigned readings. In class we note similarities and differences of the content of the five elements in this process of ultimate
transformation, pointing to the explicit discussion in URL, Chs. 2 & 3.
Then we discuss the content of the data that describes specific rituals,
initiations, and liturgies.

Readings:

URL Ch. 3 "Creation of Community through Sacred Rituals"

"Initiation and Puberty Rites," from J. S. Mbiti, *African Religions and Philosophy*

"Periodic Worship of the Zunis," from R. Benedict, *Patterns of Culture*

"The Mythic Structure of Classical Judaism," from J. Neusner, *The Way of the
Torah*

Films: "Sanctus," & "Hindu Sacrament of Thread Investiture"

5th week: Type 2 continued

Students read assigned readings. In class we continue to analyze the
data, highlighting the particular forms that express the elements of the
process of ultimate transformation in this type. Again, the discussion of
the critiques focuses on a comparison of the reasons given by the advocates and by the critics for their respective value judgments.

Readings:

"Myth, Ritual, and History in Christianity," from St. Paul, Romans 5:1-6:11; I
Corinthians 11:23-32

"Celebration and Renewal: The Catholic Mass," from *Sunday Missal Prayerbook
and Hymnal*

"Myth, Ritual, and National History Seen in 'Two American Sacred Cer-
monies,'" from C. Cherry, *American Quarterly*, Vol. 21

"The Sacred and the Profane," from J. E. Smith, *Experience and God*

"Obsessive Acts and Religious Practices," from Sigmund Freud in *The Standard
Edition of the Complete Psychological Works of Sigmund Freud* and *The Collected Papers of Sigmund Freud* (critique)

"The Ethics of Belief," from W. K. Clifford, *Lectures and Essays* (critique)

First Examination (on traditional religious types I & II)

*6th week: Introduction to Type 3: Living in
Harmony with Cosmic Law*

Students read assigned readings. In class we discuss the five key elements in the process of ultimate transformation as found in Type 3. We

note the particular expressions in the data that indicate the content of each element.

Readings:

URL, Ch. 4 "Living in Harmony with Cosmic Law"

"Chinese Religion," from L. G. Thompson, *Chinese Religion: An Introduction*

"*Li*: Rites and Propriety," from N. E. Fehl, *Li: Rites and Propriety in Literature and Life*

"On *Li*" (Rites, Propriety, Rules of Decorum) from *Hsun Tzu: Basic Writings*

Film: "Dadi's Family" (Video Cassette)

7th week: Type 3 continued

Students read assigned readings. In class we continue to analyze the data, highlighting the particular forms that express the elements of the process of ultimate transformation in this type. Again, the discussion of the critiques focuses on a comparison of the reasons given by the advocates and by the critics for their respective value judgments.

Readings:

"What *Karma* Explains," from C. Humphreys, *Karma and Rebirth*

"Hindu Dharma," from S. Radhakrishnan, *The Hindu View of Life*

"The Laws of Manu," trans. G. Buhler, in *Sacred Books of the East*

"On the Religious Sanction of Social Fictions," from P. Berger, *The Precarious Vision* (critique)

"Morality as Social Convention," from R. Taylor, *Good and Evil: A New Direction* (critique)

8th week: Introduction to Type 4: Attaining Freedom
Through Spiritual Discipline

Students read assigned readings. In class we note similarities and differences in the content of the five key elements in the process of ultimate transformation, pointing to the explicit discussion in URL, Chs. 4 & 5. Then we discuss the content of the data that describes specific meditation techniques, teachings of spiritual masters and descriptions of enlightenment experience.

Readings:

URL, Ch. 5 "Attaining Freedom Through Spiritual Discipline"

"Interviews with Yasutani Roshi," from *The Three Pillars of Zen*, ed., P. Kapleau

"Training in Zen," from Abbot Z. Shibayama, *A Flower Does Not Talk: Zen Essays*

"Dialogue between Ch'an Master Yung-Chia and the Patriarch," from *Original Teachings of Ch'an Buddhism*, trans., Chang-Yuan

Film: "Mood of Zen"

9th week: Type 4 continued

Students read assigned readings. In class we continue to analyze the data, highlighting the particular forms that express the elements of the process of ultimate transformation in this type. The discussion of the critiques focuses on a comparison of the reasons given by the advocates and by the critics for their respective value judgments.

Readings:

"The Way of Mindfulness," from Nyanaponika Thera, *The Heart of Buddhist Meditation*

"Introduction to Yoga," from S. K. Majumdar, *Introduction to Yoga*

"On the Nature of Pure Consciousness," from Shankara, *Upadeshasahasri of Sri Sankaracharya*

"On Determining Truth," from H. Feigl, "Philosophy of Science" in *Philosophy* (critique)

"On Whether Mystical Insight Is an Adequate Solution to Suffering," from D. C. Vijayavardhana, *The Revolt in the Temple* (critique)

Second Examination (on traditional religious Types 3 & 4)

10th week: Type 5 Fulfilling Human Relationships

Students read essays which explore the shift from transcendent ultimate reality to progressive fulfillment of comprehensive value. Then, the students analyze psychotherapy, encounter groups and self-actualization as means to ultimate transformation for some people.

Readings:

"On Faith as Illusion," from W. T. Stace in "Man Against Darkness," in *The Atlantic Monthly*, 1948

"Evolution and Transhumanism," from J. Huxley, "Transhumanism," in *New Bottles for New Wine: Essays by Julian Huxley*

"Ethics without Religion," from K. Nielsen in *The Ohio University Review*, Vol. VI, 1964

"URL, pp. 105-8, and Ch. 6, "The Religious Significance of Fulfilling Human Relationships"

Film: "Actualization Therapy"

11th week: Type 5 continued

Students read assigned readings. In class we continue to analyze the data, highlighting the particular forms that express the elements of the process of ultimate transformation in this type. The discussion of the critiques focuses on a comparison of the reasons given by the advocates and by the critics for their respective value judgments.

Readings:

"Education in Approval," from A. S. Neill, *Summerhill: A Radical Approach to Child Rearing*

"On the Religious Character of 'Integrity Groups'," from O. H. Mowrer in "The Problem of Good and Evil Empirically Considered with Reference to Psychological and Social Adjustment," *Zygon: Journal of Religion and Science*, IV, No. 4, 1969

"Man's Search for Himself," from R. May, *Man's Search for Himself*

"Psychoanalyst—Physician of the Soul," from E. Fromm, *Psychoanalysis and Religion*

"On Man as God's Creation—Not Man's," from A. C. Outler, *Psychotherapy and the Christian Message* (critique)

"Nice People or New Men," from C. S. Lewis, *Mere Christianity* (critique)

12th week: Introduction to Type 6: Social-Political Revolution

Students read assigned readings. In class we note similarities and differences in the content of the five key elements in this process of ultimate transformation, pointing to the explicit discussion in URL, Chs. 6 & 7. Class discussion focuses on the content of the data which calls for social revolution, describes injustices and advocates justice, equal opportunity and appropriate distribution of wealth.

Readings:

URL, Ch. 7 "The Religious Significance of Social Responsibility"

"Human Being and Social Alienation," from J. Cone, *Black Technology and Black Power*

"The Revolution as the Moral Ideal," from Liu Shao-Ch'i, "How to Be a good Communist," trans. W. T. de Bary, in *Sources of Chinese Tradition*

"Female Liberation as the Basis for Social Revolution," from R. Dunbar in *Sisterhood is Powerful: An Anthology of Writings from the Women's Liberation Movement*

13th week: Type 6 continued, and Summary Discussion

Students read assigned readings. The discussion of the critiques focuses on a comparison of the reasons given by the advocates and by the critics for their respective value judgments. The summary discussion centers on the significance of living in a world community which has diverse "ways of salvation." Also, a comparison of assumptions found in various religious forms highlights the importance of personal choices in the student's own religious awareness and behavior.

Readings:

"Religion and Morality," from J. E. Smith, *Journal of Religion*, Vol. 29, 1948 (critique)

"The Spiritual Source of Morality," from S. Radhakrishnan, *An Idealist View of Life* (critique)

Final Examination

III. Reflections on Classroom Experience

This approach to introducing students to the nature and forms of religion has been used for more than two decades in a variety of class settings. It has been used in small denominational colleges, private universities, and large state universities. In this section I will, first, describe the situation, student profile and response that I have experienced in using this approach. Then, I will present three issues that arise in this course; and, finally, describe other courses that have used this approach.

(1) *Teaching experience*: I have used this approach at Southern Methodist University (Dallas) in the Religious Studies Department, and at the University of California, Berkeley in a Religious Studies Program. In both situations most of the students took the course as an elective within a general humanities distribution requirement. Most students were first and second year students, though some juniors and seniors also took the course. Most were students who had not declared majors, had majors in a humanities field other than religious studies, or were registered in another school of the university—usually art, business or engineering.

The size of classes has ranged from twenty-five to forty-five, though during the last few years I have tried to hold to a limit of thirty-five. The classes had approximately equal numbers of men and women. While there were normally a range in ethnic and social background, most students were white middle class. Most, likewise, were nominally members of one or another Christian denomination, but they indicated on a questionnaire used the first day of class that generally they are only "somewhat active" in their religious life. At either end of the religious spectrum, the classes included a few professed atheists or staunchly "uncommitted," as well as a few witnessing (Christian) fundamentalists. Scattered throughout the classes were a few Jews, Hindus, Muslims, and Buddhists.

Most of the students enter the class with an image of religion that derives from their own (positive or negative) experience with institutional Christianity; often they define "religion" as belief in certain religious doctrines or moral rules. The majority has no more than a TV or movie knowledge of Eastern and African traditional religions, or of Islam. When students come into this course they have not approached religion as a general, universal human experience, and have not subjected their own experience to any form of analytical reflection or significant critical assessment. They do not know how to read religious texts or how to see films of religious life from different cultures in order to discern religious intentionality; nor have they compared different forms of religion within general religious categories. Likewise, there is a tendency for them to interpret a religious phenomenon at only one level of meaning, and to seek simple interpretations of religious truth.

Despite the narrow experience of religion by the students when they enter this course, most of them are willing, and often eager, to explore alternate religious options. They are curious about other peoples' religious life, and make an effort to enter imaginatively into the thought, practice, and life-stance of "strangers." Most often they appreciate a systematic conceptual framework in which they can understand the variety of religious life. Many come to the class frustrated with the conflicting religious claims of good and intelligent people (within their own experience), and value an understanding of religious life that delineates alternate structures of valuation as an important factor in accounting for different religious claims. Because the course is structured to present critiques of each "way"—and they soon learn that the assumptions within the critiques of one way can become the assumptions of the advocates of another way—the students perceive that they themselves participate in one or another set of evaluative assumptions that have consequences for their own lives.

While students sometimes are frustrated by the need to learn a new vocabulary (rapidly) as they read the advocates' statements from different cultures, they also learn the power of concepts and imagery to structure the deepest sensitivities and moral commitments of human beings. More importantly, by the end of the course, most students discover that in an attempt to attain comprehensive well-being, people have emphasized different dimensions of human life, sometimes concentrating on symbolic construction of a world of meaning, other times developing a spontaneous attitude which frees one from one's own construction, manifesting one's place in the natural rhythm of the universe, or transforming one's life through an extraordinary ecstatic experience.

The exams in this course provide the occasions for students to demonstrate their knowledge of a variety of religious expressions from different cultures, their interpretive skills to understand the meaning of specific data in relation to the paradigm of ultimate transformation, and their sensitivity to the kinds of justifications and critiques that have been given for different ways of ultimate transformation. The final exam is a take-home essay exam with several options. Students may present their analysis of some traditional religious expression that has not been directly taken up in class; they may locate a contemporary non-traditional religious (i.e., ultimately transforming) practice other than the forms discussed in class and analyze its religious character; or they may present their own "way of being religious" (which may, of course, include elements of different types examined in class), with a discussion of at least two alternate ways that they reject. Each of these options requires a description of one or more specific cultural expression, and an analysis of religious intentionality within a general concept of religion. Many students choose to present their own religious way, showing an understanding of key elements in their personal expression of comprehensive value.

(2) *Issues Raised*: The specific data that are analyzed within each "way of salvation" are selected because they demonstrate the content of the elements in that way. Students need to be cautioned against assuming that all religious phenomena fit into one or another "type." To the contrary, many religious phenomena (including the students' personal experiences and behavior) combine the content of different "ideal" types or models.

Despite the fact that each of the great religious traditions include various "ways of ultimate transformation"—as shown by locating data from several major traditions within each way—students tend to identify their *image* of a tradition with one type. This oversimplification needs to be challenged.

Because this approach attempts, within a general notion of ultimate reality, to include both (i) various understandings of a transcendent reality and (ii) various immanent developmental ultimate realities (in the non-traditional "ways"), the question can be raised regarding the wide scope of what can be included within the formal notion of ultimate reality. I hold that one pays a price for whatever definition of ultimate reality one uses. The breadth allowed in this definition makes possible a comparison between some human phenomena which function religiously without conforming to some historically defined form of (traditional) religious life.

(3) *Other courses that use or include this approach*: Over the years instructors have told me how they use this ways-of-ultimate-transformation approach. Besides courses similar to that described above, other kinds of courses can include this approach:

(a) A two-semester or two-quarter introduction to religion can focus on the traditional ways during one term, and non-traditional (humanistic) ways another. Instructors who have a semester for the traditional "ways" often include an introductory segment on different approaches to the study of religion that have been used during the past century. This allows for a discussion of the nature of religion as exposed through different disciplines, e.g., sociology, anthropology, and philosophy for one segment, leaving the rest of the term for an examination of the four traditional ways. In the second semester or quarter, the focus is on non-traditional ways, with an emphasis on the relation of religion to culture. A whole term on this aspect allows time for an exploration not only of psychotherapy and political-economic revolution as a "means of ultimate transformation" (as in the course outline described above), but can include a consideration of the religious significance of art, reason and technology in the modern world. A semester-long unit also allows time for mentioning other cultural forms, e.g., sports or entrepreneurship, which function for some people as a means for ultimate transformation.

(b) Another use of this approach in a one-term introduction to religion is to take this approach, summarized in *Understanding Religious Life*, as one segment in a three-fold analysis of the study of religion. The other two segments often explore a social science approach, and a philosophical approach (including rational-critical and existential foci) to an explanation and assessment of religious life.

(c) A third use has been to introduce students to different types of traditional religious life during the first segment. Then the class has briefly studied the basic concepts, practice, and institutional forms of two religious traditions—usually one Western and one Eastern tradition—showing the specific ways in which a tradition maintains some internal tensions, as different schools or denominations emphasize one or another means of ultimate transformation within that tradition. For example, the Christian tradition includes a sacramental emphasis in Roman Catholicism as well as a personal ecstatic experiential emphasis among the Pentecostals; the Buddhist tradition includes the theravada monastic meditation emphasis as well as the Japanese Jodo-shin trust in the power of Amida's Vow as a means for ultimate transformation.

In each of these alternate uses we see that the approach of examining "ways of ultimate transformation" can be used differently in light of the instructor's inclination. Sometimes it provides an overarching interpretive principle, and a stimulus, for students' self-reflection on their own religious assumptions; other times it is presented as one of several possible approaches to the study of religion. Sometimes the comparative concept "way of ultimate transformation" defines religion as a general concept; alternatively it can function to raise methodological questions, or help illumine the study of specific religious phenomena. In any event, the approach centers on the issue of the nature of religion as this is expressed by advocates from diverse cultural forms. It helps to develop skills in understanding another person's deepest commitments and religious behavior, provides a general conceptual framework for relating diverse religious phenomena, and stimulates the students' reflection on their own religious assumptions.

PILGRIMAGE
As A Thematic Introduction To The Comparative Study of Religion

RICHARD R. NIEBUHR

1. Background; 2. Designing the Course; 3. Sample Syllabus;
4. Curricular Setting of the Course; 5. Teaching the Course
6. Personal Reflections on the Course

1. Background

About ten years ago Diana Eck, William Graham and I began developing a course on pilgrimage, which I describe in the following pages.

We wanted to provide an introduction to the comparative study of religion designed specifically for undergraduates at Harvard College. The need for such an introduction arose from two roughly concurrent events: the authorization by the Faculty of Arts and Sciences of a limited enrollment honors concentration in the Comparative Study of Religion and the departure of our colleague, Wilfred Cantwell Smith, to take a post at Dalhousie University. Wilfred had been offering a two semester introduction to the religions of the world in the Humanities division of the General Education program, which at that time was still in effect in the college. No one was prepared to offer a course similar to Wilfred's yet we wanted a course that would be inclusive, if not comprehensive, in scope. For that reason we considered the feasibility of a thematic ap-

proach and ultimately decided that pilgrimage would satisfy our purposes.

We designed the course on pilgrimage and taught it as a team, offering it for the first time in the fall of 1978. Diana is a scholar of comparative religion and a specialist in Indian religions and culture; she had done
extensive research on the city of Banaras, a principle pilgrimage center in
India. Bill is also a scholar of comparative religion and a specialist in
Islamic religion and culture. Hence he was already familiar with the Hajj
and also had a strong interest in sacred mountains and mountain pilgrimages. I came to the course from the unlikely background of many
years of teaching modern western religious thought. However, as the
chair of the Committee on the Study of Religion at Harvard, I was devot-
ing a very substantial amount of my time to the new undergraduate concentration and working closely with these two colleagues on all aspects
of this program, including the planning and implementation of new
courses.

Before offering the subject as a public lecture course open to the general student population, we experimented with the materials and format
over a period of time in a seminar for sophomore concentrators in the
Comparative Study of Religion. In fact, it was only after having arranged
these sophomore seminars around the pilgrimage theme—while also ex-
perimenting with several other topics, such as the holy or sacred—that
we realized the special advantages of pilgrimage as an organizing principle, as something to think about and think with, in the process of leading and accompanying undergraduates into their first study of religion. I
will identify some of the advantages we discovered in a subsequent section.

2. Designing the Course

We were already well acquainted with each other and so had a solid
working basis on which to make decisions about what to include and
what to leave out of the course. As we looked into sources, we rapidly
became aware that there were far more materials than we could possibly
include in a single course. All of us were heavily involved in other
teaching and administrative responsibilities; hence we had to build on
the strengths we already possessed and then make the difficult judgments about what materials to add to our existing repertoire. Looking
back from this point in time, I am sure we all would acknowledge that
we could well have chosen to follow any one of a number of different
routes. But our own interests were bound to come to the fore, and that

fact, I believe, is not necessarily a defect. Courses of this nature are properly somewhat personal in character.

We had to decide whether to confine ourselves to pilgrimage in the narrowest sense (ritual pilgrimage) or to include other allied kinds of journeys. Some scholars of religion recognize only ritual pilgrimage as true pilgrimage. The attached syllabus shows that we chose the wider field of view. I will mention some of our reasons a few lines further along.

We distinguished between prototypical wanderings, sojournings, flights, and goings forth (Abraham and Sarah, Hagar and Ishmael, Moses and the people of Israel, the Buddha Shakyamuni) and pilgrimage actions derived from such prototypes. We deliberated whether to limit ourselves to legendary and historical journeys or to include materials of a literary character that recount a pilgrimage-like journey or employ pilgrimage as their organizing metaphor. The line between mythical, legendary, and historical, on the one hand, and fictive, on the other, is fine indeed. We opted for the second alternative. A conference on pilgrimage in Pittsburgh in 1981, organized by E. A. Morinis of Simon Fraser University, afforded an opportunity to discuss this issue with other scholars of pilgrimage. I continue to believe that written records of pilgrimage and pilgrimage stories, however highly polished, constitute significant forms of the repetition, preservation, and expansion of pilgrimage acts and pilgrimage-consciousness.

One important consideration influencing our thinking was our intention to have the course exhibit the fact that the study of religion is the study of an arena in which multiple cultural patterns converge and shape each other. In its various forms pilgrimage has played its part not only in affecting trade and commerce, geographic consciousness and centers of political power, but artistic forms as well. We wanted the course to exhibit both humanistic and social scientific approaches and to embrace both popular and "high" culture. We were much aware of the liberal arts and sciences setting in which we were working.

We also had to decide the sequence in which we would present our materials. We elected to proceed tradition by tradition (the most plausible method for an introductory course). We concentrated on Judaism, Christianity, Islam, Indian religions, and Japanese religions. And, of course, we omitted vast amounts of material, whole continents such as Africa and South America. We treated medieval European pilgrimage rather lightly, unless we could recruit informed guest lecturers. We included the "Great Migration," from England to New England in the

1630s, because the chronicles of that event pointedly invoke the Abraham epic and Exodus as types of the crossing of the Atlantic and settling in a promised land. Though we were tempted, we could not include the American westward migration in the nineteenth century. We did not know whether to begin in the East or the West. We chose to do the latter on the grounds that we could better orient students to the methods and aims of the course by beginning with Western materials. Is it more effective to start with the exotic or the putatively familiar? We still do not know.

3. Sample Syllabus

Note: This syllabus represents our most ambitious version of the course. In 1981-82 we attempted three lectures and discussion group meetings each week. In other years we followed the pattern of two lectures a week plus a discussion group meeting.

HARVARD UNIVERSITY RELIGION 10 FALL TERM 1981-82

"Pilgrimages: A Thematic Introduction to Religion"

Course Meetings:	Monday, Wednesday, Friday at 9:00
	Weekly discussion meetings.
	Three evening film showings

Instructors:	Teaching Fellows:
William A. Graham	Thomas Head
Diana L. Eck	Lindsey Harlan
Richard R. Niebuhr	Mark Hagar

Guest Lecturer: Marc E. Saperstein

In this course we use pilgrimage as our unifying theme in an exploration of human religiousness. We do not maintain that pilgrimage is equally important in all religious traditions. It is but one of a number of religious phenomena that are widely present in religious life. We shall use pilgrimage as a trajectory to follow into the religious dimensions of human experience in disparate times and places. Necessarily we shall omit much and stress pilgrimage and journey themes. We intend to use this theme as a point of departure for exploring the great variety of religious life: its symbols, rituals, and myths; its laws, doctrines, and customs; and its faith and vision. The task is made easier by the wealth of ideas and images associated with pilgrimage: sojourn in a strange land, search for healing and wholeness, quest for wisdom or solitude, return to the center, exodus and deliverance, wayfaring and warfaring, fording the stream, following the path, ascending the heights, coming home.

————————

Class Meeting Schedule

I.   RELIGION & PILGRIMAGE: INTRODUCTORY ISSUES

M	21	Sept.	Pilgrimage: The Journey & the Goal (E)
W	23	Sept.	Pilgrimage as Microcosm of Religion (N)
F	25	Sept.	Myth & Mythic Language in Religion & Pilgrimage (G)
M	28	Sept.	Symbol & the Symbolism of Pilgrimage (N)
T	29	Sept.	EVENING FILM: "To Find Our Lives"
W	30	Sept.	The Meaning of Ritual (E)

Discussion meetings W-F: "The Sacred & the Profane"; also Huichol pilgrimage

F	2	Oct.	Religion, Pilgrimage & the Physical World (G)

II. PILGRIMAGE & THE "WESTERN" TRADITIONS

M	5	Oct.	Abraham, "A Wandering Aramean..." (G)
W	7	Oct.	Exodus: Deliverance & Creation (N)

Discussion meetings W-F: Biblical Narratives of Epic Wanderings

F	9	Oct.	Jerusalem: The City on a Hill (E)
M	12	Oct.	HOLIDAY
W	14	Oct.	Pilgrimage & the Cult of the Saints in Medieval Christianity (Thomas Head)

Discussion meetings W-F: Medieval Christian Pilgrimage and the Holy

F	16	Oct.	Spiritual Pilgrimage in Medieval Christianity (Head)
M	19	Oct.	"The Pilgrim's Progress": Symbolism of the Narrative (N)
W	21	Oct.	"The Pilgrim's Progress": The "Straight Way" & the Development of the Narrative (N)
F	23	Oct.	MIDTERM EXAMINATION
M	26	Oct.	"City on a Hill": The Puritan Migration to a New Land (N)
W	28	Oct.	New Land: Thoreau's Sojourn at Walden (N)
F	30	Oct.	"Galut": Jewish Exile among the Nations (Marc Saperstein)
M	2	Nov.	Returning Home: Jewish Pilgrimage to Jerusalem (Saperstein)
W	4	Nov.	Islam, Ritual, & Pilgrimage (G)
F	6	Nov.	FILM: "Mecca, the Forbidden City"
M	9	Nov.	The Hajj: Ritual and Worship (G)
W	11	Nov.	HOLIDAY

Discussion meetings W-F: "In the Heart of the Seas" by S. Y. Agnon

F	13	Nov.	The Cult of the Saints & Tomb Pilgrimage in Islam (G)
M	16	Nov.	The Mystical Path in Islam & "The Conference of the Birds"

III. PILGRIMAGE & THE "EASTERN" TRADITIONS

W	18	Nov.	The Gods of India & the Polytheistic Imagination (E)

F   20   Nov.   The Sacred Geography of India (E)
M   23   Nov.   Pilgrimage to the City of Light (E)
W   25   Nov.   FILM: "Ramdevra: A Popular Pilgrimage in Rajasthan"
F   27   Nov.   HOLIDAYS
M   30   Nov.   Leaving Home: Pilgrimage & Renunciation (E)
Discussion meetings W-F: Interpreting Hindu images
W   2   Dec.   The Buddha and His "Going Forth" (E)
EVENING FILM SHOWING: "The Footprint of the Buddha"
F   4   Dec.   Relics, Healing, & Miracles (E)
M   7   Dec.   Nature, Gods, & Pilgrimage in Japan, I (G)
W   9   Dec.   Nature, Gods, & Pilgrimage in Japan, II (G)
Discussion meetings W-F, Suzuki readings: Zen, Shinto & Japanese pilgrimage
EVENING FILM SHOWING
F   11   Dec.   Meditation & its Setting in Japan (N)
M   14   Dec.   Basho: Poet & Pilgrim (N)
W   16   Dec.   Basho's Road through the Far North (N)
Discussion meetings W-F: "The Narrow Road To The Deep North"
F   18   Dec.   Concluding session & discussion

Course Requirements

Regular attendance at lectures, section meetings, & film showings.

Regular reading of assigned materials in correlation with the schedule of lectures and discussions. Part of the final grade for the course will depend on section discussion participation.

There will be three short essay assignments, 2-4 pages each, to be submitted in the course of the term. These will be due at the beginning of the hour on the following days: 7 Oct., 13 Nov., and 2 Dec., 1981. The specific topics for each will be handed out well in advance.

There will be a midterm examination (one hour) and a final examination (three hours). The midterm and one hour (=1/3) of the final examination will cover subjects treated in the course lectures, films, discussion, and readings. The other 2/3 of the final examination will be a two-hour essay that may be prepared in advance of the examination. Each student will choose his or her topic beforehand to write on during the allotted time in the examination. The topic chosen must be "cleared" with the appropriate section leader in advance of the examination.

The midterm is scheduled for the 23rd of Oct.; the final for Thursday, the 28th of January 1982.

[Note: In some years we altered the requirements and asked for a 15 page term paper in place of the brief essays. Students received a 10 to 15 page bibliography to assist them in writing their papers.]

The following books have been ordered for purchase:

S. Y. Agnon, *In The Heart of the Seas*
Fariduddin Attar, *The Conference of the Birds*
Basho, *The Narrow Road to the Deep North*
John Bunyan, *The Pilgrim's Progress*
Edward Conze, ed., *Buddhist Scriptures*
Diana Eck, *Darsan, Seeing the Divine Image in India*
Mircea Eliade, *The Sacred and the Profane*
Huston Smith, *The Religions of Man*
D. T. Suzuki, *Zen and Japanese Culture*
H. D. Thoreau, *Walden*

All required readings are on reserve. Readings marked with an asterisk (*) may be found on reserve in a single volume entitled "Pilgrimages: Religion 10." In the third week a packet of a few important readings will be available in class, at cost. These materials are marked below with a double asterisk (**).

Note: *The Religions of Man*, by Huston Smith, is not explicitly required reading but may serve as introduction and background for relevant sections of the course, as needed.

Schedule of Readings

Wed 30 Sept.
Mircea Eliade, *The Sacred and the Profane*
*Victor Turner, "The Center Out There: Pilgrim's Goal"
*Peter Furst, "To Find Our Life: Peyote Among the Huichol of Mexico"
      [recommended]
*Mircea Eliade, "Methodological Remarks on the Study of Religious Symbolism"
      [recommended]
*Barbara Meyerhoff, "Organization & Ecstacy: Deliberate & Accidental Communitas Among Huichol Indians & American Youth" [recommended]

Wed 7 Oct.
The Abraham Epic: Genesis 11:10 - 25:11
Moses & Israel in the Wilderness: Exodus 1-24, 32-34; Deuteronomy 1-11; 29-34
Huston Smith, chap. 7, "Judaism" [recommended]

Wed 14 Oct.
** Felix Fabri, selections from *The Book of the Wandering of Friar Felix Fabri*
**Thomas a Kempis, *The Imitation of Christ*, Bk. II
**William Langland, selections from *Piers the Ploughman*

Houston Smith, chap. 8, "Christianity" [recommended]
The Gospel of Luke, 19:28 - 24:50 [recommended]

Wed 21 Oct.
John Bunyan, *The Pilgrim's Progress* (Part I ONLY)

Wed 28 Oct.
Henry David Thoreau, *Walden*

Wed 4 Nov.
S. Y. Agnon, *In the Heart of the Seas*
Psalms of Ascent to Jerusalem: 48, 84, 87, 122

Wed 11 Nov.
Ahmad Kamal, *The Sacred Journey* (copies on reserve), pp. 3-46, 51-72, 82-93
**Selections from the Qur'an (G. Sale translation, 1734)
Muhammad Asad, *The Road to Mecca*, chap. 12, "The End of the Road"
William A. Graham, "Islam in the Mirror of Ritual" (on reserve, separately bound)
        [recommended]
Huston Smith, chap. 6, "Islam" [recommended]

Wed 18 Nov.
Ahmad Kamal, *The Sacred Journey*, pp. 97-108
Fariddudin Attar, *The Conference of the Birds*

Week of 23 Nov. - No section meetings

Wed 2 Dec.
Diana L. Eck, *Darsan, Seeing the Divine Image in India*
Mira Reym Binford, "Mixing in the Colors of Ram of Ranuja" (on reserve, separately bound)
*Agehananda Bharati, "Pilgrimage in the Indian Tradition"
Edward Conze, ed., *Buddhist Scriptures*, pp. 34-66 ("The Legend of the Buddha
        Shakyamuni")
*Diana L. Eck, "Banaras, City as Symbol"
Heinrich Zimmer, *Myths and Symbols in Indian Art & Civilization* (chap. 1 or 2, for
        use in 3rd essay assignment)
Huston Smith, chaps. 2 ("Hinduism") & 3 ("Buddhism") [recommended]

Wed 9 Dec.
*Joseph M. Kitagawa, "Three Types of Pilgrimage in Japan"
D. T. Suzuki, *Zen and Japanese Culture*, chaps. 1, 2, 11
*Sokyo Ono, *The Kami Way*, chaps. 1, 2 (Shinto) [recommended]
Suzuki, *Zen and Japanese Culture*, chaps. 4-6, 8, 9 [recommended]
Huston Smith, chap. 5 ("Taoism") [recommended]

Wed 16 Dec.
Basho, *The Narrow Road to the Deep North*, Introduction & pp. 71-143
Suzuki, *Zen and Japanese Culture*, chap. 8

---

4. Curricular Setting of the Course

Enterprises like this course on pilgrimage are inevitably affected by the nature of the institution in which they are situated as well as by the particular faculty who teach it. And they must be adapted to the student constituency and to the distribution requirements affecting students. I should mention then the general institutional and curricular context in which our course took its place. In the mid 1970s Harvard College was shifting from a General Education program to a Core Curriculum program mandatory for every undergraduate. Courses offered within such programs sometimes attract large enrollments. For a number of reasons, we chose not to offer the pilgrimage course in the General Education program. (The Core Curriculum program, either by design or accident, excluded courses on religion.) One of our reasons was that we wanted the course to be sufficiently focused and intense to provide potential concentrators with an adequate first course in the comparative study of religion. But it was available to other students as a way of satisfying the requirement that they elect two or more regular courses in the humanities, if they preferred not to follow the General Education route. This mix of concentrators, potential concentrators, and non-concentrators worked well. The average enrollment over the five years we have taught the course has been 80 to 90 students.

Other introductory as well as advanced courses were and are available to students. "Conceptions of the Afterlife" (Jane Smith), introductions to Islam (Smith and Graham), to Buddhism (Masatoshi Nagatomi and David Eckel), courses on Judaism offered by Marc Saperstein and various courses devoted to methods and issues such as "Magic, Science, and Religion" (Stanley Tambiah), "The Interpretation of Religious Experience" (Niebuhr), and a course on ritual that Diana Eck developed.

5. Teaching the Course

We varied the content of the course from year to year, continually reconsidering what was most important, most illuminating, and what materials best complimented each other.

Each of us teaching the course attended all lectures to insure continuity not only in theme but in tone and style. Each could then refer to what colleagues had said earlier and would be saying later. To avoid the well known disadvantages of "parade" courses, we kept lectures by visitors to a minimum. Normally, we scheduled two lectures and a third hour for small discussion group meetings each week. For the latter purpose we employed one or more advanced graduate students to reduce the size of the discussion groups and sometimes invited one of them, if especially qualified, to give one or two lectures. For the most part, we drew upon men and women working in the field of the comparative study of religion. At that time adequate basic texts in the history of religion were hard to come by, but some such text was necessary, and we made do. We supplemented by providing additional background information in our lectures.

We also made considerable use of film, often scheduling showings in the evening, outside regular class hours; and we used slides as well, for the most part drawn from our own travels or reproduced from books, e.g. Buson's illustrations of Basho's travel narrative. Visual materials, we found, do add significantly to the content of the course, but they can also be a pitfall, since students are often unskilled in "reading" the visual and cannot concentrate for long on a graphic image. They are trained to listen but not to see; one undergraduate confessed to me that he regularly dozed during the presentation of film and slides. Similarly, I had to work hard to learn how to employ such materials effectively and still have a long way to go; the temptation to use too much persists.

Courses are significantly affected by the classroom space in which they are located. This fact holds especially for courses involving visual materials. Harvard is woefully lacking in well designed classrooms with adequate seating arrangements, audio-visual equipment, acoustical properties, and ventilation. Finding a minimally satisfactory classroom was always difficult, and our fortunes varied from year to year.

I believe that whatever success we met with, which of course is impossible to quantify, derived in large measure from the fact that all of us doing the teaching were fascinated by the material and enjoyed working with one another.

6. Personal Reflections

A) Previously, I knew nothing about the phenomenon of pilgrimage, save for the biblical narratives in Genesis and Exodus that we use in the course and John Bunyan's *The Pilgrim's Progress*, which I had long admired for its author's incomparable style and acuity of social and psychological observation. Teaching is, of course, the most effective means of learning, and in doing background research I rapidly became aware that Protestant popular culture, despite the sixteenth century Reformers' censures of the pilgrimage-penitential system, continued to draw heavily on the pilgrimage motif. No doubt it did so partly because theological strictures change social habits only slowly, if at all; and partly because the pilgrimage motif is so conspicuous in the Bible, not only in the Old Testament but in the Letter to the Hebrews as well as in Paul's metaphors of the "contest" and the "race" (blended with the "armor of God" imagery in Ephesians 6). The vastly popular emblem books of the seventeenth century, such as Francis Quarel's *Emblems: Divine and Moral*, amply testify to this fact and help to explain why so receptive an audience awaited the publication of Bunyan's story. But seventeenth century Puritan sermons and pastoral treatises also vividly exemplify the theme.

One major lesson that I learned as a consequence of my participation in the project is that the pilgrimage motif is a natural catalyst for the combining of elements of personal and communal religious experience, especially those elements that "attract" interpretation in metaphors of temporal and spatial motion. Pilgrimage provides an apparently irresistible syntax for configuring ritual action and religious envisionment of the cosmos. It constitutes a deep pattern of religious being-in-the-world, a pattern that surfaces in many places including some that one could scarcely anticipate. For example, it not only dramatizes and valorizes particular physical and visible journeys with religious significance, it also symbolically reinterprets such inward and invisible events as conversion. Again, with its variable ingredient or sub-symbols it not only reinterprets specific "limens" or thresholds (such as leaving home, resolving to return to one's center, death) but the whole process of human life. Through its symbolical efficacy it identifies the changeableness and motility of human life with the laws and energies that make up the religiously imagined ultimate order of things. The Pilgrimage-Idea is a highly versatile "interpretant" that shapes the life-moments of persons and communities and redirects their course. A modern William James could easily write a *Varieties of Pilgrimage Experience*. I suspect this characteristic cannot be predicted of every thematic approach to the comparative study of religion, but with respect to pilgrimage there is no longer doubt in my mind.

B) As a teacher of modern Western religious thought and theology, I found the theme of pilgrimage as a means of access to the larger field of

comparative religion to be intellectually rewarding and personally exciting for a number of reasons.

i)   It provides a valuable perspective on the ever elusive dynamic
unity of spirit, mind, and body, a unity that is utterly central to our endeavor to understand human religiousness. It demonstrates how gestural
symbolization and other kinds of somatic action assist individuals and
communities to envisage the inexplicable givenness of their lives—their
origins, duties, and destinies.

ii) Pilgrimage, in its virtually inexhaustible forms, vividly exhibits
multiple ways in which the narrative-dramatic and the reflective-medi-
tative dimensions of religious life modify and shape each other.

iii) It underscores the inseparability of solitary and communal
religion.

iv) It illustrates the constant interplay between inherited forms of
religiousness and the shifting patterns of cultures.

v)   It contributes to our appreciation of the fact that religion in all
of its dimensions is not only historically but topographically situated.
Just as selves are social, incorporating the communities from which they
come and to which they aspire so they are topoplastic selves, outwardly
and inwardly shaped by the sites and regions in and toward which they
toil.

vi) As symbolic action it is condensed as well as multivalent and
lends itself especially well to instruction in a liberal arts setting, because
it relates directly to the fields of literature, history, anthropology, sociology, art history, semiotics, phenomenology or religion, philosophy of
religion, and no doubt others as well.

C) Instructors, like students, are so various in their backgrounds and
temperaments that it is not particularly helpful to generalize about ourselves and methods of teaching. However, one issue that inevitably presents itself in this case is the distinction between "authentic" pilgrimage
and quests, journeys, and migrations that ostensibly have different characters. Of course, many other topics and phenomena in religion pose a
similar difficulty.

The issue can lend itself to fruitful discussion in the classroom,
whether at the outset of the term or at a later point. Without doubt many
students are anxious for a definition of the subject matter at the very outset to give them orientation and relief from the anxiety of the unknown.
Pilgrimage affords instructors a provocative challenge in the art of
defining. Restricting the course to one quite specific type of pilgrimage is
attractive. Such an approach has the obvious merit of making the phe-

nomenon concrete and more easily controllable, but it runs the danger of severing pilgrimage from the wider field of culture-shaping and culture-preserving energies in which it has actually always existed. But the very fact that pilgrimage is embedded in this wider field makes it the challenging and illuminating subject that it is.

Pilgrimage is, of course, but one modality of religiousness, yet its capacity to reflect and to interpret the cosmos of human piety makes it attractive as a subject of interpretation and research both at a first-course level and as a topic for advanced seminars.

Pilgrimage Out West

JOHN STRATTON HAWLEY

I have never had the good fortune to take the Harvard course on pilgrimage. But it was famous even in its infancy, and when I went to teach at the University of Washington I asked if I could have a look at the syllabus. The favor was graciously granted. Now the problem was mine: how to adapt a Harvard course (of which I had never heard a single lecture) to the curriculum of a major state university 3000 miles away?

Our best students, it is true, were comparable to those at Harvard or any other first-rate school. But they were few: a great spectrum filled in just behind them, and many were not there to reap the benefits of liberal education. They were engineers, accountants, foresters, and nurses, people who might never take another religion course again. Still, they were interested—nothing forced them to elect this course to fulfill their humanities requirement—and they knew that religion was something they would meet out there in the real world. They already had.

The course was called "Comparing Religions," and what would most easily have satisfied the hundred students who showed up at the first lecture would have been a survey of doctrine. "This is what Buddhists believe." "Now here comes Islam." I wanted, however, to do a thematic course in which it would be shown that religion has to do not only with ideas but with practice, and in which one would have the chance to gauge in what measure it is its own thing and in what measure a part of the culture in which it finds itself. Hence my interest in Harvard's pilgrimage idea. It seemed to provide a vehicle for raising all those issues at the same time that it offered the opportunity to present images of people's religious *lives*—some visual material that might stick in the mind after the words ceased echoing in the head (a half-life of five minutes or less, I would estimate). My hope was that the single theme of pilgrimage would enable students to grasp something intelligible and comparable in the five traditions we would study. But I also hoped that the motif would seem basic enough—who has not thought of life as a journey?—that it could serve as a flashlight for exploring these five dark rooms. In short, the purpose of the course was not just to teach about pilgrimage but to let pilgrimage teach us about five disparate traditions in which it has played an important role.

Course Materials

At this point let me show you the basic course materials, so that you can form an impression of what we did.

(1) *Syllabus.* The course outline gives a schedule of meetings of the entire class, which were devoted mostly to lectures. Some classes were given over to discussion, but we found that the course worked much better when there could be section meetings once a week; a good teaching assistant does wonders to heal wounds inflicted by a sometimes ill-organized instructor.

In the first year the course was offered, however, we did not have the luxury of regularly scheduled small-group meetings, since no funds had been set aside for a teaching assistant. So to meet the need for discussion, some of the students themselves organized weekly discussion groups, and in some ways that was the best solution of all.

RELIGION 203:
COMPARING RELIGIONS COURSE OUTLINE

Weeks 1 and 2 - World Religions: A Family Portrait
Introduction

Mcn., Sept. 26	Comparing and religion: two fundamental human urges

Five cameos

Tues., Sept. 27	Hindus: *darsan* (seeing, sight, point of view)
Wed., Sept. 28	Buddhists: the *bo* tree
Thurs., Sept. 29	Jews: *pesah* (Passover)
Mon., Oct. 3	Christians: the Magnificat
Tues., Oct. 4	Muslims: "There is No God but God" (film)

Summation

Wed., Oct. 5	Discussion: grouping the religions on a single canvas.
	Note: Your one page essays on this topic are due

	in the class hour.
Thurs., Oct. 6	Major theoretical attempts to group world religions.

Week 3 - Introduction to Pilgrimage

| Mon., Oct. 10 | Pilgrimage and the work of Victor Turner |
| Tues., Oct. 11 | "The Wizard of Oz" as a pilgrimage narrative |

Weeks 3 and 4 - Hinduism: Pilgrimage as Centering and Crossing

Wed., Oct. 12	Brindavan, the forest of Krishna
Thurs., Oct. 13	Brindavan: analysis
Mon., Oct. 17	Benares, the city of Siva
Tues., Oct. 18	Benares, continued: "Indian Pilgrimage: Kashi" (film)
Wed., Oct. 19	Benares and Brindavan
Thurs., Oct. 20	Govardhan, the mountain of God

Week 5 - Buddhism: Life as Pilgrimage

Mon., Oct. 24	The Life of the Buddha
Tues., Oct. 25	"Footprints of the Buddha" (film)
Wed., Oct. 26	Following in the Buddha's footsteps
Thurs., Oct. 27	Siddhartha and *Siddhartha*

Week 6 - Pilgrimage in Japan

Mon., Oct. 31	Pilgrimage to Mt. Fuji, with the film "Mt. Fuji"
Tues., Nov. 1	Japanese pilgrimage
Wed., Nov. 2	Discussion and review
Thurs., Nov. 3	*Midterm examination*

Week 7 - Reading week

No classes; the instructor is out of town.

Week 8 - Judaism: Going up to Jerusalem

Mon., Nov. 14	The wandering of the patriarchs
Tues., Nov. 15	From tent to temple
Wed., Nov. 16	Jerusalem, the holy city
Thurs., Nov. 17	Pilgrimage to Jerusalem

Week 9 - Christianity: Another View of Jerusalem

Mon., Nov. 21	The pilgrimage of Jesus: Israel's journey recapitulated
Tues., Nov. 22	The sacrifice of Jesus and the sacrifice of Isaac
Wed., Nov. 23	Medieval pilgrimage in Europe
Thurs., Nov. 24	Thanksgiving holiday

Week 10 - Islam: Pilgrimage Prescribed

| Mon., Nov. 28 | Jerusalem for Muslims |
| Tues., Nov. 29 | Mecca, center of all Islam |

| Wed., Nov. 30 | "Mecca, the Forbidden City" (film) |
| Thurs., Dec. 1 | Discussion: the three Abrahamic faiths |

Week 11 - America: Conclusion

Mon., Dec. 5	America as pilgrimage
Tues., Dec. 6	The old Jerusalem and the new
Wed., Dec. 7	Review and conclusion: the self and the other

(2) *Readings*. As I made out the list of assigned readings, I included a cluster of questions intended to give students a broad idea of why they were being subjected to this particular menu of materials. These questions sometimes served as springboards for discussion in small group meetings; sometimes they were merely there as background. Any reading selection prefaced by an asterisk was one that could be found in the course reader, which was available for purchase.

RELIGION 203: ASSIGNED READING

Weeks 1 and 2

W. C. Smith, *The Faith of Other Men* (San Francisco: Harper and Row, 1962 and subsequent printings), pp. 1-111.

Huston Smith, *The Religions of Man* (San Francisco: Harper and Row, 1958 and subsequent printings), pp. 1-159.

Week 3

*Victor Turner, "The Center Out There: Pilgrims' Goal," *History of Religions* 12:3 (1973): 191-230.

*Karen McCarthy Brown, "Pilgrimage is Good to Think with," paper delivered to the American Academy of Religion, 1979.

*E. Alan Morinis, "Theoretical Perspectives on Pilgrimage," in his *Pilgrimage in the Hindu Tradition* (Delhi: Oxford University Press, 1984), pp. 233-62.

CONSIDER: Why do people go on pilgrimage? Do Turner's suggestions explain the phenomenon to you? Does Brown's perspective help? Think of the pilgrimages—journeys—that you have gone on in trying to evaluate the worth of these theoretical suggestions.

Week 4

Diana L. Eck, *Darsan: Seeing the Divine Image in India*, 2nd rev. ed. (Chambersburg, PA: Anima Books, 1985), pp. 1-75.

Diana L. Eck, "Kasi: The City as Symbol," *Purana* 20:2 (1978): 169- 92.

J. S. Hawley, "Pilgrimage to Brindavan," in his *At Play With Krishna* (Princeton: Princeton University Press, 1981), pp. 3-51.

*E. Valentine Daniel, "Equilibrium Regained," chapter 7 of *Fluid Signs* (Berkeley: University of California Press, 1984).

CONSIDER: How Benares and Brindavan compare as goals of pilgimage, and how they represent two different strands of Hindu religion. Also, think about how such places as these two—sacred centers—aid in the centering of human lives.

Week 5

*Ashvaghosha, "The Legend of the Buddha Shakyamuni," translated in Edward Conze, ed., *Buddhist Scriptures* (Harmondsworth: Penguin Books, 1959 and subsequent printings), pp. 34-66.

Hermann Hesse, *Siddhartha*, trans. Hilda Rosner (New York: New Directions, 1951 and subsequent printings), entire.

*Edwin Bernbaum, "Heaven on Earth beyond the Himalayas," *Asia* 3:2 (1980): 37-41.

CONSIDER: What the relation is between the story of the Buddha's life as narrated by Ashvaghosha and the story told by Hermann Hesse. Does Hesse's version of Siddhartha's pilgrimage depart from that lived out by the Buddha or merely reinterpret it?

Week 6

No new reading assignment. Prepare for the midterm exam.

Week 7

This is a reading week. You have no classes, but plenty to read, as follows:

Huston Smith, *The Religions of Man*, pp. 217-348 (on Islam, Judaism, and Christianity).

Week 8

Genesis 12:1-25:11 (the epic of Abraham).

Exodus 1-24, 32-34 (the Exodus and the wanderings in the desert).

Psalms 48, 84, 87, 122 (songs of ascent into Jerusalem).

S. Y. Agnon, *In the Heart of the Seas* (New York: Shocken Books, 1967 [originally in Hebrew, 1947]), entire.

CONSIDER: How similar the Jewish conception of Jerusalem is to the Hindu conception of Benares. Are there similarities between the journey of the Jewish pilgrims recounted in Agnon's story and the journey of Siddhartha as told by Hesse? What is definitively Jewish about the Jewish veneration of Jerusalem?

Week 9

Luke 19:28-24:50 (Jesus' entry into Jerusalem and his passion).

The Book of the Wanderings of Felix Fabri, pp. 279-90 (arrival in Jerusalem) and pp. 340-91 (visit to the Holy Sepulchre).

*John Bunyan, *The Pilgrim's Progress*, selections, as given in *The Norton Anthology of English Literature*, vol. 1, pp. 1168-78.

CONSIDER: The Christian and Jewish Jerusalems. Is it the same place? Is the journey there the same? In thinking about Bunyan's *Pilgrim's Progress*, a narrative of interior pilgrimage, do you notice any similarities with Hesse's *Siddhartha*? Any differences?

Week 10

*Ahmad Kamal, *The Sacred Journey*, selections. Note that the account of the *hajj* is prefaced by a glossary of terms relating to the *hajj*.

*Muhammad Asad, *The Road to Mecca*, pp. 344-75 ("End of the account of the *hajj*" is prefaced by a glossary of terms relating to the *hajj*).

*Muhammad Asad, *The Road to Mecca*, pp. 344-75 ("End of the Road").

*Malcolm X, *The Autobiography of Malcolm X*, pp. 323-47 ("Mecca").

CONSIDER: The major moments of the *hajj*. Try to get straight in your mind what they are. What logic do they present? To what extent is the Muslim *hajj* similar to Jewish and Christian pilgrimages to Jerusalem, and to what extent is it different? Do you find Turner's concepts useful in illuminating the significance of the *hajj*?

Week 11

*Robert Bellah, "Civil Religion in America," *Daedalus* 96:1 (1967): 1-21.

*John Winthrop, "Christian Charitie. A Model Hereof," with introduction, in H. Sheldon Smith et al., *American Christianity*, vol. 1:97-102.

*Henry David Thoreau, *Walden*, selections: "The Pond in Winter" and "Conclusion."

*Mark Juergensmeyer, "California as Religion," paper delivered to the American Academy of Arts and Sciences, 1980.

CONSIDER: Your own experience as Americans, even West Coasters, and the American experience as seen by others. How important is the motif of pilgrimage in it all?

(3) *Exams.* As a further gesture toward focusing this mass of material for the benefit of a student body all too accustomed to the comfort of a single textbook, I adopted the practice of handing out study questions well before the midterm and final examinations. The exam questions were drawn from among these and we devoted one day of class time before the midterm, and two days before the final, to review sessions. Certain questions lent themselves to being answered in a dramatic form. One question on the final, for instance, typically dealt with the meaning

of Jerusalem for Jews, Christians, and Muslims. So I asked class members to volunteer to represent these communities and present their various points of view before the assembly—to be amplified with comments, criticisms, and additional perspectives from the floor. Besides the exams, I required a short written exercise early in the course, but more of that below.

Course Rhythms

I had some trepidation about jumping directly into the study of pilgrimage with people who presumably had never been exposed to the comparative study of religion before, so I turned the first two weeks of the course into the world's fastest introduction to world religions—or at least the five that were principally to concern us here. This presented students with the opportunity to do some frantic reading in the famous Smiths—Wilfred and Huston—to try to get some sense of major emphases in whatever traditions were totally unfamiliar to them. I chose *The Religions of Man* and *The Faith of Other Men* for this task because they are extremely well written and because they are quite different in their approaches. I made elaborate apologies for the gender language in the titles and made it clear that I did not want the students to go and do likewise in anything they wrote for this course.

In class, meanwhile, I focused on what I called "five cameos." These were lectures intended not to be surveys of the five traditions under study but to introduce them by means of some element in the tradition that could stand as symbolic of the whole. The premise was that by looking for an hour at some significant moment or aspect in the lives of Hindus or Jews, one could learn something about what the whole tradition means as practiced. This was a version of the approach so often taken by Wilfred Smith, and with great success in *The Faith of Other Men*. Like the motifs Smith chose for adumbration in that book, these were selected with an eye to exploring the way in which religion infects different aspects of life. In addressing Christianity through the *Magnificat*, for example, I talked quite a bit about Bach and worked through various passages in his setting of the text. By coming at Judaism through the Passover celebration, we were approaching a tradition through what and how it eats. My Jewish wife provided samples of Passover fare for academic contemplation.

In each case, moreover, it was possible to establish a relation between the symbol we were focusing on and the role played by pilgrimage in the tradition of which it was a part. Hindus, for example, expect to see something (*darsan*) at the culmination of their journeys, a phenomenon one can recognize in many traditions but one that has particularly to do with images in the Hindu instance. Passover is one of the three times during the year when Jews are specifically bidden to assemble at Jerusalem; indeed, it is a celebration of pilgrimage itself. And the film "There is No God but God" devotes a significant amount of attention to the Muslim pilgrimage to Mecca (*hajj*).

At the conclusion of these five days, a one- or two-page essay was expected from the students. They were to imagine themselves as photographers faced with the task of shooting a family portrait of the five religious traditions we were considering. Each tradition was to be represented as a single person, a device whose appropriateness I urged them to question but for present purposes to accept. The photographer's task, then, was to determine how the various members of the family of world religions should be arranged to allow for the best—perhaps the most accurate—portrait. Which tradition belonged in close proximity to the next? How close? In what position? Should the portrait reflect action on the part of the subjects? Each student was to sketch out the photo he or she would have taken and to explain, briefly, the criteria used for composing the photograph in such a way.

On the day these little essays were due, the class was devoted to discussing the various options that had been chosen and debating the merits of each. One immediate lesson was that no one scheme is adequate; one perspective will not work. Another effort was to examine the often unquestioned assumptions that went into the preparation of these exercises. A third fruit, I always hoped, would be an increased realization of the sorts of things one would need to know to do such a portrait more satisfactorily or in greater detail. And a fourth, frankly, was that the whole exercise broke a good deal of the ice that needs to be cleared away before a class of that size can feel comfortable talking with one another. On the following day I tried to show how various options the students took had been used or avoided in major scholarly attempts to work out a framework for describing the relations between these and other religious traditions.

At that point the course "began." From the third week on, our agenda was specifically pilgrimage. Unavoidably, I devoted the first day to the thoughts of Victor Turner, but I followed up with something perhaps a little less orthodox: a discussion of "The Wizard of Oz" as a pilgrimage narrative. We considered specifically Turnerian categories but looked at the story from other perspectives as well—Christian imagery about the road to Jerusalem, for example—and I was always surprised how at how firm and accessible a place the Oz story has in the minds of most American 20-year-olds. That, too, was something I asked about: why was it so?

Then we launched into the traditions themselves, beginning with the Hindu. My thought in beginning with Hinduism, of course, was that it was necessary background for Buddhism. Moreover, if one began in the East one could bring the course to a conclusion in the West, closer to home. I still think this approach has a compelling logic, but I will admit that to begin with Hinduism, particularly when one has so little time to devote to it, can be awfully baffling to the students. I tried to minimize their bafflement by focusing on two pilgrimage cities—Benares and Brindavan—and using them not only as contrasting (yet in other ways similar) examples of pilgrimage behavior but as symbols of two sides of Hindu religion generally: the *saguna* (immanentist, imagist, Vaisnavite) and the *nirguna* (transcendental, aniconic, Saivite). Obviously these are very broad strokes of the brush, but I hoped they would serve to give some sense of major tensions and complementarities within the tradition. That was a point I wanted to make early on: religious traditions are not, as the photographer exercise would seem to suggest, monolithic entities.

In some years, when other aspects of the course's design permitted, I have complemented this look at two cities with a study of various mountain pilgrimages: Govardhan, Sabarimalai, Shambhala, Siripada, Mt. Fuji. As the names suggest, these mountains span the border between Hinduism and Buddhism, so they provide a transition from one to the other that suggests how closely tied Buddhism can be to the Hindu network out of which it emerged. On the other side of the coin, I usually try to spend some time with Buddhism in its Chinese or Japanese form to show how different Buddhism can be from its Hindu—and Buddhist—past.

In other years I have de-emphasized mountain journeys and jumped directly into a consideration of the Buddha's life as a pilgrimage account. This introduces a personal perspective on pilgrimage that is at least in part appropriate to the central preoccupations of Buddhism. Then we look at ways in which this pilgrimage has been ritualized and replicated—both by people who would call themselves Buddhists and by some who might not. Hermann Hesse comes in here, and I feel somewhat apologetic for using him since *Siddhartha* has often been read already by people in the class, but he is useful as an example of how a story can spread beyond the boundaries of a single tradition. It also points to the expansive, missionary thrust in Buddhist history. Furthermore, it creates the possibility of asking just what the relation is between Hesse's characters and Asvaghosa's. The "cameo" lecture on the *bo* tree also comes in handy at this point, as background for Buddhist pilgrimage. And that brings us up to the midterm, which deals with the Eastern traditions.

When we suddenly find ourselves immersed in stories of the biblical patriarchs (and matriarchs), many students breathe a sigh of relief. Here at last is something they feel they know something about. But soon it turns out that this too is new. Most are unaware of the tension that accompanied the transformation of a nomadic people into a nation with a center at Jerusalem, and on the other side of the same coin, I am always intrigued to sense the skepticism with which non-Jews in the class meet the Jewish devotion to that city, that particular place. Christians, particularly Protestants and particularly Americans, have a tendency to think of religion as something not intrinsically related to nationhood or place. Though they know about Israel from what they hear on the six o'clock news, they are often unprepared for the depth of Jewish devotion to Zion, both historically and emotionally. Agnon's *In the Heart of the Seas* makes it palpable, even though it is a work of imagination that makes substantial use of legend.

When we come to Christianity in the following week, many students are sure they are home free. Judaism remains slightly exotic for most, but this, after all, is Sunday School. One response to this is Fabri's *Wanderings*, since his vivid adoration of the city of Jerusalem—the city itself— and his conviction that it is the navel of the earth comes as something with which most students, often particularly the Christians, have a hard time identifying. So what is for many the "home" tradition becomes strange or at least complex—always a good thing. In fact, the very use of pilgrimage as an important connecting theme among religions is something that students are apt to greet with a certain amount of skepticism and surprise: does Christianity really have all that much to do with pilgrimage? At this moment it becomes clear that, at least for significant numbers of Christians and for considerable stretches of Christian history, it did indeed, and that is a good lesson. One of the objects of any course that deals with cross-cultural understanding is surely to help the students appreciate that whoever they are, they are a minority in the world and in world history, and often it is the study of one's own tradition that makes this point easiest to grasp. To sense that your own perspective on things makes you a stranger, even an outsider, to many you had assumed to be your comrades ought to be a breath of some sort of fresh air.

Since Christians usually learn about Jesus in Christian institutions, and sometimes under the restraining eye of ritual, Christian students are often least likely to expect a blast of fresh air insofar as he is concerned. Hence I have often had vivid response to the two lectures in which I attempt to depict Jesus's story as a narrative of pilgrimage events staged by pilgrimage motifs recorded in the Hebrew Bible. In short, I try to make Jesus very much the Jew as he moves inexorably (was it inexorable?) toward Jerusalem. Most students are astonished, for instance, to hear that the account of the great transfiguration along the way presupposes and reenacts the great experience at Sinai, and it seems a happy circumstance that the early lecture on the Passover helps at least as much to understand Jesus's last days as does the one on the Magnificat. It seems to be a matter of some revelation that Jesus's life is not only a symbol for other Christians' journeys, but that it has a symbolic component itself. I try to read it as in some ways a restatement of the pilgrimage of Israel.

When we turn to Islam, many of the same motifs emerge in new form. We look at the Holy City from what is now a third perspective, then turn to Mecca and the *hajj*. Here is pilgrimage writ large, and the students' reaction to the film "Mecca, the Forbidden City," in which the *hajj* is presented by Muslims—specifically the Saudi Arabian and erstwhile Iranian governments—always impresses me. Often one senses in their reaction to it an element of what can only be called awe. By having dwelt on the relation between Jesus's conception of himself (or that held by the Gospel writers) and the sacrifice of Isaac, the stage is set for the role played by the sacrifice of Ishmael in the ceremonies of the *hajj*, and Jewish and Christian attitudes toward the Jerusalem as *axis mundi* set the stage for Muslim convictions in regard to Mecca and its *ka'ba*.

Jewish students are used to having to put up with Christian misinterpretations of "their" scriptures, but most Christian students have never had to confront the ongoing tale of biblical hermeneutics in its Islamic form, so it is always salutary to see these old "prophecies" fulfilled one more time than, from a Christian point of view, they ought to have been, and to sense that the New Testament may be no more implied by the Old than the Quran is by the Bible. The learning of such lessons is perhaps not a necessary outgrowth of the study of pilgrimage on a global scale, but the pilgrimage theme does provide a vivid format for making such learning possible.

Finally the course comes truly home as in its closing hours we turn to America. Most of the readings have to do with what for Americans are classical subjects—the Mayflower, Walden, civil religion—and I try to flesh this out with pilgrimage motifs in early American hymns, especially those that draw on the Psalms for their subject matter and phraseology. The course is taught not in Cambridge, however, but in Seattle, and that makes it particularly appropriate to devote some attention to the westward thrust of American history. Mark Juergensmeyer has always helped me with this by presenting some version of his fine lecture on "California as Religion," where Hollywood and the Golden Gate fill in any blanks left by Oz. There is always the chance to do the ritual singing of that Northwest favorite, "Acres of Clams," too, and I never go through this week of the course without recalling what it was like to strap my skis on my Volkswagen in Connecticut late one fall and head for Aspen, not knowing if or when I would ever come back. I did come back, of course, but Washingtonians can easily identify with the sense of lost mission and cramped space that attended my journey "back East."

The themes of pollution and overuse that inevitably come to the surface when American pilgrimage is in the air suggest a foray into science fiction as the primary modern medium for pilgrimage narrative and a naturally American genre, but somehow there is never quite enough time to get into it. We close, instead, by going back over where we have been in the form of a review for the final exam. As I have said, I try to choreograph as much of this as is possible into class presentations and debates closely related to the study questions for the final.

At the very end I often tell of two contradictory preoccupations that I had when I was a little kid. The one was to wonder at my good fortune to have been born an American, poised at the apex of history and heir to the progress of civilization, a force that had shot like a slow-burning rocket from its launching pad in the ancient Near East across the terrain of classical Greece and Rome, past the glories of medieval Europe, and straight on over the Atlantic to come to rest in our own huge land. What could be more logical, more splendid? And how lucky I was to have been born at the end of the rocket's rainbow.

My other preoccupation seemed to point in another direction altogether. It was a fantasy I had that I was one in a pair of twins, but my brother had become lost from view. I knew where he was, though. He was in Thailand, perhaps, or China—somewhere just halfway around the world, wherever that was, and every once in a while I would go to the globe to try to figure out where you would end up if you dropped a plumbline through the middle of the orb from Lombard, Illinois. To meet this other little boy was at times my greatest hope, and it never occurred to me that by the logic of my other picture of the meaning of time and space he had been condemned to the dark side of the planet and the underside of history.

Having told these stories to the class, I would propose that any comparative course—certainly one in comparative religion—presents one with the possibility of a meeting between self and other, and with the prospect of having to revise one's sense of one's own destiny in light of what other people have claimed as theirs. The particular fascination of a course on pilgrimage is finding not only that the sense of trajectory on the part of self and of one's others is often comparable, but that sometimes the trajectories actually intersect. The challenge of such a course—and I'm afraid this tends to come out in full sermonic mode—is to recognize ourselves in others, to recognize others in ourselves, and to be honest but not frightened about the distances between us. After all, not just traditions but even selves are composite entities: witness the widely divergent preoccupations with identity in my own childhood. Comparison is a thing not just without but within. It's in our bones as human beings, and we should cultivate it for all it's worth.

Problems and Opportunities

The first major problem with this course from the students' point of view was that it did not always deal with religious traditions as "isms," and there was no way to avoid fielding questions asked from that perspective. Nor should there have been: one has to meet a question as asked. But the thematic way of doing things—particularly if the theme is something actual and ritual as well as something contemplated—does create a framework within which the "ism" expectation is suitably on the defensive, and given that framework it was often possible to show that such questions only address part of a larger reality.

A related problem is the one having to do with history: the expectation that everything ought to be understood first and foremost in historical context. I must admit that I share this mindset to a degree and feel apologetic for giving the historical dimension of things short shrift, so I have occasionally presented thumbnail sketches of the origin and spread of Buddhism and Islam at some point when those traditions are under discussion—usually early on. Yet I have not found a way to work this into the course as systematically as perhaps I should. One obvious way to do so would be to substitute a historically oriented introduction to world religions for Huston Smith's book right at the outset, but I am hesitant to lead off with something less spirited than he makes possible, and I comfort myself with the knowledge that the other two basic courses in religion at Washington are thoroughly historical in their format.

Another difficulty has to do with the nature and extent of the readings I assign. Some students have complained that these are too diverse, too costly, or that they are just plain too much. In response to this reaction I have paired the list down a bit since the first time I taught the course, but I am hesitant to cave in too completely to the student who said, "It's too bad there wasn't a summary of all the readings so we could get general points rather than having to read the whole thing."

The pilgrimage course has other difficulties too, but most of them are personal. I have a tendency, for instance, to encourage discussion even in a class of a hundred. While most students appreciated the life this often gave to the class, some regretted the sidetracks it inevitably opened up. A somewhat more Prussian approach might serve me well, and I congratulate anyone to whom a sense of clear-headed discipline comes more naturally than it does to me.

The course has some strengths, too. Though some students feel that more time should be devoted to the religions close to home—after all, this might be their only religion class, and there are things they want to know—the majority recognize that the use of a single theme gives them a chance to look at a vast array of material from a more or less manageable point of departure. They appreciate the fact that each tradition gets "equal time." Most students say that my extensive use of slides is a good thing, an antidote to the printed word, but occasionally I have heard the lament that my collection of visual materials having to do with the Western traditions ought to be as good as what I can show for Hinduism and Buddhism. It's a fair criticism, and again one that others teaching this course might well escape.

One feature of the course that has almost always received good reviews was my occasional use of guest lecturers. I have always set up the "cameos" and the course problematic myself, since I do not want to yield too soon to the possible vagaries of a "parade" course. But when we got to the place in the course when a whole week (think of it!) is devoted to a single tradition, I like to persuade various colleagues to do one of the week's lectures—something close to his or her expertise. This has the effect of altering voice and perspective on a regular basis, but not at the cost of continuity, and of giving the students a chance to see how other people handle such material.

It suggests also what further resources the university has for pursuing the study of religion, and to show that a major theme such as pilgrimage is of interest to scholars of various orientations, not just my personal quirk. One of the hallmarks of the Washington program is that we have an ongoing faculty seminar on themes in comparative religion. Guest lecturers bring the spirit of that discussion into the classroom, and the fact that not all of them are on the religion faculty as such illustrates that religion is the sort of thing that overflows disciplinary boundaries.

At its best a course like this stands a good chance of meeting the objectives that Karen Brown sets for a religion course in her essay in the Berkeley volume of this series: it presents beliefs as intrinsically related to social settings; it leaves a series of connected and, I hope, enduring images in the mind; and it suggests that to understand ourselves we must make an effort to understand others, some of whom share our beliefs and behavior, some of whom do not. I hope the course also qualifies as a basic entry in the humanities curriculum envisioned in the Chicago volume of this series, since it focuses so directly on what Judith Berling calls there "multiple worlds" and since it focuses to a considerable extent on interpreting constructs—"texts," one might say—that are in Marilyn Waldman's terms "masterpieces" of human creation. I refer to Mecca, Jerusalem, Benares and the rest, not just in their outer form, but as imagined realities—cities of the mind, to be approached from within. Yet we see not just the masterpiece, the beckoning ideal, but the flawed manifestation as well—the beggars, the wars, the journeys uncompleted—and time and again a student must decide whether the tarnish is so deep as to obscure the bright vessel forever. I personally hope the answer is "no," but there is no way I can remove the urgency of the question. I can only insist that it needs to be asked not selectively, but universally.

❧VI❧

"Healing" as a Theme in Teaching the Study of Religion in a Liberal Arts Setting

LINDA L. BARNES

One way to compare religious traditions is by selecting themes that seem, in a variety of ways, to appear throughout a number of them. That is, we select what look like instances of recurring similarity and explore this similarity in some depth not only to see what it tells us about the common experiences of being human, but also to observe where it conceals important differences in the expression of this experience. The task of this paper is to reflect on the implications of one theme which has drawn increasing attention in a number of disciplines, and which has begun to enter the field of the study of religion—namely, the theme of healing.

On one level, healing can be studied as a phenomenological category. Anthropologists have found it useful to study other cultures through their healing traditions,[1] noting that as we see who falls ill, under what circumstances, to whom a sick person goes, and what coping strategies are available, we learn much about the values of the culture as well as

---

[1] From the medical anthropologist's point of view, for example, the objectives of a comparative frame are several-fold. The first is ethnographic: we seek information about the other culture. Second, we seek to explore fundamental issues within a cross-cultural context, and to develop a frame to ask what has been omitted. Third, we want to compare a healing system's theory with its actual practice, to see where discrepancies between the two occur. The issue is to "reconstruct entire systems of medicine and to compare their cognitive and social structure." (Arthur Kleinman, lecture).

about our own culture in comparison.[2] This, of course, can hold true not only for a study done on the basis of current field research in a contemporary setting; it also holds for the study of a tradition's history, as we find being done in much of the "new history."[3]

Healing also permits us to study the interaction of traditions. We find this, for example, in the introduction of Eastern traditions such as acupuncture into North American culture, or in the use of Western biomedical methods in non-Western countries. This makes healing a possible lens through which to survey certain historical processes.

We could argue, of course, that anthropological and historical approaches are all that are needed to study healing, and that other dimensions can be taken up in courses on psychology or medicine. It is true that all such courses could treat the theme in a comparative way, and that each could acknowledge the religious dimensions of healing. So, how might we make a case for including a course on healing in a program on the study of religion in a liberal arts school?

In the first place, healing as a theme forces us to look at some of the ways in which categories such as "religious/non-religious," "sacred/profane," or "sacred/secular" do not necessarily serve as appropriate distinctions in many traditions. Rather, healing is an integral part of the religious tradition in some cases, and religion often has to do with healing. As a result, healing as a theme allows us to question some of the very categories with which our disciplines operate.

In a lecture at the Center for the Study of World Religions, Tom Csordas, from Harvard's Department of Social Medicine, argued that religion dealt with breakdowns in the normal functioning of things. Healing was a way of re-establishing a threatened order, and religion was a technique for healing. Arthur Kleinman, also of the Department of Social Medicine, suggested in a talk that same evening that religion was what came in when one recognized human finitude and had to face the fact of one's own finitude and death. It was not simply a technique for overcoming illness, but a total response to the *fact* of death and illness. It is what we do when there is no other solution.

These are different ways of thinking about religion. In the one, religion becomes a particular type of healing technique; in the other, a different category having to do with consolation. The one has to do with the

---

[2] Ravi Kapur, lecture.

[3] See, for example, Theodore K. Rabb and Robert I. Rotberg, eds., *The New History: The 1980s and Beyond: Studies in Interdisciplinary History* (Princeton: Princeton University Press, 1982), 227-78.

acceptance of finitude as it involves suffering and illness; the other, with the struggle against and the effort to overcome it. Csordas also observed that the gulf between departments such as those of religion and anthropology in the study of healing went back to perceptions in the social sciences, according to which religious healers were seen as either mentally ill, suffering from schizophrenia or epilepsy, or as indigenous psychotherapists. In both cases, the psychological analogy was dominant. These approaches, however, neglected two things: the experience of the participants, and "the non-specific mechanisms by which healing was efficacious."

This absence, Csordas noted, traced back to Durkheim, who had proposed that the sacred could be explained in terms of the social, with people recognizing something greater than themselves in the form of society, and worshipping that. In the social sciences, then, the Other was assimilated into the social. This eliminated the sacred as an analytic category, which led to the elimination of the study of the sacred in healing. For phenomenologists such as Otto, van der Leeuw, and Eliade, however, the sacred is a fundamental capacity of the human being.[4] This makes religious experience and the sacred a preliminary premise.

These two different starting points raise other issues. The liberal arts, after all, have been known to view the study of religion with some suspicion, fearing that religion courses may erect platforms for the preaching of particular faith positions. This has burdened the study of religion with the need to appear "objective" and "scientific" in the manner of the social sciences (despite the awareness within the sciences themselves of the impossibility of absolute objectivity). Nevertheless, the study of religion has sometimes felt obliged to report only what can be observed and quantified, and to feel a certain shyness about discussing anything related to the experience of what some might take to lie at the very heart of religion—be that God, Heaven, or the Void.

Therefore, professors find themselves having to ask whether they are to address and present the subject matter as outsiders who see religion as essentially derivative—whether psychologically or sociologically—and who therefore imagine it as a secondary phenomenon, or as religious people affirming a religious mode of being.[5] Do we, in other words, as-

[4] Lecture by Tom Csordas, at the Center for the Study of World Religions, Harvard, Spring 1989.

[5] John B. Carman, Introduction to MS on "Divine Polarities: Contrast and Harmony in the Mystery of God," p. 1.

sert that being religious is a primary, defining quality of being human?[6] If we take the role of outsider, then there would appear to be little problem in attempting a scientific approach to the study of religion. Accordingly, we would seek to explain the content of the various religions by means of explanatory paradigms drawn from the various humanities.

If, however, we had the sense that the second response were somehow more true, then the study of religion would require us to invert the order of our investigation: we would then explore how the various cultures (and the various expressions of a culture, such as the humanities themselves) represent the ways of being religious—of attempting to state questions of ultimate concern, and of articulating the relationship within and with the cosmos. This would result in quite a different stance and hence a different course. We would then be saying that however useful the various interpretative strategies and disciplines might prove in teaching about the theme of healing, they would still fail to explore the relationship between this phenomenon and human being as basically religious being.

To suggest a sense of what this latter approach might look like in practice, I will review three courses on healing that have been taught at Harvard University.

I. Hindu Systems of Healing

Professor Ravi Kapur, a psychiatrist invited from India to hold a joint appointment at the School of Social Medicine and the Divinity School at Harvard, taught a course titled "Hindu Systems of Healing." He opened his course with a discussion of some of the differences between biomedical and Hindu ways of conceptualizing and experiencing the body, health, and illness.

In juxtaposing their own system with one unfamiliar to them, he asked the students to begin to reflect critically on their own assumptions as well as on the implications of those assumptions. In subsequent sessions, he spoke about yoga (including his own experience of having taken a year away from his clinical practice to study under the instruction of a guru) and about folk healing. As part of his presentation on folk healing, Kapur introduced three levels of analysis: 1) a phenomenological description of healing practices themselves; 2) how the healers themselves explain and understand what they do; and 3) how we might develop metaphors and analogies with which to convey to a Western audi-

---

6 See Wilfred Cantwell Smith, *Towards a World Theology* (Philadelphia: Westminster Press, 1981).

ence something of the experience of the healing process as perceived by those who practice and receive it.[7]

Kapur invited two other speakers, both of them psychiatrists, to supplement his own presentations. One of them, Mitchell Weiss, had specialized in the study of a particular healing system (Ayurveda), while the other, Arthur Kleinman, also a medical anthropologist, raised questions from his own work about problems that arise when one attempts the comparative study of different healing traditions. Thus, throughout the course, Kapur introduced methodological questions and interpretive strategies at the same time as he was presenting case material. In other words, he was teaching ways to conceptualize healing itself. (See, for example, the class session on "Idioms of Distress" which addressed how cultures perceive, describe, and respond to illness.) Having been trained in and practiced Western medicine and psychiatry, yet also having interacted with and experienced traditional Indian systems of healing, Kapur was able to move back and forth with some fluency between the two systems of thought and practice.

It was in the third session of the course that he looked at the use of Western psychiatric styles of treatment as used in an Indian setting, and explored some of the various ways in which Indian personality and experience make it problematic to assume that we can simply transplant a Western system of healing to Indian soil. Nor was he talking about grafting Indian styles of healing onto Western psychiatry while leaving the psychiatric approach intact. Rather, he was exploring a new synthesis that would recognize the contributions of both systems and bring them together in some new way (as, for example, in using meditation deriving from yoga as a treatment for psychiatric patients). His discussion of these alternatives was itself an instruction for the students in how to think not only in theoretical but also in applied terms.

Because this was a course being offered in a Divinity School setting, Kapur deliberately emphasized the more scientific and clinical ways of talking about the course materials, whereas in a medical school setting he would have given more explicit emphasis to the philosophical and religious questions. We see here a concern for prompting students to stretch not only their assumptions about healing, but also the patterns of thought informed by their involvement in a particular discipline.

This suggests that our approach to teaching itself can contribute to communicating something of the world view about which we are teaching. Kapur, for example, hoped to say something about the Hindu way of

[7] Kapur, lecture.

seeing life through his very interaction with students, through the kinds of questions he asked, and through the way he selected, organized, and presented the material of his courses. In other words, the teacher has the potential to embody and communicate the moral and spiritual values intrinsic to what he or she is teaching.[8] While this is not to say that the teacher should play guru, it is to insist that students do look to teachers as possible models, and that we need therefore to be conscious of how our own teaching style constitutes part of the course material.

Kapur described three types of students as having been interested in his course. The first, a small group of medical students, had no quarrel with the general project of comparing Western medical systems with certain Indian systems of healing. They did feel, however, that the course was not "objective" enough, and that it was lacking in the more quantifiable elements their background had led them to expect. By this they appear to have meant that it was not a course taught according to models of Western scientific precision in its discussion of illness, healing strategies, and curing. The implication of their critique was that Western science represents the authentic model by which to assess medical reality.

At the other extreme was a group that was highly critical of the Western bio-medical model. Seeking academic sanction for their rejection of this system, they expected a polemical approach in the course, and seemed to want to set up an icon to the Indian healing traditions—one flickering in torchlight and smelling of incense. Some of them seemed to assume that the course would transform them into apprentice Indian healers. They felt that Kapur allied himself with the medical students, while it was Kapur's perception that they were basically in search of therapy themselves. It was also such students who proved highly dissatisfied when they discovered that they were expected to demonstrate a high level of critical and analytical insight in reflecting on both the Indian and Western systems.

A third group of students came to the course out of a growing sense of doubt as to the efficacy of an exclusively Western, biomedical approach to healing. What distinguished this much smaller group from the second group was, perhaps, a quality of thoughtfulness and a concern for a more than superficial consideration of both traditions in the interest of coming up not only with a broader understanding of healing, but also with a new way of imagining human potential in relationship to world and cosmos. One of these students, for example, was doing a joint graduate program in medicine and anthropology, and had undergraduate training

---

[8] Kapur, conversation.

in the study of religion. He wrote a provocative study for his term project on the entry of the Indian Ayurvedic tradition into American culture.

The issue raised by this diversity of students is an inter-disciplinary one. The challenge of such a course is not just a matter of the professor's own ideogical orientation, but those of the students as well, all of whom bring their own pedagogical expectations. Given the blend of students from the Divinity School, the Medical School, the School of Education, the Department of Anthropology, and the undergraduate program, the questions raised by the students themselves introduced an interdisciplinary approach. Kapur also took care to invite student reflection on the basis of their own experience. In this connection, he raised the issue of practical experience or practicum in courses on the study of religion. Arguing that no one objects to the use of scientific experiment as a way to teach the Western scientific mode of knowledge, why, he asks, should there be any objection to including such disciplines as yoga or meditation in a course on the study of religion?

It is worth noting that, during the following semester, he also gave a course at Harvard Divinity School in which he combined theoretical texts on yoga with practical instruction. The students were held responsible not only for the textual material but were also expected to practice yoga every day and to record their physical, emotional, and mental responses. Thus, he combined the experiential with the theoretical and attempted to do so in an observable way.

What was it that made these courses relevant to the study of religion? Here we would have to understand healing and health as Kapur defined them:

> What is health? Even the World Health Organization understands it as a state of complete physical, social, and mental well-being. But this is a static entity, which some of us see as more dynamic. What is also there is a spiritual dimension, without which we could be wolves, and still be "healthy." The spiritual dimension involves whether a person can live in a balanced relationship in the cosmos, in relation to feelings, imagination, and fantasies beyond this world. Healing is religious because to become whole means accepting the spiritual in us—our relationship with the cosmos, and not just our physical, mental, or social state. There is an understanding of health in all religions which goes beyond the cultural understanding. Religion can "heal" by presenting this ideal and asking people to move toward it. Order, growth, and transcendence are essential to human existence. Healing incorporates all three (or must, if it is to be true healing).

> I am interested in the process of human transformation, in the historical, psychological, and existential correlates of this quest, and in the methods people

adopt to follow this quest. Over the years of my medical practice, I have come to realize that true healing is also a process of transformation where the person achieves a higher order of integration rather than just being restored to a previous state of health.[9]

Here we encounter two important issues. The first is Kapur's assertion that health necessarily involves a spiritual dimension. But equally important is the issue of transformation: that a person is not simply restored to some previous state, but rather moves on to some sort of new being which gathers up his or her experience in some new way. This paradigm is one that can be used in connection with the healing process, but which applies equally well to various ritual processes.

The temptation is to assume that, at the conclusion of either the healing or the ritual (or, for that matter, of the healing ritual or ritual healing), everything returns to some ongoing state of normalcy. Yet we then fail to account for the ways in which people integrate the new into the familiar, arriving at a synthesis which they may still identify as identical to the prior state, but which has been altered by the transitional process of illness and/or ritual.[10]

II. Healing and Power: Female Participation in Mexican Popular Religiosity

Dr. Sylvia Marcos, a visiting professor at Harvard and a practicing psychotherapist from Mexico, taught a course on women in Mexican popular religiosity in which she presented an analytical and critical framework designed to train students to rethink a variety of assumptions. She did so by focussing on the experience of women, using this as a way to discuss dynamics of power. She drew on video presentations of curing ceremonies, slides of goddesses, priestesses, healers, and other Mexican women, and recordings of curing ceremonies. The students also

---

[9] Kapur, lecture and conversation.

[10] Kapur, discussion. See, also, James Loder, *The Transforming Moment* (San Francisco: Harper and Row, 1981). Loder develops a sequence of moments which plot the process of transformation. The first of these is an awareness of a conflict (conscious conflict); the second, a setting aside of the conflict when one has struggled, without success, to find a solution (pause); third, the emerging of a new image with which to conceptualize and imagine the situation; fourth, a period of integration, during which one reorients one's way of knowing to take the new image into account; and, finally, a presenting of the new way of seeing to one's community for confirmation or contradiction. Loder has looked at how this paradigm is intrinsic to authentic learning, and one might explore ways of adapting it to describe the process of transformation undergone in illness and recovery.

read excerpts from Aztec codices and interviews with healers now practicing in Mexico.

Critiquing Western categories of illness and religiosity for their inability to recognize (and for their failure to take seriously) what Mexican popular tradition has perceived as illness, Marcos analyzed the power dynamics built into Western therapeutic systems. Presenting materials on a range of women healers, she showed how modern practices trace back to ancient times, yet now also incorporate biomedical techniques. This allowed her to raise questions about what it has meant for women to be healers, what varieties of power they have derived and transmitted as priestesses and as healers; and what this has meant historically. (For example, in the Aztec tradition, a woman might have been highly respected for skills which, at certain points in European history, would have caused her to be burned as a witch.)

In this sense, the course was a training ground in how to study the history of people who have not been at the center of the historical record. Her course raised questions concerning the nature of women's experience in comparison with that of men in ways intended to give one a far richer perspective on how a given culture envisioned its own ills and the process by which these were healed.

The design of this course represented not only an approach to the study of healing; it was also an attempt to teach how a Third World feminist scholar would deconstruct generally accepted historical accounts in order both to bring into relief women's reality and way of composing meaning, and to critique the primacy of a Western biomedical model of healing. Marcos made her concern clear at all times, and made it equally clear that her course was, indeed, part of a political as well as a religious concern. It was also a rethinking of therapeutic styles. The course was polemical, and consciously so.

III. Psychological Healing in Cross-Cultural Perspective

Healers in some systems are perceived as those people qualified to recognize and respond to social tensions and ills. Among the Kalihari !Kung, for example, "as the healer accumulates power, he or she begins treating broader problems, such as hostilities between villages."[11] The paradigm is one of healing what Raboteau refers to as both the body personal and the body social. Without the one, the other remains incomplete. Moreover, the fact that healing in non-Western cultures often oc-

---

[11] Richard Katz, "Education as Transformation: Becoming a Healer among the !Kung and the Fijians," *Harvard Educational Review* 51:1 (1981): 77.

curs in a group context presents an individual-oriented culture such as ours with compelling questions. If history is made by groups, then might we not argue that healing must also occur at the level of the group as well as at that of the individual?

Prof. Richard Katz, at the Harvard School of Education, began his course on Psychological Healing by discussing the assumptions we make about ways in which psychological healing is conceptualized, and methods intended to effect this kind of healing. He presented case material as data about specific traditions, and as a way to look at how transformation is understood to occur in the contexts of the Kalahari !Kung, Fijians, Native Americans, Hispanics, and psychotherapy. Many of the healing ceremonies involved were ones we would describe as religious rituals, even as many of the readings themselves also suggested a religious content: "Education for Transcendence," "Lame Deer: Seeker of Visions," "Puerto Rican 'espiritismo'," "Modern Man in Search of a Soul," "Religion, Psychiatry, and Problems of Everyday Life." Katz moved back and forth between talking about education, healing, and transformation. This would suggest that, while the course did not predominantly address religious concerns, it was constructed in such a way that, with some shift in focus, it would easily have lent itself to becoming a course that could be taught in the study of religion.

Katz dealt primarily with the experience of the healer. While he did not overlook the experience of the patient, he was mostly concerned with exploring alternative models of therapy and treatment in which the process of becoming a healer, in fact, initiated the healer's own development or transformation. This thread he continued to trace in sessions on the healer's education and life history, the healing power, and the healing ritual as the locus of transformation.

Katz's major concern here was one of application. How were the educator, the therapist, and the healer to rethink what it means to enter into the illness sequence of another person, or to confront their own illness? The students in the course were, in this sense, intended to integrate alternative strategies into their own vocabulary and to risk their own transformation in the process.

Further Methodological Thoughts

In examining this process of illness, healing, and transformation through which a person moves, Arthur Kleinman proposed to Kapur's class that there are three constants in every healing system. Together, these comprise the process of healing: 1) the problem is restated according to a system. It is made into a symbolic entity or object 2) which is then manipulated according to some ideologically or theoretically determined practice (praxis). 3) This is followed by the enunciation of the transformation. The healer pronounces that the person or group is healed, or changed, according to the rhetoric of the cure. The message itself has its own power. For example, if a charismatic healer tells a person to drop the crutches because she or he is healed, then healing, independent of how the person may, indeed, feel, is understood by the group to have occurred.[12]

Another way to envision the healing process is as a sequence of moments, each of which opens into several possibilities:

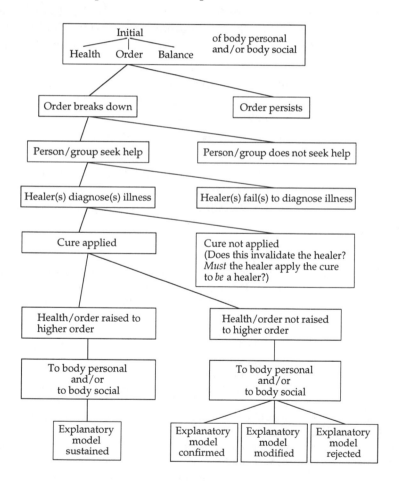

This reflection on the process of healing might serve as a strategy for organizing a course. We might also draw on the following questions proposed by other professors who have taught courses on healing.[13] They raise some of the issues these teachers have felt were important in their own courses.

Illness: How is illness explained (what is the disease etiology)?[14] What is it that gets sick and what dies—do other traditions distinguish between the body, mind, and spirit as we do? Does illness carry moral implications, and what personal/social bonds does it rupture (or what ruptures does it represent)?

Health: How are health and wholeness imagined, and on what understanding of the Self are these images based? What is the vision of right order in the body, the Self, human relationships, and the cosmos? What power dynamics in the culture do these images imply?

Diagnosis—A Question of Discourse: What is recognized as proper diagnostic procedure? How does the healer take the patient's understanding of illness and rephrase it into a new, specialized terminology—the language, or discourse, of the healer?

Healers: Who can be a healer and why? By what process does one enter this role? Is there a difference for men and for women? What is the nature of the relationship between the healer and the patient, as well as between the healer and the community? What is the source of the healing power—that is, of the healer's authority (i.e., a degree, or divine sanction)?

---

[13] These questions were suggested in conversations with Professors Sylvia Marcos and Ravi Kapur as I observed their classes, and with Lamin Sanneh, Albert Raboteau, Lawrence Sullivan, Karen McCarthy Brown, and Charles Long in the context of conversations related to the preparation of materials for this NEH project.

[14] We must, for example, distinguish between "disease" and "illness." "Disease is a value-free entity—it is a deviation in the structure and function of the body. Illness is a value-judgement by a person or by a society about something harmful, uncomfortable, or distressful. In the physical domain, what is considered uncomfortable, or stressful is shared by most people (although even this is not uniform): we want the ability to procreate, the absence of pain, a lasting state in which the body is disregarded as much as possible, and longevity. So much is, for the most part, held in common between cultures...

Insofar as disease is the more consistently quantifiable of the two, it is the part of experience more deliberately addressed by the bio-medical approach to healing. This approach is unable to take into account the ways in which the deviations in structure and function of the body may be related to situations that the culture considers to be harmful, uncomfortable, or stressful." (Kapur, lecture)

Intervention: What is understood by good care? Is it productive (helping to attain certain ends and benefits, as with vitamins), protective (against present and future dangers, as with inoculations), or punitive (to regulate, punish, and/or harm, as with suppressive drugs or lethal injections)?[15] Why is it thought to work?

Aftermath and Social Reintegration: What is meant by efficacy—how do people know that someone has been cured, and what is the nature of the transformation? How are failures explained?

Many of these questions were raised in these three courses, either through lecture and discussion or through the readings. Insofar as multiple healing systems were under study, no single set of conclusions can be drawn. Rather, the courses provided the occasion to explore a range of alternatives, thereby prompting the students involved to challenge many of their own presuppositions. It is true that these three professors were, themselves, critical in various ways of some of the biases in Western medicine—particularly those that neglected to understand the patient as a relational being. This, if anything, constituted an underlying common influence that oriented these courses. It was, moreover, not inconsistent with concerns that led many of the students to take the course in the first place. To this extent, therefore, it functioned as a somewhat tautological element. The larger set of questions, however, could just as easily be oriented in other directions, according to the concerns of instructor and students.

Teaching Healing as a Theme in the Liberal Arts

A given university may choose to offer only one course on healing. Yet even in one course, the instructor can raise questions that students will be able to address at a basic level, but which also point beyond themselves to questions of greater complexity. Therefore, graduate students will also be able to engage in the materials. The course could then occur at any point in a student's education and would not necessarily require previous background.

The theme of healing itself also permits a number of ways to organize and present the material. For example: 1) We can look at the theme as part of the history of a particular tradition (as with the rituals and meaning of healing in the Christian tradition from the time of the early church to the present). 2) We could study a healing tradition in connection with one of the humanities. 3) We might also look at a number of traditions

---

15   Albert Raboteau, conversation.

and compare them through the use of sub-themes, such as illness, diagnosis, intervention, and efficacy.

For any of these approaches, we could certainly draw on the data, insights, and methodologies of anthropology, sociology, psychology, and bio-medicine. At the same time, in doing so, it would seem important to make explicit and to teach students how to scrutinize the objectives, advantages, and limitations of each of these approaches. That is, we would have to make some effort to expose the presuppositions of any of these other interpretive strategies, including that of the study of religion itself.

If we chose to work with the equivalent of a Great Books approach, we would have to look at what various peoples and traditions have perceived to be the individuals, groups, and practices that manifest powers or qualities valued by the culture. What persons and works of this sort have so reshaped the imagination of the culture that later developments have all had to take this particular forebear into account or be held ignorant? Why does the culture, as it evaluates itself, hold such a person or classic or practice in esteem? Likewise, what power relationships do these values imply and sustain? Who defines the canons of taste and who determines what constitutes health?

As the teacher attempts to determine what constitutes worthy content for a course and how to present it, she or he faces the contemporary reality of the student population in all its diversity. One can no longer assume a homogenous social background, academic preparation, or social orientation and set of values among the student body. Moreover, to speak of this as the "cultural deprivation" of these students—that is, to speak only of what students don't know—is to disclose a personal bias as to what constitutes knowledge. Many students do, indeed, lack what the university has designated as culture. What knowledge they do possess is often categorized as useless, trivial, or pernicious—if, indeed, it is even thought of as knowledge at all.

It is ironic that the professor who may dismiss as an asset the kind of memory that can recall and synthesize years of song lyrics, soap opera plots, complicated dance steps, and other aspects of popular culture may, at the same time, be the same professor who values oral tradition in other cultures and who cannot understand why the students fail to find it meaningful.

This is not to claim that memory alone be equated with learning or wisdom. It is to ask how well the professor who claims to speak the tongues of other traditions can bridge cultural gaps within his or her own setting. How much, for example, has she or he tried to penetrate the world of meaning of the student who comes ill-prepared by university standards, in order to make an effective translation. How can we claim to talk about understanding the world of the Other and to teach students to do so when what we embody in our encounters with them is a basic dismissal of the various values they may bring? Does our very approach then not contradict what it is we claim we are teaching them to do?

Charles Long has suggested that healing itself, understood in a variety of ways, can serve as an analogy to the process of education. For example, the healer may re-enact some process symbolically, as when a shaman performs a symbolic recapitulation of the birth process. On the other hand, we can also talk about healing as bringing out the health intrinsic to a person, seeing the person as an original, whole Self which has somehow been obstructed and which needs to have the obstructions transformed in order to recover the original knowledge and well-being of the Self. This would be like the idea of education as "educare," the leading out of the Self.[16] These are only a few suggestions, but they and others bear thinking about insofar as healing implies a kind of teaching the Self about how to undergo transformations toward wholeness.

It is worth noting that, over a period of some four years, at least four courses in healing were offered at Harvard (the courses discussed do not include the work being done in the Departments of Social Medicine and Anthropology). Of the professors teaching these courses, however, only one—Lamin Sanneh from the Center for the Study of World Religions at Harvard—was actually on the religion faculty; the others were involved in disciplines other than religion who, nevertheless, felt the study of religion to be a significant forum within which to present their work. The challenge, here, is to integrate a topic whose importance is now recognized in other disciplines, and integrate it more fully into our thinking on the teaching of religion.

This will require us to look more carefully at our own assumptions about the relationship between body, mind, and spirit. For example, insofar as both body and mind are the loci of distress and suffering, and healing in the broad sense is the attempt to remove or transcend these experiences, healing intersects with the concerns of religion. It suggests ways in which religious experience itself concerns what is immediate and visceral. This is important insofar as it constitutes one way to convey the relevance and meaning of religious experience to students.

The study of healing raises yet another, somewhat less obvious concern as well: If students receive the message that they are to sally forth

---

[16] Charles Long, conversation.

from the university as rugged individuals trained to confront the world through competition, is the university truly preparing them to enter a world in which it is profoundly dangerous to overlook the ways in which we are all interrelated? Is a liberal arts education then really preparing its students with worthy images of responsible adulthood? Might the alternative not be a more ecological vision in which the health of the world (both as natural and a social environment) as well as that of the nation or community, of the family, and of the person are all intimately connected?

To think according to a relational paradigm derived from this way of thinking about healing does not mean to overlook the differences. "Healing" need not mean the restoration of some archetypically "correct" way of being and doing. We have, after all, no common myths of eternal return. But to reflect on what we mean by healing calls us to reflect, too, on what we mean by community at all levels. We might argue that if one of the aims of the liberal arts education is to cultivate the understanding of diversity, then one contribution of the theme of healing might be to reflect on how to hold all that diversity in relationship *as* an expression of wholeness.

One possible version might be that of a much extended community which allows for diversity and which protects the right of the minority to dissent. Let us acknowledge, of course, that this is a particular vision of democracy which insists on the value of pluralism for the health of the whole. It seems a perspective that is consistent, however, with the very nature of the liberal arts and with a theme in which transformation means the process of increasingly comprehensive integration.

HINDU SYSTEMS OF HEALING

R. L. Kapur, Ph.D., F.R.C. Psych. (RLK)
Visiting Professor, Depts. of Social Medicine and Divinity

M. Weiss, M.D., Ph.D. (MW)
Instructor, Depts. of Psychiatry and Social Medicine and Health Policy

Required Reading:

1. Kakar, S. (1982)   *Shamans, Mystics, and Doctors* (SMD) (Knopf)
2. Frank, J. (1974)   *Persuasion and Healing* (P&H) (Shocken Books)
3. Carstairs, G. M. and   *Great Universe of Kota* (GUK) (California Press)
   Kapur, R. L. (1976)
4. Leslie, Charles (ed.)   *Asian Medical Systems* (AMS) (Univ. of Calif. Press)
   (1976)

Schedule of Meetings and Readings:

Sept. 19   1. Introduction to the Course (RLK and MW)

2. Comparison of Western and Indian Approaches to Healing, Part I: Western Approaches (RLK)

Readings: Basham, A. L. (1976), "The Practice of Medicine in Ancient and Medieval India" (AMS, pp.18-43)

Bolling, G. M., "Disease and Medicine—Vedic," in James Hastings et al. (eds.), *Encyclopedia of Religion and Ethics*, Vol. 4:762-72, New York: Scribner

Jaspers, Karl (1963), "The Concept of Health and Illness," in *General Psychopathology*, pp.779-90, Manchester University Press

Capra, F. (1983), *The Turning Point*, pp.123-63, 305-358, New York: Bantam Books

Eisenberg (1977), "Disease and Illness," in *Culture, Medicine, and Psychiatry* 1:1:9-23

Sept. 26   1. Comparison of Western and Indian Approaches to Health and Illness, Part II: Indian Approaches with Reference to Ayurveda (MW and RLK)

2. Towards Delineation of Similarities and Differences in Western and Indian Approaches (Discussion)

Readings: Bhattacharya, D. (1983), "Psychiatric Pluralism in Bengal India," in *Social Science and Medicine* 17:947-56

Obeyesekere, G. (1976), "The Impact of Ayurvedic Ideas on the Culture and the Individual in Sri Lanka," *AMS*, pp.201- 226

Brahmananda, Gupta (1976), "Indigenous Medicine in Nineteenth and Twentieth Century Bengal," *AMS*, pp.368-82

Oct. 3   Classical Healing Traditions of India: Concepts of Illness and Healing in Ayurveda (MW)

Readings: Jolly, J. (1977), *Indian Medicine*, 2nd. rev. ed., Munshiram

              Venkoba, Rao, A., "India," in J. G. Howells (ed.), *World History of Psychiatry*, New York: Brunner/Mazal, pp. 624- 49

              Weiss, M. G. (1980), "Caraka Samhita on the Doctrine of Karma," in Wendy O'Flaherty (ed.), *Karma and Rebirth in Classical Indian Traditions*, Berkeley: Univ. of California Press

Oct. 10   Yoga and Health (RLK)

Readings: Kapur, R. L., "A Brief Report on Experiential Study of Yoga" (ms.)

              Tarmini, I. K. (1961), *The Science of Yoga*, Madras: Theosophical Publishing House

              Srahl, Fritz (1975), *Exploring Mysticism*, Pelican

              Vahia, N. S. et al., "Value of Patanjali's Concepts in the Treatment of Neurosis," in Arieti et al., *New Dimensions in Psychiatry*, New York: John Wiley and Sons, pp.293-304

Oct. 17   Folk Healing Traditions in India, Part I: A Description of Types of Healers and Their Practices—Historical and Anthropological Perspectives (RLK and MW)

Readings: Kakar, S. (1982) *SMD*

              Trivedi, J. K. and Sethi, B. B. (1979), "A Psychiatric Study of Traditional Healers in Lucknow City," *Indian Journal of Psychiatry* 21:133-37

              Somasundaram, O. (1973), "Religious Treatment of Mental Illness in Tamil Nadu," *Indian Journal of Psychiatry* 15:38-84

              Kapur, R. L. (1979), "Role of Traditional Healers in Mental Health Care in India," *Social Science and Medicine* 130:27- 31

Oct. 24   Folk Healing Traditions of India, Part II: Case Studies
Readings: As for Oct. 17

Oct. 31   Comparative Assessment of Indian and Chinese Healing Traditions: Guest lecture by Dr. Arthur Kleinman (AK)

Readings: Kleinman, A. (1980), *Patients and Healers in the Context of Culture*, Berkeley: Univ. of California Press, Chs. 7, 8, and 9

Nov. 7   Guest lecture by Prof. Nancy Shields
              Topic and readings to be announced. Case studies.

Nov. 14   Idioms of Distress: Characteristic Clinical Presentations and Patterns of Help-seeking (RLK)
              Symptoms and Signs of Illness Patterns: Other Problems

Readings: Carstairs, G. M., and Kapur, R. L. (1976) *GUK*

Nichter, Mark (1981), "Idioms of Distress," in *Culture, Medicine, and Psychiatry* 5:379-408

Beals, A. R. (1979), "Strategies of Resort to Curers in South Asia," in *AMS*

Malhotra, A.K., "Dhat Syndrome: A Culture-bound Sex Neurosis of the Orient," in *Archives of Sexual Behavior* 4:519-28

Nov. 21   Psychotherapy with Indian Patients (AKL)

Readings: Hoch, E. M. (1974), "Pir, Faqir, and Psychotherapist," in *The Human Context*, Vol.6, pp. 668-76

Hoch, E.M. (1977), "Psychotherapy for the Illiterate," in Arieti et al., *New Dimensions of Psychiatry*, New York: John Wiley and Sons, Vol.2: 75- 92

Neki, J. S. (1973), "Guru-Chela Relationship: The Possibility of a Therapeutic Paradigm," in *American Journal of Orthopsychiatry*: 755-66

Surya, N. C. (1975), "Ego Structure in a Hindu Joint Family," in Caudill, W., and Lin, T. Y. (eds.), *Mental Health Research in Asia and the Pacific*, Honolulu

Frank, J. (1974), "Non-Medical Healing: Religious and Secular," in *P&H*

Dec. 5   1. Observations of a Western Psychiatrist on Psychotherapy in India (MW)

2. Comments from an Indian Perspective (RLK)

Readings: Hoch, E. M. (1973), "Psychotherapy in India," in *Indo-Asian Culture*, pp. 74-81

Roland, A. (1981), "Towards a Psychoanalytical Psychology of Hierarchical Relationships in Hindu India," in *Ethos* 10:232-53

Wig, N. N. (1983), "DSM III: A Perspective from the Third World," in R.L. Spritzer et al., (eds.), *International Perspectives on DSM III*, Washington: American Psychiatric Press

Dec. 12   Involvement of Traditional Healers in Primary Health Care (RLK)

Readings: Taylor, Carl (1976), "The Place of Indigenous Medical Practitioners in the Modernization of Health Sciences," in *AMS*, pp. 285-99

Montgomery, E., "Systems and Medical Practitioners of a Tamil Town," in *AMS*, pp. 272-84

Dec. 19   Course Summary and Panel Discussion on the Healing Process (RLK, MW, and AK)

❧VII❧

The Strange in the Midst of the Familiar:
A Thematic Seminar on Sacrifice

Michael D. Swartz

Introduction

It is often said about religious studies, as of anthropology and other disciplines, that one of its goals is "to make the strange familiar and the familiar strange." Though this idea has been expressed in many ways and by many thinkers,[1] my first introduction to the concept was through Bertolt Brecht's idea of *Verfremdung*. The *Verfremdungseffekt*, often inadequately rendered as "alienation effect" and thus mistaken for mere ironic detachment, is intended to serve the goal of the didactic, epic theatre of making the familiar strange and thus laying bare social and economic relationships taken for granted.[2] As a student of esoteric trends in ancient Judaism, such as Merkavah mysticism and magic, I have also endeavored to make the strange familiar—to help students and readers understand the structures and logic of seemingly irrational types of religious behavior. An implication of this latter objective is that the aim of education is not only self-knowledge, but understanding of unfamiliar ways of

---

[1] See J. Z. Smith's discussion of V. Shklovsky's notion of "defamiliarization" in *Imagining Religion* (Chicago: University of Chicago Press, 1982), xiii.

[2] A lucid exposition of Brecht's theories on theatre can be found in his *Messingkauf Dialogues*, trans. J. Willet (London: Methuen & Co, 1965); on the so-called "A-effect" see pp. 76-83. On Brecht's self-conscious approach and its implications for anthropology, see J. Spencer, "Anthropology as a Kind of Writing," *Man* (N. S.) 24 (1989): 152-53.

thinking and living. These are certainly not the only goals of a course in religious studies, but they can be important ones.

A related goal is to get students to think critically about religion. This deceptively simple statement can mean several things. Depending on the academic setting and the instructor's interest, it can mean teaching students to evaluate the claims of religions to truth and their rhetoric, helping students clarify or develop their own world-views or values, or getting students to understand religious behavior as a form of human behavior inseparable from other forms of human behavior. My own interest, and that reflected in this paper and the seminar which it presents, is in this third type of critical thinking.

In addition to these critical goals, we should not lose sight of the value of teaching specific things. Our students should be able to identify and understand religious concepts, persons, dates, works of literature and the like which play an important part in the culture and discourse of our world.

The cross-cultural thematic course can be a valuable way of advancing these (admittedly ambitious) goals. By comparing ostensibly similar types of behavior or concepts as they appear in two or more religious cultures, we can learn something specific about them—such as the patterns and priorities of each—and learn something applicable to other phenomena we study—such as the uses and limits of our categories and the range of behavior encompassed by them. A particularly valuable effect of such comparison is the shock that results upon juxtaposition of disparate phenomena.[3]

With these and other interests in mind, I have taken part in developing and teaching, together with Professor Benjamin C. Ray, a seminar for majors in religious studies at the University of Virginia based on the theme of sacrifice and the study of religions.[4] This paper is a description of this seminar and how it relates to the goals stated above.

---

[3] On this type of juxtaposition in the classroom, see J. Z. Smith, "'Narratives into Problems': The College Introductory Course and the Study of Religion," *JAAR* 56: 735-36.

[4] This seminar grew out of conversations with Professor Ray, and with Professor Gary A. Anderson; many issues relating to it were discussed in a special group at the NEH Summer Seminar at Harvard. Professor Ray and I led the seminar in the Spring of 1989. Another majors seminar on the theme of sacrifice has been taught in the department by Professor Robert L. Wilken. All of these colleagues have written on sacrifice and integrate the topic into their own courses. Their help in developing and clarifying issues related to the seminar and this paper is much appreciated.

The Majors Seminar

Because of its size and diversity, and for historical reasons, the undergraduate religious studies curriculum at the University of Virginia is organized into traditions (such as Judaism, Christianity, and Buddhism,) and what are called "cultural areas" (such as ethics and religion and literature). By the time the student is in his or her fourth year, that student will usually have been introduced to at least two religious traditions. We have found that students do not usually come to the department wanting to study "religion" in the abstract; rather they come curious about, for example, Judaism, Hinduism, the New Testament, or medical ethics, and simply continue to take courses in the department.

The majors seminar is required for all majors, and is usually taken in the student's fourth year. It is designed to give a sense of religious studies as a diverse field, but one which involves a set of skills which can be learned. The subject matter can be practically anything as long as it meets the goals of the seminar; past and proposed subjects have included "defining religion," "cosmologies," and "Gods of Flesh, Gods of Stone." Although it has been taught by individuals, we believe the seminar to be most conducive to team teaching. We want students to become acquainted with the notion that there is diversity in ways of studying religion, and the interplay between the instructors in the course of discussion is a step towards representing that diversity.

There are distinct advantages to presenting a thematic comparative seminar near the end of a student's undergraduate education in religious studies rather than at the introductory level. At this level of work, students should be sufficiently sophisticated about the study of religion and aware of the limits of the seminar to understand that we are not presenting any of the traditions in its fullness, and that sacrifice is not a central theme in all of them. For example, understanding of sacrifice is central to the understanding of biblical Judaism. However, in presenting Vedic sacrifice we are not necessarily presenting the richness of Indian, or even Vedic religion. In addition, students, having become acquainted with one or more traditions, will have something to compare the subject matter to. They will also have met some of the historical and textual problems inherent in the study of a tradition.

Sacrifice as a Problem

Attitudes to sacrifice are often a barometer of our embarrassment about religion. This alone would make it a worthy subject for study. But there are several reasons for considering it as a theme for a course in the study of religion.

As the syllabus below points out, sacrifice is both strange and familiar to us. Sacrifice seems to modern eyes the most irrational—even immoral—aspect of some religions, including that of ancient Israel. But at the same time, sacrifice is a common conceptual term in religions, and ritual sacrifice is considered by Catholics to occur in the Eucharist. Sacrifice was a key issue in the Reformation, which deeply informs modern views of religion.[5] The question of the depiction of the Temple sacrifice in the Jewish liturgy was an important issue in the Reform movement in modern Judaism.[6]

Sacrifice as a subject for a thematic course has the further advantage of illuminating the relationship between thought and action in religion. It is an activity with conceptual implications. In many traditions, it is among the most physical of ritual activities. This allows us to consider seriously religious traditions in which the enterprise of theology does not play a central role. At the same time, the theological dimension of sacrifice plays an important part in Christianity as well as its ritual dimension, so theology is not ignored as a subject for study.

Through studying sacrifice, the students will also become acquainted with such issues as ritual, sacred space, purity, anthropomorphism, and the relationship between myth and ritual. They probably will have met some of these themes in previous courses, but here many of them can come together.

The Seminar

Our syllabus is presented below. The seminar is held once a week. In addition to listing the class schedule and readings, the syllabus presents some of the goals and reasons for the seminar as it is structured. The syllabus endeavors to make it clear that the subject of the seminar is really the study of religion rather than simply sacrifice.

---

[5] In laying the blame for the inadequacies of older approaches to the study of religion squarely in the laps of nineteenth-century anthropologists, we often ignore the role of conflicts which have their roots in the Reformation. See K. Thomas, *Religion and the Decline of Magic* (New York: Charles Scribner's Sons, 1971), 51-77; and M. Douglas, *Natural Symbols* (New York: Pantheon, 1982), 37-53.

[6] See J. K. Petuchowsky, *Prayerbook Reform in Europe: The Liturgy of European Liberal and Reform Judaism* (New York: World Union for Progressive Judaism, 1968).

REL 400: MAJORS SEMINAR
SACRIFICE AND THE STUDY OF RELIGION

Instructors: Benjamin C. Ray and Michael D. Swartz

What does a religious studies major do, anyway?

Rel 400 is a seminar on the study of religion. Here we will learn ways in which the academic study of religion is carried out by looking at one important and complex aspect of religious behavior: sacrifice.

What does sacrifice mean? Can killing be a religious act? Can there be a bloodless sacrifice? When the ancient Jews and the contemporary Nuer sacrifice cattle, are they doing the same thing? Can we put that activity in the same category as the ritual killing of human beings by the Aztecs? Is the Eucharist a sacrifice? How do we approach such questions?

It is often said that a goal of religious studies is "to make the strange familiar and the familiar strange." Sacrifice is both strange and familiar to us. It is hard for most of us to conceive of the ritual slaughter of animals as a religious act with profound meaning for people. Often, when we study religion, we are concerned with extracting pure ideas from the data we learn; we don't want to get involved in the messy details. But religion involves action as well—ritual, biological, political and social activity. Sacrifice is one of the most puzzling and interesting of these activities.

Sacrifice is also something familiar to us. The Temple and the biblical sacrificial system take up at least one-fifth of the Torah (the core of the Hebrew Bible). Its destruction in the first century was a traumatic and formative event in the history of Judaism. Jesus lived in a Judea dominated by that Temple, and Christians debate to this day whether sacrifice is a significant part of Christian theology and worship. One cannot know the Vedas, African religions, Mesoamerican religions or even—some would argue—American civil religion without understanding sacrifice. We use the term in ethics, in war, and in baseball.

More important, sacrifice is a good way of understanding and testing the wide variety of methods of studying religion. How do we interpret what we see when we ask about a phenomenon such as sacrifice? In this seminar we will see how this phenomenon is interpreted from the anthropological, sociological, historical, psychological, and theological perspectives. All of these are part of Religious Studies. Using the term sacrifice, we can test our definitions of categories we use to describe religion. How, if at all, can we compare religions?

As majors in religious studies, you have become acquainted with one or more religious traditions or disciplines. The purpose of the Majors Seminar is to stop and reflect on what is being majored in. In this seminar we will ask how we learn and interpret what we know about religion. We will do so by focusing on one dimension of religion, that of sacrifice. You will learn to read theoretical essays in the study of religion critically, and to apply the methods you learn and develop to the study of specific religious phenomena.

I. Class Requirements

A. *Participation in class discussion* is absolutely essential to this seminar. Much of the class time will be spent discussing issues raised by the readings, by the instructors, and by fellow class members. The extent to which you take part in this discussion will be a significant indicator of your success in this class.

B. *One report* (about three pages, double-spaced) on a specific class topic, to be read and discussed in class. This report will be a summary of the main points of the subject, and should include a brief evaluation of the readings. You will use the assigned reading and supplementary materials.

C. *Two six-to-eight-page papers* to be presented and discussed in class. These are to be critical evaluations and applications of the methods used in the study of sacrifice in an individual religious tradition. The first paper will deal with one of the traditions studied in the first half of the seminar. The second will deal with the traditions covered in the second half. Because of the structure of the seminar, most students should thus have the opportunity to present papers on traditions both familiar and unfamiliar to them from their previous study in the department.

D. *A one-page essay* defining sacrifice and explaining your definition, to be read and discussed at the final class session.

II. Required reading:

1. Bible: Any reliable translation.
2. B. C. Brundage, *The Fifth Sun*. Austin: University of Texas Press, 1979.
3. M. Douglas, *Purity and Danger* 1966, repr. London and New York: Ark, 1988.
4. M. Eliade, *The Myth of the Eternal Return or, Cosmos and History*. Trans. W. R. Trask. 1954, repr. Princeton: Princeton University Press, 1974.
5. E. E. Evans-Pritchard, *Nuer Religion*. New York: Oxford, 1956.
6. Other selected readings.

Class Schedule

1. Introduction to the seminar

2. Israelite sacrifice: In Theory
   • B. Levine, "On the Presence of God in Biblical Religion," in J. Neusner, ed., *Religions in Antiquity: Studies in Religion presented to Erwin Ramsell Goodenough* (Leiden: E. J. Brill, 1968), 71-87; J. Levenson, "The Jerusalem Temple in Devotional and Visionary Experience," in A. Green, ed., *Jewish Spirituality from the Bible to the Middle Ages* (New York: Crossroad, 1986), 32-61.

3. Israelite sacrifice: In Practice
   • Leviticus 1-5, 16; Numbers 19; E. Leach, "The Logic of Sacrifice," in *Culture and Communication* (Cambridge: Cambridge University Press, 1976), 81-93; B. A. Levine, "Biblical Temple," *Encyclopedia of Religion*, 2:202-16.

4. The trajectory of sacrifice in Judaism: purity; The Temple and its afterlife
  • Douglas, 1-57; J. Neusner, "Map Without Territory," *History of Religions*, 19 (1979): 103-27.

5. Sacrifice in Early Christianity?
  • F. M. Young, *Sacrifice and the Death of Christ* (London: SPCK, 1975), 47-82.

6. In Catholic and Protestant Christianity
  • J. A. Jungmann, *The Mass of the Roman Rite* (New York: Benziger, 1951-55), Vol. I, Pt. 3: Sect. 1, nos. 3 and 5; Vol II, Pt. 4: Sect. 1, no. 3; sect. 2, nos. 12, 13; S. Campbell-Jones, "Ritual in Performance and Interpretation: The Mass in a Convent Setting," in M. F. C. Bourdillon and M. Fortes, eds., *Sacrifice,* (London: Academic Press, 1980), 89-105; F. Clark, *Eucharistic Sacrifice and the Reformation,* (second ed., Oxford: Blackwell, 1967), Chapters 4 and 6.

7. Perspective: Theories of Sacrifice and Ritual
  • V. Valeri, "The Elements of Sacrifice," in *Kingship and Sacrifice: Ritual and Society in Ancient Hawaii,* trans. P. Wissing (Chicago: University of Chicago Press, 1985), 62-75; Eliade, chs. 1-2; C. Geertz, "Religion as a Cultural System," in *The Interpretation of Cultures* (New York: Basic Books, 1973), 87-125.

8. Student Papers

9. Sacrifice in Africa
  • Evans-Pritchard, Chapters 8-11.
  • Film: "The Nuer"

10. Aztec Sacrifice
  • Brundage, Chapters 1-3, 5, 8-9; D. Carrasco, "Star Gatherers and Wobbling Suns: Astral Symbolism in the Aztec Tradition," *History of Religions* 26 (1987): 279-94.

11. Vedic Sacrifice
  • H. Hubert and M. Mauss, "The Scheme of Sacrifice," in *Sacrifice: Its Nature and Function,* trans. W. D. Halls (Chicago: University of Chicago Press, 1964), 19-49;
  • Film: "The Altar of Fire."

12. Sacrifice and Modernity
  • J. Z. Smith, "The Bare Facts of Ritual," in *Imagining Religion* (Chicago: University of Chicago Press, 1982), 53-65; W. L. Warner, "An American Sacred Ceremony," in *American Life: Dream and Reality.* (Chicago: University of Chicago Press, 1953), 1-26.

13. Student Papers

14. Student Papers; Concluding Assignment: A one-page definition of sacrifice to be discussed in class.

Additional Items on Reserve:

Anderson, G. A. *Sacrifices and Offerings in Ancient Israel.* Atlanta: Scholars Press, 1987.

Bourdillon, M. *Sacrifice.*

Broda, J., Carrasco, D., and Moctezuma, E. M. *The Great Temple of Tenochtitlan: Center and Periphery in the Aztec World.* Berkeley: University of California Press, 1987.

Burkert, W. *Homo Necans.* Berkeley, University of California Press, 1983.

Eilberg-Schwartz, H. "Israel in the Mirror of Nature: Animal Metaphors in the Ritual and Narratives of Ancient Israel." *Journal of Ritual Studies* 2 (1988): 1-30.

Hamerton-Kelly, R. G., ed. *Violent Origins: Walter Burkert, Rene Girard and Jonathan Z. Smith on Ritual Killing and Cultural Formation.* Stanford: Stanford University Press, 1987.

Clark, F. *Eucharistic Sacrifice and the Reformation.*

Daly, R. J. *Christian Sacrifice: The Judaeo-Christian Background before Origin.* Washington: The Catholic University of America Press, 1978.

_____, *Origins of the Christian Doctrine of Sacrifice.* Philadelphia: Fortress Press, 1978.

Levine, B. A. *In the Presence of the Lord.* Leiden: E. J. Brill, 1974.

Commentary

The seminar schedule interlaces the more theoretical readings, such as Geertz, Leach, and Hubert and Mauss, with the readings that focus on a specific subject (such as Levine, Brundage, and Young). Although the readings emphasize the social sciences, a variety of social-scientific approaches appear, including the structuralism of Leach, Warner's Durkheimian approach, the symbolic approach of Valeri, and those of other seminal thinkers such as Evans-Pritchard and Geertz. The approaches also range from the grand, cross-cultural schemes of Eliade and Hubert and Mauss to approaches, like those of Geertz and Neusner, which insist on studying systems whole and observing a phenomenon in systemic context. In our class discussions, we have brought our respective research methods to bear on the material, such as my textual and historical orientation and Professor Ray's ethnographic experience.[7] Students are encouraged in their papers to test the applicability of one of the methods studied in the theoretical readings to some of the data learned in the more specific readings and sources—acknowledging at the same time that these latter readings have methods and biases as well. The result of these exercises, we hope, is the student's growing confidence in his or her ability to do what the student of religion does in bringing analytical skills to bear on a subject.

[7] See Smith's remarks on making students aware of the process of textual study: "Narratives into Problems," 737.

At the same time, the syllabus also reflects my conviction that students ought to know not only how to approach a given problem; they ought to know about something in particular. By the end of the semester they will have gained specific knowledge and, we hope, a clearer understanding of such concepts as Temple, Eucharist, agni, and Memorial Day. They will also have produced a definition of sacrifice which is the product of their own thinking about, and, inevitably perhaps, relationship to, religion. And they will have read a few classics in religious studies such as Eliade's *The Myth of the Eternal Return* and Mary Douglas' *Purity and Danger*.

Problems and Benefits to the Approach

In thematic courses, there is often the danger of over-conceptualization. In studying those themes which focus on an activity, such as sacrifice or pilgrimage, sacrifice or pilgrimage as an *activity* quickly becomes reified into the abstract *idea* of sacrifice (self-sacrifice, altruism, and ethics) or the *idea* of pilgrimage (journey, quest, and personal growth), which is then related to other abstract ideas—especially those with which the instructors and students are more familiar. Students are often more comfortable with this intellectualist approach. It is thus important that, at least from time to time, the instructors bring the focus of discussion back to religious behavior from the concepts it inspires.

There are many problems in religious studies not covered here. We do not define religion for the purposes of this seminar, nor do we ask the students to do so. However, the assignment of defining sacrifice is designed to confront the student with the value and the problems involved in such definitions. Defining a term such as sacrifice, which would seem, on the face of it, to be easily identifiable, should make students more aware of the categories they use.

Sometimes the subject matter seems so alien to the students that it takes a while to get warmed up to it. In our case, the students became most enthusiastic in the classes in which Aztec sacrifice was discussed and in which Warner's presentation of Memorial Day was read together with Valeri's theory of Hawaiian sacrifice. Here the juxtaposition of those cultures raised provocative questions of the relationship between war and human sacrifice, and the role of the community's values in transcending the individual. No doubt the students' enthusiasm was due to the dramatic subject matter, but these topics also served as a catalyst for the approaches the class had learned in the weeks before. It would be an interesting exercise to place the discussions of Aztec sacrifice and Memorial Day sacrifice near the beginning of the seminar, to confront the students at the outset with some of the most striking implications of comparison of religions.

By the same token, students tended to resist the particulars of sacrifice. It was necessary to emphasize that studying such a subject requires the patience to probe its details and to analyze, step by step, the process the activity involves; that the disciplined study of a religious phenomenon necessitates going through its particulars to arrive at a theoretical picture. Toward this end, ethnographic films can be a great help. They often bring the immediacy and texture of ritual behavior into the classroom. It is one thing to read of sacrificial blood and where it is collected in a ritual; it is another thing to see it gushing from an animal. In films we were able to observe details left out in the written ethnographic accounts. Students, who are usually accustomed to worship conducted in reverent silence or solemn song, are often struck by the apparent casualness of participants in many rituals. This observation can be a springboard for discussion about the relationship between feeling and ritual behavior and Western ambivalence about ritual. It is also as important that our students look at film and video critically as it is that they read critically. The subject matter was also made vivid in a class session in which Professor Gerald P. Fogarty, a colleague who is both a historian of religion and a Catholic priest gave an account of what he does when he performs the Eucharistic sacrifice in the Mass.

Notes on the Topics

The seminar begins with sacrifice in biblical and post-biblical Judaism. It is important to understand biblical sacrifice in order to understand the concept of sacrifice as we use it—that concept being the biblical institution as seen through Hellenism and Christianity. To most of us, biblical sacrifice is the strange in the midst of the familiar. The Book of Leviticus must be one of the least-studied biblical texts in the classroom. Many earlier scholars saw sacrifice as a late form of degenerate priestly religion. Others tended to "biblical exceptionalism," arguing that Israelite sacrifice was more noble, sophisticated, ethical and less "magical" than that of surrounding cultures.[8] But sacrifice is not only an essential part of biblical religion; it is important for understanding post-biblical Judaism.

The article by B. A. Levine, "On the Presence of God in Biblical Religion," is an eloquent essay on the mythic assumptions behind this element of biblical religion. I believe that every treatment of biblical reli-

---

8   On earlier views of biblical sacrifice see Anderson, *Sacrifices and Offerings*, 4-14.

gion should include it. Although too technical for the average student, Levine's *In the Presence of the Lord* is a seminal work in the study of Biblical sacrifice. Also important for its attention to issues in the history of religion is Anderson's *Sacrifices and Offerings in Ancient Israel.*[9]

As noted above, films and visual materials should be used and discussed whenever possible. This includes diagrams or pictures of temples and ritual sites as recorded or imagined. If visual materials on the Samaritan Passover sacrifice can be found, they would prove an interesting addition to the unit on sacrifice in Judaism.

From the more theoretical perspective, Hubert and Mauss presents perhaps the simplest and most influential view of sacrifice. For this very reason we decided not to place it at the beginning of the seminar; it can seduce students away from subtler thinking about the phenomenon. The short passage by Valeri is an excellent summary of theories of sacrifice. His own theory (pages 70-75), despite the unfamiliar terminology employed, is a useful and provocative one.

The seminar could accommodate other topics and cultures than the ones we have selected. We did not deal with sacrifice in Greek and Hellenistic religion, but there are sophisticated treatments of it, such as those of W. Burkert and M. Detienne.[10] It must be remembered that in the Greco-Roman world after 70 CE, Jews and Christians were the exception rather than the norm in not holding sacrifices. Attention could also be paid to the critique of sacrifice in Buddhist thought. Another interesting tack could be to discuss rituals which look like sacrifice in religious cultures which profess no active sacrificial ritual, such as the Islamic pilgrimage ritual at Mt. Arafat, or the Jewish folk ritual of *kapparot*. The use of the concept of sacrifice in ethics was also not explored systematically in the seminar.

Conclusion

This discussion is meant to serve not simply as a suggestion for a seminar, but as an example of one approach to the teaching of religious studies and a discussion of sacrifice as an aspect of the field often overlooked in teaching. Similar courses could be built, for example, around

[9] See also Levine's commentary to Leviticus in *The JPS Torah Commentary: The Traditional Hebrew Text with the New JPS Translation* (Philadelphia: Jewish Publication Society 1989), v. 3. Another view of biblical sacrifice is offered in J. Milgrom, *Cult and Conscience: The Asham and the Priestly Doctrine of Repentance* (Leiden: E. J. Brill, 1976).

[10] Burkert, *Homo Necans*; see also M. Detienne and J-P. Vernant, *The Cuisine of Sacrifice Among the Greeks* (Chicago: University of Chicago Press, 1989), which contains a good bibliography.

the rubrics of religion and magic,[11] or religion and war.[12] Behind this approach is the hope that our students will be able to find a way of understanding religion analytically in their encounters with it, even as they participate or make choices in their religious lives. For historians of religion, this approach to teaching can be seen in continuity with the historical approach to the study of religion we practice in our scholarship. As Brecht observes:

> If empathy makes something ordinary of a special event, alienation [*verfremdung*] makes something special of an ordinary event. The most hackneyed everyday incidents are stripped of their monotony when represented as quite special. The audience is no longer taking refuge from the present day in history; the present day becomes history.[13]

[11] This theme shares many features with the theme of sacrifice, having been a crucial element in the debate over the nature of religion at least since the reformation. At the same time, such a course would also emphasize the study of magical rituals and texts themselves, and their rhetoric and inner logic.

[12] This course could be based on the premise that students often find it difficult to see religious issues as plausible motivation for war, revolution, mass suicide, and other forms of social violence.

[13] Brecht, *Messingkauf Dialogues*, 76.

❧VIII❧

The Symbol of Destruction and the Destruction of Symbol:
Sacrifice as a Thematic Course Focus

WILLIAM R. DARROW

As I see it, they satisfy two or three primitive human urges with this huge sacrifice. One was mentioned previously: sacrificing animals instead of human
beings. Sheep instead of Isma'il. Kill animals, in order to refrain from killing
human beings. It is also the best possible practice in the use of knives, in shed-
ding blood, seeing blood. Women, men, and children, knives in hand, take
such delight in carcasses, for procuring provisions, or simply for the thrill of it.
Several times I saw people cutting up carcasses just for fun, and such a gleam
of delight in their eyes...

—Al-e Ahmad, *Lost in the Crowd*, p. 90

"Sacrifice" in its strict etymological sense of "making sacred" might
be said to be all that we study in comparative religion. The establishment
of a boundary between a sacred and a profane realm and the fabrication
of objects that bear the sacred in the profane realm and thus connect the
two might always appear to be the focus of our work. But just as the sa-
cred/profane dichotomy may be parochial, there is also much about this
strict appeal to etymological origins that misleads. If we were to select a
term from another language to name our category, we would be led in
other directions and toward other origins. With the Indo-Iranian *yajna*
we would focus on "worship." Using the Semitic *qurban* we would emphasize the sense of drawing near. The Greek term *thuein* would make us
see the smoke's ability to bridge the two realms of gods and men. The
Chinese *jisi* would connect our category with the notion of "display."
The German term *opfer* directs us to the crucial intersection of the ideas of
victim and offering. Nevertheless sacrifice has been seen as a unitary and

113

central concept in the comparative study of religion and one of major significance in the history of that study. Therefore sacrifice provides a rich focus for a thematic course to introduce students both to the range of human religious expressions and to the process of constructing heuristic concepts that allow students of religion to illuminate, compare, and contrast the materials of human religious history.

To delimit the focus of such a course I will begin by provisionally defining "sacrifice" as "the ritual destruction of an object as an offering to the divine." We should recognize at the outset that sacrifice is a concept that seems to have a deep and special fascination and power for those who are products of the Judeo-Christian tradition. This fascination has two deeply conflicting but intertwined roots. The first is the fascination with the act of violence necessary to sacrifice. The symbolism of destruction, more specifically killing living beings, animals or even humans, both attracts and repels and therein lies its continuing power to fascinate. This violent character of sacrifice has recently become the theoretical starting point for several approaches to sacrifice (Burkert, Girard, Hamerton-Kelley).

If violence provides the first source of fascination, the substitution and displacement of that violence onto other objects or into other activities then provides the second source. There are any number of substitutions and displacements. The substitution of a ram for Abraham's sacrifice of his son is one of the richest multivalent symbols of substitution, invoking the possibility of human sacrifice and then displacing it. The cessation of the Temple sacrificial cult after the fall of the Second Temple and the rise of Rabbinic Judaism with its displacement of sacrifice into other forms of domestic worship is a self-consciously historical displacement. The Christian doctrine of atonement held that Christ's death was the final and ultimate sacrifice and Christianity's task became one of finding the appropriate manner of memorializing rather than repeating that sacrifice. Both Judaism and Christianity have consciously proclaimed the end of physical sacrifices and the cultivation of refined notions of self-sacrifice and charity. In this they are joined by Islam, although animal sacrifice remains a significant act in Islamic ritual life, experienced in the ritual life of Muslims as the experience of a Muslim pilgrim in Mecca testifies at the head of this essay. For all three the progressive movement from sacrifice and its violence to more refined moral notions seem central, although it is noticeable how easily each tradition can recover a language of the horror of sacrifice in the face of tragedy such as martyrdom, warfare, or the holocaust.

The character of the fascination of sacrifice for those who are products of the Judeo-Christian tradition should make one suspicious about the appropriateness of "sacrifice" as a cross-cultural category. We have already pointed to the issues attendant upon translating the term into several different languages and to the overdetermined sources for our fascination. To these we may add two further substantive definitional problems that need to be addressed when approaching the notion of sacrifice as a category of religious activity. First, is sacrifice a unified category or instead a collection of disparate and contradictory acts that share the common feature of the destruction of an object? Second, even if we accept the notion of sacrifice as a unified category, should the sacrificial act ever be separated from its surrounding cultic context?

The first question points to the radically different intentions behind different sacrifices. No typology can be exhaustive but the subtypes of sacrifice include: tribute, praise, thanksgiving, sustaining the world, supplication, catharsis, purification, communal celebration, and expiation. Religious traditions that have sacrifice in fact divide them up into such subtypes and do not necessarily employ a single overarching concept to identify all of them. The rules and character of each ritual depends on its purpose.

The complexity of such typology led earlier generations of scholars, seeking for a unitary vision of sacrifice, to posit one as primary, the source of all sacrificial activity. E. B. Tylor thought the origin lay in the process of giving in expectation of a return gift in a closed system of forced exchange. W. R. Smith saw the origin of sacrifice in the celebration of a communal meal between the human and the divine and thus tried to correct Tylor's mechanistic view. Frazer's focus on the sacrificial death of a weakened king can be seen as a type of world sustaining approach to sacrifice, while the more recent theories of violence and sacrifice by Girard stresses the cathartic function of sacrifice as an outlet for violence. All these theoretical formulations, despite sometimes great sophistication, have stressed the unitary nature of sacrifice based on a notion that one type of sacrifice was the original type: a mode of explanation that leads one to monocausal and monolithic interpretations.

The result of these different theoretical grapplings may be unconvincing, but they have left us with our category. The theoretical insights heavily inform much of the writings we will use in the course. There is an irony here in that the category remains, the phenomenon exists, even if it is one that has been constituted for the most parochial reasons and whose original or purest form cannot be agreed upon. With this we can return to our preliminary definition and pose a second and broader question. Is it appropriate to separate sacrifice from a wider category of offering? (Baal) Is the offering of first fruits at a harvest festival easily differentiated from the sacrificial destruction of a living being? Related to this is the question of whether a sacrificial offering in a curing rite or rite of passage can be separated out from this cultic context and called "sacrifice." In the end the separateness of our category may appropriately collapse and the coincidence of violence, symbolization, and power that seems to lie at the center of our concept of sacrifice may be critically inspected. This in the end is the purpose of the course proposed here.

The course brings together five themes which are interwoven throughout the syllabus. We have already alluded to them in this initial discussion, but I want to expand on them briefly before turning attention to the actual course syllabus.

The Symbol of Destruction

Violence, the symbol of destruction, is at the heart of one main strand of the course. Blood and gore are our object. The transgressive and criminal character of sacrifice is central to our conceptualizations. This line of approach might be labeled psychoanalytic since it begins with Freud. But the disciplinary identity of this theme is not quite so clear. Frazer contributed to it with his fascination with the necessary sacrificial death of a weakened king. Bataille, Girard, and Burkert have continued this theme with theories of differing subtlety and breadth. The relation of sacrificial action to the character of human aggression is at issue here. Sacrifice creates the illusion of being close to the wild, the dangerous, the uncontrolled; of stripping away culture and revealing the natural.

The Destruction of Symbol

If sacrifice first takes us into what appear to be powers of the unconscious and the expression of inchoate desire, at the same moment we discover the embeddedness of sacrificial activity in a whole range of symbolic systems. Sacrifice is always an act in culture and thus is by definition never a "natural" act. Culture places a structure of categories on the "natural world" and provides the symbol systems in which we exist. The object that is destroyed is always symbolically constituted. Thus sacrifice raises the question of symbol for us, even if it is primarily the destruction of a symbol that marks its character. Sacrifice is never random violence, no matter how much its horrific character is emphasized.

It is always an object of value, of wealth, that is sacrificed. In addition, in the case of animal sacrifice, it is always a domesticated animal, an animal who by definition exists on the boundary between nature and culture. That animal must often be purchased, an act which underlines the embeddedness of the sacrificial object in the systems of exchange and value. The embeddedness of the sacrificial object in the symbolic codes of cuisine and food is central to an understanding of much sacrifice. The play with notions of purity and pollution in sacrifice brings in a culture's cleanliness code. Finally, the scapegoat's ability to symbolize the guilt of a social entity in a scapegoat sacrifice or the victim's ability to release the symbolic energy to restore a collectivity are two powerful symbolic aspects of some sacrifice.

Hegemony and Patriarchy

If sacrifice manages to straddle the nature/culture line with delightful ambiguity and power, it is also crucial to point out that sacrifice as a symbol of power is appropriated by the hegemonic forces in society as a source of legitimacy. The role of kings and priests in sacrificial cults underlines the crucial interconnection between sacrifice and power (Coombs-Shilling, de Heusch, Valeri, Zito). Sacrifice and the ability to conduct sacrifice appears to have been a powerful source of legitimacy which in many ways survives to the present. The right of a government to demand individual sacrifice in war may not be as far different as we might have thought from older concepts of human sacrifice.

Ritual

Focus on sacrifice is a symptom of religious studies' preoccupation with ritual activity. Ritual seen as enacted truth, the performative character of religious expression, has become central to contemporary religious studies. As a focus sacrifice allows students to recognize some of the sources that have contributed to this development, some of the features of that focus, and perhaps to explore some of the limits of such a focus.

Category Formation

Finally, there is much that is both problematic and overdetermined about our category of sacrifice. A focus on this category allows students to recognize the problems attendant upon cross-cultural categories. By always problematizing the sources of the category, while at the same time recognizing the heuristic value of "sacrifice," such a course as this can become a valuable practicum in the character of cross-cultural study.

PROPOSED SYLLABUS

Week 1   The Character of a Sacrificial System: The Nuer
                Evans-Pritchard, *Nuer Religion*, pp. 177-286

Week 2   Sacrifice as Transgression and Crime
                Freud, *Totem and Taboo*

Week 3   Sacrifice and Patriarchal Power
                Kristeva, *The Powers of Horror: An Essay in Abjection*, pp. 1-132
                Jay, Nancy, "Sacrifice as Remedy for Having Been Born of
                Woman"

Week 4   The Sacrificial Scheme
                Hubert and Mauss, *Sacrifice: Its Nature and Function*

Week 5   Sacrifice as Ecstatic Violence
                Bataille, *Theory of Religion*

Weeks 6-7   Sacrifice in Greece
                Hesiod, *Theogony*
                Detienne, "Culinary Practices and the Spirit of Sacrifice"
                _____, "The Violence of Wellborn Ladies: Women in the
                Thesmophoria" both in *The Cuisine of Sacrifice*
                Euripides, *The Bacchae*

Weeks 8-9   The Fate of Sacrifice in the Semitic Religions
                Yom Kippur: The Day of Atonement
                Genesis 22, Leviticus 16
                Agnon, *Days of Awe*, pp. 183-279
                        High Holy Day Prayerbook, Avodah Service
                Sacrifice and Atonement in Christianity
                    Epistle to the Hebrews
                Sacrificial Models in Islam
                    Combs-Schilling, *Sacred Performances* pp. 221- 71

Weeks 10-11 The Fate of Sacrifice in India
                Rig Veda 10.90; Chandogya Upanisad 3.14-5.24
                    Bhagavad Gita
                John Parry, "Sacrificial Death and the Necrophagous
                Ascetic"
                Charles Malamoud, "Indian Speculations on the Sex of the
                Sacrifice"

Week 12   Sacrifice and Ritual: Process and Sham
                Turner, "Sacrifice as Quintessential Process Prophylaxis or
                Abandonment"
                Smith, "The Bare Facts of Ritual"

Notes on the Syllabus

The Nuer (Week 1)

We begin with a classic ethnographical account of the sacrificial system of the Nuer. This reading should be supplemented by the anthropological documentary *The Nuer* (1970) which will give students a good sense of the lived space of the Nuer and also illustrate an animal sacrifice. The graphic footage will be very helpful in exploring students' reactions to the killing of animals in sacrifice and the source of those reactions. Since the experience of repugnance is an important theme it is a graphic way to place the issue at the outset. Evans-Pritchard's focus is on Nuer blood sacrifice whose intent is piacular. He specifically excludes the wider range of offerings and dedications that the Nuer practice, but his discussion of the substitution of an animal by a species of cucumber opens the issue of substitution. His unforgetable discussion of the implements of sacrifice, the spear, nicely opens the question of the symbolism of sacrifice. His presentation of the movement of sacrifice—presentation, consecration, invocation, and immolation—establishes a schema that will be important throughout the course and is well grounded in some of the earlier literature that will be studied subsequently.

Freud (Week 2)

The following five weeks are designed to provide a range of theoretical approaches to sacrifice organized around the general themes of the symbol of destruction and the destruction of symbol. *Totem and Taboo* introduces the range of issues connected with the first issue: that of the character and power of violence. A reading of Freud establishes four issues that will be central to the course. These are: the question of "origins" of sacrifice; sacrifice as transgression and crime; the totemic substitution and communal celebration; and finally the question of patriarchy and jural authority. Freud meant his speculations in *Totem and Taboo* and *Moses and Monotheism* to be historical, but it would not be productive to focus on the problem of the historicity of Freud's vision of the primordial killing of the father or for that matter the dubious evidence for totemism. The important issue is to discuss why Freud considered finding origins, a foundational story, the necessary strategy in approaching the problem of the totemic meal and the vision of displaced violence and substitutionary destruction that lies at the base of the totemic feast that Freud saw at the heart of sacrificial practice.

Sacrifice and Patriarchal Power (Week 3)

The Freudian scheme of a primordial patricidal crime and its displacement into a sacrificial feast opens quite directly attention to gender issues in connection with the concepts of violence and sacrifice. These are issues that have been of wide interest to contemporary feminists, especially those influenced by psychoanalytic thought. Nancy Jay's essay raises the question of the relation between males, sacrifice, and power and explores why it is that women sacrificers are so exceedingly rare, an issue that Evans-Pritchard will already have raised. Unfortunately her essay does not explore the psychoanalytic issues involved, but does lay the background for a reading of the first portion of Kristeva's *Powers of Horror*.

Kristeva's essay allows us to explore the interconnections between sacrifice and the abject and Other. She provides a scheme that lets us explore the cultural construction of the visceral reaction we have to sacrifice's power. The abject, the disgusting, the repugnant, exercises its fascination because it exists at the edge, on the margin of defilement. It is constituted by what is excluded from what is clean and proper. It is the site of a sublime power and is the place of the unnamed other. Freud's reconstruction of the primal murder makes explicit the power of the violation of one taboo, murder of the father, but leaves the role of the incest unexplained. Without the incest taboo the desire for murder cannot be understood. This is Kristeva's correction to Freud. The unexamined role of the incest taboo points directly to the other who is woman who inhabits the site of the abject. Woman is feared and desired as the abject, created as a victim upon whose body the order of society is imposed. Sacrifice is the mode in which the boundary is maintained in the moment of its violation. Women are excluded from this action but are the site on which this takes place. Sacrifice may be replaced by internalization and moralization, by the establishment of a law of purity and holiness, but the character of its constitution as a "persecuting machine" persists throughout these transformations.

The Sacrificial Scheme (Week 4)

Hubert and Mauss address the problems of the opposing intentionalities of sacrifice by focusing on the general scheme of sacrifice that all share. This enables them to affirm the unity of sacrifice. That scheme involves both the definition of the actors in the sacrificial drama and the stages of that drama. The bulk of the data they drew upon was from a comparative reading of Hebrew and Indian priestly traditions. Their work thus also functions to introduce two of the sacrificial systems we return to later in the course. The book is noticeably text based and stands rather uncritically in the priestly traditions from which the texts derive. The centrality of the sacred/profane dichotomy and the role of the victim in connecting these two realms lies at the heart of their analysis. The acts of consecration and sanctification are the mechanisms that make the connection possible. The social function of sacrifice is also central. The destruction of victims nourishes the social forces and gains advantages both for those who enact the sacrifice and for society as a whole. The power of sanctity provides protection and restores equilibrium. While sacrifice is quite explicitly criminal, Hubert and Mauss do not dwell on the violent and transgressive character of sacrifice. They move rather easily into the moralization and internalization of sacrifice, which they see in Christianity though do not pursue in the cases of Judaism and Hinduism.

Sacrifice as Ecstatic Violence (Week 5)

If Kristeva explicity critiques Freud's approach to violence and crime for what he has left out, Bataille implicity critiques Hubert and Mauss for what they have left out: the ecstatic power of sacrifice and the need for ecstasy. Bataille's work begins with an analysis of the reasons for human desire for immanence, which arose in the consciousness which separated us from our animality. With consciousness came the creation of objects, things in the world that are in circulation and exchange. Sacrifice provides the opportunity for the destruction of such an object and the ecstatic recovery of intimacy through violent action. It is a deliberate destruction of the exchange system of the circulation of things. This destruction is made possible by the production of surpluses. Bataille sees the modern world as characterized by a different attitude toward surpluses. They are no longer destroyed in the classical sacrificial model, but put to use. This creates a new sphere, separate, outside the economic, industrial, or military sphere. In this new sphere violence is now turned outwards rather than inwards. The promise of the recovery of a lost intimacy through sacrificial violence is no longer attainable and the increasing levels of violence in modernity testify to the increased desperation with which modern human beings seek for the lost intimacy of ecstasy. Girard's theory of violence and the sacred and the necessary cathartic character of violence has its most immediate origins in Bataille's work and I find Bataille much richer and subtler than Girard's rather mechanistic theory, but Girard's *Violence and the Sacred* would be another appropriate reading here and would have the additional advantage of leading us more directly into the next topic: the place of sacrifice in ancient Greece.

Sacrifice in Greece (Weeks 6-7)

The structure of the remainder of the course is to explore more specifically some of the themes developed in the first part of the course and to encourage the reading of a selection of primary texts to provide students with the experience of reading primary materials. The materials on Greece derive from reading two texts, Hesiod's *Theogony* and Euripides' *Bacchae*. The first provides for an exploration of the cosmogonic role of violence and sacrifice in the construction of the world. The two secondary essays open issues of the classification of food and the symbolic system of cuisine. What one sacrifices and thus eats is a central issue as is the issue of who eats what of a sacrificial offering. The story of Prometheus in the *Theogony* exegeted by Vernant in "At Man's Table: Hesiod's Foundation Myth of Sacrifice" in Detienne and Vernant, *The Cuisine of Sacrifice* allows one to explore these themes in the context of the literary reworking of myth. The two secondary articles actually assigned provide further background in both texts and practices. The *Bacchae* provides a further rich opportunity to explore the literary reworking of sacrificial imagery as well as allowing one to again raise the gender issues posed by Kristeva. The sacrificial offering of Pentheus to Dionysus by the maddened female officiants of the cult allows one to reopen issues of horror and the abject in the context of a play which self-consciously explores the different registers of sacrificial action and display.

The Fate of Sacrifice in the Semitic Religions (Weeks 8-9)

The final two major sections of the course return to the materials on which Hubert and Mauss based their work: the Semitic and the Indian worlds. In both cases we are investigating the survival of sacrificial imagery and conceptions and the way they are reworked in the face of religious change. I have drawn materials from the three heirs of Semitic sacrificial practice: Rabbinic Judaism, Christianity, and Islam. There are admittedly some dangers in this selection because a lot of materials are being covered that will not be familiar to students and because there is an admittedly triumphalist view that the doctrine of atonement, in either its Jewish or Christian models, successfully preserves what is morally powerful in sacrifice, while Islam preserves what is morally repugnant. It is my hope that this course will above all teach students to question the sources of their feelings of repugnance, but I want to be clear here that there are grave problems that might waylay a class.

We read Genesis 22 to set the Abrahamic myth as the foundation myth for placing sacrifice in the Semitic tradition while Leviticus 16 introduces the sacrificial doctrine of atonement. This lays the basis for a close reading of the celebration of *Yom Kippur* and more specifically the supplemental *avodah* liturgy where the temple sacrificial is recalled. The *Letter to the Hebrews* opens the question of the Christian reworking of the doctrine of atonement and the sacrificial view of Christ. The material taken from Islam return us to the actual practice of sacrifice in an Islamic context, of the power connected with the ability to conduct those ceremonies as well as the wider presence of sacrificial conceptions in the Islamic view of sexuality. The context is the Great Sacrifice held in connection with the pilgrimage to Mecca, reference to which stands at the head of this essay, and its use by the Moroccan royal house to legitimate itself. There is a danger that concluding here will reinforce students' prejudice that Islam is "more primitive" or "less moral" than Judaism and Christianity. It is up to the instructor to address this conclusion directly and at the same time to explore continuities in the theme of atonement in the three traditions.

The Fate of Sacrifice in India (Week 10-11)

Concluding with the culture of India allows us to focus on three issues: the survival of sacrificial models in later religious history; the spiritualization of sacrifice; and finally the connection between sacrifice and power, in this case priestly power. While a number of scholars have explored the continuing significance of sacrifice in Indian religious culture (e.g., Bolle, Biardieu, and Brian Smith), the concepts that are usually taken to be central to Indian religious culture do not include sacrifice. The proposed readings attempt to redress this by focusing on sacrifice as a continuing spiritual reality in India. To be sure it is a spiritual reality that has been much more noticeably emptied of its horror than we have seen in the Greek and Semitic contexts, an issue that would be rich to explore in the classroom.

Readings of primary texts include the "Sacrificial Origin" text from the Rg Veda; Upanisadic expansions of the notion of sacrifice as a model for thinking about religious insight and transformation and finally the Gita. The Gita, of course, presents cultic sacrificial practice as but one of three modes of religious action in the world and in fact provides a very important vision of the correct attitude toward sacrificial action. But while it presents the alternative ways of knowledge and devotion as different from and, in some readings, as superior to the way of sacrifice, it is notable how the sacrificial mode of action establishes the character and content of the other two modes. The proposed secondary reading by Malamoud provides an interesting introduction to the first modes of speculation on the sacrifice in the *Brahmanas*. The article by Parry presents the dominance of sacrificial imagery in the death practices for normal human beings and the special status of one type of full renunciant who do not participate in this system.

Sacrifice and Ritual: Process and Sham (Week 12)

The two concluding readings allow us to place the consideration of sacrifice in the larger arena of ritual studies. Turner's article, by focusing on process, attempts to move beyond the limitations imposed both by typologies of sacrifice and the narrow stress on sacrificial scheme. It concludes with an examination of the possibility of speaking both of the interiority and the performative aspects of ritual. Jonathan Smith's article casts a critical gaze on the notion of ritual as repetition and as presentation of an attainable ideal. Smith wants to focus rather on the disjuncture between ritual life and everyday life as what is being illustrated by ritual activity.

I want to thank chronologically those people who have listened to this course as it has developed and provided timely help: Lisa and Steven Wright, Jacob Meskin, Peter Just, and David Edwards.

SELECT BIBLIOGRAPHY

Agnon, S. Y., *Days of Awe* (New York: Schocken, 1948)

Al-e Ahmad, Jalal, *Lost in the Crowd*, trans. John Green
(Washington: Three Continents Press, 1985)

Baal, Jan van, "Offering, Sacrifice and Gift," *Numen* 23 (December 1976):
161-78

Bataille, Georges, *Theory of Religion*, trans. Robert Hurley (New York:
Zone Books, 1989)

Beidelman, T. O., *W. Robertson Smith and the Sociological Study of
Religion* (Chicago: University of Chicago Press, 1974)

Biardieu, Madeleine, and Charles Malamoud, *Le Sacrifice dans L'Inde ancienne* (Paris: Presses Universitaires de France, 1976)

Bolle, Kees W., "A World of Sacrifice," *History of Religions* 23 (1983): 37-63

Bourdillon, M. F. C., and Meyer Fortes, eds., *Sacrifice* (New York: Academic Press, 1980)

Burkert, Walter, *Homo Necans: The Anthropology of Ancient Greek Sacrificial
and Myth*, trans. Peter Bing (Berkeley: University of California
Press, 1983)

Combs-Schilling, M. E., *Sacred Performances: Islam, Sexuality and Sacrifice* (New York: Columbia University Press, 1989)

Detienne, Marcel, *Dionysus Slain,* trans. M. and L. Muellner (Baltimore: Johns Hopkins University, 1979)

Detienne, Marcel and Jean-Pierre Vernant, *The Cuisine of Sacrifice Among the Greeks,* trans. Paula Wissig (Chicago: University of Chicago Press, 1989)

Duverger, Christian, "The Meaning of Sacrifice," in *Fragments for a History of the Human Body,* ed. Michel Feher with Ramona Naddaff and Nadia Tazi, Part III (New York: Zone Books, 1989), 366-85

Evans-Pritchard, E. E., *Nuer Religion* (Oxford: Clarendon Press, 1956)

Foley, Helene P., *Ritual Irony: Poetry and Sacrifice in Euripides* (Ithaca: Cornell University Press, 1985)

Hamerton-Kelly, Robert G., ed., *Violent Origins: Walter Burkert, Rene Girard and Jonathan Z. Smith on Ritual Killing and Cultural Formation* (Stanford: Stanford University Press, 1987)

Henninger, Joseph, "Sacrifice," in *Encylopedia of Religion,* ed. Mircea Eliade, vol. 12 (New York: Macmillan, 1987), 544-57

Heusch, Luc de, *Sacrifice in Africa: A Structuralist Approach,* trans. Linda O'Brien and Alice Morton (Bloomington: Indiana University Press, 1985)

Hubert, Henri H. and Marcel Mauss, *Sacrifice: Its Nature and Function,* trans. W. D. Walls (Chicago: University of Chicago Press, 1964)

Jay, Nancy, "Sacrifice as Remedy for Having Been Born of Woman," in *Immaculate & Powerful: The Female in Sacred Image and Social Reality,* eds. Clarissa W. Atkinson, Constance H. Buchanan and Margaret R. Miles (Boston: Beacon Press, 1985), 283-310

Kristeva, Julia, *Powers of Horror: An Essay in Abjection* (New York: Columbia University Press, 1982)

Letvin, Alice Owen, *Sacrifice in the Surrealist Novel: The Impact of Early Theories of Primitive Religion on the Depiction of Violence in Modern Fiction* (Ph.D. Thesis: Washington University, 1980)

Malamoud, Charles, "Indian Speculations about the Sex of the Sacrifice," in *Fragments for a History of the Human Body,* ed. Michel Feher with Ramona Naddaff and Nadia Tazi, Part I (New York: Zone Books, 1989), 74-103

O'Flaherty, Wendy Doniger, *Tales of Sex and Violence: Folklore, Sacrifice, and Danger in the Jaiminiya Brahmana* (Chicago: University of Chicago Press, 1985)

Parry, Jonathan, "Sacrificial Death and the Necrophagous Ascetic," *Death and the Regeneration of Life*, ed. M. Bloch and J. Parry (Cambridge: Cambridge University Press, 1982)

_____, "The End of the Body," in *Fragments for a History of the Human Body*, ed. Michel Feher with Ramona Naddaff and Nadia Tazi, Part II (New York: Zone Books, 1989), 490-517

Rudhardt, Jean and Olivier Reverdin, eds., *Le sacrifice dans l'antiquite*, (Entretiens sur l'antiquite classique XXVII) (Geneva: Fondation Hardt, 1981)

Segal, Charles, *Dionysiac Poetics and Euripides Bacchae* (Princeton: Princeton University Press, 1982)

Smith, Brian K., *Reflections on Resemblance, Ritual, and Religion* (New York: Oxford University Press, 1989)

Smith, Jonathan Z., "The Bare Facts of Ritual," *History of Religions* 20 (1980): 112-27

Smith, W. Robertson, *The Religion of the Semites: The Fundamental Institutions* (New York: Shocken Books, 1972)

Turner, Victor, "Sacrifice as Quintessential Process Prophylaxis or Abandonment?" *History of Religions* 16:2 (1976): 189-215

Valeri, Valerio, *Kingship and Sacrifice: Ritual and Society in Ancient Hawaii*, trans. Paula Wissing (Chicago: University of Chicago Press, 1985)

Vaux, Roland de, *Studies in Old Testament Sacrifice* (Cardiff: University of Wales Press, 1964)

Zito, Angela Rose, "Re-presenting Sacrifice: Cosmology and the Editing of Texts," *Ch'ing-shih wen- t'i* V:2 (December 1984): 47-78

❧IX❧

Mysticism: A Popular and Problematic Thematic Course

FREDERICK J. STRENG

Many religious studies departments offer a course in (comparative) mysticism. Students flock to such courses. Yet, even a casual conversation with religious studies teachers indicates that one cannot be sure just what content, structure, and purpose one will find in a course called "mysticism." These facts indicate something of the lure, complexity and confusion in the use of this term as a theme for exploring an important dimension of religion.

What is mysticism? Is it a state of consciousness, a discipline, an art, or a quality of living? Is it all the above? Perhaps "mysticism" does not refer to a single thing, but is a general "umbrella" or "family" concept which covers distinct, but related, experiences and activities. Is the wide scope of content and activity included in the theme "mysticism" simply an extreme form of the suggestive and evocative character of any significant thematic category, which seeks to deepen and stretch our comprehension of life that is given focus by that theme? Is there any organizing principle, or set of disciplinary assumptions, that illumine the "reality" of all mystics' experiences, attitudes, and life styles? Are some procedures better than others for confronting the "otherness," the ineffable character in the mystical experience, as well as the "otherness" of strange cultural concepts and imagery through which the ineffable character is expressed? Similarly, can mystical procedures evoke an awareness of the universal center—the ground of all possibilities, the core of all actuality—that provides an essential relatedness, continuity, or even identity,

127

between all apparent difference of cultural forms? These are some of the basic questions raised in using "mysticism" as a thematic approach to the study of religious life.

Mysticism has been regarded by some scholars and some religious adepts as the essential religious experience. Whether one agrees with this claim or not, there are important expressions in the major world religions (as well as outside them) that have been termed "mystical." These have included certain states of consciousness ranging from total quietness and serenity to impassioned, ecstatic, and awesome experiences. These states, according to advocates, have provided the deepest insights into the nature of existence and, likewise, enabled trans-noetic and trans-emotional awareness. Such activities as contemplative prayer, meditation, fasting, and initiation rites are seen as both conditions for, and expressions of, a transformation of thought, will, and emotions that is articulated as "union with the One," "Divine Love piercing one's heart," and "manifesting the Suchness of things."

How can we structure a *study* of mysticism in a humanities curriculum so that we do justice to its perceived ineffable character, its power to transform lives and its concreteness within particular historical, social, and psychological conditions? Do we look at specific mystical writings by religious saints and practices of spiritual teachers from different religious traditions in an attempt to understand mysticism in a specific historical context and within the specific imagery which they use? Do we try to develop, through imagination and abstraction, a cross-cultural religious vocabulary to form generic terms within which we can compare and interrelate specific expressions? Do we adopt basically behavioristic or humanistic psychological terms to account for (either life-enhancing or pathological) extraordinary experiences within personality development and social behavior? Do we develop a theory of religious consciousness which is part of a general theory of consciousness in order to understand the character of validity claimed by some or all mystics? Do we engage in at least preliminary mystical practices themselves to develop an empathy for—if not actually achieve—a state of awareness characterized by equinimity, loss of ego-images, and insight?

I. *Assumptions of this course*: The goals of the course "Mysticism: East and West," outlined below, are (1) to understand the religious intention(s) of mystical exponents from several different religious traditions and cultures, (2) to explore the nature, or general characteristics, of that family of religious expressions called "mysticism," and (3) to develop personal, emotional, and aesthetic sensitivities that can be combined with reflective skills for assessing the value of the mystics' claims. To achieve these goals the course is structured around reading and discussion of mystical thought and practice as presented in five books by contemporary authors. Four of the books each present the understanding and advocacy of mystical practice from several major religious traditions: Buddhism, Christianity, Hinduism, and Islam. The fifth book is a sympathetic psychologically oriented discussion of mystical experience which provides a basis for reflection about the relation of the differences and similarities found in the advocates' claims from different religious traditions.

While I have used classical mystical texts (in English translation) in other years, the course described below uses contemporary advocates and sympathetic interpreters of each of the four religious traditions. Since these are written for the contemporary English-speaking market, they are generally easier for students to comprehend than the classical texts. However, their use also requires more explantion of the tradition's matrix—its assumptions and conceptual formulations—during class discussion than does the use of classical texts. These books sometimes refer to the historical background of mystical ideas and practices, but they do not give much information about particular historical traditions. Their main purpose is to evoke a sense of depth awareness, the joy of insight and freedom, and give preliminary information on the procedures for expanding conventional consciousness. Perhaps the most important psychological benefit for the students in using contemporary spokespersons is that the mystical claims and practices are perceived as a live option for people today.

The procedure for learning was to read and discuss in some detail the contents of each book in series in about two-and-a-half weeks per book. After the books by spokespersons from Buddhism and Christianity were read, each student wrote a paper of 2,000-2,500 words comparing some important aspect of mystical awareness found in each of the two traditions. The papers focused on such topics as spiritual and meditation practices, the character of the mystical experience(s), and assumptions and formulations about the nature of ultimate reality, the cosmos and the human condition. Selected student papers, or aspects of papers centering on a common issue, were read in class as the basis for a summary discussion of material covered during that five-week period. Similarly, during subsequent weeks, the books by Hindu and Muslim interpreters were read, and their contents discussed in class prior to the writing of a paper comparing aspects of mystical awareness from each of the traditions studied.

The final three weeks concentrated on the question of the relation of mystical expressions in distinct religious traditions to some possible overarching mystical experience, quality of living, or psychological structure; the issues were focused by a reading and discussion of Ken Wilber's *No Boundary*. This book was selected because it presents, through a fairly easy-reading style, a position different from the dominant orientation structured into the course. Wilber presents mystical experience as a single transcendent consciousness with "no-boundary"; in the course we viewed mystical experience as an umbrella term for a family of different states of consciousness that have significant overlapping characteristics together with different experienced structures (and therefore different understandings) of "no-boundary."

The final paper could take one of three forms. It could be an analytical paper on some general concept, practice, image, or institution within the general concept of "mysticism" which uses information from at least the four traditions considered in the course to document similarities and contrasts within the common element chosen. Secondly, it could be a theoretical paper that describes the nature of mystical experience and practice as documented by an appeal to the data found in the volumes from each of the traditions taken in the course. (Very few students have chosen this option!) A third option is a personal statement on the significance of mystical experience and practice for oneself which is based on two kinds of resources. The first is the personal experience of the student who has participated in regular meditation or contemplation for at least this semester (usually in connection with a Zen center, Yoga institute, or some practicing community). The second is the assigned readings of the mystical traditions considered in the course.

This course is listed as an upper division undergraduate course. While there are no prerequisite courses for taking "Mysticism: East and West," this course presumes a willingness by each student to read carefully the assignments before class and come prepared to discuss the material. In order to integrate the material in the readings with the students' personal sensitivities and with general notions of mysticism, I asked them to keep in mind various questions—questions which often served to structure class discussions. These include the following: What are the basic metaphors used by the authors to communicate the ineffable mystery which they affirm? What are the most significant procedures used by the spiritual masters or advocates for becoming aware of the nature of life at its most profound level? What are the basic notions of the self, the religious problematic of the human condition, and the nature of ultimate reality as portrayed by the authors? Which spiritual qualities, such as purity, love, or illumination, are emphasized? How is the nature of true knowledge, insight, or understanding described? What conditions, according to the advocates, aid the transformation of desire, motivation, and will?

The texts for the course (in their order of use) are:

Shunryu Suzuki, *Zen Mind, Beginner's Mind* (New York: Weatherhill, 1970), abbreviated below as ZMBM;

Morton T. Kelsey, *The Other Side of Silence: A Guide to Christian Meditation* (Paramus, NJ: Paulist Press, 1976), abbr. as OSS;

Martin Lings, *What is Sufism?* (Berkeley, University of California Press, 1977), abbr. as WS;

Georg Feuerstein, *The Essence of Yoga* (New York: Grove Press, 1974), abbr. as EY; and

Ken Wilber, *No Boundary: Eastern and Western Approaches to Personal Growth* (Los Angeles: Center Publications, 1979), abbr. as NB.

The course outlined below is designed as a one-semester course, with classes meeting three hours per week. Films that were shown in class are also noted.

II. *Course outline:*

1st week:	Introduction to the study of mysticism in a college curriculum
2nd week:	ZMBM Prologue and Part 1, Right Practice ZMBM Part 2, Right Attitude Film: "Mood of Zen"
3rd week:	ZMBM Part 3, Right Understanding
4th week:	OSS pp. 1-41 Encountering God OSS pp. 42-79 The Spiritual World Film: "Bernini—The Esctasy of St. Teresa"
5th week:	OSS pp. 83-122 Preparation for the Inward Journey OSS pp. 125-77 Uses of Imagination
6th week:	OSS pp. 179-236 Developing Imagination 1st PAPER DUE: discussion of student papers
7th week:	WS "The Originality of Sufism," The Universality of Sufism," "The Book," "The Messenger" Film: "The Sufi Way"
8th week:	WS "The Heart," "The Doctrine," "The Method," "The Exclusiveness of Sufism"
9th week:	WS "Sufism throughout the Centuries" EY pp. 17-37 from Part I: Yoga as Search for Oneness Film: "Awareness"

10th week:	EY pp. 38-95 from Part I, including chapters on "The Wheel of Life and Death," "The Crisis of Inner Awakening," and "Ethical Integration"
11th week:	EY pp. 96-144 from Part I, including chapters on "One-pointed Consciousness," "Degrees of Absorption" and "The Ultimate Transcendence"
12th week:	2nd PAPER DUE: discussion of student papers NB Chs. 1 & 2 Who Am I?
13th week:	Chs. 3-6 Questions: Are the boundaries of selfhood real? Are there levels of selfhood? Film: "Time Is"
14th week:	NB Chs. 7-10 Questions: How does one deepen self- discovery? Can one transcend ego-identity?
15th week:	Summary, and discussion of students' reflections for the final paper

III. *Reflection on classroom experience*: This course is one of several attempts I have made over the last twenty-five years to teach a course in (comparative) mysticism. As indicated in the opening remarks, there are various approaches to the subject—a theme which can include a wide variety of data which are of deep interest to many people, but which perhaps reflects as much (or more) the scholar's implicit definition or the general concept of "mysticism" as the concrete historical expressions of religious experience. A legitimate concern is whether or not "mysticism" as a general concept is simply a product of the reflective (Western) study of comparative religion. I believe that as presented in many scholarly interpretations, it is, indeed, a "construct" derived from the study in comparative religion. As such, however, it may still provide a useful interpretive instrument for understanding important religious experiences. While as a construct, "mysticism" is in danger of being simply an abstract idea about religious life unconnected to the historical and cultural context in which it emerges, a general notion of mystical experience and practice can pose interesting questions about the existential assumptions, the social and psychological processes, and evaluative dispositions that people use to attain and express a profound awareness of life. In order to address the question of the possible usefulness of a course on mysticism I will first describe my experience in teaching the course outlined above and then compare this approach to other courses on mysticism.

(1) Class experience: I have taught the course outlined above at Southern Methodist University (Dallas) as an advanced undergraduate course, composed of about fifteen students. The classroom setting is a seminar

room, with most students sitting around a large table; it is conducive to discussion. The students are usually equally divided between men and women, most coming from white middle class families. About one third are religious studies majors, the others majoring in other departments in the humanities and social sciences, or registered though other schools in the university. This is an elective—though it is one course that fulfills a distributional requirement for religion majors—without prerequisites. Only about half of the students have had at least one other course in the department of religious studies. Most are nominally members of one or another Christian denomination, and most have little information of religions other than Christianity. At the same time, two or three have practiced meditation in Zen, Yoga, or Sufi communities. Self-introductions by each member of the class at our first meeting indicate that most students identify mysticism with extraordinary or transcendent experience, and that they are motivated by curiosity about it.

The use of materials by advocates and sympathetic interpreters of particular spiritual disciplines involves the students immediately in the religious assumptions about the nature of existence and the possibilities of consciousness. S. Suzuki's essays in *Zen Mind, Beginner's Mind*, for example, engage the students directly by confronting their attitudes about themselves, their self images and personal experiences. His claims challenge them to think about their feelings and perceptions in a new context. In class discussions we focus on specific passages—chosen by the students or the instructor—which need clarification, or which are particularly provocative, in order to call attention to the character of the shifts in consciousness advocated. At times their questions are the occasion for a brief lecture that draws on philosophical explanations, stories, and descriptions of practice from other parts of the Buddhist tradition. The material derived from the Buddhist tradition is meant to further explain the concepts, maps of consciousness, attitudes, and techniques that have structured the Zen approach to spontaneous living. The goal of this segment of the course, however, is to evoke in the students a sense of the possibility of liberation from self-imposed physico-psycho-social-moral—i.e., karmic—bondage. For each class I have a list of issues found in the assigned reading; sometimes—especially during the first discussions of each book—I organize the discussion around them; other times I call on different students to state what they think are the key issues in the reading.

As we move through the second text, M. Kelsey's guide to Christian meditation, the students are asked not only to grasp the author's understanding of the basic concepts, imagery, and theological assumptions in relation to Christian spiritual practice, but a (small) part of class time is devoted to a preliminary comparison of Christian and Buddhist answers to the questions emerging from the general notions of mysticism (as given above in the section on the assumptions of the course). Again, the primary concern is for students to engage the religious intention of the spiritual discipline, in this case the practice of prayer and meditation as a proper response to God that leads to loving others. Reference to other Christian theological notions, sacraments, faith or Biblical interpretations are discussed in class only for the purpose of understanding the historical, cultural and institutional context out of which Kelsey's assertions arise. Throughout the course students are admonished to imagine empathetically what it would be like to see the world from the perspective represented by the reading. This requires learning a particular vocabulary, imaginatively structuring their perception of the world in those terms, and sensing the emotional weight and aesthetic value of the terms that give the world meaning, "purify one's heart," or release one from conventional habits of thinking.

The readings and discussions on Yoga and Sufism from the seventh through the eleventh weeks of the course likewise focus on understanding the religious intention found in these disciplines. Attention is given to the authors' formulation, imagery, and analysis of mystical experience and practice found in Hinduism and Islam. It is important to note that these authors are sympathetic interpreters of these particular spiritual practices, so they stand in a little different relation to the traditions that they explore than do the first two authors. Also by the time we are dealing with the third and fourth mystical expression, students are making comparisons between aspects of the thought, experiences and practices from the different traditions that are often surprising, and sometimes insightful. They see, for example, that ritual and trust in a spiritual authority are significant, if not ultimate, elements in spiritual discipline; they recognize that theological and ontological concepts can provide a basic orientation to self-understanding, but that concepts and images function in various ways in different mystical traditions, as well as in different levels of mystical paths.

By the time students have demonstrated a basic grasp of some important aspects of mysticism in four religious traditions and are reading a text that seeks to provide a synthesis of all the approaches, they have participated in discussions on, and written analyses of, the differences and similarities of different mystical phenomena. The final assigned reading raises the possibility that the variations one finds in the concrete expressions of spiritual disciplines are secondary concerns. Much more important, according to the author of *No Boundary*, is the inner core experience of the highest level of consciousness, which is perceived as a different order of awareness than that used in historical-social description or reflective analysis. In a consideration of this possibility, students are asked to evaluate the evidence from their reading, and their own life experiences. The final papers indicate (without surprise) that some are persuaded, some are not. At least they have all been confronted with the claims from different religious traditions that there are modes of awareness through which people can respond to, or actualize in themselves, the ultimate resource for well-being; and they have had to consider the relation of their own learning processes to the possibility of a radically different order of knowledge.

Some issues that arise from this approach to a course on mysticism are:

(a) Does the lack of considerable historical and cultural information about the traditions in which mysticism emerges prevent a grasp of the religious intention by the students? Indeed, an understanding of the historical, linguistic, and cultural context is important for interpreting the meaning of the statements that the students are asked to read. Those few students who have had a general introduction to various religious traditions, to cultural histories, or to a typological introduction to religious life in the East and West have an advantage, especially at the beginning of the study of each book. The more they know of the histories and cultures, the better. At the same time, those students who are engaged with the material, and undaunted by early confusion, ask questions about the assigned readings. Most students are able to specify basic differences and similarities in different mystical expressions on the basis of their reading and class discussion.

(b) Does the focus on differences in mystical apprehension, as it arises out of different religious traditions, prevent a grasp of the transcendent character of mystical experiences? I have tried to deal with this question head on by having the students read and discuss a book at the end of the semester that emphasizes mystical awareness as a trans-historical and trans-rational mode of awareness. This forces students to come to grips with this issue, and is resolved by each student according to his or her reflection and experience.

(c) Is a brief examination of mystical experiences and practices from four different traditions too much for a single semester? I have also taught courses in comparative mysticism using materials from two traditions and from three traditions in one semester (see below), and conclude that different sorts of learning take place by comparing material from two, three or four traditions. A brief exposure to, and analysis of, four traditions seemed to work well to achieve the goals set for this course.

(d) Does the emphasis on the religious intention of mystics distort an understanding of mystical phenomena in that it does not give equal time for considering physiological, psychological, and sociological explanations for the phenomena? It is clear that this course does not provide a full picture of all the conditions which contribute to the rise of mystical experiences. This situation is recognized during the first day of class; at the same time it provides the occasion to talk about the nature of the investigative questions, foci and procedures for analysis in religious studies as a distinct approach to understanding human life within a university.

(2) A comparison with other courses using the theme of mysticism: One option is to compare the mystical expressions from two traditions, one Eastern, the other Western. I have used this approach by comparing Christian and Buddhist mystical material. It allows time for interpreting mystical expressions within the context of other religious practices (for example, ritual and ethical concerns) within each tradition, and for taking into account the historical development of different mystical disciplines and experiences within a single tradition before making comparisons between representatives from each tradition. In this kind of course the focus is, first, on the relation of different mystics and mystical expressions to the beliefs, social authority, monastic communities, daily activities of both monastics and laity, and symbolic expressions found within a single tradition. It allows students to examine the lives of mystics and their relation—as spiritual models, sources of power, and teachers, for example—to the life of a religious and cultural community. Then similarities, as well as contrasts, between practices, ideas, imagery and spiritual qualities sought in each tradition can be noted. This approach places "mysticism" within concrete historical moments, and focuses on the cultural and biographical contexts for which mystical awareness is relevant. Less time is spent on specifying general characteristics of mysticism in this approach than in the one outlined in the first two sections above.

Another option is to study in detail "classic" religious texts which present basic spiritual practices and religious concepts in relation to mystical awareness, such as perfect insight, union with God, or identity with the source of all. For example, I have taught a one-semester seminar in which we examined translations of texts found in the Buddhist, Christian, and Hindu traditions: the Mahayana Buddhist text *Perfection of Wisdom in Eight-thousand Lines*, St. John of the Cross' *Ascent of Mount Carmel*, and selections from two writings of the Hindu seer Shankara, *A Thousand Teachings*, and his *Commentary on the Brahmasutra*. As we began the study of each text, I gave an introduction to the historical and cultural context in which these writings were found, including a summary statement of the key philosophical or theological notions that had been prominent in the tradition up to the point when these writings appeared.

The seminar sessions in this option focused primarily on the content of these texts. Except for the classes in which I gave an historical introduction, one of the students presented a prepared short (3-5 page) statement of the central religious concerns found in the assigned reading for that day. Then we discussed the meaning of the most important sections of that reading, highlighting the imagery, the religious notions, the relation of epistemological assumptions to the spiritual practice proposed, and the characteristic attitudes and inner qualities that were advocated in the text. In class discussion a considerable amount of time was also devoted to the clarification between diverse cosmological, psychological, and ontological notions, the qualities of experience described, and techniques for achieving their specified spiritual goals. As students became familiar with the second text, we noted points of comparison with aspects of the spiritual path found in the first text. Similarly, aspects of mystical awareness found in the third text were compared to parallel aspects found in the first two texts. The term paper required a comparison of some general element of mystical experience, presuppositions, imagery or practice found in the writings that were read and discussed in class.

Both of these latter options focused on more limited material than that found in the approach outlined for "Mysticism: East and West." The two-tradition option concentrated on particular mystical experience and practice as emerging from, and functioning as part of a historical tradition. The three-tradition course emphasized an analysis of the mystical assumptions, procedures and purposes enshrined in classical texts that are still authoritative for a segment of the tradition in which they are found. In both of these approaches the educational task was to explore the meaning of mystical awareness as other people, in different times and places, have witnessed to it. While most students found such exploration significant, they had to take a step in a different direction to ask what value this kind of human experience had for them. This existential question is more at the heart of the educational task of the course outlined in the first two sections. The contemporary statements drawn from four traditions sought to evoke a response in the readers, and engage them directly in considering new attitudes and expanded consciousness. Such a course pays the price of foregoing an encounter with religious classics, and the pleasure of enjoying the richness of only two traditions; perhaps it is not too high a price if the trade-off is an existential engagement with contemporary interpreters who contribute to a reflection on mystical consciousness as a human possibility today.

Spiritual Practices in Historical Perspective

CAROL ZALESKI

We are all familiar with students who become drawn to the comparative study of religion as an extension of their own search for spiritual direction. This search can express itself in many different forms, one of which I see embodied in the students who tell me that they became interested in studying religion after taking classes in meditation or yoga. For some, the initial motivation was a desire to understand parents who had been caught up in the spiritual movements of the 60s and 70s; no doubt we will begin to see more of such students as we enter the 90s.

One of the remarkable features of the "meditation boom" (as journalists like to call it) is its links to the academic study of religion. As a cultural event, the quest for spiritual instruction is located today not only in ashrams and zendos but also, and for many followers primarily, in bookstores. Browsing in the bookstores of cosmopolitan urban centers or college towns, contemporary seekers encounter a jumble of religious scriptures and classics as well as popular, hybrid concoctions; they pick up a Qur'an, a copy of *Zen Mind, Beginner's Mind*, a self-help book sprinkled with Vedanta aphorisms, *The Zohar*, Ouspensky, *The Dead Sea Scrolls*, a modern interpretation of *The Cloud of Unknowing*; they read accounts of hidden schools of self-knowledge and spiritual transformation, intimate encounters between masters and disciples, and exalted meditative attainments by yogins and monks. And then they take our courses; they take them because they recognize that they need help to become discriminating readers of the religious texts that have become accessible to such an unprecedented degree. Those of us who are scholars and translators of this material are in some ways responsible for the exciting jumble in the religion sections of our bookstores; and since we have placed these sacred texts in their hands, they are perhaps justified in asking us for a user's manual.

"Spiritual Practices in Historical Perspective" was designed in part to reach such students—not to supply a user's manual, but with the modest aim of drawing them into a more historically informed way of interpreting the spiritual choices available to them. The course is described in the catalogue as "a critical examination of the proliferation of spiritual techniques in contemporary Western society, and an historical introduction to the sources from which these practices originate."

In its earliest, and in some ways most successful form, I gave this course as a freshman seminar (part of a program of small ungraded colloquia for freshmen). Fifteen students were admitted to the seminar; fifteen well-scrubbed, enthusiastic young men and women in their first semester of college, almost falling over themselves in their eagerness to learn about meditation and to understand the contemporary spiritual scene. Because few of the participants had any background in the study of religion, the seminar functioned also as a thematic introduction to world religions. Our first "field trip" was a group walking tour of the bookstores of Harvard Square.

Offering the course at an upper level introduced new problems, as I became inundated with applicants from the Divinity School as well as the college. Some qualified applicants to the course were not admitted because I felt that their long years of experience in a particular spiritual practice might create an imbalance in a class which had been designed primarily for undergraduates without extensive background; but some "overqualified" students were admitted nonetheless if they seemed willing to enter into the spirit of the course.

There were a few students whose unrealistic expectations about the course (one applicant wrote, "excitement tingles through both my body and mind at the possibility of the various fieldtrips"), or omnivorous appetite for spiritual practices, made me wary. If their applications described galloping along the circuit from ashram to analysis and from temple to mudbath, I tended to turn them away. But I also aimed for diversity, and found it to a degree that surpassed my expectations: a freshman of Jewish background greatly influenced by his Buddhist sociologist father; a young Ismaili Muslim woman; a Divinity School student who worked in a stress reduction clinic; a sophomore whose only exposure to the subject was a cautionary course in high school about the "cults"; a young Catholic woman contemplating joining Opus Dei; an architecture student from Germany interested in Yogananda; a sophomore follower of Bahai, a Polish Catholic hospital chaplain; an Orthodox Jew; and so on.

The following outline provides a map of the course as taught in the fall term 1988-89 at Harvard; I will comment further below on its advantages and pitfalls as an example of comparative and thematic teaching.

SPIRITUAL PRACTICES IN HISTORICAL PERSPECTIVE

I. Course Description (from the syllabus):

In recent decades, an extraordinary number and variety of spiritual disciplines have become influential in our society. The purpose of this course will be to gain historical perspective on the forms of spiritual practice that are currently attracting disciples, and to explore the reasons for this fascination with methodical spiritual technique.

The course will focus on Buddhist meditation, yoga in the Hindu tradition, and contemplative prayer in the Christian tradition, as well as clinical studies of meditation and biofeedback. We will study both the contemporary practice and the historical roots of each tradition, reading classic texts like the Maha-Satipatthana-Sutta, contemporary spiritual "best-sellers," and interpretive works by historians of religion, psychologists, and social scientists who have investigated the cultural significance of the quest for methodical spiritual discipline. In order to acquire some practical understanding of our subject matter, we will also pay visits to local centers and meet with practitioners and teachers of the disciplines we study.

Each tradition will be considered from several angles, including: social setting, teaching methods, the role of the body, the training of attention, and the relationship between personal effort and surrender to a higher power.

Formal requirements for the course include participation in classes and field trips, individual consultations with the instructor, a final research paper, and a report to the class on outside reading, to be accompanied by a 3-5 page paper which is distributed to everyone in advance. These reports provide background on topics related to but not fully covered in our common reading; and sharing them with the class helps to foster an atmosphere of scholarly collaboration.

II. Schedule

Week 1: Orientation

At the first meeting, I characterize the course as part of a larger enterprise of becoming alert to popular religious ideals and longings as they are manifested both within and outside the mainstream religious institutions of our society. It is a matter of fine-tuning our cultural antennae. At the same time, the desire to understand the contemporary religious situation motivates us to begin a serious historical investigation of foundational works.

This historical perspective is vital if we are to understand how contemporary spiritual practices are shaped by the prevailing ethos.

My introductory comments set boundaries on the course: "Spiritual Practices" is not intended as a catchall for the exploration of spirituality or mysticism in general, altered states of consciousness, new religious movements, or New Age thought. Part of the group's task is to clarify our assumptions about what "spiritual practice" or "spiritual discipline" means; this is to be accomplished by continually revising our definitions, and by grappling with the historically situated character of terms like prayer, *meditatio, contemplatio,* yoga, *dhyāna, smṛti,* and *samādhi.*

Readings for the first week include Herbert Benson's *The Relaxation Response* (a popular bestseller which looks at meditation from the perspective of behavioral medicine, and proposes a simplified form of TM as a stress reduction technique) and Donald Meyer's provocative essay on "The Discovery of the 'Nervous American'" in *The Positive Thinkers).*[1] I pair these readings in order to propose a hypothesis which the course will test: that contemporary appropriation of traditional forms of spiritual practice has direct antecedents in the therapeutically oriented spiritual philosophies (such as New Thought) which attracted a large popular following in nineteenth-century North America.

A visual collage of meditative practices is provided by "Meditation: The Inward Journey," a film which I would recommend for its fidelity to popular images of meditation rather than as a serious entry into the his-

---

[1] Herbert Benson and Miriam Z. Klipper, *The Relaxation Response* (Avon, 1976). Donald Meyer, *The Positive Thinkers: Popular Religious Psychology from Mary Baker Eddy to Norman Vincent Peale and Ronald Reagan* (rev. ed., Middletown, Conn.: Wesleyan University Press, 1988), chap. 1; this is an expanded and updated version of a book first published in 1965, tracing the influence of New Thought and other manifestations of "healthy-minded" religion on North American culture.

torical study of spiritual disciplines.[2] We view this film again at the end of the course in order to determine whether we have acquired a more nuanced understanding of these images and of the connotations of "meditation" in contemporary thought.

In the first week, I hand out the following list of questions to provide further orientation:

Questions for Consideration

What are people looking for when they seek instruction in meditation or prayer? Is there any connection between worshipping and "workshopping"?

Are there any characteristically American forms of spiritual practice? What happens when traditional meditative or yogic techniques are transplanted in contemporary North American soil?

Where do contemporary Jews and Christians turn when they wish to find direction in methods of prayer, meditation, or contemplation? To what extent do they draw on the classics of their own spiritual heritage? What new forms have arisen from the meeting of East and West?

What is the role of the teacher in contemporary and traditional forms of spiritual instruction?

What is the significance of the social setting in which spiritual instruction and practice take place?

How do different spiritual disciplines treat the body? What is the relationship between the training of the intellect and the training of the spirit?

What are the goals of the various traditions of spiritual discipline: therapy? repentance? devotion? self-mastery? self-knowledge?

Why do many traditions stress the importance of training the attention?

How do different traditions understand the relationship between contemplation and action? Between effort and grace?

Week 2: Meditation in the Theravāda Buddhist Tradition

We begin with Buddhism because of its special character as a missionary religious tradition based on the meditative experience of its founder, and as a tradition for which meditation remains a central ritual and soteriological symbol.

---

[2] "Meditation: The Inward Journey" is produced by the Hartley Film Foundation, Cat Rock Road, Cos Cob, Conn. 06807, and available for purchase or rent from their catalogue.

Our primary reading is Nyanaponika Thera, *The Heart of Buddhist Meditation*, a lucid treatment which provides an annotated translation of the Mahā-Satipaṭṭhāna-Sutta and an anthology of other foundational texts on right mindfulness from the Pali Canon.[3] We also read part 1 of Daniel Goleman's *The Meditative Mind*, a popular work by the psychology editor of *The New York Times*, which discusses the teaching of Buddhaghosa's *Visuddhimagga* and introduces in a simplified and accessible form the classic Buddhist distinction between *śamatha* (Pali *samatha*) and *vipaśyanā* (Pali *vipassanā*).[4] *Śamatha*, which means "calming," is associated with *samādhi* (concentration; also a general term for meditative discipline) and is described in the classic texts as unfolding in eight stages of meditative absorption (*dhyānas*). *Vipaśyanā*, which means "insight" or "discernment" is associated with *prajñā*, as the ultimate realization of the principle of right mindfulness. Although this distinction is understood in different ways by the various Theravāda and Mahāyāna schools, and can lead to classifications which are too rigid, it provides a helpful focus for further discussion of the different aims and methods of meditative practice. We can now begin to ask whether a particular practice involves focusing on a single meditation subject and screening out distractions (as in the essentially yogic technique of *ekāgratā*, "one-pointedness"), or whether it involves "bare attention" and inclusive global awareness. The encounter with Theravāda Buddhist literature on meditation also introduces a way of thinking about the relation between meditation, morality, and an intermediate category: the taking of precepts as a mode of purification preparatory to spiritual training (a topic to which we return when we read Patañjali).

A visit to the Cambridge Insight Meditation Center presents the class with a thriving North American adaptation of a form of Vipassanā meditation taught in the forest monasteries of Thailand and Burma. This is the first of our "field trips."

Other works which I have used for this week include Donald Swearer, ed., *Secrets of the Lotus: Studies in Buddhist Meditation*, half of which is devoted to Theravāda meditation; Winston King, *Theravāda Meditation: The Buddhist Transformation of Yoga*; and Amadeo Solé-Leris, *Tranquility and*

---

[3] Nyanaponika Thera, *The Heart of Buddhist Meditation* (York Beach, Maine: Samuel Weiser, 1965; first published by Rider & Co., 1962).

[4] Goleman, *The Meditative Mind* (New York: Jeremy P. Tarcher, 1988); an expanded version of *The Varieties of the Meditative Experience* (New York: E. P. Dutton, 1977).

Insight.[5] For students who have no background in the study of Buddhism, I usually recommend Walpola Rahula, *What the Buddha Taught.*[6]

Week 3: Zen

The previous week's readings and discussion on "mindfulness" techniques as a distinctively Buddhist contribution to the spiritual disciplines provide an appropriate vantage point for considering Zen.

Readings for this week range from evocative treatments like Shunryu Suzuki's, *Zen Mind, Beginner's Mind* to works of historical scholarship such as excerpts from Heinrich Dumoulin's history of Zen Buddhism (most helpful has been his essay on "The Yogic Element in Buddhism").[7] Last year I was able to include Kenneth Kraft's *Zen: Tradition and Transition*, a fine anthology of essays by contemporary scholars and practitioners.[8]

Two topics are central to this week's discussion: the characteristics of *zazen* and the structure of Zen communities in Japan and North America. Our material on Zen communities comes from three different sources: a student report on daily life in a Japanese Zen monastery (based on the charming rendition in *Unsui: A Diary of Zen Monastic Life*, along with D. T. Suzuki's *The Training of the Zen Buddhist Monk* and relevant essays in *Zen: Tradition and Transition*);[9] screening of a film which chronicles daily

---

[5] Swearer, ed., *Secrets of the Lotus* (New York: Macmillan, 1971). King, *Theravada Meditation* (University Park, Pennsylvania: Pennsylvania State University Press, 1980). Solé-Leris, *Tranquility and Insight* (Boston: Shambhala, 1986). Concise accounts of Buddhist meditation can also be found in Winston King's article in *The Encyclopedia of Religion* and Robert Gimello's "Mysticism and Meditation" in *Mysticism and Philosophical Analysis*, ed., Steven T. Katz (New York: Oxford University Press, 1978).

[6] Rahula, *What the Buddha Taught* (New York: Grove Press, 1974).

[7] Suzuki, Shunryu, *Zen Mind, Beginner's Mind: Informal Talks on Zen Meditation and Practice*, ed. Trudy Dixon (New York: Weatherhill, 1970). Suzuki Roshi was a Sōtō Zen master who came to the United States in 1958 and stayed to lead the San Francisco Zen Center. He died in 1971.

Dumoulin, Heinrich. *Zen Buddhism: A History* (New York: Macmillan, 1988), vol. 1, chap. 2.

[8] Kraft, ed., *Zen: Tradition and Transition* (New York: Grove Press, 1988). For historical background, see especially John R. McRae, "The Story of Early Ch'an," pp. 125-39, Philip Yampolsky, "The Development of Japanese Zen," pp. 140-56, and T. Griffith Foulk, "The Zen Institution in Modern Japan," pp. 157-77. The volume also includes lucid essays on *zazen, dokusan* and *kōan* training, the Zen poetic tradition, and problems of authority and change as Zen adapts to the West.

[9] Giei Satō and Eshin Nishimura, *Unsui: A Diary of Zen Monastic Life*, ed., Bardwell L. Smith (Honolulu: University of Hawaii Press, 1973). D. T. Suzuki, *The Training of*

life at a North American Zen center and records the community's response to the unexpected disclosure of their teacher's alcoholism and sexual misconduct;[10] and a visit to the Cambridge Buddhist Association, a meditation center established in consultation with D. T. Suzuki, and currently led by Maurine Stuart Roshi, a well-known Zen teacher and concert pianist from Canada.

To focus on Theravāda and Zen Buddhist practice as representative of Buddhist meditation is of course to make major and perhaps unforgivable omissions. As a small corrective, I usually recruit students to give in-class reports on the most significant areas of omission: devotional meditative practices characteristic of Pure Land Buddhism, and visualization exercises found in Vajrayāna and other esoteric Buddhist sects. This allows us to add to our repertoire at least some initial consideration of the tension between effort and grace ("self-power" versus "Other-power") and the ambiguity of images and imagination in spiritual practice.

Week 4: Yoga

Since yoga is such a multivalent term, I have approached this segment of the course in several different ways. One year, we focused entirely on Mircea Eliade's *Yoga, Immortality, and Freedom*, which led us into a wide-ranging discussion of background assumptions in Indian thought, archaic elements in yoga, the symbolism of initiatory passage through death and rebirth, and apparently paradoxical features in the evaluation of the physical cosmos.[11] Even the most optimistic New Agers in the class could not help but notice the difference between the "acosmism" of classical Hindu yoga and the appropriation of yoga in the West as a way to cultivate health, vitality, and attunement to an essentially friendly universe.

Another year, we spent most of our time comparing translations of Patañjali's *Yoga Sūtra*. In both years, there has been some effort to correlate Patañjali's summary of the eight "limbs" of yoga with Buddhist

---

the *Zen Buddhist Monk* (New York: University Books, 1959; originally published in Kyoto by the Eastern Buddhist Society, 1934). Relevant essays in *Zen: Tradition and Transition* include Morinaga Sōkō, "My Struggle to Become a Zen Monk," pp. 13-29, T. Griffith Foulk, "The Zen Institution in Modern Japan," pp. 157-77, and Kenneth Kraft, "Recent Developments in North American Zen," pp. 178-98.

10 "Zen Center: Portrait of an American Zen Community," written and produced by Anne Cushman, directed by Lou Hawthorne (1987); available in videotape from the Hartley Film Foundation.

11 Eliade, *Yoga: Immortality and Freedom* (2nd aug. ed.; Princeton, N.J.: Princeton University Press, 1969).

classifications; and considerable discussion of the significance of the body and breath in spiritual practice.

For our field trip, we visit the Nityananda Institute, where classes in *haṭhayoga* and *kuṇḍalinīyoga* and meditation are given by members of a community founded by the late Swami Rudranandra (also known as Rudi). An American follower of Bhagavan Nityananda (the saint of Ganeshpuri), Rudi was recognized as a Swami by Nityananda's disciple Swami Muktananda. Visits to the Institute have included a brief introduction to the classic yoga *āsanas*, as well as a meeting (and rather free-wheeling discussion) with Swami Chetanananda, Rudi's successor, who delivers the teachings of Kashmir Śaivism seasoned with a generous dose of midwestern American iconoclasm and humor.

Weeks 4 and 5: Prayer and Contemplation in the Christian Tradition

The first question that arises when we shift to the Christian tradition is whether we will be able to find practices and teachings on spiritual discipline that are even roughly commensurate with what we have encountered in previous weeks.

The issue is complicated by the fact that the recent revival of interest in the classics of Christian contemplative life has been influenced both by exposure to Asian spiritual traditions and by the continuing presence in our culture of what William James called "the religion of healthy-mindedness."

Two of the works we consider, *The Way of a Pilgrim* and *The Cloud of Unknowing*, have become minor bestsellers precisely because they remind people of mantra yoga or Zen, and because, taken out of context, they seem hospitable to contemporary psycho-spiritual interpretation. *The Cloud of Unknowing*, for instance, can be found in several modern translations and has been adapted by figures as diverse as Ira Progoff (who treats it as a manual for psychotherapy) and the Cistercian monk Basil Pennington (who combines the author's advice on prayer with TM and the Jesus prayer). Readings in this medieval classic can thus be a way of bringing the question of translation and cultural assumptions to the surface. In one year, I asked a student to give an in-class report comparing the different versions of *The Cloud of Unknowing*.

For an overview of Christian spiritual disciplines, we read Kallistos Ware, "Ways of Prayer and Contemplation: Eastern" and Jean Leclercq, "Ways of Prayer and Contemplation: Western."[12] Both authors discuss

---

[12] In *Christian Spirituality: Origins to the Twelfth Century*, eds., Bernard McGinn and John Meyendorff (New York: Crossroad, 1985), 395-414 and 415-26.

the divergent ways in which Christians have sought to obey the biblical injunction to "pray without ceasing" (Luke 18:1 and 1 Thess. 5:17). Ware sketches the teachings of the Desert Fathers—and their more systematic successors—on prayer and attention, spiritual combat and *theoria*; *metanoia* and remembrance of God; repetition of the Name of Jesus; and divine union. Leclercq introduces the Western monastic traditions of *oratio*, *lectio*, *meditatio* (that is, meditating on the word of God as embodied in a memorized passage of scripture), and *contemplatio*; his essay emphasizes the centrality of the Psalter in monastic prayer, and the intimate connection between the contemplative life and the life of penance and asceticism.

In order to highlight the importance of the Bible and the liturgy for Christian spiritual practice, I have brought students to a monastery for Vespers, and accompanied this excursion with an excellent pamphlet on the Divine Office, by the Anglican nun and scholar Benedicta Ward.[13]

My hope is that this introduction to liturgical and monastic prayer will help to correct some distortions which might be reinforced by our other readings. A certain imbalance is built into the course, since one of its objectives is to examine the historical roots and the contemporary cultural significance of contemplative literature that has had a "cross-over" appeal, attracting non-Christians and nontraditional Christians. Primary readings have therefore focused on spiritual practices like the Jesus prayer (first popularized in North America by *Franny and Zoey*), and on works of contemplative literature which appear less overtly Christocentric or communal in emphasis, such as the following: *Writings from the Philokalia on the Prayer of the Heart*, *The Way of a Pilgrim*, Thomas Merton, *Contemplative Prayer*, *The Cloud of Unknowing*, and Basil Pennington, *Centering Prayer*.[14] Hybrid forms like the mantra prayer of Dom John Main, Jean-Marie Déchanet's Christian yoga, and William Johnston's Christian Zen have also received attention in different years.

---

[13] Benedicta Ward, SLG, *Liturgy Today: The Divine Office and the Eucharist* (Oxford: Fairacres Publications, Sisters of the Love of God, 1971, 1978).

[14] *Writings from the Philokalia on the Prayer of the Heart*, trans. E. Kadloubovsky and G. E. H. Palmer (London: Faber and Faber, 1951); *The Way of a Pilgrim*, trans. R. M. French (New York: Harper and Row, 1974); Thomas Merton, *Contemplative Prayer* (Garden City, N.Y.: Doubleday, 1971); *The Cloud of Unknowing and Other Works*, trans. Clifton Wolters (Harmondsworth, Middlesex, England: Penguin Books, 1978); M. Basil Pennington, *Centering Prayer: Renewing and Ancient Christian Prayer Form* (Garden City, N.Y.: Doubleday, 1982).

Works of Carmelite and Ignatian spiritual direction are among the major omissions for this section; again, I call upon student reports to help fill in the gaps.

Week 6: Alcoholics Anonymous

The last time I offered this course, the segment on Alcoholics Anonymous was dropped for want of time, much to my regret. A. A. and other Twelve Step programs constitute one of the most potent forces for spiritual transformation in our society, exhibiting the characteristically therapeutic orientation of North American spiritualities. Now that it has become fashionable in New Age circles to describe every personal or social ill as an "addiction," the Twelve Step programs have become even more popular, despite the fact that they run counter to the endemic optimism of the New Age by calling for an experience of genuine and sometimes ego-shattering conversion.

Topics treated in our week on A. A. have included: differences and similarities between "sin" and "addiction"; the relation between "self-power" and "other-power," or effort and grace, in Twelve Step programs; and the question of whether or not A. A. constitutes a methodical spiritual discipline. In place of a field trip, I usually invite a guest speaker; in the past, some students on their own initiative have attended open meetings. Readings for this week are drawn from *Alcoholics Anonymous* (the "Big Book"), *Alcoholics Anonymous Comes of Age, Twelve Steps and Twelve Traditions, Not-God: A History of A. A.* and various A. A. pamphlets.[15] Alcoholics Anonymous is a popular subject for student reports; there have been reports on biographies of Bill W., on William James's discussion of alcoholism and conversion, on women in A. A., and on the recent critique of A. A. by Herbert Fingarette.[16]

Week 7: Biofeedback and Clinical Studies of Meditation

At the end of the course, we come back full circle to Herbert Benson and others who have attempted to adapt meditation to a clinical setting. Our reading is drawn from Patricia Carrington, *Freedom in Meditation*, which summarizes the major clinical studies of meditation, and three

[15] Alcoholics Anonymous books and pamphlets can be ordered for free or at nominal cost from the central offices located in major cities throughout the U.S. and abroad, or from Alcoholics Anonymous World Services, Box 459, Grand Central Station, New York, NY 10163.

[16] Fingarette, *Heavy Drinking: The Myth of Alcoholism as a Disease* (Berkeley: University of California Press, 1988).

journal articles.[17] Student response to these readings has varied; on the one hand, the image of scientists in white coats wiring up yogins in saffron robes strikes most of them as amusing and slightly preposterous, if not downright offensive. And they have learned (or so I hope) to resist the idea that one can simply strip away cultural and religious trappings in order to isolate and test the phenomena of meditation.

On the other hand, students tend to be sympathetic to the therapeutic aims of the stress-reduction techniques, open to being evangelized by the "gospel of relaxation," and intrigued by the new world of discourse that opens up when traditional religious language gives way to the terminology of modern behavioral psychology: "deautomatization," "primary process thinking," "state-dependent learning," and so on. A visit to the health center for a demonstration of biofeedback completes this unit; participants are invariably charmed by the possibility of a more playful, albeit technological, approach to the regulation of inner states.

The course concludes with final student reports, and with what one might almost call testimonials by the participants as to the ways in which the course affected them or changed their outlook on spiritual practices. There is no question that a course like this engages students personally; and the field trips and in-class reports help to create a sense of community in which students feel comfortable expressing their concerns. In order to maintain the academic coherence of the endeavor, I always stress from the beginning that the course will not provide direct spiritual instruction of any kind; to play the guru in this kind of setting would be a distasteful as well as irresponsible undertaking.

III. Relevance to the question of "comparative religion"

One of my motives for creating a course on "Spiritual Practices" was that I share my students' fascination with, and sometimes inchoate longing for, methods of spiritual instruction in which the capacity for a deeper quality of attention is cultivated. Among our other concerns, the course therefore devotes considerable time to discovering what each tradition is saying about the nature of attention.

[17] Carrington, *Freedom in Meditation* (2nd. ed.; Kendall Park, N.J.: Pace Educational Systems, 1984); Ilan Kutz, Joan Z. Borysenko, and Herbert Benson, "Meditation and Psychotherapy," *The American Journal of Psychiatry* 142:1 (January 1985): 1-8; Roger Walsh, "The Consciousness Disciplines and the Behavioral Sciences: Questions of Comparison and Assessment," *The American Journal of Psychiatry* 137:6 (June 1980): 663-73; Jon Kabat-Zinn, "An Outpatient Program in Behavioral Medicine for Chronic Pain Patients Based on the Practice of Mindfulness Meditation," *General Hospital Psychiatry* 4 (1982): 33-47.

Although the literature of spiritual direction abounds with observations about attention, watchfulness, receptive awareness, and mindfulness, this dimension of religious life tends to be neglected by scholars of religion. One reason for this neglect may be that the phenomena of attention are difficult to place in relation to more familiar religious categories like cognition, affectivity, and will. Having inherited a preoccupation with analysing the religious affections and evaluating the cognitive status of religious experience, we are predisposed not to notice when the religious people we study express interest in the human capacity for attention.

Mystical experience, on the other hand, is commonly considered to have, in William James's terms, a "noetic quality." A course on mysticism, then, is also an exploration of ultimate questions of religious truth and meaning. Inevitably it will attract students who consider the mystical testimony of the world's religious traditions to be a universal thesaurus of perennial truth.

Although the "Spiritual Practices" course has much in common with courses on mysticism, its scope tends to be restricted to what might be called the "entry level" of mystical training rather than its consummation. This means that even though questions of meaning and truth arise, we have fewer occasions to engage in the exhilirating—and sometimes stupefying—endeavour to discuss the ineffable or to resolve the debate over perennialism.

The plural form, "Spiritual Practices," helps students appreciate the idea that our subject matter is a "family of religious expressions" (as Frederick Streng says of mysticism in the essay that precedes this). "Spiritual practices" is a way of speaking about a variety of things people do, for a variety of reasons, rather than a name for a single generic category of experience. "Spiritual discipline," like "mysticism," has a more generic sound to it, but can also be treated as a collective name, with connotations that vary according to cultural context. The value for comparative study of a term like "spiritual discipline" does not stand or fall on our ability to develop a fixed, univocal definition that will always be valid cross-culturally. The inherent ambiguities in our terminology give the course an open-ended and unfinished character which I find at once limiting and intellectually liberating.

My motives for teaching "Spiritual Practices" do not entirely coincide with my students' motives for taking it. Part of what fascinates me about this subject is that the quest for spiritual disciplines in our society mirrors and runs parallel to the recent history of that spiritual quest (or quest for understanding) which we call comparative study of religion. Teaching this course has increased my awareness of the ways in which the comparative study of religion reflects, and influences, contemporary religious consciousness.

To ask whether we can use a term like "spiritual discipline" generically, or whether it is legitimate to say that *dhyāna* means "meditation," is analogous—though not identical—to asking whether a monastic tradition from India or East Asia can be translated to North America without serious distortion. In either case there is the concern—both scholarly and existential—to be true to a tradition and yet communicate successfully under changed conditions. Earlier in this volume, John Carman and Frederick Streng suggested that comparative study is an enterprise of cultural translation in precisely this wider sense: as scholars and teachers of comparative religion we often find ourself applying a term or concept derived from one tradition to an altogether different situation; and if we are conscientious, we do so in a gingerly and "self-consciously ambiguous" fashion, ever mindful of the differences.

The difficulties of translation appear in an acute form when we look at the quest for spiritual discipline in our society. We see a situation in which cultural translation has been occurring at a rapid and indiscriminate pace, sweeping along a vast number of thoughtful and well-meaning people who feel cut off from their own past and unsure of what it would mean to remember (or discover for the first time) the all-important differences. Members of newly organized meditation groups have been forced to make instant decisions about which features of a culturally alien religious tradition to save and which to discard. Lack of consensus on these issues has often become a source of schism and disillusionment.

The students in "Spiritual Practices" agonize over this very question. As the course progresses, it becomes apparent that even our most sophisticated authors can be accused of approaching spiritual traditions selectively, taking what they like and rejecting what they don't like. And the field trips expose us to markedly different kinds of teaching centers and communities, different styles of leadership, and different ways of facing the challenge of translation. Whether to chant (and if so, in what language?), to do prostrations, to swear obedience to one's teacher, to wear special clothing, to take monastic vows or create new forms of lay commitment, to preserve the distinct features and institutional separation of traditional lineages and sects—all of these puzzles emerge as crucial ones, and students begin to wonder whether there are any common criteria (other than subjective ones) for solving them.[18]

This brings up one of the problems pointed out by Kendall Folkert: in our consumerist society, comparative study of religion can all too easily collapse into a form of comparison shopping. "Spiritual Practices" is especially liable to fall into this trap, and my only way to prevent it is to make this one of the explicit concerns of the course. The phenomenon of comparison shopping won't go away just because we expunge it from our curricula; so perhaps it is best to meet it head on. Although it is historically distorting to think of comparing the world's religions, the contemporary world has to some degree already refashioned itself around this distortion; religious people of non-Western as well as Western cultures increasingly see themselves as subscribing members of a "religion."

This would become even more painfully obvious in a thematic course on conversion—a phenomenon often neglected by comparative religionists. The complex interactions between religion and culture are viewed quite differently by a convert from one tradition to another than they are by a scholar of comparative religion; and yet conversion, like shopping for spiritual disciplines, is a part of the history of human religiousness which needs to be counted in.

As the field of the study of religion matures, it is discovering its own place in the history of human religiousness, growing more conscious of its integral connection to the surrounding culture, and becoming less inclined to assume that its judgments are unbiased. This is a discovery which comparative and thematic courses like the ones described in this volume are uniquely suited to help us communicate to our students.

---

[18] On these issues in the Zen context, see Kenneth Kraft, "Recent Developments in North American Zen," and Martin Collcutt, "Epilogue: Problems of Authority in Western Zen," in *Zen: Tradition and Transition*, pp. 178-98 and 199-207.

When discussing these issues with students, it is important to point out that the traditions are not static; significant adaptations to modernity are likely to have occurred already before a particular practice gets imported to North America or Europe.

❧XI❧

Understanding the Self: East and West: An Interdisciplinary Study of a Theme

FREDERICK J. STRENG

Comparative themes can provide a conceptual lens through which a person can see relationships between once-hidden aspects of life, and raise new questions about human experience and expression. Themes are interpretive lens which shape what is, and what can be, seen. They can be derived from imagery, practice or inner qualities found in particular religious and cultural traditions; they can emerge from a discipline of study, such as philosophy, anthropology, or biology; or, they can be suggestive general terms drawn from common human experience whose usage is shaped by particular cultural experience and explained by theories reflective of different academic disciplines. Within the last option is the concept and general human experience of the "self." It is a useful theme for exposing different cultural patterns of awareness, for investigating the assumptions of different disciplinary interpretations, and for evoking personal sensitivities to the evaluative aspects of knowing and living as a human being.

Assumptions of this course: This course explores the meaning of specific expressions of self-consciousness, and reviews various theories used to explain them. We study a range of human experience found in the East and the West, and examine theories of the self from the perspectives of different academic disciplines: comparative religion, philosophy, psychology, and biology. The goal of the course is to aid each student in the formulation of his or her position (with justifications) on the nature of personhood in light of significant descriptions and reflections that draw from Western and Eastern sources.

Two assumptions pervade the structure of the course and the selection of assigned materials. The first is that the distinction between authentic and inauthentic living is a meaningful one. This is to say that human life cannot be understood completely in terms of biological survival. To exist as a biosocial organism is a necessary condition for, but not a sufficient account of, the nature and meaning of human existence. At the core of human experience is the felt urge to perceive and choose the better over the worse, happiness over sadness, and authentic living over inauthentic. Religions and cultural philosophies highlight the human need to distinguish between self-deception and insight, the cultivation of righteousness plus rejection of evil, and the development of inner qualities such as integrity, kindness, and courage rather than their opposites.

A significant part of what human self-consciousness means is the capacity to formulate an image of superlative value, and to work toward actualizing this value through social strategies and personal effort. While a human being is born with the genetic capacity to develop into a person, socialization and personal development are as important as the genetic conditions for becoming truly human. Along with psycho-social conditions over which a person may have little control the individual constructs some personal sensitivities, dispositions, and skills which provide general orientations and set parameters within which evaluations are made. In this course we probe the character, assumptions, and attitudes of some claims that have been called "authentic" human living because they function to direct the learning process toward "authenticity."

The second assumption is that an understanding of the "self" in the last quarter of the twentieth century requires a consideration of a plurality of human experience and of diverse approaches to the subject. Thus the content includes an analysis of Eastern and Western expressions and diverse theoretical reflections of the self, of both traditional religious and humanistic views of authenticity, of male and female experiences in self-identity, and explanations from the biological and behavioral sciences as well as those based on religious intuitions or extraordinary experience. The *process* of viewing different understandings of the self in relation to different approaches to understanding and explanation, exemplifies a general humanities approach in university education. By imaginatively participating in the assumptions, developing different vocabularies, and focusing on diverse questions about the self, students can engage in the dialectic process of empathically entering into an "other" human experience, and returning to their own standpoint for assessing and integrating the variety of possibilities into a coherent view. Stated another way, this course assumes that self-consciousness is itself varied; and that the vocabulary, the orientation, and attitudes of the perceiver already contribute to the understanding that is available. Thus, there is a concern to develop a sensitivity to the concepts, existential assumptions and modes of consciousness in human self-awareness, and to various approaches that have consequences for one's self-identity and behavior.

These two assumptions, indeed, reflect a self-consciousness of the times in which we live, in which there is an explosion of information about the variety of notions about the self in different cultures and a continuing discovery about the mechanisms of perception, learning, memory, feeling, and conditioned behavior. They also provide a (hopefully healthy) tension between the relativity of views and the need to affirm a stance in which authentic living can be achieved without total (or even sufficient) knowledge of all the dimensions of selfhood. Most of the class sessions are devoted to a discussion of assigned reading. This emphasizes the development of skills in reading comprehension, ferreting out the assumptions found in approaches and claims, and communicating the alternatives as preparation for a continuing life-long exploration and development of selfhood. Rather than accumulating information from lectures on different approaches, students are asked to read assigned material carefully and discuss the issues, keeping in mind the questions of *how* we can know who and what we are. This places the reflection about the use of reason, empirical analysis, and intuition within the patterns and processes of experienced life.

Each student brings some uniquely personal, and some general, information concerning self-consciousness to this course. We first attempt to gain a basic conceptual clarity about often-used terms such as "person," "self," "self-identity," "consciousness," "choice," and "quality of experience." A beginning clarity can emerge as the class reads the perspectives and (value-laden) reflections on the nature of authentic selfhood in Part I by representatives from humanistic psychology, Christianity, and Buddhism. In the second segment we raise a central issue in the empirical and philosophical study of the self: the mind/body problem, or more particularly, the relation of the brain processes to evaluative choice within self-consciousness. Finally, in the third part of the course we explore various dimensions of human experience by relating our immediate experiences of selfhood to other people's experience, and ask students to formulate a personal systematic statement about the nature of the self.

By using different approaches to the questions surrounding the human experience of selfhood students are asked to probe the hidden assumptions and unexamined imagery found in their own self-experience. They are urged to become conscious of their vocabulary as they examine the vocabulary of selfhood used by others, and to note the sensitivities evoked by images, ideas, and questions found in different perspectives. In class we point out different kinds of questions which are centered around issues that can be more aptly answered by some approaches and disciplines than others. Part of the complexity and challenge in understanding the self is the fact that a "self"—which is already partially structured by a particular language, cultural experience, interpretive framework, and evaluative sensitivity—is engaged in understanding!

Several general questions can be kept in mind as one engages the variety of perspectives. What are the primary characteristics, or constituents, of selfhood or personhood? Does the author assume that there are different orders or levels of selfhood, e.g. differentiating between a pseudo-self and an authentic self? If so, how does the authentic self relate to the general conditions for the development of a personality? How does the self function in relation to the body and other material causes? What procedures of cognition and self-awareness (if any) are assumed or stated to be necessary for an accurate apprehension of the self? Are any procedures perceived by advocates of an orientation as necessary for cultivating an authentic (or the highest quality of) selfhood? Is it possible to integrate the understandings of the different approaches, or are they simply an unreconcilable plurality of interpretive perspectives?

This course is structured as a one-semester course with classes meeting three hours per week. Each class period is a combination of a brief lecture and discussion. Films shown during class sessions have been noted.

COURSE OUTLINE:

1st week: Introduction to the study of the self as a university course

Invite discussion of self-awareness: note differences in vocabulary, dimensions of self-experience, imagery, and content.

Present course organization, calling attention to different approaches, kinds of questions and analytic models.

Film: "Everybody Rides the Carousel"

2nd week: Introduction to a humanist psychological approach to "becoming a person"

Reading: A. Maslow, *Man's Search for Himself*, Chs. 3 & 4

3rd week: Introduction to (contemporary expressions of) the traditional Christian understanding of self as combining body and spirit in response to God.

Reading: selected chapters from M. Kelsey, *The Other Side of Silence* and C. Davis, *Body as Spirit*

4th & 5th weeks: Introduction to the Theravada Buddhist approach to self-knowledge, i.e., no-self.

Reading: P. de Silva, *An Introduction to Buddhist Psychology*

Film: "Buddhism: Footprint of the Buddha—India"

1st paper: Describe and analyze the differences and similarities of the key features in the approaches to "authentic self-knowledge" in humanistic psychology, traditional Christianity, and Theravada Buddhism.

6th week: Introduction to the relation between physiological processes and the personal experience of consciousness

Discussion of the differences and similarities of human consciousness and other animal sensory response mechanisms based on study of evolutionary theory, comparative physiology, fetal and early childhood development, and social behavior.

Reading: J. Eccles & D. Robinson, *The Wonder of Being Human*, Chs. 2-5

Video-Cassette: "The Trigger Effect"

7th week: Introduction to conceptual issues when discussing the relation of brain processes to phenomenological experiences of the self.

Dangers of logical confusion due to a transference of meaning that depends on different logical referrents because of common syntactical structure, or due to a literal interpretation of a metaphorical use of a term, e.g., Do computers literally "think"?

Reading: D. M. Armstrong, "The nature of mind," found in C. V. Borst, *The Mind-Brain Identity Theory*

U. T. Place, "Is consciousness a brain process?" found in C. V. Borst, *The Mind-Brain Identity Theory*

J. Eccles & D. Robinson, *The Wonder of Being Human*, Chs. 6 & 7

8th week: Introduction to the neurophysiology of mental events: learning and memory

Reading: J. Eccles & D. Robinson, *The Wonder of Being Human*, Chs. 8-10

Film: "Left Brain, Right Brain," Parts I & II

9th week: Is the mind simply an information processing mechanism? How does "the materialist" and "the dualist" account for voluntary movement?

Reading:

P. McCorduck, "Forging the Gods," from *Machines Who Think*

J. Eccles & D. Robinson, *The Wonder of Being Human*, Ch. 11

G. Ryle, "Descartes' Myth," from *The Concept of Mind*

A. Comfort, "Forward" and "The mechanism of I-ness," from *I And That: Notes on the Biology of Religion*

2nd paper: Describe and analyze the issues, evidence and justifications in the debate between materialists and dualists over the nature of brain/mind.

10th week: Selected issues in considering the self in relation to what might be beyond the physical world. Can self-identity survive bodily death? What sort of evidence counts toward justifying belief in eternal life? What imagery of selfhood (if any) is useful to talk about life after death?

Reading:

J. Hick, "A Possible Pareschatology," from *Death and Eternal Life*

H. Küng, "End of the world and kingdom of God," from *Eternal Life*?

Film: "Life After Death"

11th week: Buddhist and Christian experiences of the spiritual journey. Here we explore personal statements of the significance of life choices for self-awareness, and the importance of self-images for ultimate commitments.

Reading:

E. Lerner, *Journey of Insight Meditation: A Personal Experience of the Buddha's Way* (24 page excerpt)

H. N. Wieman, "The Problem of Religious Inquiry," from *Religious Inquiry: Some Explorations*

A. G. Denham, "Selected Fiction: Tales I Tell Myself," *Occasional Papers*, United Methodist Board of Higher Education and Ministry, March 10, 1980

F. Tribe, "Ordinary Practice," *Kahawai: Journal of Women and Zen,*
V/1

A. Ray-Keil, "Rape as Personal and Cultural Koan," *Kahawai:
Journal of Women and Zen,* IV/1

C. Christ, "Expressing Anger at God," *Anima* 5/3 Film: "Killing
Us Softly"

12th & 13th weeks: The struggle for freedom and the development of a creative conscience: ultimate values in the development of selfhood.

The final weeks of the course focus on a discussion of the possibilities and limitations of various understandings of (personal
and ultimate) freedom and creativity. In what sense (if at all)
do human beings transcend time and materiality? What are
the justifications (if any) for considering moral choice to be
more than social reinforcement, or self-sacrificing love more
than hidden self-aggrandizement? Is the pursuit of quality-
living more than a mental-emotional compensatory fantasy?

Reading: A. Maslow, *Man's Search for Himself,* Chs. 5-8

Final paper: Each student is asked to present her or his personal
position on the nature of the self, indicating a sensitivity for
the plurality of perspectives and interpretive approaches that
have been studied during the semester, and providing justifications for his or her understanding.

Reflections on classroom experience: This course is designed to fulfill
a general education requirement for senior undergraduate students. It is
one of about twenty courses at Southern Methodist University (Dallas)
called "Capstone courses" which are described as follows:

The Capstone component of the curriculum consists of courses designed to
explore the broader intellectual and social context of a principal field of study.
The purposes of these courses are to familiarize students with the inter-relat-
edness of various specialized fields of knowledge, to assess the impact of these
fields upon society, and to evaluate their moral and ethcial dimensions.

I have taught it, or similar courses, several times with enrollments
from twenty to forty-five students. Because of the emphasis on discussion during class sessions, I have tried to limit the enrollment to thirty
students. The students are usually equally divided between men and
women, most of whom come from white middle class families. About
one-fifth are religious studies majors, about one-fourth are psychology
majors, leaving the majority from other humanities and social science
departments, or other schools of the university. Most of the students
have had no formal study in religion, philosophy, or non-Western
cultures. Also, most are nominally members of one or another Christian

denomination, while there are often several vocal students committed to a behaviorist psychological orientation.

The variety of approaches to understanding the self is both stimulating and perplexing for most students. For example, many students are intrigued by the possibility of studying the Buddhist perspective, but the effort to grasp the vocabulary and perspective of Buddhist psychology in two weeks of reading and discussion is demanding. Nevertheless, the possibility of achieving a transcendent awareness within the Theravada Buddhist orientation without a divine revelation is also an eye-opening experience for most. Likewise, for some of the humanistically and behavioristically oriented students, the traditional Christian recognition that an "authentic self" requires relating one's thoughts, feelings, and actions to a Divine spiritual resource is equally difficult to understand as a live option.

Perhaps the most critical existential issue for most students is raised during the second segment of the course. Here we consider the question of whether the general human experience of the freedom of choice (including aesthetic and moral evaluation) is only a "false echo" in the neurological mechanism of the brain. We focus on the power of the imagery and assumptions within the description of brain processes by both philosophers and neurophysiologists, some of whom suggest that the notion of a "self" or "mind" separate from the brain is simply a "ghost in the machine." This is related to questions of whether or not there is a fundamental difference between human learning or self-consciousness, on the one hand, and either "language" used by lower animals, or "artificial intelligence" by computers, on the other. In considering these questions, again, we focus on the assumptions and the kinds of evidence put forward to claim a separate "self" which is dependent on, but not identical with, neuro-physiological processes, or to claim that the distinction is based on faulty reasons and emotional needs.

Having raised the issues of various concepts of authenticity in the first segment, and of the arguments and evidence for the mind/brain question in the second segment, students have a general framework for considering in the final segment the questions of the self in reference to "life after death," transcendent goals for living, and notions of personal freedom and conscience. We look at specific examples of religious and moral claims in the contemporary world and suggest various possibilities for formulating the notions of human freedom, creativity, and ideal virtues (e.g., love, justice, peace) in light of both human conditionedness and potential. The final paper, which requires the student to present his or her understanding of the self in light of the issues raised during the semester, is at first regarded by many as an impossible task. Even though we use the discussion in class sessions during the final week to structure several options with their implications for one's personal awareness and behavior, many feel it is asking too much to take a position and defend it. I am happy to say (on the basis of unsolicited penned statements at the end of their papers) that many found this to be a rewarding exercise.

Despite the fact that most students affirm the value of exploring the nature and expressions of the self as outlined in this course, several concerns regarding the material and structure of the course can be raised. Briefly they can be summarized as follows:

The readings listed here are given by way of example. Each has been used in the course, and some provoke more response than others. Perhaps there are better readings.

Readings from religious traditions other than Christianity and Buddhism might be used. This would structure the juxtaposition of ultimate claims in a different way.

There are several subtopics in the debate between the materialists and the dualists on the nature of brain/mind. These have been considered in a cursory manner. Though they are interrelated, one gets easily seduced into a discussion that touches many points briefly.

This course is oriented more toward problems of interpretation, assumptions, and perspectives than toward empirical description or lengthy analyses of specific arguments. This approach engages most students who have taken the course; at the same time they express frustration at the rapidity of shifting perspectives, and the emphasis on problematic questions rather than on definitive answers.

❧XII❧

Bourgeois Relativism and the Comparative Study of the Self

LEE H. YEARLEY

It has happened to all of us, of course. We come on a sentence that not only causes us to pause but also leads us to start a process of painful reflection. This happened to me when I was reading (not studying) a book of Adorno's. Bourgeois toleration, he said, is consciously relativistic and neutral and subconsciously disposed to protect the status quo in both individual and society. My reflections on that sentence led me to replace a successful introductory course I had been teaching with a very different kind of course. The course I created is the major subject here, but the process I went through casts light on that course and may contain lessons that others will find useful.[1]

The course I eliminated had been a remarkable success by the usual standards as well as by the more important standards. An introduction to comparative religious thought, the enrollments were high enough to cause substantial staffing problems and the evaluations were usually embarrassingly good. (Thankfully they were not universally good, a sure sign that something is amiss.) More important, talking with students, watching them develop over the course, and seeing them appear in other courses made me think the course was doing many good things. Why then destroy it?

---

[1] The theoretical framework for the course I will describe is presented in my contribution to the Chicago volume in this series, "Education and the Intellectual Virtues," in *Beyond the Classics? Essays in Liberal Studies and Liberal Education*, eds., F. E. Reynolds and S. L. Burkhalter (Atlanta: Scholars Press, 1990).

The reflections generated by the line in Adorno made painfully evident to me that whatever might be its beneficial effects, the course also helped to support a kind of bourgeois relativism. The relativism I refer to is not the product of a sophisticated intellectual position. It is only the raw notion that people have no clear cut ways to adjudicate conflicts among ways of life or ethical judgments, and therefore they ought to (or perhaps only can) embrace fully the ways of life and judgments they presently have.

I teach in a university where the undergraduates, with few exceptions, are immensely talented, very energetic, and aim to take their place as leaders within the society. Most are or hope to be members of the "bourgeoisie," in at least most of the major senses of that complicated word. They are, however, also struggling with issues about what they owe to other people and to their own souls. That struggle is both intense and poignant because they are drawn to pursue conventional forms of success and the material benefits and status they bring. Relativism becomes for many of them, I think, a way of justifying the comfortable way of life to which they are antecedently drawn. It furnishes answers to questions that might lead them to change what they do and who they are. It becomes, then, a way of justifying a "status quo" in themselves and their society from which they now gain, or can gain, a tremendous amount; except, of course, in the spiritual realm.

My course was helping them to justify their attitudes. Indeed, it was doing in its own idiosyncratic way what I believe many introductory courses in comparative religions often do. I aimed to present a powerful set of integral and radically different perspectives on a particular theme. I then questioned whether we had any rational grounds on which to adjudicate among the truth and value of them.

The old course, Varieties of Religious Thought, proceeded as follows. I began by examining what most modern philosophers—or sophisticated, secular people—would consider the marks of good thinking; e.g., how one weighs evidence or decides if claims are true or merely plausible. The account was standard, and it is powerful. Perhaps most important, much higher education attempts to instill in students an appreciation and finally adoption of this kind of thinking. I then tried to show how much religious thinking either contradicts or stands in tension with that ideal. (I also noted in passing how much thinking about other important matters also conflicts with that ideal.) Several brief examples of religious thought were considered in making the general point; for example, how and why one could defend the notion of transmigration; how and why one might argue for a strong distinction between teachers and saviors.

In the remainder of the course, I focused on the topic of meeting death, either one's own imagined death or the death of another. I examined treatments of it in various religious traditions. Some time was also spent trying to make the idea of death vivid, given that few students thankfully have much first hand experience, and most have trouble really envisaging their own end. (A classicist I know believes in the Socratic notion that philosophy is the art of learning how to die; he sometimes despairs, in his phrase, of teaching philosophy to people who believe they are immortal. The statement is, I think, an exaggeration in the direction of truth.)

Brief comments were made about the traditions the thinkers or texts represented, but the main point was to examine the way people presented and argued for their views. My major preoccupation was always to highlight differences, even at times to argue for near incommensurability. Indeed, I presented a typology based on the notion that there are three radically different ways of being religious, and that they loosely fit with Western, South Asian, and East Asian kinds of religions.[2]

The course had almost no discussion of how we might go about adjudicating conflicts among ideas. In fact, choosing death as the central subject made that kind of discussion almost impossible, given the mystery that surrounds it and the various complicated issues which circle around any answer. Moreover, we moved so quickly over so much ground that students had little chance to engage various thinkers at a level that allowed them seriously to make their own judgments, however provisional they might be.

I created the course in the early 1970s. At that time I thought I needed to demonstrate two ideas vividly and academically. First, that people could live in very different ways, ways usually built on religious beliefs, and yet still be recognizably human. Second, that the kind of procedural, calculating reason we in the culture often take for granted was only one way—and often a feeble way—to deal with the more substantial ques-

---

[2] For a description of this typology, see my "Three Ways of Being Religious," *Philosophy East and West* 32:4 (1982): 439-51; a related piece is my "A Comparison Between Classical Chinese Thought and Thomistic Christian Thought," *The Journal of the American Academy of Religion* LI:3 (1983): 427-58. I present a significantly different picture of comparisons, one closer to the new course, in my book: *Mencius and Aquinas: Theories of Virtue and Conceptions of Courage* (Albany: State University of New York Press, 1990) in the series, F. Reynolds and D. Tracy, eds. *Towards a Comparative Philosophy of Religions*.

tions about life's meaning we faced. (I was, I now see, yet another example of how the late sixties and the Vietnam War made this agenda compelling.)

These goals surely still have much to be said for them. By the early 1980s, however, the times (and thus I) and the audience had changed, and I had not fully realized it. I now faced people for whom relativism was a given and toleration an ideal. I kept needing to remind myself that these students had grown up with television shows that depicted, in visually exciting ways, how different were other cultures. They also lived with talk shows that often presented fundamentally different approaches to life, if in an anecdotal and unintellectual atmosphere. As a friend said to me, our students at age ten were watching documentaries on head-hunting tribes and talk shows where satanic cults were the subject.

My course ran the risk of becoming yet another version of those experiences. It surely was less colorful, and it met them at a less impressionable time. But it also carried the weight of academic authority, involved reading eloquent testimonies about religious ideas, and led students to the engagement produced by the writing of papers that will be evaluated. Moreover, as I now understood, these students (and I) had much to gain by deciding that relativism was a truth by which one could live, or even must live, as it served to preserve a status quo that was apparently beneficial for them (and me).

The old course had, of course, a justification. In some educational situations a version of it even might be needed. I doubt, however, that the real challenge of cultural relativism is best approached anywhere simply by focusing on differences and presenting a large number of cases. In my situation the course clearly needed to be changed. And so I changed it.

I still believed, passionately believed, in comparative courses and in an approach to variety that used themes. The new course resembles the old one in ways that reflect that belief and other of my general educational ideals. Both courses reflect specific principles: for example, coverage is basically unimportant; powerful and diverse ways of thinking have to be considered; the subject must be of existential import; the high tradition is the focus; and the course should help foster dispositions that will remain after much else has been forgotten. Other principled differences between the two courses are, however, clear. Fewer things must be done more slowly; a significant but more manageable topic must be the focus; both diverse ideas and ways to adjudicate among, or at least think about, them have to be presented and centrally dealt with; and students have to encounter a subject matter about which they already have strong if inchoate ideas to which they feel committed.

The subject I chose was conceptions of the self as they vary within and among cultures. Different texts and issues have been highlighted at various times but a representative selection is as follows. I usually start with an accessible short, contemporary work that helps students to see issues and to entertain ideas that make intuitive sense to them. (A major purpose of the text is also to provide a good basis for initial discussions in sections.) Charles Taylor's article on human agency has worked well. He argues for a position (e.g., a cognitive theory of the emotions) that differs from most modern notions but underlies many religious positions. Most important, he distinguishes between strong and weak evaluations. Weak evaluations arise when I decide among a number of desires all of which I would like to fulfill if I could. Strong evaluations arise from a decision about what kind of person I want to be, and I think of my desires in the contrastive terminology of worthy and unworthy. Many students believe they are strong evaluators and discover, usually to their dismay, that they are weak evaluators.

We then examine, for the bulk of the course, selections from a variety of classic texts. I usually begin with Aristotle. (I believe Aquinas has an even more compelling picture, and one that is more significant religiously, but formidable difficulties accompany the task of helping students, in a brief time, understand Aquinas's genre and vocabulary.) Aristotle's picture is a powerful and traditional one. Moreover, it gives students a chance to read and begin to understand what appears to be difficult and, to some, even impenetrable material.

Indeed, using such a text manifests one of my key aims in the course. I aim to present students with difficult classic texts and help them to see just how rewarding it is to work through them. (This goal can be reached, I think, only if we give students brief selections; that is, try to do less more slowly.) As humanists teaching beginning courses, one of our most crucial jobs is to show students that texts, especially texts from different times and cultures, have riches that can be obtained if they are properly mined. Those riches provide us with insights, legitimate pleasures, and new approaches that we can acquire from no other source. Learning that lesson is among the most important the humanities can give, and it may endure long after the material in the course, and even my name, are long forgotten. (When planning a course, I always ask myself how students who took the course might in twenty years be different than they would be if they had not taken the course. Their having learned this lesson provides one of the few clear answers.)

Aristotle presents a clearly worked out, abstract picture of what the self is. It even can be presented in diagramatical form, and I use a variety of handouts here and throughout the course to introduce materials. (An added advantage of using them is that you can then show how the diagrams cannot really capture the thought's subtleness.) Beginning with Aristotle enables students to understand just how many of their own views are variants of the Aristotelian picture. That is, it allows them to see that ideas about habits, say, or about distinctions between deliberative and theoretical rationality are parts of a specific tradition's way of thinking. They are not ideas that simply arise from human experience, they are ideas that arise from a particular tradition's way of conceptualizing experience.

I attempt to "sell" Aristotle, to show students that he presents a clear and defensible picture of who and what a self is, that he gives us a conceptual framework that allows us better to understand our own often inchoate experience. In the remainder of the course, however, I challenge most elements of his framework. But I do so in a way that hopefully enables or even forces students continually to think out what they think a self is. Indeed, as the course progresses many come to realize that we all know we have a self and that it is very important, but that what exactly it may be, or even how best to think about it, is less than clear.

I often, immediately after Aristotle, introduce brief selections on specific topics from Christian writers that raise basic questions about Aristotle's ideas on selfhood. One example is the account, in the second chapter of Augustine's *Confessions*, in which he argues that he stole pears not in order to realize any good but to act against all goods, to rebel against the whole order of things. Another is Aquinas's account of spiritual sloth (edited for easier use) in which he argues that people may find themselves in the distressing position of being unable to act to achieve those goods they truly love.

My main project, however, is to look at three East Asian accounts and then to return to two Western accounts. All of them challenge the sensibleness, or profoundity, of Aristotle's account. I normally start with Mencius for several reasons, not the least of which is his immense importance to the Confucian tradition. His depiction of the self can, at first reading, appear to fit easily into Aristotle's account. Showing students that it does not makes them aware of the need to be suspicious of one's own inital readings of texts from radically different cultures. That process also illustrates for them how unconscious presuppositions can control our interpretation of foreign ideas.

Another reason to use Mencius is that the outlines of his view of the self can be grasped relatively easily once it is explained. (This is another place where a lengthy handout, complete with textual references and a description of key terms, can be very helpful, especially for the serious student.) Moreover, many students find Mencius' view persuasive if sometimes because they think, quite mistakenly, that it matches some of the most optimistic views of humanistic psychology.

I aim, then, in treating Mencius to show how his ideas both relate to and differ from Aristotle's—e.g., no theoretical reason exists in Mencius but he does share with Aristotle a concern for virtue. I also aim to show how his mode of presentation—the mixture of aphorism, story, image, and argument—corresponds to almost no Western genre and yet serves needs and produces results that Western forms do not. Throughout, I underscore why Mencius would develop the picture he does; what evidence he looks to, what forms of argument he finds convincing, and what spiritual ideal animates him.

We then move to the *Chuang Tzu*, a (probably) third century BCE Taoist text. Mencius and Chuang Tzu often argue about similar ideas. Examining two thinkers who can be said to share a common discourse is important; it happens nowhere else in the course and is one reason they were chosen. Moreover, the issues they worry about usually differ markedly from those with which Aristotle deals.

Most critical, however, is that Chuang Tzu questions our ability to know what we think we know. His use of powerful images and arguments puts such skepticism in an especially compelling way. Few are the students who will not, in some way, be touched by the virtuoso performance the book contains. Facing this challenge about what we can know, although critical in itself, is particularly important insofar as it affects questions about how to understand the self.

Indeed, Chuang Tzu's views on knowledge link closely with his views on the self. He attacks any idea that the self resembles a solid something. But he also presents us with an eliptical but powerful set of images about what the self is. By means of these images he tries to use language to move people beyond language so that they can grasp what is, for him, a saving vision. His attempt, then, allows students to study how one may present a radical view of the self through a medium, language, that necessarily can only at best point to it. The character and viability of such attempts will be examined with all the figures who follow.

Finally, Chuang Tzu allows us to see our first "non-ameliorative" picture of the self. That is, he argues people ought not simply try to ameliorate those problems that appear in normal human perception and action. Rather, they must break radically with ordinary life if they are to reach full human flourishing. Chuang Tzu's depiction of that flourishing state is both strange enough and compelling enough that the real bite, and difficulty, in this approach is illustrated well.

The third East Asian text or figure is one that presents a "discovery" or "monistic" model; that is, a model where people discover what they truly are by finding a higher, subsistent reality, a Mind that transcends but connects with all individual minds. This model, evident in different ways in various religions, presents probably our first explicitly metaphysical view of the self. That is, the position makes no sense outside of specific and controversial ontological beliefs, and proponents presume that people can obtain the needed knowledge.

From this perspective, it seems clear, people do not develop a self whose natural capacities will grow if they are nurtured. Rather they discover a hidden ontological reality that defines and saves them. No matter what specific human beings, their particular instantiations, may do, this true self continues to exist. This self is obscured by such impediments or defilements as errant passions or misguided perceptions, so to reach the true self these impediments need to be overcome. The real self consists of a permanent set of dispositions that are covered over, but that can be uncovered or recovered.

Occasionally I have used Buddhist texts, e.g., the *Platform Sutra*, to present this view. Usually, however, I use a neo-Confucian, normally Wang Yang-ming. My choice rests on practical considerations. Even with a text like the *Platform Sutra*, a set of complex new terminology and ideas must be explained, and we already are awash with different kinds of ideas. Moreover, the use of a neo-Confucian allows me to highlight, if in passing, an important idea. That idea is how a conception of the self can change radically within a tradition, even when figures in the tradition think it has not. Wang Yang-ming considers himself a follower of Mencius, but Buddhist views have become dominant enough to provide the spectacles through whch he sees Mencius.

We end the course by returning to the West and treating two modern figures, Kierkegaard and Freud. Kierkegaard's *Sickness Unto Death* is again an initially forbidding text that when read closely becomes for many a very powerful intellectual experience. It presents, from within the Western tradition, a set of compelling criticisms of the principles that underlie Aristotle's vision of the self; for instance, the principle that in most cases to know the good is to do the good. These criticisms rest on Kierkegaard's employment of ideas that have become important parts of our modern understanding. An especially notable instance is his emphasis on self deception, on the willed obscuring of understanding in order to protect the self from having to face the implications of some idea or fact.

Moreover, Kierkegaard works from and deepens a variety of insights or perturbations that many students have. Kierkegaard's treatments of how despair works and his sense for the difficulties that conformism generates, all strike cords in most of today's students. Furthermore, his argument that these notions demand the kind of radical solution that religion offers sets well, and firmly in a Western context, an idea that has appeared previously, notably in Chuang Tzu and Wang Yang-ming.

Finally, Kierkegaard presents a highly sophisticated picture of the different levels of selfhood that rests on his brilliant, if controversial, perspective on the alternative ideas of the self the West has produced. We can use, and test, Kierkegaard's categories in a way he never imagined by placing each of the East Asian figures we have studied in one or another of the stages he thinks constitutes the hierarchy of selfhood. Seeing the insights and distortions that occur when we do this teaches a valuable lesson about the importance of the comparative enterprise and the pitfalls, and pratfalls, in it. (Many students, incidentally, choose to write on this subject if given the opportunity.)

Freud is the final figure considered, and I teach texts of his that may seem irrelevant; e.g., his essay on narcissism. I approach him through such texts because most students are familiar only with the vulgar, common renditions of Freud. More important, he is often at his worst when directly analyzing religion and at his best when examining phenomena that characterize religion, such as obedience or a sense of self-validating wholeness.

I end with Freud for various reasons. Unlike other positions considered, his is an avowedly secular, even scientific, view; he attempts to reduce, to explain in other terms, most common ideas of religion and the self. Moreover, the vocabulary and some of the insights in Freud resemble those found in Kierkegaard, and yet they are set within a different framework and used for very different ends. (I usually introduce both Kierkegaard and Freud by describing Hegel's views on the modern problems of selfhood and consciousness.)

Furthermore, studying him also allows us to examine how his ideas both resemble and differ from those modern ideas about the self that the cultural dominance of humanistic psychology has made convincing to many students. Treating Freud allows us to return, after a long journey, to some common contemporary pictures of the self. Seeing them in Freud also enables us to understand how they arise from a well worked out theory, but a theory that may seem to be suspicious or at least peculiar. Finally, in concentrating on the late Freud, we end with a most striking picture of the self. Freud aims to dissolve normal pictures of selfhood and to replace them with a view that not only correlates with but seems as strange as a view like Chuang Tzu's. That is, I can end by making unfamiliar the apparently familiar, just as I hoped previously to make the seemingly unfamiliar begin to look familiar.

Many of the goals that characterized the old course are still present here: presenting variety, doing comparisons, calling in question basic notions, choosing a topic of existential import, treating classic texts, eschewing any attempt at coverage. But the differences are fundamental. Relatively few texts are considered, and they are considered as closely as time constraints allow. Moreover, the topic is one that can be more easily controlled, and the issues surrounding it can be better defined and analyzed. Some issues are tracked through almost all the figures. Examples are the character of reason and emotions and relationship between them; the nature and source of saving dispositions; the specific problems that lead to the self's deformations; the description and evaluation of the the link between our more clearly animal and more clearly human sides; the need for transcendent forces to be present if the self is to be actualized; and the form of and rationale for different kinds of self-cultivation.

Perhaps most critical, I can show students that we have criteria that enable us to decide (if obviously within the boundaries of our own finitude) that some answers are better than others. I can also help them learn that, even where we lack answers, there are better and worse ways to think about the questions. Over the course of the quarter, then, students learn to do something many of them doubt is possible: they can think well or badly about matters about which they care deeply. (They may even realize that such thinking manifests intellectual virtues and will, in turn, determine how they feel.) Students can also begin to understand that who they become will depend, in significant ways, on their willingness to do such thinking and feeling. Finally, the course also allows them to understand how best to go about a task that is of crucial importance to all of us today. That task is the sympathetic yet critical comparison of different views of the self, and thus of human flourishing.

Aquinas was right, I think, when he said that all teachers can best be described as deficient secondary causes. At our most potent, we are but faint forces in a world that contains dramatically effective powers. And yet what we try to produce is both valuable and rare. The enterprise can be a noble one, then, especially if we remain constantly aware of how our activity can aid what is problematic or what is best in the culture to which we belong.

APPENDIX

The syllabus for my course is over six pages long, and I will not burden people with it. I will, however, cover three subjects that may be of help to people interested in teaching a course like this. (I will, incidentally, send copies of the handouts I made up and use in the course to anyone who requests them; e.g., a four-page handout on Mencius's idea of the self.)

I. Texts

I feel particularly strongly about two texts. With Aristotle, I use T. Irwin's translation of the *Nichomachean Ethics* (Hackett, 1985). With Chuang Tzu, I use A. C. Graham's translation, *Chuang-tzu The Seven Inner Chapters and Other Writings From The Book Chuang-tzu* (George Allen and Unwin, 1981). Both allow students (and teachers) to make real progress in their understanding of the text, in part because of the translation, in part because of accompanying notes, glossaries, etc. A number of good translations of the Aristotle are in print; the main alternative to Graham is B. Watson; note that Graham has done a reconstruction of parts of the text.

With Mencius, D. C. Lau's translation is good and has a helpful introduction (*Mencius*, Penguin Books, 1970); J. Legge's translation is also excellent but the language has a Victorian flavor and is difficult for students to penetrate (*The Works of Mencius*, orginally published in 1895 and reprinted by Dover in 1970.) The only available full translation of Wang Yang-ming is *Instructions for Practical Living and Other Neo-Confucian Writings by Wang Yang-ming*, translated with notes by Wing-tsit Chan (Columbia University Press, 1963). People may also find helpful the background provided in A. C. Graham's *Two Chinese Philosophers Ch'eng Ming-tao and Ch'eng Yi-chuan* London: Lund Humphries 1958; as noted below, I have used selections from it in the course. With Kierkegaard, the translation by the Hongs of *The Sickness Unto Death* is best (Princeton University Press, 1980). Using the translations of Freud from the *Standard Edition* is highly recommended; many of the books are available in paperback but the papers are not. The multi-volume edition of Freud that P. Rieff edited and Collier publishes has good selections, well organized by theme, but the translations are older ones. Finally, the paper by Charles Taylor, "What is Human Agency?" is found in his *Human Agency and Language, Philosophical Papers 1* (Cambridge: Cambridge University Press, 1985), pp. 15-44.

II. Written Assignments

Examples of the general written assignments in the course follow. (The course is taught on a quarter system and reflects that unhappy situation.) With the first two assignments, I give very specific questions that set an issue and point students to particular, short (i.e., 3-5 pages) passages in the texts. Special office hours are held before the papers are due and some of the most important teaching in the course occurs during them.

1] A 4-6 page typed paper on Aristotle that responds to one of 5-10 questions I hand out, some of which will deal with his relation to Taylor or to the Christian ideas we briefly examined.

2] A 4-6 page typed paper on East Asian conceptions that responds to one of 5-10 questions that I hand out.

3] A 10-12 page final paper that should cover the following points:

a] how a proponent of a conception of the self from Aristotle, East Asia, or the modern West would analyze a conception of the self arising from one of the other—e.g., if you take Aristotle you must analyze either an East Asian or a modern Western conception.

b] how the latter conception would respond to the analysis given of it.

c] how you would evaluate both the analysis and the response.

III. Readings

Examples follow; I have omitted recommended readings.

1) The piece by Charles Taylor is noted above.

2) Aristotle: *Nichomachean Ethics*

Roman numerals refer to book, arabic numbers to the section in the book; page numbers refer to the Irwin translation.

a] General Background I: 3,4; 7-10 [pp. 3-7; 13-27] VII, 1 [pp. 172-74] (on types of people)

b] The Human Soul I,13 [pp. 29-33]

c] Excellences of Thought VI: 1-7 but read in the following order: 1,2,3, 6,7,4,5 [pp.148-59]

d] Excellences of Character: virtues, dispositions, and the "mean" II: 1-7 [pp. 33-49]

e] Bravery as an Example of an Excellence of Character III: 6-9 [pp. 71-79]

f] Mildness and Shame IV: 5, 9 [pp. 105-7; 114-15]

g] The Great-Souled Person (magnanimity) IV, 3 [pp. 97-104]

h] Self-Love and Friendship IX, 8 [pp.253-56]

i] The Contemplative Life X: 7,8 [pp. 284-91]

3) Mencius: The *Mencius* is separated into books, parts, and sections. 1a7, for example, is book one, part A, section 7; page numbers refer to the Lau translation.

1a7 [pp. 54-59]
2a2 [pp. 76-80]
2a6,7 [pp. 82-83]
3a5 [pp. 104-5]
3b1,2,9 [pp. 106-7,113-15]
4a1,4,10-12, 17,18 [pp.117-19;122-25]
4b11-14, 26, 19 [pp.130-31, 133-34]
5b1 [pp. 149-51]
6a1-20 [pp. 160-70]
6b1,2, 13 [pp. 171-72, 179-80]
7a1-7,13-17, 26-27, 40,41,44 [pp. 182-85;187-88, 191-92]
7b 21,23-26,31,32,35,37 [pp. 198-204]

4) Chuang Tzu: readings from the Graham translation noted above: pp. 116-125; 43-72; 81-99

5) Wang Yang-ming: readings are the Chan translation noted above:
"Inquiry on the *Great Learning,*" pp. 269-80
#5, pp. 9-12
#139 pp. 107-110
226,227,229,231, pp. 201-3
168,169,171, pp. 150-57

Background readings from A. C. Graham, *Two Chinese Philosophers* noted above; these readings may also be helpful in understanding the two other Chinese texts.

    ix,x [through the second full paragraph]
    8-13 [through the second full paragraph]
    31-36 [to the paragraph break]
    44-58 [chapter four]
    61-62 [up to the quotation]

Soren Kierkegaard: *Sickness Unto Death,* pp. 13-96; 110-14. [Reading the whole is recommended]

Sigmund Freud: *New Introductory Lectures on Psychoanalysis,* pp. 139-54 [end of first full paragraph]; pp. 8 [first full paragraph]-20 [to first full paragraph]; pp. 51-98. Other selections have included Freud's essays on narcissism, masochism, mourning, and selections from *Civilizations and its Discontents.*

❧XIII❧

"Scriptures and Classics": An Introductory Course in the Study of Religion

WILLIAM A. GRAHAM

The origin of the course on "Scriptures and Classics" that I am about to describe is both easy and difficult to trace. Most obviously, it stemmed from nearly a decade of my own work on the Qur'an as scripture and on the problem of scripture itself (Graham 1986, 1987, 1989). Less obviously, it came as a result of the kinds of experiences that led to and fed my original interest in Qur'an and in scripture: walking the streets of old Cairo listening to the cadences of Qur'an recitation in the nights of Ramadan, admiring the reverential ritual care with which the Torah scrolls are handled in a local synagogue, contemplating fabulously illuminated biblical and psalter manuscripts from medieval Europe, and sitting in a Gujarati village temple where a learned Jain *muni* expounded to an attentive audience of monks and laypersons the meaning of passages from sacred texts. Such experiences give the deeper impetus to approach the teaching of an introductory comparative course in religion through the phenomenon of scripture.

On the surface, the study of sacred texts seems to be too traditional and obvious an entrée into the study of religion to be very exciting in today's classroom. And, indeed, the idea of introducing students to religion through consideration of some of the greatest religious and cultural classics of human history does represent in some ways an "old-fashioned" answer to the perennial question of religious-studies programs: "How do we teach the basic comparative course in religion?" Not only is it unabashedly "textual" in its focus on scriptures and classics (rather

179

than, for example, non-literate, "popular" religion); it is also relatively
unconcerned with programmatic "methodology" in the study of religion.
While many questions of method and approach in studying religion
comparatively are raised, no markedly theoretical writings are considered; instead, primary texts form the substance of the course reading.
Furthermore, the particular religious traditions whose texts are included
are almost exclusively those "great" or "world" traditions that have prevailed in the dominant civilizations of history. These and other aspects of
my "Scriptures and Classics" course deserve some explanation even before we look at its specific content. Here two questions in particular merit
consideration:

First, why concentrate on written texts rather than, for example, practices or symbol systems? My own answer is that I am convinced of the
invalidity of the notion that in focusing upon only the "great" or
"classic" texts of various communities we skew the study of religion seriously in favor of the elite, or "high" traditions of those communities.
Scriptures become scriptures only because communities of persons find
in them, through generation after generation, the most compelling
blueprints for life that they can conceive, the expression of the highest to
which they aspire, and the most tangible link to transcendence that they
know. This is as true for the uneducated masses as for the intellectual
and religious elites, for literacy and education have most often little to do
with access to such texts. While a scripture is, at a very basic level, a literate phenomenon, it is by no means only accessible to the literate or
other elites in a given context.

The overwhelming majority of persons who have "had a scripture"
have had access to it not through their own reading of the printed or
written page, but through hearing and learning by heart the sacred
words read aloud by others; through reciting, chanting, or singing these
words from memory; and through everyday oral use of formulae and
vocabulary drawn from holy writ. In short, scriptural texts build a fundamental part of the "background" of meaning, reference, and symbolism for all religious thought and action in any context. The human being
is a verbal animal above all, a language-maker and language-user; verbal
texts are the natural expression of his or her fundamental religious sensibility, and whether these texts are written down, memorized, or both,
they are living elements of religious life at all levels of society, from that
of the underclasses to that of the nobilities.

Second, why include "classics" as well as "scriptures"? At one level,
to underscore that not only so-called "scriptures," but all truly great

texts, can be mined to some degree for what they can tell us about the religious values of the tradition that has accorded them "classic" status. (Our subject in such a course is, after all, most fundamentally religion itself.) At another level, the course is centrally concerned with the importance of critical self-consciousness about the problematic nature of all of our neat categories, from "religious" or "secular" to "scripture" or "classic." (One need only think here of the Western practice of distinguishing between "Confucian classics" and "[Chinese] Buddhist scriptures", where the Chinese use the same term, *ching,* for both.)

In the end, one must be willing to accept that both "scripture" and "classic" are, first, important points of entry into other religious worlds, and, second, descriptive categories with which to think, not rigidly delimited pigeon-holes into which all important texts can be neatly placed. Scriptures are those texts that have special sacrality and primary authority in a religious community, typically those that are read from or recited in worship and prayer, and often those that are used magically and treated with special veneration that can border on bibliolatry. They demand always interpretation, exegesis, so that they never stand utterly alone. They are perceived as an ontological unity, however varied their origins and sources. "Classics" on the other hand are variously conceived and defined, but always represent in some fashion a key element in the self-definition and self-understanding of a given cultural, ethnic, national, or other group tradition. They are of interest to the historian of religion because they reveal a great deal about the fundamental Weltanschauung of the tradition(s) that consider(s) them central.

Perhaps most fundamentally, both categories of text are of interest to the teacher of religion or, indeed, of the humanities generally, because they represent the best of any given tradition; they present to us the eagle-flights of the human spirit, the most profound moral standards and ethical systems, the deepest insights into human mortality, suffering, compassion, courage, and joy, and the closest human approach to transcending the merely human or mundane. They are, in short, vessels bearing the very life-blood of the great religious traditions, and thus a fine access both to each of these traditions in their particularity and to all of these as concrete instances of the religiousness that has been such a defining characteristic of the human.

Background. The course in question is one of a series of introductory courses that those of us primarily involved in the undergraduate program of concentration in the Comparative Study of Religion have taught almost every year since the inception of the concentration in 1974. The first of these was a course on pilgrimage (described above in the present book, pp. 51-63 by Richard Niebuhr). Other such introductory courses in comparative religion have dealt with ritual and, most recently, under Diana Eck, interreligious dialogue. Each of the courses is aimed primarily at (1) undergraduates looking for a first or only elective in the study of religion, (2) potential undergraduate religion concentrators, and (3) sophomores already accepted into the honors-only concentration at the end of their freshman year. Because of the peculiarities of the Harvard context, where little distinction is made between undergraduate and graduate courses save in the case of seminars, and where students cross over naturally and easily to take courses in other faculties, our introductory courses function also *de facto* as a staple in the "history of religions" area of the Harvard Divinity School's basic curriculum. Thus we always have between thirty and fifty per cent enrollment from M.T.S. and M.Div. candidates in the Divinity School in any one of these introductory courses. Such diversity of enrollment has its advantages and disadvantages, but it inevitably makes teaching a basic course in the general history of religion a more challenging endeavor than otherwise. We have also found that many masters students in Divinity have had little or no previous exposure to the study of religion in a comparative context—that is, in the global context of human religiousness as a whole, as opposed to that of solely Christian or Jewish, or perhaps Western European culture and history. Nevertheless, this and our other basic courses have been conceived primarily as undergraduate offerings and continue to be oriented above all to an undergraduate audience of potential or beginning religion concentrators and students seeking an elective course in religion.

The Course: General Remarks. As the latest version of our introductory course in religion, "Scriptures and Classics" is relatively new, and indeed, still *in nascendi*, since at this writing (fall, 1989), I am giving it only for the second time. (Our pilgrimage course, by contrast, has been given a number of times over a ten-year period.) I taught the course for the first time in the fall term of 1987-88, but only after giving both undergraduate and graduate seminars on the topic the preceding spring. (I might note that these seminars proved invaluable as means of developing the larger, lecture-based course. They provided excellent experience with the subject matter and reading assignments and ideas for lectures and discussion topics in the larger course [which involves, because of large enrollment—presently about 140—almost of necessity a "lecture" format.])

In the course, we meet twice a week for lectures, questions, and such discussion as can be sustained in a large group. Everyone meets in addition once a week in one of eight or nine smaller sections of about fifteen persons for discussion of the week's reading. Exclusive of holidays, the usual Harvard term has approximately seventeen weeks. Of these, two are devoted to reading period, two to examination period, and the remaining thirteen to class meetings. As for "Scriptures and Classics" requirements, there are three assigned essays, all with some choice as to exact topics and due dates (see below), a midterm exam (replaced, in 1989-90, by a rewrite of the first essay), and a three-hour final exam.

Goals of the Course. The course is conceived, as my earlier remarks indicate, with three major purposes in mind. One is to introduce undergraduates to the general study and history of religion and to the historically "major" traditions of human religiousness. A second is to explore the specific and significant religious phenomenon of scripture. A third is to consider (and, explicitly or implicitly, to compare) how different traditions have confronted the truly major issues of human existence. Finally, integral to all of these purposes is the fundamental aim to encourage students to read and think critically and to write literately.

(1) In introducing students to the general study of religion in a comparative context, a topical theme such as scripture allows one to focus on a variety of religious phenomena and diverse aspects of religious life. When reading *Gilgamesh*, the issues of myth and legend, polytheism, and life after death all come easily to voice and discussion; when exploring the Bhagavad Gita, questions of morality, of duty, of devotion, and of religious experience arise naturally; when wrestling with selections from the Lotus Sutra, the idea of a "scripture" as well as problems of "skill in means," meditation, ritual, polemic, and myth are readily apparent; when reading the Genesis narratives, questions of tradition, faith, community, obedience to God, and many more must be faced; and when confronting the *Chuang-tze*, mysticism, quietism, and several other matters have to be discussed. In this way, one can cycle through a series of problems and concerns of *homo religiosus* while reading some of the great texts of history.

Along the way, by virtue of the necessity for some contexutalization and some background (through reading, lectures, and discussion meetings) for each text considered, students are further obliged to acquire at least a rudimentary acquaintance with and sensitivity to basic ideas and aspects of some of the major religious traditions of past and present. I make no attempt to sketch systematically the history, institutions, or ideas of whole traditions, but I do encourage students to develop through their required and recommended reading some fundamental knowledge of what Buddhists, Muslims, or others say their faith is, how they express and practice it, and what the bare outlines of the history of their tradition are.

(2) The course explores what I feel to be a deceptively obvious and "simple" phenomenon in the history of religion, namely "scripture", in order to show both how complex and how arbitrary and culture-bound any such category actually is. The topic, to be sure, need not have been scripture—myth, mysticism, conversion, and the like would also have done well (as have pilgrimage and ritual in our curriculum at Harvard). Still, scripture has some unique advantages, including the aforementioned opportunity to expose students to the highest-quality materials from the various traditions.

In particular, I consider it important in treating scripture to introduce students at the outset of their study of religion to problems of Western and modern category-formation and the related problems of reductionism, generalization, and cross-cultural comparison. In this regard, the addition of "classics" that many would not want to call "scriptures" to the title and to the reading list gives a kind of foil for the overtly liturgical or doctrinal texts that most would agree should be called "scripture." This allows us to address specifically our own vocabulary and conceptualization and our assumptions about what makes a text "religious." I try especially in the lectures to sensitize students to the necessity for self-consciousness about the biases their own experience, language, and faith give to any study of persons, groups, and texts that are religiously and culturally "other" than themselves, their communities, and their texts.

(3) Part of the excellence of scriptures and classics as subject matter for such a course is the range of fundamental issues of human life this topic offers the beginning student of religion. That texts such as those we read have spoken with such vigor and ever-renewed urgency to countless generations of religious persons and groups is testimony to their unstinting concern with issues timeless and generally meaningful or problematic, even though they do so in specific and culturally distinctive ways. Life, death, friendship, sex, worship, faith, morality, meaning, tradition, identity, and many more fundamental themes of human experience lie naturally to hand for each reader of the texts in such a course. This aspect of the subject matter is particularly important and helpful for a general audience of undergraduates who may be making the first

and/or only foray of their academic careers into religious studies. It gives them a fruitful basis for both discovery of how much they share in common with apparently "foreign" and even "strange" human beings in other times and places and also how singular every person's and every community's particular thought and way of life is. To see the strange as familiar is important; perhaps more important is to discern the striking contrasts in the ways in which widely diverse but equally intelligent, equally faithful, equally sincere, and equally flawed human beings have struggled to articulate and to remain true to their understanding of the highest-order truth, duty, and potential for human existence.

(4) The final major aim of the course is to encourage students to read, think, and write well. To this a great deal of attention and a significant proportion of teaching energies and time in the course are devoted. The emphasis on careful reading and thinking about the material is a primary element in the work of the sections. Having students write several short papers during the term is (if sufficient formal written and oral feedback is given with grades) a far superior way of improving reading, writing, and thinking abilities than is a single long term paper written during reading period and returned at the final examination with written comments alone. The requirement in the present version of the course that all students rewrite their first paper on the basis of the teachers' written comments has proven an especially important step toward the goal of improving students' writing.

Section Discussions. In 1987-88, I used the initial offering of the course to experiment with team-taught discussion sessions each week. Each member of the teaching staff was responsible for advising and grading the work of his or her own section (ca. 12-15 students), but each section and leader were paired with another section and leader, and each week both paired teachers worked together in two discussion sections rather than alone in one. To judge from the evaluations, this seems to have been successful; certainly in a course with such diversity of materials, it provided in general both moral and tangible support to teaching fellows in weeks in which the readings were far from their specialities. Further, because of complementary specializations between the two teachers in each pair, students had easy access to a wider range of resources than otherwise. In the end, only one of the five team efforts broke down at midterm, with the two sections meeting separately with their respective leaders thereafter. While I think that the "team" approach can be a success in this kind of comparative course, I am using a one-teacher, one-section format in 1989-90, apparently with good success.

To help ensure the quality of the reading, writing, and discussion experience, we hold weekly teaching staff meetings of one and one-half to two hours. In these mini-seminar staff sessions, we share ideas for the coming week's discussion meetings, go over grading problems and examination questions, and deal with other pedagogical and personal issues that arise in the separate sections. Furthermore, we discuss and put into final shape at each meeting a detailed handout containing the following week's assignments, several study questions for discussion preparation, and suggested further readings for those interested and those writing papers on the week's text. This kind of regular staff attention to the ongoing work of the course has been in my estimation a major factor in whatever success we have had with the course.

Lectures. In the 1987-88 lecture meetings, I tried consciously various approaches, since this was a first-time offering. This year, I have modified many aspects of the lectures. Those that are listed in the current syllabus below should be taken only as indicative of the kinds of topics broached. In general, I try to deal with specific problems of understanding and meaning in each text (or part of each text) that we read. I also address specifically many of the aforementioned problems, or "meta-issues" raised in the texts: life, death, friendship, sex, worship, faith, morality, meaning, tradition, identity, and the like.

Beyond these efforts, I try throughout to raise at selected junctures important general and theoretical questions for the study of religion. Some of the major ones that I try to touch upon are as follows:

Can we distinguish "scripture" from "classic" in any systematic way? (Similarly, can we distinguish "culture" (or "world view") from "religion"?)

What themes or other qualities distinguish or seem to recur in "scriptures" and "classics"? (What is both generic/human and specific/culture-bound in each text?)

Can we distinguish "primary scripture" from "secondary scripture" (e.g., Qur'an from Hadith, Torah from Mishnah? Is "canon" a useful or cross-culturally meaningful term?)

What are the self-images of particular scriptures? (And what definitions of "scripture" might be distilled from such self-images?)

Do literate traditions constitute the best [or worst?] medium for studying religion? (Is the "big tradition"/"little tradition" dichotomy tenable or helpful? Are oral and written cultures mutually exclusive? Do great texts give us adequate insight into key matters of a given tradition?)

What is the ongoing history and use of great religious texts in a community or communities? Do the functions of scriptural texts offer adequate means for identifying and categorizing texts as "scripture" or "classic"?

What is meant by widely used terms or concepts such as myth? ritual? mysticism? revelation/inspiration? "theology"? "ethics"? Heilsgeschichte? hagiography? eschatology?

How do we deal sensitively and empathetically yet critically and historically with traditions alien to us? or with our own? (With respect to alien scriptures, can we overcome the barriers of translation to any acceptable degree?)

With respect to lecture format, the most successful sessions are often those that are most interactive—i.e., those in which the class is challenged to think out loud about and raise either issues such as those above or the texts themselves. Also notably successful have been the lectures that focused on the text for the week with relative specificity, whether they took the form of an *explication du texte* or a discussion of issues, such as "mystical thought," "religion and culture," or "hagiography," suggested by the text.

In closing, I should mention that what does come through from one's students in such a course is above all the ceaseless fascination and appeal of the truly great texts of our common human heritage, above all those of profound religious dimensions. This is what makes such a course more than a mere survey of "world scriptures"; indeed, what makes it a pilgrimage along some of the great paths of the human spirit and a potentially engaging introduction for students to the study of human religiousness. Mark Twain's adage about a "classic,"—"Something everyone wants to have read and no one wants to read,"—is amusing and makes a point, but it belies the endless fascination exercised upon each new generation by "scriptures and classics" such as those treated in the course I have been describing.

William A. Graham

SELECT GENERAL BIBLIOGRAPHY

Bruce and Rupp
 1968   F. F. Bruce and E. G. Rupp, eds. *Holy Book and Holy Tradition.* Grand Rapids, Mich.: William B. Eerdmans.

Childs
 1979   Brevard S. Childs. *Introduction to the Old Testament as Scripture.* Philadelphia: Fortress Press.

 1984   *The New Testament as Canon: An Introduction.* Philadelphia: Fortress Press.

Coburn
 1984   Thomas B. Coburn. "'Scripture' in India: Towards a Typology of the Word in Hindu Life." *JAAR* 52: 435-59.

Curtius
 1953   Ernst Robert Curtius. *European Literature and the Latin Middle Ages.* (orig. Ger. ed. 1948; 2nd rev. ed. 1954) Eng. trans. by Willard R. Trask. Bollingen Series, no. 36. New York: Pantheon.

Denny and Taylor
 1985   Frederick M. Denny and Rodney L. Taylor, eds. *The Holy Book in Comparative Perspective.* Studies in Comparative Religion, ed. Frederick M. Denny. Columbia: University of South Carolina Press.

Graham
 1986   "Scripture." In Mircea Eliade et al., ed. *The Encyclopedia of Religion.* 16 vols. (New York: Macmillan) 13:133-45.

 1987   William A. Graham. *Beyond the Written Word: Oral Aspects of Scripture in the History of Religion.* Cambridge, New York, etc.: Cambridge University Press.

 1989   "Scripture as Spoken Word." In Miriam Levering, ed., *Rethinking Scripture: Essays from a Comparative Perspective.* Albany, N.Y.: SUNY Press. Pp. 129-69.

Lanczkowski
1956   Günter Lanczkowski. *Heilige Schriften. Inhalt,Text-gestalt und Überlieferung.* Stuttgart: W. Kohlhammer, Urban-Bücher.

Leipoldt and Morenz
1953   Johannes Leipoldt and Siegfried Morenz, *Heilige Schriften. Betrachtungen zur Religionsgeschichte der antiken Mittelmeerwelt.* Leipzig: Otto Harrossowitz.

Morenz
1950   Siegfried Morenz. "Entstehung und Wesen der Buchreligion." *Theologische Literaturzeitung* 75: 709-716.

O'Flaherty
1979   Wendy Doniger O'Flaherty, ed. *The Critical Study of Sacred Texts.* Berkeley: Graduate Theological Union, Berkeley Religious Studies Series.

Smith
1967   Wilfred Cantwell Smith. *Questions of Religious Truth.* New York: Charles Scribner's Sons.

1971   "The Study of Religion and the Study of the Bible." *JAAR* 39: 131-40.

1989   "Scripture as Form and Concept. Their Emergence for the Western World." In Miriam Levering, ed. *Rethinking Scripture: Essays from a Comparative Perspective.* Albany, N.Y.: SUNY Press. Pp. 29-57.

van der Leeuw
1963   G[erardus] van der Leeuw. *Religion in Essence and Manifestation.* (orig. Ger. ed. 1933). Eng. trans. J. E. Turner with Appendices . . . incorporating the additions of the 2nd Ger. ed. [1956] by Hans H. Penner. New York and Evanston: Harper and Row, Harper Torchbooks.

APPENDIX: SELECTED COURSE MATERIALS

Rel. 13   **Harvard University**   **Fall 1989-90**

COURSE SCHEDULE

M 18 Sep.   Introduction: "Scriptures" and "Classics"
W 20 Sep.   Religion, Religious Texts, and History
F 22 Sep.   Myth and History

M 25 Sep.   *Gilgamesh:* Defining the Human
W 27 Sep.   Section discussion: *Gilgamesh*
F 29 Sep.   *Gilgamesh:* Questions and Reflections

M 02 Oct.   Veda, Upanishads, and Gita: An Overview
W 04 Oct.   Section discussion: The Upanishads
F 06 Oct.   The Upanishads: Questions and Reflections

M 09 Oct.   HOLIDAY
W 11 Oct.   Section discussion: The Bhagavad Gita
F 13 Oct.   The Bhagavad Gita: Questions and Reflections

M 16 Oct.   The Buddhist Vision and Buddhist "Scriptures"
W 18 Oct.   Section discussion: Selections from Buddhist Scriptures
F 20 Oct.   Buddhist Scriptures: Questions and Reflections

M 23 Oct.   Pilgrim and Poet: Basho as Japanese (and Buddhist?) "Classic"
W 25 Oct.   Section discussion: Basho, *Back Roads to Far Towns*
F 27 Oct.   *Back Roads to Far Towns:* Questions and Reflections

M 30 Oct.   Religion and Culture, Scripture and Classic: The Case of the *Analects*
W 01 Nov.   Section discussion: *The Analects*
F 03 Nov.   *The Analects:* Questions and Reflections

M 06 Nov.   The *Chuang Tzu:* Renunciation or Mysticism?
W 08 Nov.   Section discussion: *Chuang Tzu*
F 10 Nov.   *Chuang Tzu:* Questions and Reflections

M 13 Nov.   The *Aeneid* as "Western" Classic
W 15 Nov.   Section discussion: The *Aeneid*
F 17 Nov.   The *Aeneid:* Questions and Reflections

M 20 Nov.   Exodus and Torah: Questions of Religious and Cultural Paradigms
W 22 Nov.   Section discussion: Selections from the Torah

F 24 Nov.   THANKSGIVING HOLIDAY

M 27 Nov.   Abraham in Three Traditions: Considering Western Monotheism
W 29 Nov.   Section discussion: Selections from the Torah
F 01 Dec.   Torah: Questions and Reflections

M 04 Dec.   The New Testament: Recasting Scriptural Authority
W 06 Dec.   Section discussion: Selections from the New Testament
F 08 Dec.   The New Testament: Questions and Reflections

M 11 Dec.   The Qur'an: The Culmination of Western Scriptural Consciousness
W 13 Dec.   Section discussion: Selections from the Qur'an
F 15 Dec.   The Qur'an: Questions and Reflections

M 18 Dec.   Conclusion: Scriptures, Classics and Religious Life

COURSE REQUIREMENTS

The basic work of the course is done in and for section meetings. These discussion meetings provide the central opportunity for exploration of the texts read in the course. Section and lecture preparation sheets with required and recommended readings for each week will be distributed. Section participation (including completion of brief assignments) is *mandatory* for successful completion of the course.

Three short essays are due during the term, each one to be submitted to your section leader *at the beginning of the section meeting on that particular topic.*

There is no mid-term, but there is a final examination. A portion of the final examination will address the Reading Period assignment. This assignment is *Black Elk Speaks*, a text drawn from the Native American tradition of the Oglala Sioux, which is essentially without written texts. Because it is essentially a text that records the oral narratives of Black Elk, it presents a sharp contrast to the other texts to be studied during the term. A study sheet for *Black Elk Speaks* will be provided for the final exam.

For purposes of grading, the different elements of the work of the course will be valued roughly as follows:

> Class Participation 25%
> Essays (#1, #2, #3 combined) 50%
> Final Examination 25%

BOOKS RECOMMENDED FOR PURCHASE

Basho. *Back Roads to Far Towns.* Trans. S. Corman and S. Kamaike. Mushinsha/ Grossman, 1968; repr. White Pine, 1986.

The Bhagavad-Gita. Trans. B. S. Miller. New York: Bantam, 1986.

[Black Elk]. *Black Elk Speaks*. Trans. J. G. Niehardt. Washington Square, 1959.

Buddhist Scriptures. Trans. Edward Conze. Middlesex: Penguin, 1959.

Chuang Tzu: Basic Writings. Trans. Burton Watson. New York: Columbia University, 1964.

[K'ung fu-tzu]. *The Analects of Confucius*. Trans. Arthur Waley. Middlesex: Penguin, 1979.

The Epic of Gilgamesh. Trans. N. K. Sandars. Middlesex: Penguin, 1960.

Readings in the Qur'an. Trans. Kenneth Cragg. New York: Mentor, 1938.

[Upanishads]. Selections from The Upanishads (photocopy). Trans. F. Max Müller, in *The Sacred Books of the East* (Oxford: Clarendon Press, 1884), vols. 1, 15.

[Virgil]. *The Aeneid of Virgil*. Trans. Allen Mandelbaum. New York: Bantam, 1961.

Also Recommended

Smart, Ninian, *The Religious Experience of Mankind*. Third edition. Scribner's, 1984. An historical survey of major and minor traditions of world religion. Very useful as an introduction or quick reference source for particular traditions.

Smith, Huston, *The Religions of Man*. New York: Harper & Row, 1958. Repr. Perennial. Offers very general and highly interpretive introductions to the major world religious traditions. We suggest it for purchase by those with no previous background who want lively, readable, and sensitive, but less historical, introductions to most of the traditions whose texts we shall read.

Zaehner, R. C. *The Concise Encyclopedia of Living Faiths*. London: Hutchinson, 1959. Repr. Macmillan (PB). This is a more historically, as opposed to philosophically, oriented survey of the major world religious traditions only (no smaller or former traditions are treated).

WEEKLY ASSIGNED READINGS

Introductory Week: Background Readings

Required Background:
William A. Graham, "Scripture," in Mircea Eliade, et. al., eds. *Encyclopedia of Religion* 13:133-45.

Recommended:
Wilfred Cantwell Smith, "The Study of Religion and the Study of the Bible" and "Scripture as Form and Concept: Their Emergence for the Western World," in Miriam Levering, ed. *Rethinking Scripture*, pp. 18-57.

Readings for Section 1: Gilgamesh

Primary Source (and primary focus of discussion):

N. K. Sandars, trans., *The Epic of Gilgamesh*, pp. 7-48, 61-119.

Required Background:
Thorkild Jacobsen, "Mesopotamian Religion: An Overview," in *Encyclopedia of Religion* 9: 447-66.

Recommended:
Thorkild Jacobsen, *The Treasures of Darkness: A History of Mesopotamian Religion*, esp. chs. 5-7; B. Thorbjørnsrud, "What Can the Gilgamesh Myth Tell us about Religion...in Mesopotamia," *Temenos* 19 (1983): 112-37; Alexander Heidel, *The Gilgamesh Epic and Old Testament Parallels*; Samuel N. Kramer, "The Epic of Gilgamesh and its Sumerian Sources," *Journal of the Amer. Oriental Society*, 64 (1944): 7-23; T. F. Gaster, "Semitic Folklore," in the *Standard Dictionary of Folklore, Mythology and Legend*, *s.v.*; For those interested in comparing a different scholarly translation (by E. A. Speiser): James B. Pritchard, ed., *Ancient Near Eastern Texts Relating to the Old Testament*, pp. 72-97.

Readings for Section 2: The Upanishads

Primary Source:
Selections from the Upanishads in F. Max Müller, trans., *The Sacred Books of the East*, vol. 1, pp. 92-109 (Chandogya Upanishad, part VI: 1-16) and vol. 15, pp. 1-24 (Katha Upanishad, entire), pp. 73-77, 85-91, 113-17, 130-36, 173-85, and 204-9 (Brhadaranyaka Upanishad, parts I: 1-2 and 4, II: 5, III: 6-8, IV: 4-5, and VI: 2 respectively).

Required Background: Thomas J. Hopkins, *The Hindu Religious Tradition*, chs.1 and 2.

Recommended:
R.E. Hume, *The Thirteen Principal Upanishads*, 2nd ed., introduction, pp. 1-72; S. Radhakrishnan, *The Principal Upanishads*, introduction, pp. 17-44; Paul Deussen, *The Philosophy of the Upanishads*, 2nd ed., trans. A. S. Geden; J. S. Helfer, "The Initiatory Structure of the Kathopanishad," in *History of Religions* 7 (1968): 343-67; F. H. Holck, "Death Themes in Plato and the Upanishads," in *Journal of Religious Studies* 8 (1980); Walter Kaebler, "The Brahmacarin: Homology and Continuity in Brahmanic Religion," in *History of Religions* 21/1 (1981); and S. P. Singh, *Upanishadic Symbolism*.

Readings for Section 3: The Bhagavad Gîtâ

Primary Source:
Barbara Stoller Miller, trans., *The Bhagavad-Gita*, p. 19-154.

Required Background:
Thomas J. Hopkins, *The Hindu Tradition*, chs. 4, 5.
Franklin G. Edgerton, trans., *The Bhagavad Gîtâ*, pp. 103-135 [from translator's essay].

Recommended:
On Hindu Scripture: J. A. B. van Buitenen, "Hindu Sacred Literature," in *Encyclopaedia Britannica* III, s.v. Robert C. Lester, "Hinduism, Veda and Sacred Texts," in F. M.

Denny and R. L. Taylor, eds., *The Holy Book in Comparative Perspective*, pp. 126-47. Thomas B. Coburn, "Scripture in India: Towards a Typology of the Word in Hindu Life", *Journal of the American Academy of Religion* 52 (1984): 435-59.

On the Hindu Tradition: R. C. Zaehner, *Hinduism*, pp. 80-146. For more specifically on the Gîtâ: J. A. B. van Buitenen, trans., *The Bhagavad Gîtâ in the Mahâbharata*, pp. 1-29. (For those who wish to consult another translation of the Gîtâ, the translations of Edgerton and van Buitenen (see above), as well as the translation of R. C. Zaehner (above), are recommended.

Readings for Section 4: *Buddhist Scriptures*

Primary Sources:

Edward Conze, trans., *Buddhist Scriptures*, pp. 34-66 (part 1, ch. 2), 145-68 and 181-217 (part 2, chs. 3, 4, and 5).

Required Background:

Walpola Rahula, *What the Buddha Taught*, pp.1-66.

Luis O. Gomez, "Buddhism in India," in Mircea Eliade, et. al., eds., *Encyclopedia of Religion* 2: 351-72 and (skim) 372-82.

Recommended:

R. C. Zaehner, *The Concise Encyclopedia of Living Faiths*, pp. 267-347; Takeuchi Yashinori and John P. Keenan, "Buddhist Philosophy," in *Encyclopedia of Religion* 2: 540-47; Lewis R. Lancaster, "Buddhist Literature: Canonization," in *Encyclopedia of Religion* 2: 504-9; Hirakawa Aira, "Buddhist Literature: A Survey of Texts" in *Encyclopedia of Religion*, vol. 2, pp.509-529; Edward J. Thomas, *The Life of the Buddha as Legend and History*, passim; Hans Wolfgang Schumann, *Buddhism: An Outline of its Teachings and Schools*, pp. 17-83; Edward Conze, *Buddhism: Its Essence and Development*, pp. 27-118.

Readings for Section 5: Matsuo Bashô

Primary Source:

Matsuo Bashô, *Back Roads to Far Towns*, trans. Cid Corman and Kamaike Susumu (Freedonia: White Pine Press, 1986).

Required Background:

Robert S. Ellwood and Richard Pilgrim, *Japanese Religion* (Englewood Cliffs, N.J.: Prentice Hall, 1985), pp. 83-108.

Richard B. Pilgrim, "The Religion-Aesthetic of Matsuo Bashô," *The Eastern Buddhist*, n.s., 10 (1977): 35-53.

Recommended:

(General background on Zen and haiku): Daisetz T. Suzuki, *Zen and Japanese Culture*, Bollingen Series, 64, ch. 1 ("What is Zen?") and ch. 7 ("Zen and Haiku").

(On Bashô): William LaFleur, *The Karma of Words* (Berkeley: Univ. of California Press, 1986), ch. 8 ("The Poet as Seer: Bashô Looks Back"), pp. 149-64. James H. Foard, "The Loneliness of Matsuo Bashô," in Frank E. Reynolds and Donald Capps, eds., *The Biographical Process*, pp. 363-91. Charles E. Hambrick-Stowe, "Two Pilgrims: Bunyan and Bashô," in *The Japan Christian Quarterly* 51 (1985): 161-70. The best monographic study is Makoto Ueda, *Matsuo Bashô*.

Readings for Section 6: The Confucian Analects

Primary Source:

D. C. Lau, trans., *The Analects of Confucius*, pp. 59-160.

Required Background:

Frederick Mote, *Intellectual Foundations of China*, pp. 3-52.
Herbert Fingarette, *Confucius—The Secular as Sacred*, pp. 1-17.

Recommended:

(On Confucian Philosophy): Benjamin I. Schwartz, *The World of Thought in Ancient China*, pp. 56-134; Donald J. Munro, *The Concept of Man in Early China*, pp. 49-83.

(Topical essays): Tu Wei-Ming, *Confucian Thought: Selfhood as Creative Transformation*, and *Humanity and Self-Cultivation: Essays in Confucian Thought*.

Readings for Section 7: Chuang Tzu

Primary Source:

Burton Watson, trans., *Chuang Tzu, Basic Writings*, pp. 1-140.

Required Background:

A. C. Graham, trans., *Chuang Tzu: The Inner Chapters*, pp. 3-33.

Recommended:

(On Taoism and Chuang Tzu): Max Kaltenmark, *Lao Tzu and Taoism,* trans. Roger Greaves, pp. 70-106; Benjamin I. Schwartz, *The World of Thought in Ancient China*, pp. 186-254; Victor H. Mair, ed., *Experimental Essays on Chuang Tzu,*.

(On Lao Tzu): Kaltenmark, pp. 5-69. D. C. Lau, trans., *Lao Tzu—Tao Te Ching*; Holmes Welch, *Taoism: The Parting of the Way*, pp. 18-87.

Readings for Section 8: Virgil's Aeneid

Primary Source:

Allen Mandelbaum, trans., *Virgil's Aeneid*, books I-VI (Skim books III and V).

Required Background:

R. D. Williams, "The Aeneid," in *Cambridge History of Classical Literature*, vol. 2, Latin Literature, pp. 333-69 (Ref. Room: PA 60003. L3);

R. D. Williams, "The Aeneid," in T.S. Pattie and R.D. Williams, eds., *Virgil: His Poetry through the Ages*, pp. 24-56.

Recommended:

(General): Wendell Clausen, "An Interpretation of the Aeneid," in *Virgil: A Collection of Critical Essays*, ed. Steele Commager, pp. 75-88; W. A. Camps, *An Introduction to Virgil's Aeneid.*

(On Characters and Theme): Barbara J. Bono, "Virgil's Dido and Aeneas," in her *Literary Transvaluation: From Vergilian Epic to Shakespearean Tragicomedy*, pp. 7-40; C. H. Wilson, "Jupiter and the Fates in the Aeneid, " *Classical Quarterly*, n.s. 29 (1979), pp. 361-71; Robert Coleman, "The Gods in the Aeneid," *Greece and Rome* 29 (1982), pp. 143-68; C. M. Bowra, "Virgil and the Ideal of Rome," in his *From Virgil to Milton*, pp. 33-85.

(On Virgil's Influence): Meyer Reinhold, "Vergil in the American Experience from Colonial Times to 1882," in John D. Bernard, ed.,*Vergil at 2000*, pp. 185-205; T. S. Pattie, "The Popular Traditions," and "Virgil's Imitators," in *Virgil: His Poetry Through the Ages*, pp. 84-108; Marjorie Donker, "The Waste of Land and the Aeneid," *PMLA* 89 (1974): 164-73.

(On the Nature of the Text): J. W. Jones, "The Allegorical Traditions of the Aeneid," *Vergil at 2000*, pp. 107-132; T. S. Eliot, *What is a Classic?*; C. M. Bowra, "Some Characteristics of the Literary Epic," in his *From Virgil to Milton*, p. 1-32.

Readings for Section 9: Torah I

Primary Source:

Exodus 1-15 and Deuteronomy 26: 5-10 (Subject: The Exodus). Skim as background to the Exodus: Genesis 37-50 (Joseph and the coming of the Israelites to Egypt).

Required Background:

Yehezkel Kauffman, "The Genesis of Israel," in *Great Ages and Ideas of the Jewish People*, pp. 3-29.

Recommended:

(General): Howard Greenstein, *Judaism—An Eternal Covenant*, pp. 16-35.

(Exemplary Figures): L. Ginzberg, *The Legends of the Jews* (JPS 1910) vol. 1, ch. V "Abraham," pp. 183-308; Ibid., vol. 3, "Moses in the Wilderness," pp. 80-118; "Abraham," in *Encyclopedia Judaica*, vol. 2, pp. 111-24; "Moses," Ibid., vol. 12, pp. 371-410.

(On the Nature of Biblical Religion): L. Strauss, "Jerusalem and Athens," *The City College Papers*, pp. 3-21; Y. Kauffman, *History of the Religion of Israel*, pp. 1-245.

Commentary: U. Cassuto, *A Commentary on the Book of Genesis*; and *A Commentary on the Book of Exodus.*

Readings for Section 10: Torah II

Primary Source:

Exodus 19-24, and selections from the Midrash on portions of this to be handed out in class (Subject: the Covenant at Sinai); [for lecture on Friday, 1 Dec.:] Genesis 12-22, the Abraham epic.

Required Background:

E. E. Urbach, "Torah," *Encyclopedia of Religion* 14: 556-65;

Judah Goldin, "Midrash and Aggadah," *idem*. 9: 509-515

Readings for Section 11: New Testament

Primary Source:

The Christian Bible: Matthew; Romans 1-4, 9-11; Galatians; Hebrews.

Required Background:

Krister Stendahl, *Paul among Jews and Gentiles and Other Essays*, pp. 1-23.

Jaroslav Pelikan, "Praeparatio Evangelica," *The Christian Tradition*, vol. I: *The Emergence of the Catholic Tradition*, pp. 11-27.

Recommended:

(Historical Background:) Norman Perrin and Dennis C. Duling, *The New Testament: An Introduction*. 2nd ed., pp. 3-37.

(Jesus and His Gospel:) Pheme Perkins, *Reading the New Testament* (New York: Paulist Press, 1978), pp. 65-108.

(The Synoptic Gospels:) Helmut Koester, *Introduction to the New Testament*, vol. 2: *History and Literature of Early Christianity* (Philadelphia: Fortress, 1982), pp. 44-49, 59-64.

(Paul and His Letters:) Pheme Perkins, ibid., pp. 129-67.

(History of Interpretation:) Robert M. Grant, with David Tracy, *A Short History of the Interpretation of the Bible*, pp. 3-187.

(Canon:) R. M. Grant, "The NT Canon," *The Cambridge History of the Bible*, ed. P. R. Ackroyd and C. F. Evans, pp. 284-308.

(Diversity in Early Christianity:) James D. G. Dunn, *Unity and Diversity in the New Testament*, pp. 1-7, 369-88.

(Exegetical Method:) Leonhard Goppelt, *Typos*, trans. D. H. Madvig, pp. 127-52, 161-78.

Readings for Section 12: The Qur'an

Primary Source:

Kenneth Cragg, trans. and ed., *Readings in the Qur'ân*, "God and His Praise," pp. 89-92; "God n Creation: Man and Nature," pp. 93, middle of 94-bottom of 107; "Prophets and Messengers," pp. 113-14 top, 117 mid-122 top; , 128 mid -137(end of S.12), 139 bot-142 top, 145 bot-149 top, 150 bot-153 top, 166 mid-170 top; "The Prophet Preacher and Meccan Years," pp. 177-80 top; "Society and Law," pp. 296-97; "Unfaith, Judgement and Last Things," pp. 349 mid-350.

Required Background:

Fazlur Rahman, *Islam* , pp. 25-42.

W. C. Smith, "Is the Qur'an the Word of God?" in W. Oxtoby, ed., [W. C. Smith,] *Religious Diversity*, pp. 22-40.

Recommended:

H. A. R. Gibb, *Mohammedanism* (see chapter on Qur'ân) and "al-Kur'an," in *Shorter Encyclopedia of Islam*, pp. 273-86. Michael Cook, *Muhammad*, esp. pp. 67-72 (on Muhammad and the Qur'an); W. Montgomery Watt, ed., *Bell's Introduction to the Qur'an*; W. Montgomery Watt, *Muhammad, Prophet and Statesman*; Tor Andrae, *Mohammed: The Man and His Faith*, rev. ed. trans. T. Menzil; Patricia Crone, *Meccan Trade and the Rise of Islam*, (See introduction and ch. 10).

❧XIV❧

Religious Studies 202: Words, Truth, and Power

MIRIAM LEVERING

I. Introduction

This is a course that focuses on the roles of words and texts in religious life. It approaches that topic globally, conveying in its form the message that human religious life, being human, is both profoundly diverse and at the same time a single ongoing spectrum of possible experience. It assumes that on this topic comparison is possible and fruitful—that, for example, the study of certain notions of mantra in South Asia will illumine certain notions of prayer in the Jewish tradition, both through similarities and differences. It uses the schematic proposal of Walter Ong that there is in the history of cultures a pattern shaped by the evolution of technologies of the word to focus the comparisons within loosely comparable cultural types and historical moments.

This course is one that different teachers could take in a variety of directions, drawing on their own strengths while still truly introducing the comparative study of religious life. The topic also seems to be ideally suited to a team-taught approach. Beyond this, the course could be taught as a religious studies offering in a broader liberal arts "core" or "general ed" program as part of an interdisciplinary approach to the questions revolving around the uses and limits of hearing/reading, speaking/writing, language and text. I believe that this topic within the comparative study of religion can be well used to demonstrate to students and colleagues in the liberal arts what religious studies and the comparative study of religion is about. At the same time, the topic allows

Religious Studies students and faculty to build bridges with other liberal arts departments.

I would like at the outset, however, to make a disclaimer. This is a course about the connections religious traditions have perceived or denied between words and truth and words and power. It is not based on the assumption that the best way to introduce students to religious traditions is to ask them to read the "religious classics" or "scriptures" of those traditions. It does not assume that texts are the greatest expressions of those traditions or that reading texts is the best way to find out "what people believe." A course on this topic clearly risks reinforcing these notions. Both the course design and the instructor's guidance should steer the course away from such shoals.

a. The topic

There are four aspects of this topic that deserve attention:

(1) How people experience truth mediated through words, and the power of words to form and transform them, relates directly to their theologies/cosmologies, and to their psychologies/epistemologies.

(2) Further, these experiences are also related to the institutions and dynamics of authority and power in a society. Priests, sacred kings, prophets, all understand differently the relations of words to ultimate truth and to legitimate power. Foucault has brought to our attention the ways in which discourse establishes relationships of power. Feminists and other persons aware of the effects on consciousness of domination and subordination have called attention to the fact that words that seem "natural" and "religiously appropriate" to the dominant group may do so in part because they reinforce the structures of domination, and may in fact close off avenues to the experience of ultimate truth and sacred empowerment to the subordinate group—or perhaps to both groups.

(3) Also, how people experience truth and power in words relates to how they seek to include words in their relationship with the sacred, in their religious projects (reading "religiously," prayer, chanting, etc.). When people come to words with the expectation of encountering the Ultimate, they find more in and through them than the outsider with no such expectations could possibly have predicted.

(4) In addition, how people experience truth and power in words relates to the technologies used in communicating, preserving, and transmitting words within the culture. (More on this below.)

In designing this course, I have hoped to make it possible for the student to attend to some extent to all of these aspects.

b. Secular and sacred texts

One reason this topic is particularly well suited to bridge-building between religious studies and other fields in the liberal arts is that the topic of the relations between words and truth and words and power allows us to cross the boundary between the "religious" and "secular" uses and understandings of language and text in the West. The ways in which that boundary has been drawn and re-drawn in the West is the result of a particular history. It certainly has not been drawn in the same way in other cultures. Exploring the heuristic usefulness both of ignoring it, of seeing interrelations across it, and of raising once again the question, what is the nature of that boundary and where does it really lie—in other cultures and in our own—could prove fruitful for religious studies and for the liberal arts. For example, in this version of the course I explore what it means to have a distinction in our culture between "scripture" and "classic," by pursuing comparison with the Chinese case.

Although the topic of "scripture" and "sacred text" is only one of the topics of the course, it is an important one. One of the aims of the course is to make it possible to explore new approaches to the subject that can enable even the introductory student to move well beyond the fixed ideas about scriptures with which students often come to the comparative study of religion.

c. The topic of post-modernism

I have mentioned above that I believe this course would contribute well to a "core" or "general education" curriculum in the liberal arts that raises questions and offers approaches to understanding language and "textuality." Readers of this essay are certainly far from unaware of the various post-modern movements in literary criticism, philosophy, and the "human sciences" that tackle directly the question of the relation of words to truth and power.

In general, the intellectual movements of the post-modern era, particularly that of Derrida, are highly challenging to certain religious world views (though not of course to others—Zen, for example). To raise these issues in an introductory course at a comprehensive state university like the University of Tennessee in the form in which they are raised by post-modern intellectuals would of course be folly. Yet I believe that similar kinds of questions can be raised by looking at the range of views on the connections between words and truth and words and power within historical religious traditions.

d. How the course uses Ong's typological framework

In the syllabus below, I have followed departmental guidelines that encourage instructors of introductory courses to select one tradition from each of three cultures—India, China, and the Mediterranean world—and from small-scale traditions. From the Mediterranean area I have chosen the Jewish tradition. From India I have chosen to emphasize both Hindu ideas about the ultimate power of sound and word, and the shape and nature of the sacred texts of the Indian Buddhist tradition. From China I have introduced the Confucian classics and the Taoist suspicion of any referential theory of words and concepts.

As mentioned above, I have chosen to adopt as a framework of organization Walter J. Ong's proposal that changes in the technologies of words lead to radically different psychological, religious, and cultural possibilities. I do not intend to subscribe to the whole of Ong's view of history and consciousness (to me it seems that his overly simple typology results in ideas that have at once too much and too little explanatory power).

It may be useful to offer a few explanations here of how I see the relation between the "Ongian typology" and the materials I have selected from the Hindu, Buddhist, Jewish, and Chinese "small-scale" traditions.

1. The word in oral cultures

> In the beginning was God,
>> Today is God
>> Tomorrow will be God.
> Who can make an image of God?
>> He has no body.
>> He is as a word
>>> which comes out of your mouth
> That word!
>> It is no more,
>> It is past, and still it lives!
> So is God.
>>> [traditional pygmy song]

The "Ongian argument" (shorthand for a line of thought put forward by Eric Havelock, Jack Goody, Marshall MacLuhan and others, and developed further by Walter Ong) says that in a primarily oral culture, words are an event, powerful, transforming, creative of relationship between the speaker/reciter and the hearer, and deeply formative of the persons who memorize them in order to preserve them. By contrast, in a culture like our own, words are often not events but artifacts, objects of our distanced evaluation. In an oral culture the word only exists in the moment of its being spoken and recited; thus it can not be treated as an object in the same way that it can when written. It is spoken and recited in the presence of hearers—thus its meaning is alive ("present"), because it is an event of speaking and hearing between persons, not an item to be stored and read without the writer present. Thus it is, in Ong's words, more "alive" than the written word, which is dead, and has to be resurrected by the reader. Likewise, it is natural that the word should be associated with power in oral cultures, since it takes energy, power, to speak it, and it is always combined with sound energy.

In another sense it is more alive as well: although effort is often made to pass on the valued words of the tradition intact, using various kinds of formula to make exact or approximate transmission possible, nonetheless one can always alter them, often unconsciously, to respond to the needs of the present. Thus a gap between past meanings and present needs does not arise.

The lack of a written form of transmission shapes the rhetorical style of orally preserved traditions. Building on the work of Havelock, Lord, and others, Ong points out the following characteristics:

(1) thinking in lists and formulas which make for easy memorization. As Ong says in Chapter 3 of *Orality and Literacy*: "In an oral culture, sustained thought is tied to communication. But even with a listener to stimulate and ground your thought, the bits and pieces of your thought cannot be preserved in jotted notes. How could you ever call back to mind what you had so laboriously worked out? The only answer is: think memorable thoughts. In a primarily oral culture, you have to do your thinking in memnonic patterns, shaped for ready oral recurrance." (Ong, p. 34)

(2) Clustering. To add vividness an oral culture groups objects together with certain clauses, epithets, etc.: e.g., "the beautiful princess," "the brave soldier."

(3) Redundancy. To keep speaker and hearer abreast of the flow of the discourse the speaker moves forward slowly, with much repetition of what has already been said.

(4) Conservativism. What has been learned in the past must be repeated over and over again to remain readily recallable. Primary attention is thus not focused on intellectual experimentation, but on keeping what has been learned alive. Knowledge is still fluid, however, in that

old themes and exressions can be reorganized in response to new knowledge, which then becomes "traditionalized."

(5) Embeddedness in (present) situation, and in community. Oral cultures, where the word is experienced as an event the center of which is
the human community, see the cosmos as "an ongoing event with man at
its center."

In oral cultures, only words that are memorized can be transmitted;
thus there must be a continual effort of repetition to keep things important to the tradition in memory. Words in chirographic cultures can be
stored in archives, analyzed, combined in new combinations. Thus writing makes possible a kind of freedom in relation to the word, freedom to
treat it as an object. Writing makes possible new different activities of
thought, dependent on objectifying and distancing, impossible in oral
culture.

On the other hand, the writer and reader in chirographic (writing)
cultures lose the intimate presence of the memorized, recited, or orated
word; as they become isolated readers, pursuing meaning in the silence
and solitude of a library, they lose the sense of participation in a living
community created by the oral word as event. (Cf. Ong, "Maranatha...")
A consequence (though Ong seems to say self-contradictory things here)
is that greater religions are created (the "world religions," according to
Ong, take form because they have the power of the technology of writing—they can create and interpret scriptures), yet the power and immediacy of the living word, the union between the knower and the known,
is not easily retained in the chirographic religions; these religions are
challenged to find ways to allow the dead letter of the written words of
the tradition to become again the living, and (necessarily, to Ong) spoken
word.

In this course we look at the attitudes toward words and truth and
words and power in a few instances in small-scale societies. Then we
look at the Hindu tradition, where sound, particularly the sound of
words, is, in one interpretation, the powerful creative energy of the universe itself. This understanding and practice may be the most radical
identification of words with sacred truth and sacred power that we can
find in the history of religions. We look as well at the Buddhist understandings of mantra, and at the Vedas, which until recently were transmitted entirely orally.

Beyond this, the Buddhist scriptures give us an excellent window
through which to see the characteristics of orally transmitted traditions.
The now-written-down Buddhist sutras are still marked today by many

formal and rhetorical features attributable to their having been transmitted orally for centuries after the Buddha's death. One finds in them many formulas and numerical categories (the four noble truths, the eightfold path, etc.) that are "memorable thoughts." One finds most of the other characteristics of oral traditions mentioned above: clustering, redundancy, embeddedness in the moment and in community, and conservatism.

2. Sacred word in chirographic cultures

The power of memory, and even more so the use of writing, make possible in many cultures a process of "crystalization" of the sacred traditions into "scriptures," "classics," and "canons," a process which brings about new relationships with true and powerful words, and new ways of making those words a part of one's relations with the sacred.

Chirographic cultures is Ong's term for cultures that possess the technology of writing, but not the technology of printing. In such cultures, of course, reading and writing are the practices of an elite group; most people still live in a largely oral culture. The adoption of the technology of writing seems to some (e.g., Plato) to bring losses as well as gains (cf. current fears about the computer). Will it result in loss of the word as a possession of memory? Or will it result in the treatment of word as simply an object, rather than as living voice, as personal address? Does the fixing of tradition stifle creativity, or merely rechannel it into new forms? Will it result in loss of the living intimate contact with (and control of) the words of the memorized traditions, loss of the mental powers of persuasive speech and spoken argument and discussion?

Yet the opportunity to write down the treasured words of the tradition, if only as an aide-memoire, is usually seized (not always: cf. case of the Hindu Vedas). With this comes, of course, written "scriptures" and "classics." With the fixing in writing of scriptures and classics comes the need for hermeneutics, as well perhaps as a second complementary scriptural process: e.g., the oral Torah to keep the written Torah a process rather than an anachronism. Also, the question arises of the shape and boundaries of the written form. The shapes that emerge (genres, canons) will be related to the needs of the community and its institutions—the shape of its religious practice and of its systems of transmission. In some cases, what will occur is some kind of canonization: a monastic curriculum; a lectionary; a canon as "the book of the church," to provide a unity in common worship or practice; a canon as a standard[1] as well as a principle for excluding heretics and heresy; a canon as a way of providing and fixing yet another theological reflection on the traditional materials.[2] Where the narrative or doctrinal record is understood to be the primary and most authoritative bearer of the tradition (in contrast, for example, with meditation or monastic rule), "scripture," "classic," and "canon" will take on special meanings and significances.[3]

Reading, writing, "study," can all now acquire importance in the religious life; the acts themselves, and the artifacts produced by writing, can acquire symbolic sacred meanings.

At the same time, the question of whether or not, or to what degree and in what sense words can convey sacred truth, and were meant by their (divine or ultimately sanctioned) speaker/author to convey sacred truth, arises in the age of rising chirographic civilizations. Just as the "scripture" and the "classic" are taking on power and authority, a new scepticism of the word, and of reliance on scriptural authority, arises:

a. Recognition of the arbitrariness of the language creation process arises (cf. the Chinese Taoist Chuang-tzu); of its self-contradictoriness. (cf. the philosophy of the Buddhist Nagarjuna)

b. Recognition of the possibility that Truth is beyond the power of words, of Names, to capture. (Nagarjuna, Chuang-tzu)

c. Recognition that pious but slavish or compulsive (grasping) adherence to tradition-sanctioned words, names, images, can limit vision or provide an escape from truth. (Zen Buddhism)

The course looks at these developments as they appear in the history of several different bodies of scripture. The effects of originally oral development and transmission are also evident in the Jewish scriptures, as are the effects of the value eventually placed within a chirographic culture on having a fixed written form. It appears from existing texts as though the sacred traditions of the Jewish people went through three

[1] More common in the Greco-Roman world than elsewhere: Cf. David L. Dungan, "The Cultural Background of the Use of the Term 'Canon' in Early Christianity," in *Aufstieg und Niedergang der romischen Welt*, Bd. II Heft 26, ed., W. Haase und H. Temporini (Verlag: Walter de Gruyter, 1991).

[2] Cf. James A. Sanders, *Torah and Canon* (Philadelphia: Fortress Press, 1972).

[3] Cf. Kendall W. Folkert, "The 'Canons' of Scripture," in Miriam Levering, ed., On the subject of canon, see also Jonathan Z. Smith, "Sacred Persistence: Toward a Redescription of Canon," in idem., *Imagining Religion: From Babylon to Jonestown* (Chicago and London: University of Chicago Press, 1982), 36-52; and Martin S. Jaffee, "Oral Torah in Theory and Practice: Aspects of Mishnah Exegesis in the Palestinian Talmud," *Religion*, no. 15 (Oct. 1985): 387-410.

stages of transmission. (1) First, they were passed down orally; (2) then they were written down but continued to be primarily oral; they were not fixed (what was written influenced what was told orally, and vice versa); (3) finally, as is evident with the Qumran texts for the first time (cf. Theodore H. Gaster, *The Dead Sea Scriptures*, the Pescherim), they were fixed in their written form such that any additions or reinterpretations could not be made by amending the text, but had to be made in commentary. Over time we see a similar shift in the means of preserving and transmitting prophetic oracles: first they were given and remembered orally (cf. Isaiah 4-5 for examples of oral structuring); then they were dictated (cf. Jeremiah); finally, under conditions of the exile in which the communities addressed were not in one place, they seem to have been partially in written form from the beginning (cf. Ezekiel).

Before the fixing of a written form, the question of how the revelation and the story of God's actions of earlier times was relevant to the current community could be addressed as one retold the story. With the fixing of a written form, that question becomes problematic, giving rise to wonderful reflections on the truth and power of revealed words to changed communities over time (e.g., God's message to Habbakuk in his own time was not the message to us; God intended those same words to give us in our time a different message).

As the role of the written Torah (Hebrew Bible) in Jewish life illustrates, in a chirographic culture a book is accorded great value. In a culture with writing but without widespread use of printing, where texts must be copied by hand to be reproduced, a book is a rare treasure, and even the privileged are likely to own only a few. If the only book in a family is the Bible, how special will the relationship be with the words of that book.

The course also raises the less explored question of what changes came about in the Buddhist tradition as the transmission and even composition of scriptures came to be primarily in written rather than oral form.

3. Can words symbolize or express "sacred" truth and power in print and electronic cultures?

Print cultures and electronic cultures bring further transformations of our relations to truth and power in words. As Ong has pointed out, our technologies extend our powers, but they also change us. A challenge posed to contemporary religious traditions by changing technologies of communication and the increasingly pluralistic societies those technologies make possible is how to find the right place for tradition-sanctioned words in a world in which words are so numerous and the truths they express are perceived as so provisional and partial that they have little authority, and in which no single canon reflects the realities in which we live. And what are we to make of the greater and greater role that images have to move us directly without any need for words?

RELIGIOUS STUDIES 202: WORDS, TRUTH, AND POWER

PART I. Introduction to the Issues of This Course

Week I:
A. KINDS OF RELIGIOUS WORLDS ENCOUNTERED IN THIS COURSE
1. The I-Thou model—as self and as community, one finds oneself in relationship to a Holy Other. Language, the Word, is the best metaphor for the encounter, transformation, and empowerment experienced in the relationship—since Word comes from the Other, and yet can only be understood if the self/community allows itself to be addressed, even constituted, by that word.

Four sub-types:
a. Ecstatic communication with the realm of spirits
b. Personal apprehension of a holy presence
c. Sacred action: myth, sacrament, and holy rite
d. Prophecy, justice, and the sanctification of commandment
Reading:

> Denise L. Carmody and John T. Carmody, *Shamans, Prophets and Sages*, pp. 31-32; 53-55 and 56-57.

> Streng, Frederick, *Understanding Religious Life*, second edition, Part II, Chapter 5, 6, and 7.

2. The sage/yogic model—words (or alternatively, an analysis leading to the transcendence of words) function to move consciousness from "ordinary consciousness" to rational understanding, "sageliness within and kingliness without" (the sage as creator and participant in social harmony) "unitive consciousness," "pure awareness," or the actualization of true, authentic selfhood. Buddhism, "Neo-confucianism," Taoism.
Reading:

> Streng, *Understanding Religious Life*, 2nd ed., Part II, Chapter 8.

> Carmody and Carmody, *Shamans, Prophets, and Sages*, pp. 113-15.

Week II:
B. Introduction to the Ongian Historical Typology
1. orality in oral cultures;
2. literacy and chirographic cultures;
3. print cultures;
4. post-print (electronic) cultures
Reading:

> Ong, Walter J., "Maranatha: Death and Life in the Text of the Book," *Journal of the American Academy of Religion*, XLI, no. 4 (1977): 419-49.

QUESTIONS:

1. Words, and the power of speaking, cursing, and naming, have been understood by many to *be* sacred power, or to be the best metaphor for sacred power. For others, religious experience and knowledge of the sacred has been experienced as mediated, and words, even when not themselves regarded as sacred or creative powers (i.e., their sacredness is derivative rather than primary) have been among the most powerful bridges. Are they experienced as bridges differently by people in different kinds of cultures? Or are the ways in which they are experienced similarly obscured by the different ideologies concerning the word, the mind, and the sacred/reality in different cultures?

2. Ong's argument is that certain kinds of thinking, and certain kinds of approaches to knowledge, are impossible in oral cultures, while others common to oral cultures are impossible in writing or type cultures. What are these, and how do they relate to the uses people make of sacred texts?

3. People in oral cultures typically understand the power and significance of words differently from those in writing and type cultures. Do they know something that we of type cultures need to know? Or is there no bridge back into the past world?

4. What do you make of Derrida's argument, that it is nonsense to suggest that in the spoken word the meaning of the speaker is translated more immediately and purely into words than in writing? Derrida suggests that by the very nature of language such immediate and pure relation between meaning and speech is impossible— "difference" enters in, to the same degree as in writing. Thus the desire to associate word and sacred meaning, or word and sacred power, is a vain and deluding aspiration, "nostalgia." Cf. Christopher Norris, *Deconstruction: Theory and Practice* (London and New York: Methuen, 1982).

Part II. The Word in Oral Cultures

A. Characteristics of Oral Cultures
Reading:
> Brian Stock, *The Implications of Literacy* (Princeton, N.J.: Princeton University Press, 1983), pp. 14-17.

B. How the Connections Between Word and Truth and Word and Power Have Appeared in Oral Cultures
1. The word as creative, powerful
Reading:
> Marcel Griaule, *Conversations with Ogotemmeli*, pp. 16-40.

2. The word in epiphany/revelation
Reading:
> Halifax, Joan, "Shamanic Voices," pp. 70-75. From Lame Deer and Richard Erdoes, *Lame Deer: Seeker of Visions.*

> Smart, Ninian and Richard D. Hecht, *Sacred Texts of the World: A Universal Anthology*, pp. 359-65. (Black Elk's vision of the grandfathers)

Week III:

3. The power of the word in true and powerful communication: prayer and incantation

Reading:

> Momaday, Scott, "The Man Made of Words." Lecture on cassette tape. On language and prayer and the image of the world and the human presumed by them in the Native American tradition.

> Twitty, Ann, "Voice Above, Voice Below," *Parabola*, vol. viii, no. 3:39-47.

4. Word as channel of power; Mantra and "magic"

Reading:

> Applegate, Richard B., "Introduction: The Power of the Word," in Eknath Easwaran, *The Mantram Handbook*, pp. 9-34.

> Easwaran, Eknath, ibid, Ch. 1 "What the Mantram Is," pp. 37-53, and "Some Great Mantrams," pp. 55-77.

5. Mantra and ritual in Hinduism

Reading:

> Lester, Robert C., "Hinduism: Veda and Sacred Texts," in Denny and Taylor, eds., *The Holy Book in Comparative Perspective*, pp. 126-47.

Week IV:

Reading:

> Alper, Harvey, "Regression Toward the Real" (mantra in Indian thought, particularly in the Kashmiri Saiva tradition), *Parabola*, vol. viii, no. 3:72-81. (Deals with the later tradition)

> Hopkins, Steven, "*Sabdatattva*: Symbolism of Word and Speech in Indian Tradition." (Unpublished paper)

B. Early Buddhism as an Oral Tradition:

1. The Buddha's oral discourse: preaching and debate. How orality shaped the transmitted tradition: the oral "sutra"—numerical categories, formulas for memorization, etc. The symbol "Dharma"—truth, norm, teaching in words.

Reading:

> Smart and Hecht, pp. 231-38; 241-44;

> Ray, Reginal , "Buddhism: Sacred Text Written and Realized," in Frederick M. Denny and Rodney L. Taylor, eds., *The Holy Book in Comparative Perspective*, pp. 148-60.

2. The "first council"—arriving at a sanctioned (yet not finally closed) oral text

Reading:

> McDermott, James, "Scripture as the Word of the Buddha," *Numen*, vol. xxxi, fasc. 1 (July, 1984): 22-39.

Week V:

3. Pilgrimage, story, and the Buddhist community: The development of Jataka tales and of the legend of the Buddha's heroic career and its connection with the rise of the importance of pilgrimage to places associated with the Buddha's life.

Reading:

> Reynolds, Frank E., "The Many Lives of Buddha: a study of sacred biography and Theravada tradition," in Frank E. Reynolds and Donald Capps, eds., *The Biographical Process: studies in the history and psychology of religion*, pp. 37-61.

C. Later Orality in Buddhism: Tantra and Mantrayana

1. Development of an esoteric tradition, initiations

2. Mantra in Tantric Buddhism

Reading:

> Blofeld, John. *Mantras: Sacred Words of Power.*[4]

D. Pre-Textual Judaism as Oral Tradition as Reflected in the Existing Texts

1. Torah as story that tells one of one's identity: canon as marked by and resulting from a dynamic process of reinterpretation of the meaning of that story.

Reading:

> Sanders, James, *Torah and Canon* (Controversial but stimulating understanding of Torah and canon as story process.), pp. 1-53.

Week VI:

2. Prophecy (commissioned communication)

Reading:

> Sanders, *Torah and Canon*, pp. 54-90.

> Bartlett, David L., *The Shape of Scriptural Authority*, Ch. 2, "The Authority of Words," pp. 11-27.

> Carmody and Carmody, Shamans, Prophets, and Sages, pp. 56-60.

> Heschel, Abraham, The Prophets, Ch. 1.

3. The Name of God, God's "Word" and God's "Voice" in the Hebrew Bible

Reading:

> Hebrew Bible: Genesis 32; Exodus 3; 1st Kings 19; Jeremiah 1.

> Heschel, Abraham Joshua, *God in Search of Man* (Philadelphia: Jewish Publication Society of America, 1955), pp. 136-44.

---

[4] Although scholars may wish to take issue with Blofeld's treatment at some points, this book has the advantage of being readable.

PART III. Scripture and Classic: Preaching and Teaching in Chirographic Cultures

Week VII:

A. The Origins of Our Own Concept of "Scripture" in the West:
Reading:
> Smith, Wilfred Cantwell, "Scripture as Form and Concept: Its Emergence for the West," in Levering, ed., *Rethinking Scripture*, pp. 29-57.

B. The Transition to Oral/Chirographic Culture in the Buddhist Tradition: What the Written Dharma has Meant to Buddhists
1. Among Buddhists, all written canons are sectarian canons—the growth of the use of writing technology and the growth of sects; new forms—commentaries, treatises, philosophical arguments—are now possible.
Reading:
> Kogen Mizuno, *Buddhist Sutras: Origin, Development, and Transmission*, Chs. 1-3; 9; 7-8 (pp. 13-55; 157-79; 11-156).

2. The rise of Mahayana—its understanding of Dharma, sutra, Buddhavacana, the Dharma preacher; opening up the question of authoritative tradition and the nature and use of text; acceptance of text as a written phenomenon; vast multitude of texts.
Reading:
> MacQueen, Graeme, "Inspired Speech in Early Mahayana Buddhism II," in *Religion*, vol. 12, no. 1 (January, 1982): 49-65.
>
> Hurvitz, Leon, trans., *Scripture of the Lotus Blossom of the Fine Dharma (The Lotus Sutra)*, Chs. 10 and 14.

3. Dharma and sutra in Mahayana Buddhism: text as sacred symbol
Reading for the instructor:
> Schopen, Gregory, "The phrase 'sa prthivipradesas caityabhuto bhavet' in the *Vajracchedika*: notes on the cult of the book in Mahayana," *Indo-Iranian Journal*, vol. XVII (1975): 147-81.

Reading for the student:
> *Lotus Sutra* readings (above).

Week VIII:
5. The written sutra and teaching and preaching in later Buddhism; the reciting, copying, and commenting on sutras as turning the wheel of dharma and as a karmic act.
Reading:
> Levering, Miriam, "Scripture and its Reception: a Buddhist case," in Levering, ed., *Rethinking Scripture*, pp. 58-101.

6. Speech, silence, and the highest wisdom.
Reading:
> Robert, Thurman, trans., *The Holy Teaching of Vimalakirti*, especially Chs. 7 and 9 (pp. 56-63 and 73-77).
>
> Ray, Reginald, "Buddhism: Sacred Text Written and Realized," pp. 160-76.

7. "Dead words and live words": the Zen koan
Reading:
> Miura, Isshuu and Ruth Fuller Sasaki, *The Zen Koan: Its History and Use in Rinzai Zen* (New York: 1965).

Week IX:
8. Word as image and sound: the written Sanskrit syllable in later Mantrayana—textuality transforms Tantra
Reading:
> Rambach, Pierre, *The Secret Message of Tantric Buddhism*, pp. 60-87.

> Hakeda, Yoshito S., *Kukai: Major Works*, pp. 234-62.

D. "Classics," Study and Sagehood in Chinese Traditions
1. What is a classic? A "religious classic"? Why do we call these the Chinese classics?
a. A comparison with Western 'classical tradition'
Reading:
> [Georges Gusdorf.] "Humanistic Scholarship, History of." In: *Encyclopaedia Britannica* 15th ed., 1974 printing, Macropaedia, vol. 8: 1170-79.

b. Reflections on "classic" and "religious classic"
Reading:
> Bartlett, David L., *The Shape of Scriptural Authority*, pp. 27-38.

Week X:
c. The Chinese classics: General introduction
Reading:
> [Wing-tsit Chan.] "Confucian Texts, Classical." In: *Encyclopaedia Britannica* 15th ed., 1974 printing, Macropaedia, vol. 4, pp. 1104-08.

2. Confucius as the model teacher; study and moral formation in the Confucian classical tradition
Reading:
> Selections from *The Analects of Confucius*.

> Creel, H. G., *Confucius and the Chinese Way*, Ch. vii.

3. The "Four Books" and "Five Classics" as teacher
Reading:
> Taylor, Rodney L., "Confucianism: Scripture and the Sage," in *The Holy Book in Comparative Perspective*, pp. 181-202.

Week XI:
3. The Taoist challenge to the Confucian model:
Reading for students:
> Lau, D. C., trans., *Tao Te Ching* (selections).

> Watson, Burton, trans., *Chuang-tzu: Basic Writings*, Ch. 2.

E. Torah: Tanak and Talmud in Jewish Traditions

1. Torah and Talmud

Reading:

> Rosenbaum, Jonathan, "Judaism: Torah and Tradition," in Denny and Taylor, eds., *Holy Book in Comparative Perspective*, pp. 10-35.

> Heschel, Abraham Joshua, "God, Torah, and Israel," in Edward LeRoy Long, Jr. and Robert T. Handy, *Theology and Church in Time of Change*, pp. 71-90.

> Heschel, Abraham Joshua, "The Study of Torah," in Neusner, Jacob, eds., *Understanding Jewish Theology: classical issues and modern perspectives*, pp. 55-61.

> Scholem, Gershom G., "Tradition and Commentary as Religious Categories in Judaism," *Judaism*, vol. 15, no. 1 (Winter, 1966): 23-39.

Week XII:

3. Mysticism of the written word: Sacred alphabet in Judaism

Reading:

> Shawn, Ben, *The Alphabet of Creation*. A short fable about how the letter "beth" was chosen to be the letter through which creation was begun.

> Scholem, Gershon, "The Meaning of the torah in Jewish Mysticism." In his *On the Kabbala and its Symbolism*, pp. 32-86.

PART IV. In What Lies The "Scripturality" of Scripture?

A. To understand what scripture is we have to start by asking what scripture is for people after it has become scripture—how do they experience it being true and mediating power?

Reading:

> Smith, Wilfred Cantwell, "The Study of Religion and the Study of the Bible," in Levering, ed., *Rethinking Scripture*, pp. 18-28.

> Corless, Roger J., "Sacred Text, Context and Proof-text," in Wendy Doniger O'Flaherty, ed., *The Critical Study of Sacred Texts*, pp. 257-70.

> Ricoeur, Paul, "Epilogue: The 'Sacred' Text and the Community," ibid., pp. 271-76.

Week XIII:

B. The retention of orality in our encounter with scriptures—a confirmation of Ong? Are scriptures as scriptures, that is, as powerful, and thus true, necessarily oral?

Reading:

> Graham, W. A. Jr., "Scripture as Spoken Word," in Levering, ed., *Rethinking Scripture*, pp. 129-69.

C. A characteristic of scripture: that it has many uses (is true and powerful) in the religious life: to inform, to be a medium of transaction or action (performative), to transform the reader, hearer, or reciter, and to serve as symbol of ultimate sources of truth and power. The iconic and magical uses of scripture.

Reading:

Levering, "Scripture and its Reception," in Levering, ed., *Rethinking Scripture*, pp. 58-101 (review).

Ruether, Rosemary, ed., *Woman Guides*, pp. 150-53: "Terror, Glory and the Gift of Reading in a Black American Evangelist" (from Jean McMahon Humez, ed., *Gifts of Power: The Writings of Rebecca Jackson; Black Visionary, Shaker Eldress*).

Stern, Aileen, "Learning to Chant the Torah: A First Step." In Susannah Heschel, ed., *On Being a Jewish Feminist: A Reader*.

Week XIV:

D. What is it to read religiously?

Reading:

Hebrew Bible: The Song of Songs; The Book of Esther

QUESTIONS:

1. When did The Song of Songs become a great mystical text? When was it composed? When was it placed in the canon? When Bernard of Clairvaux and others read it that way?

2. Why do we read The Book of Esther as a religious text about God's action on behalf of his people when God's name is not mentioned in the text?

PART V. Print Cultures and Their Relation to the World

Ong's thesis on the effect of print on cultural attitudes toward words is that words and books become information storage, commonplace, too numerous, grist for the mill of the intellect. Words become primarily conveyors of facts.

QUESTION: Is there a religious consciousness characteristic of print cultures?
Discussion of the following topics:
A. The effects of mass literacy and mass communication:
1. the tract
2. the newspaper as "true word"
3. the decline of the authority of literate elites
B. Individualism/community and the possible continuing roles of "classics" and traditional "sacred texts" in a world where so much else is available to be read, appropriated, used in identity formation.
C. Scripture and the need for certainty and community in the print world of the bureaucratized industrial nation state: the rise of "fundamentalisms."
D. Liberation movements and the perceived power of the word.

Reading:

Gross, Rita, "Female God Language in a Jewish Context," in Carol P. Christ and Judith Plaskow, eds., *Womanspirit Rising*, pp. 167-73.

Janowitz, Naomi and Maggie Wenig, "Sabbath Prayers for Women," in ibid., pp. 174-78.

Daly, Mary, *Gyn/Ecology* (selections). (A more radical statement on women's need to create their own language.)

E. Liberation movements and the discovery of new scriptures; Alice Walker's *The Color Purple* as a new scripture of religious feminism.
Reading:

The Mudflower Collective, *God's Fierce Whimsy*, pp. 103-162.

Week XV:

PART IV. "The Word"? In Electronic Culture

QUESTION: does technology transform communication, mental processes, cultural participation?)
Possible topics:

A. The growing power of the non-verbal: images, emotions, and the electronic media
Reading:

Ellul, Jacques, *The Humiliation of the Word* (selections)

MacLuhan, Marshall, *The Gutenberg Galaxy* (selections)

B. The political commercial—uses of the "true" and "powerful" image: the use of religious and lifecycle images to create trust in a candidate in TV ads.

C. The electronic preacher/TV evangelism.

D. Relativism and detachment in the global village.

QUESTION: Is there a role for "scripture," "classic," or "canon" in electronic culture? What roles will reading and writing play in the life of the knowing self opening toward transcendence? In the building of community (communities) beyond the "life-style enclave" (cf. Ballah et al., *Habits of the Heart*)?

❧XV❧

Religion and Gender: A Comparative Approach to the Topic within Religious Studies

MIRIAM LEVERING

1. The topic of gender

We think of gender as a biological given. But in profound and important ways it is a social and religious construct. Gender as a social construct divides persons into two or more categories, sets highly charged fences between them, then establishes limits to the politically possible enactments of self for members of each category. The practices by which one expresses or enacts gender—whether sanctioned or unsanctioned, whether one stays within the fences or tries to cross them—take place as part of a field of relationships of power and carry a tremendous burden of meanings.

Religion draws upon those meanings. When religious groups convey their experience of Divine power(s), gendered imagery often pervades their expressions. Likewise, religious communities almost always are involved in establishing and sanctioning the system of gender distinctions in a society, and in maintaining or changing the practices of gender. Religious practices often enact understandings of what men and women are—and what they should hope to be.

More specifically, religion, which is often under at least nominal male control, supports or does not support the religious projects and identities of men and women differently. Women are most often supported by their religions in their search to enact ultimate meanings in a domestic, family context. Men are likewise most often supported in their search for fulfillment in leadership or accomplishment in the public realm. Religions vary in the degree of support they offer for women who seek to enact a religious vision or identity apart from the domestic realm, or in a position of leadership.

Scholars of religion have recently come to understand how much everything we study needs to be looked at with self-conscious attention to the importance of gender. Religious texts, for example, are often written down by men, and assume an audience in which males are dominant. Not only do we need to become more aware of the messages they convey about gender, we need to ask whether they reflect to any degree the religious insights of the women of the community.

Another important question that must be addressed is whether there are in fact separate religious practices of communities for men and women within a single culture or tradition. If so, what do they have to tell us about how women have been creative in meeting their own needs and telling their own stories within the religious sphere? And where women and men use the same symbols, participate in the same ceremonies and read or listen to the same stories, we need to ask whether those stories and ceremonies may not mean different things to each.

Some scholars argue that all of the living religions of the world are deeply implicated in social systems in which men keep women subordinate or marginal. We need to find out whether this has always been true. Beyond this, we need to ask what has been done or is now being done to imagine what any of the living religions would be like if it truly allowed men and women to be equal participants—or to create a situation in which that could happen.

Ideally, attention to the differences that arise in connection with gender would be a feature of every course about religious life. In practice, such attention often still tends to be token. Courses on the religions of India or China, for example, often attend seriously to the "great" texts, philosophies, and practical disciplines, while giving scant attention to the "lesser" disciplines of women's household rites—or to the way in which religion sanctions and gives meaning to family structure.

Thus it seems that at the moment in our curriculum at the University of Tennessee and elsewhere there is a need for a course that looks at the inter-relationships between power, the creating of selves or identities, gender, and religion.

2. *What one might do in a course on this topic*

One obvious way to teach such a course is to focus on the current Western feminist critique of traditional and contemporary religion as patriarchal or male-dominated, and with the creation in the West of feminist theologies and thealogies, liturgies, etc. within existing Western traditions and as new religious movements. A good basis for such a course would be Judith Plaskow and Carol P. Christ, eds., *Weaving the Visions: New Patterns in Feminist Spirituality* (Harper and Row, 1989).

Another version of this kind of course, one that would in fact allow students to evaluate the feminist critique for themselves rather than merely read what critics have written, would look at human religious history through the eyes of the feminist critics. Good courses have been taught that focus in this way on the religious history of "the West" (ancient Near-eastern religions, Hebraic religion, Judaism, and Christianity). A good example of such a course was developed by Judith Plaskow at Manhattanville. I do not know of any course that has tackled all of the world's religious history, or even all of the history of religion in literate civilizations, in this way.

Another approach is to treat gender as a topic, similar to those of suffering, death, war, or the body, which every religious tradition large or small has to address, and therefore one around which a comparative course could be built. One could survey the treatment of gender in each of the major traditions of civilizational religion, using a text such as Arvind Sharma, ed., *Women in World Religions*. This approach has the virtue of simplicity of design, and permits the issues discussed to arise from within the cultural context of each tradition. However, as Falk and Gross also note in the introduction to their *Unspoken Worlds*, it tends to prevent focused discussion of patterns that occur in many traditions.

Another approach to a thematic or comparative kind of course is to examine how women participate in religion in male-dominated cultures by setting alongside each other examples from two such cultures. A good example is one taught at Princeton University by Helen Hardacre, who drew her examples from the West and Japan. Here the organizing principle is the thesis that there are patterns of participation typically allowed or forced upon women in such cultures. For example, women's religious participation, like their social position, is often seen as marginal.

Women's bodily processes are often seen as ritually polluting, a fact which often limits women's religious participation. Women are associated with ecstatic religion, whether shamanic or mystic in type. This is particularly true where the ecstatic, shamanic, or mystical are seen as religiously marginal. Women are allowed to develop certain kinds of religious identity—for example, that of the virtuous wife and good mother, who serves fertility and nurtures the family, while keeping her sexuality within male-defined bounds; or that of the celibate nun, whose status as a valued religious person depends on her ability to transcend her sexuality. Likewise, women are allowed to exercise certain kinds of religious leadership (shamanic or prophetic), and are denied others (organizational, sagely, or priestly). These patterns can be found in many cultures, and may be grounded in frequently encountered features of gender distinctions such as those discussed in Ortner and Whitehead's "Accounting for Sexual Meanings," from the introduction to their book *Sexual Meanings* (see syllabus below). But as Emily Ahern's article on female purity and pollution in Chinese religion (see syllabus below) makes clear, seeing common patterns across cultures is not enough; the meanings of these patterns in each case need to be determined through specific studies of particular cultures. A course like this may be one context in which this can be done.

A similar course focusing on cross-cultural patterns, but with a stronger focus on women's own religious worlds, and drawing on a wider range of traditions and types of societies, is one modeled by Nancy Auer Falk and Rita M. Gross in their collection of articles, intended as a textbook, called *Unspoken Worlds*. Falk and Gross take as a principle that their selections must place "women in center stage—as men had been placed so often in the past—and meet them as subjects, not objects, with their own experiences and aspirations." (p. xv) They seek "to create an understanding of women's own enterprises, whether the world around them defined these as 'in' or 'out,' respectable or shocking." Such a course, focusing on women's experience and the religious worlds that women create, would differ from one using Sharma's *Women in World Religions* as a textbook, which places the "tradition" or "religious system" in center stage, and thus looks centrally at how the mainstream of a tradition, almost always male-dominated, defines gender and the "place" of women. Beyond this, Falk and Gross design the book around two themes: the contrast between extraordinary callings and everyday domestic concerns in women's lives; and the "level of support women find [in their religious system], whether they are called to extraordinary ventures or are bound up in everyday concerns."

Yet another possible topic for a course is that pursued by the authors of the essays in Caroline Bynum, Steven Harrell, and Paula Richman's *Gender and Religion*. Here the topic is the complex relationsip between culturally constructed gender, religious symbol, and social context. As Bynum writes in her introduction, following Ricoeur and Victor Turner, religious symbols are polysemic, and "there is no such thing as a religious symbol that is merely a sign or statement about social structure." (p. 2) And, at the same time, "all symbols arise out of the experience of 'gendered' users." (p. 3) The challenge as Bynum sees it is to develop, through concrete studies, a theory of gendered symbols, indeed perhaps even of symbol-using itself, that takes both of these theoretical understandings into account. This book deals with a wide spectrum of material from differing contexts but, unlike *Unspoken Worlds*, is not designed as a textbook. A course on this topic using Bynum's introductory essay and some of the concrete studies in this book would be very interesting, but would appeal most to very well-prepared students.

The course I present below draws on but is different from these models. It was designed to thematize not only gender, but the study of religion itself, particularly those provinces within the study of religion that have become methodologically aware of religious life as necessarily gendered. Gender as in a significant relation to religion was considered to be a world-wide phenomenon. An attempt was made to line up examples from two broad "traditions" for comparison or mutual illumination: from the West (particularly the Hebrew Bible and modern Christian and post-Christian feminist theology) on the one hand, and from Asia (Buddhist, Chinese, and Korean religions) on the other. These choices obviously bore some relation to the specific training and interests of the instructors—more about that below. The idea was that the student would not only learn something about religion and gender in these two broad cultural contexts, but would also learn how questions about religion and about gender were being raised and answered in various branches of scholarship in religious studies.

Thus, in this course we read together concrete examples of the new kinds of scholarship in religious studies that take gender into account. These included literary critical, historical, anthropological, psychological, and theological/ethical approaches. Students were asked to write a major research paper in the religious tradition and methodological discipline of their choice.

3. How we came to offer such a course

I had become interested in gender in 1979 and 1980, when I spent eighteen months in Taiwan getting to know the life of a Buddhist convent. In thinking about that experience I wondered how Buddhist monks and nuns understand themselves and are understood to fit into or contravene the larger society's gender expectations. And in so far as those gender expectations are constraining, is there both a religious and a social liberation that comes to women (and perhaps to men) by becoming a monastic Buddhist practitioner. Do the practices by which women strive to overcome the delusion of "self" as understood in Buddhism also allow them to create larger and more empowered selves than the practices of domesticity and the enactment of expected gender in lay social roles would allow? A second question I had concerned in what ways Buddhist monastic life was experienced or understood in different ways by women and by men, and in what ways the women of the convent thought that being a woman affected the course of Buddhist practice. These questions were only partially answered in that experience—more research needs to be done. But it was clear that the Buddhist women I spoke with thought that there were important differences in the male and female body, in the balance of emotion and reason in men and women, and so forth—differences that affect the ease of progress in Buddhist practice.

Since that time I have been interested in keeping up with the field of women and religion in the West, as well as with new research on women in Buddhism and Chinese and Japanese religion and society, and have offered courses in "Religion and the Experience of Women" at Oberlin College and the University of Tennesee.

After that period in Taiwan I became interested in doing more historical studies of women in Buddhism as well. I have been writing recently about records of women teachers and the rhetorical discussion by male teachers concerning successful women students of Ch'an and Zen Buddhism in China and Japan. I have also been very interested in recent years in the topic of what makes scriptures "scripture," and have drawn on the comments of women in the convent in Taiwan on that topic.

I could not have been more fortunate than to have as a colleague in this course Dr. Lee Humphreys, whose field is Hebrew narratives, and who in recent years, as the Director of the University of Tennessee Learning Research Center, has developed a strong interest in learning theory and cognitive psychology. To my own historical and anthropological interests, broadened as best I can by reading in literary theory and Western feminist biblical studies and theology, he brought strengths in literary theory, a developed interest in the narratives that include or leave out figures like Sarah and Ruth in the Hebrew Bible, and a strong familiarity with the work represented in Belenky et al.'s *Women's Ways of Knowing*.

4. *Our curricular context*

This course was given as a "proseminar"; all religious studies majors are required to take one proseminar during their junior or senior years. Thus all majors who planned to graduate in 1990 and who had not yet taken a proseminar had no choice but to study the topic of "Religion and Gender." In addition, a number of students who were not seniors or not religious studies majors joined the course, including a psychology graduate student and an older Black woman graduate student with a strong interest in theology. As occasional auditors the course enjoyed the presence of an additional faculty member in religious studies and a faculty member in social work. Whether despite or because of the widely varying kinds and degrees of student interest, the course seemed to enable everyone to make real progress in an area appropriate to her or his interest and level.

In our curriculum, this "proseminar" has several purposes. First, it should be integrative in the sense that it introduces or reintroduces students in one course to a broad range of approaches current in religious studies.

Second, it should allow students to draw on and deepen the historical studies of specific religious traditions and regions required of all students at the 300 level: courses in Buddhism, Christianity, the religions of India, of Africa, or China, or Japan.

Third, the course is used specifically as our version of the state-required "Outcomes Assessment" program, in place of an "Outcomes Exam" given to all seniors. Thus it is in a sense a prolonged outcomes exam. It must require of students a formal paper proposal, an annotated bibliography, a 20-page research paper and a formal class presentation of the finished paper. Through these steps the student can demonstrate her or his skill and imagination in the kind of thinking, speaking, and writing we hope she or he will have learned in the course of a religious studies major. This enables us to see whether, at the 200 and 300 level, we are teaching students to "do religious studies" for themselves, not simply learn the information we give them.

"Gender" seems to be a good topic for these purposes. First, it affects religious life everywhere, so that all of the student's previous exposure to specific historical traditions can be brought into play, and integrative comparisons can be made.

Second, how religion is gendered and supports gender constructions is a topic that has been approached within every discipline upon which religious studies draws: anthropology, symbolic studies, history, psy-

chology, sociology, literary criticism, theology, to name but the most obvious. The issues raised by gender difference go to the very heart of theory in all those disciplines, so that by looking at gender the real theoretical underpinnings and assumptions of all of those disciplines can be examined.

And third, to many students the topic is fresh and exciting, saving the
"outcomes" proseminar from being an opportunity merely to rehearse
once again skills and interests already developed at the 300 level.

Given that a major research paper was a requirement of the course,
our approach was to allow students very considerable lattitude in the
choice of paper topics, so that the fact of being forced to study a loaded
topic like "gender" in order to graduate would not arouse so much resistance that learning would not take place.

We were also particularly concerned that if possible this be a course
on "religion and gender," not on "religion and women"—although we
recognized that most of the courses the students had taken in the department had been, unknowingly, courses on "religion and men." We
made it clear to students that we were interested in the way religious
meanings were found in the social constructions of male gender as well
as female gender, and encouraged students to take up that topic. A number of students, male and female, chose to read John Ehle's novel *The
Winter People* which we had chosen because it makes the social perception of male gender its explicit topic. We made sure that this was thoroughly discussed in class time. I had chosen a few reading assignments,
notably Charles Keyes' "Ambiguous Gender: Male Initiation in a Northern Thai Buddhist Society," to model for students how male gender and
its ritual and symbolic transformations can be studied within religious
studies. We did a few other similar things, such as showing a videotape
of Bill Moyers' program on Robert Bly's recent workshops with men.
Nonetheless, when it came time to choose a paper topic, all the students,
including the men, chose to focus on female gender.

5. Topics, readings, and the themes of the course

It was a fortunate and fateful choice to begin the course with Belenky,
et al., *Women's Ways of Knowing: the development of self, voice and mind*. This
wonderful book reports on a large phenomenological interview study of
women in various institutions of learning (including an elite women's
college, and a clinic that teaches medicare patients how to take care of
their infants). The questions concerned how the women felt about various situations in which they had been taught something, or had come to

know something for sure. How did they know that they knew something, and how did they gain the confidence to claim it and speak it out loud? The proposals in this book concerning how women and men in our culture develop various kinds of approaches to knowing and learning, and how they develop a self and a voice, interested all the participants greatly. Belenky et al.'s studies are similar to, though broader in population studied, William Perry's studies of Harvard men, so comparisons of men's and women's feelings and strategies are possible, though in the main there seem to be only a few strong differences that correlate with gender. Doing this reading at the beginning made men feel included, since so much of what was said seemed to speak to the experience of both women and men in the course. Doing this reading at the beginning made the categories of self, voice, and the telling and interpreting of stories, including one's own story and the stories one tells as a learner and scholar, central to the rest of the course.

The next section of the course focused on the question raised in readings by Mary Daly, Carol Christ, Caroline Bynum, and Larry Shinn: how do gendered religious symbols mean? Are their meanings limited by their reference to society's gender distinctions? It is true, as Carol Christ argues, that only a female symbol for divine power can affirm women's powers and experiences, or, as Mary Daly argues, that a male Christ cannot be liberating for women? Or do these views reflect a misunderstanding of the nature of the religious symbol, as Larry Shinn suggests. In general students appreciated Bynum's nuanced discussion, but expended more energy defending Christ and her position from Shinn's criticism. The Richman and Keyes essays on aspects of Buddhist literature and practice were good illustrations of the kinds of careful study of how symbols mean that Bynum and her colleagues call for.

The third section of the course chiefly introduced students to Phyllis Trible's readings of Genesis 2-3, the Book of Ruth, and other Biblical narratives. Students appreciated these glimpses into the history of Western religion, and also took from them the lesson that a gender-sensitive reading of tradition-sanctioned story may unearth quite different meanings from those given in standard preaching and Sunday school lessons in a culture unself-consciously or self-consciously patriarchal. This subject made a bridge to students for whom church is a major part of their lives and feminist criticisms of religion were new. Some of the more feminist students, though, were quite ready to dismiss *God and the Rhetoric of Sexuality*—they wondered why Phyllis Trible would go to such lengths to rehabilitate a hopelessly patriarchal religion by finding bits and pieces that can be reclaimed through new readings.

The fourth section provided a brief novel-reading interlude. Students had a choice among Alice Walker's *The Color Purple* (a "scripture" for much of feminist religion in America, and a book that should have been required of all who have not read it); John Ehle's *The Winter People* (a novel whose theme is how masculine gender is enacted in the southern Appalachian mountains, and how a man who does not enact gender in the same way is accepted); E. M. Broner's *A Weave of Women*, which describes a community of women in Israel and their reinterpretations of traditional Jewish rituals and practices to fit the realities in their lives; and Maxine Hong Kingston's *Woman Warrior*, which deals with the myths and realities of Chinese women's lives, and the ways these serve and do not serve the Chinese-American author in her growing up.

If the third section raised the question of what an interpreter of Biblical stories does, the fifth section on anthropological approaches raised that of what an ethnologist does in interacting with and narrating the meanings of another world, as well as the question of what a teller of her own life story is doing as she constructs a fictional "self" in addressing her audience. At the same time, this section allowed us to look at the issue of whether there are common patterns in the ways men and women participate in enacting the religious meanings of a culture. The fundamental reading assignment here was Laurel Kendall's *The Life and Hard Times of a Korean Shaman*, which proved to be an excellent choice for raising both kinds of questions. Kendall's shaman teacher and friend told Kendall and other listeners stories of her own life. Following great hardships as a daughter and a wife, she became a shaman, which gave her a meaningful and powerful, if despised, expressive role in an important sector of Korean religion—the so-called "women's rituals" of god-possession which complement the Confucian rituals, the highly socially respected "rituals of male lineage," which are performed by men.

The last section on feminist and womanist theology and ethics in the United States, based on *Womanspirit Rising* and *Weaving the Visions*, turned out to be useful primarily in supplementing discussions that had already arisen and were continuing to be carried on in the context of the students' presentations of their paper proposals and of their finished papers. A number of students chose to write and present to the class fine papers on the work of Carol Christ, Rosemary Ruether, Sallie McFague, and Mary Daly. One black graduate student wrote an excellent paper on the position and needs of women in the black church to which a biblically based womanist theology must respond. Our procedure in this last section was to ask a few students, particularly active auditors who were not in the throes of writing papers, to choose and introduce readings from *Womanspirit Rising* and *Weaving the Visions*, in addition to those on the syllabus, that seemed to add new themes to our discussions. Examples were essays by Carter Heyward on sexuality and spirituality, and Paula Gunn Allen on the spiritual heritage of Native American women.

6. Fruits of the course

In some ways my ideas about the course were not fully realized in fact. I intended our discussions to be more focused both on theoretical concerns and on cross-cultural testing of theory and approach than they often became. Part of this was due to a strength of the course that was also a weakness: throughout, students were asked to introduce the readings for discussion and kick off or lead the class discussion. As students said orally or in their evaluations, the great virtue of this was that they felt empowered in hearing their own voices shaping the excellent discussions in this course. The weakness was that often the theoretical issues were not as highlighted in discussion as I had hoped they would be. Perhaps my expectations were misplaced: for example, the rather abstract issue of how a symbol works pales as a discussion topic compared to the much more concrete and emotional subject of how women cope with the marriage and family system of traditional China.

Also, something happened that I had not thought through but should have expected. Several of the brightest and most articulate students, most notably two religious studies majors and two english majors, began the course as feminists with rather developed interests in Western feminist theology. Their concerns and insights tended to make Western feminist theology and thealogy a strong component of the course from the beginning, even though I had designed the syllabus so that these topics would not be addressed explicitly until the last part of the course.

For most students the papers and presentations were a chief fruit of the course. In most cases the course served as a successful springboard that allowed them to develop a research project that fit well with their preparation and interests. As instructors we put a lot of effort into working with students to choose and refine a suitable topic. In addition to those mentioned above, students wrote papers on the following topics: An interview study of the women managers at Kroger stores in the area, asking whether their conservative (Southern Baptist and Roman

Catholic) religious backgrounds that taught that woman's place was in the home, and the conservative, male-oriented business culture of East Tennessee, affected their work circumstances and their feeling about their desire to succeed at the job. A study of how surviving incest might affect a Christian woman's feelings about God as heavenly parent. A comparison of female religious participation in India and China. A constructive theological project on the need for women's language in theology. A historical study on women finding a voice in the early American Quaker movement. A paper comparing different interpretations of the Book of Ruth. A study, undertaken by the psychology graduate student, of drawings of God by male and female children at different age levels in a Catholic school. A paper on the gender messages in the modern revival of witchcraft.

I think it is fair to say that although some found the discussions threatening and at time "unfair to men," most students became more conscious of gender as a pervasive social fact and more aware of connections between gender construction and religion than they otherwise would have been. Students also became aware of the ways in which women and men in many cultures participate and interpret differently in religious life, and the degrees to which women have had difficulty enacting fulfilling religious and social identities, finding their own voices, telling their own stories, and having their voices heard.

RELIGIOUS STUDIES 499: PROSEMINAR

Instructors: Drs. Levering and Humphreys
Topic for 1990: Religion and Gender

BOOKS FOR PURCHASE

Packet of Xeroxes

Belenky, Clinchy, Goldberger, and Tarule, *Women's Ways of Knowing: The Development of Self, Voice, and Mind* (New York: Basic Books, 1986).

Christ, Carol P., and Judith Plaskow, eds., *Womanspirit Rising: A Feminist Reader in Religion* (New York: Harper and Row, 1979).

Plaskow, Judith, and Carol P. Christ, eds., *Weaving the Visions: New Patterns in Feminist Spirituality* (New York: Harper and Row, 1989).

Bynum, Caroline Walker, Stevan Harrell, and Paula Richman, eds., *Gender and Religion: On the Complexity of Symbols* (Boston: Beacon Press, 1986).

Kendall, Laurel, *The Life and Hard Times of a Korean Shaman* (Honolulu: University of Hawaii Press, 1988).

One of the following novels:

Maxine Hong Kingston, *Woman Warrior*

Alice Walker, *The Color Purple* (only if you have not seen the movie)

E. M. Broner, *A Weave of Women*

John Ehle, *The Winter People*

Recommended for purchase:

Kendall, Laurel, *Shamans, Housewives, and Other Restless Spirits: Women in Korean Ritual Life* (Honolulu: University of Hawaii Press, 1985).

COURSE REQUIREMENTS

One research paper of 15-20 pages, due April 24; in addition, students will be asked to submit an annotated bibliograpy for the paper on March 6, and a preliminary draft of the paper on April 3.

One short paper (3-5 pages) on one of the novels (see below).

One class presentation concerning the paper proposal.

One class presentation of the finished research for the paper.

SCHEDULE OF SESSIONS

This course will have five parts representing different approaches to religion in which gender figures prominently: (1) PSYCHOLOGICAL/DEVELOPMENTAL; (2) GENDER AND SYMBOLISM; (3) gender-conscious LITERARY APPROACHES to religiously significant narratives; (4) ANTHROPOLOGICAL APPROACHES; and (5) GENDER, THEOLOGY, AND RELIGIOUS ETHICS. The number of sessions and common readings devoted to each of these parts will depend to a certain extent on student interests and needs.

Core readings for each of the five parts will be as follows:

I.   PSYCHOLOGICAL/DEVELOPMENTAL APPROACHES
Beleky et al., *Women's Ways of Knowing.*

Miller, Jean Baker, *Toward a New Psychology of Women,* Chapters 1-3. (In packet)

Keller, Catherine, "Feminism and the Ethic of Inseparability," in Plaskow and Christ, eds., *Weaving the Visions,* pp. 256-65.

Tong, Rosemarie, *Feminist Thought,* Chapter 5: "Psychoanalytic Feminism"; and Chapter 8: "Postmodern Feminism." (In packet)

II. GENDER AND SYMBOLISM: THE DEBATE
Daly, Mary "After the Death of God the Father," in *Womanspirit Rising,* pp. 53-62.

Christ, Carol P., "Why Women Need the Goddess: Phenomenological, Psychological and Political Reflections," in Christ and Plaskow, eds., *Womanspirit Rising,* pp. 273-87.

Bynum, Caroline, "Introduction: The Complexity of Symbols," in Caroline Bynum et al., eds., *Gender and Religion,* pp. 1-20.

Shinn, Larry D., "The Goddess: Theological Sin or Religious Symbol?" *Numen: International Review for the History of Religions* 31.2 (1984): 175-98. (In packet)

Richman, Paula, "The Portrayal of a Female Renouncer in a Tamil Buddhist Text," in Bynum et al., *Gender and Religion,* pp. 143-65.

Keyes, Charles F., "Ambiguous Gender: Male Initiation in a Northern Thai Buddhist Society," in Byum et al., *Gender and Religion,* pp. 66-96.

For further reading:
E. M. Broner, *A Weave of Women.*

Discussion themes: Larry Shinn argues that much feminist discussion of religion is based on an overly simple, Geertzian understanding of religious symbols. Caroline Bynum and her colleagues likewise argue that the relationship between culturally constructed gender, religious symbol, and social context is complex. "Gender-related symbols bear many relationships to society, at times affirming societal values, at times rejecting or transcending them." The challenge is to clarify how these symbols function for those who use them, how, and to whom, they "mean." What is your evaluation of this argument and approach?

III. LITERARY APPROACHES: NARRATIVES OF GENDER
      IN THE HEBREW BIBLE
Trible, Phyllis, "Eve and Adam: Genesis 2-3 Reread," in Christ and Plaskow, eds., *Womanspirit Rising,* pp. 74-83.

Bal, Mieke, *Lethal Love: Feminist Literary Readings of Biblical Love Stories* (Indiana University Press, 1987). (On reserve)

Trible, Phyllis, *Texts of Terror: Literary-Feminist Readings of Biblical Narratives* (Philadelphia: Fortress Press, 1984). (On reserve)

Trible, Phyllis, *God and the Rhetoric of Sexuality* (Philadelphia: Fortress Press, 1978). (On reserve)

IIIb. GENDER IN CONTEMPORARY NOVELS

Students are asked to read and write a short paper concerning one of the novels listed on page 1 of the syllabus.

IV. ANTHROPOLOGICAL APPROACHES

Ortner, Sherri and Harriet Whitehead, "Introduction: Sexual Meanings," in Ortner and Whitehead, eds., *Sexual Meanings*. (In packet)

Kendall, Laurel, *The Life and Hard Times of a Korean Shaman.*

Kendall, Laurel, *Shamans, Housewives and Other Restless Spirits*. (On reserve)

Ahern, Emily, "The Power and Pollution of Chinese Women," in Margery Wolf and Roxane Witke, eds., *Women in Chinese Society* (Palo Alto: Stanford University Press, 1975), pp. 169-90. (In packet)

Harrell, Steven, "Men, Women, and Ghosts in Chinese Folk Religion," in Bynum et al., *Gender and Religion*, pp. 97-116.

Mernissi, Fatima, "Women, Saints, and Sanctuaries in Morocco," reprinted from *Signs* 3:1 in Falk and Gross, eds., *Unspoken Worlds*. (In packet)

V. FEMINIST AND WOMANIST THEOLOGY AND EHICS: THE CONTEMPORARY DISCUSSION IN THE UNITED STATES

a. History and the Sacred

Christ and Plaskow, "Introduction: Womanspirit Rising," in *Womanspirit Rising*, pp. 1-17.

Plaskow and Christ, "Introduction," in Plaskow and Christ, eds., *Weaving the Visions*, pp. 1-13.

"Part 1: Our Heritage is Our Power," in *Weaving the Visions*, pp. 15-92.

Fiorenza, Elizabeth, "Women in the Early Christian Movement," in *Womanspirit Rising*, pp. 84-92.

Pagels, Elaine, "What Became of God the Mother?" in *Womanspirit Rising*, pp. 107-119.

"Part 2: Naming the Sacred," in *Weaving the Visions*, pp. 93-169.

Morton, Nelle, "The Dilemma of Celebration," in *Womanspirit Rising*, pp. 159-66.

b. Ethics and Community

"Part 3: Self in Relation," in *Weaving the Visions*, pp. 171-265.

"Part 4: Transforming the World," in *Weaving the Visions*, pp. 267-356.

For further reading:
    The Mudflower Collective, *God's Fierce Whimsey*. (On reserve)

❧XVI❧

Women in African-American Religions: The Caribbean and South America

Karen McCarthy Brown

Teaching a course on the role of women in the religions that arose as a result of trans-Atlantic slavery necessitates rethinking the way in which world religions are taught in colleges and universities. The African-American material in itself mandates perspectives different from those commonly used in religious studies departments. When an emphasis on women is added, this emphasis both reinforces and extends the critique of how we teach about the world's religions.

African-American Traditions

African-American religions in the Caribbean and South America are almost exclusively non-textual religions. So the focus on texts which characterizes so many academic offerings is the first thing to go. In my own courses textual analysis is replaced largely by interpretations of symbolic and ritual modes of communication. Deciphering religious meaning through rituals can be a very helpful way of holding worldview and ethos together. The religious philosophy remains wedded to particular values and styles and, when the reporting is rich and detailed, also to particular persons, times and places. As a consequence, the philosophical dimensions of these religions cannot readily be appropriated by students as if they were part of a disembodied thought system equally applicable anywhere in the world. It is my impression that North American students tend to "shop" among the world's religions, particularly in introductory-level survey courses. They seem to feel they can pick and choose

what is useful and meaningful to them without these choices restructur-
ing their lives or provoking serious social consequences. This priveleged
view not only has the flavor of colonialism, it also distorts the way most
people experience religion in their lives.

The organizational structures of African-American religions are multi-
cephalic. Individual temples are often loosely organized into family-like
networks (composed of the houses of those leaders initiated by a given
priest or priestess) but there is no central organization and no overarching authority in these religions. Neither are there functional equivalents
for canon or creed. One consequence is that distinctions cannot easily be
made between the so-called great tradition and popular expressions of
that tradition. The flexibility and adaptability of the African-American
traditions have supported their survival in the midst of oppression and
rapid social change, but these same qualities complicate the teaching
process. The search for orthodoxies, essences or mainstreams within
traditions has to be replaced by an attempt to draw meaningful generalizations from numerous case studies, generalizations which tend to be
more attitudinal, or even aesthetic, than dogmatic. Teaching about
African-American religions in the Caribbean and South America does
not produce neat lists and diagrams on the chalkboard.

The Africa-based religions are, moreover, not so much discrete religions as religious energy centers that are partially fueled by interconnections with traditions and institutions which are otherwise separate. Historically speaking, they are blends of different African religions with various types of spirituality (Catholic, Protestant, Masonic, spiritualist) practiced by the slaveholders. The several traditions from which they are
composed maintain some degree of separation within the resulting mix.
For example, Vodou ceremonies in Haiti are still organized by the
rhythms and moods of different African "nations." They also usually
begin with a clearly demarcated Catholic prologue. Cycles of Vodou
ceremonies frequently include attending mass in the local Catholic
church or making pilgrimages to distant churches significant for the
saints to whom they are dedicated, saints conflated with African spirits
honored in Haiti. Catholic priests routinely denounce those who serve
the Vodou spirits. But those who serve the spirits simply observe that
"that is the way priests talk," while continuing to see themselves as good
Catholics and to believe in the efficacy of Catholic ritual. Clearly what it
means to be Catholic in Haiti is heavily dependent on who is telling the
story. In the academic world, we have been more prone to listen to the
voice of the priest than that of the lay person who both was confirmed in

the church and serves the Vodou spirits, even though that lay person speaks for at least eighty-five percent of the Haitian population. These people are never called Catholics in the literature on Haitian religion. They are, however, frequently called Vodouisants, an academic term which Haitians do not use to describe themselves.

Due to these three characteristics of African-American religions (their non-textual form, multi-cephalic organization, and tendency to blur their boundaries) the teacher of a course on African-American religions confronts questions which are in fact central to the academic study of religion in general. Is the phenomenon we study composed of discrete traditions with firm boundaries or are the boundaries between traditions fluctuating, permeable, and overlapping? How does our general sense of the field shift when we attend to the rather large portion of the world's people who routinely participate in more than one of the traditions we present in the classroom as mutually exclusive? Or to take this question to a more fundamental level, what is the result of our tendency within the academy to characterize religions as things or entities? (No two "things" can occupy the same space at the same time.) Haitians still prefer to use a verbal form to identify their religion ("serving the spirits") rather than employing the noun, Vodou, which scholars of religion such as myself have nevertheless found impossible to avoid. What happens to an overall vision of the field of religious studies when particular subject matters move us to conceptualize religions in more dynamic terms, such as seeing them as styles of meaning-making continuously interacting with other such styles in a variety of social and institutional contexts?[1]

Other questions arise as well. Where do we place the emphasis in the study of religion? On texts? On symbols and rituals? On history? On case studies? Do different emphases yield different senses of what religion is? Where does the impetus for studying religions through their texts come from? Is it born from the textual focus of the academy or that of the religions themselves? If the religion itself emphasizes text, then the question becomes: what group within the tradition supports and benefits from the primacy of that text?

The root questions concern authority. Whose religion do we present in the classroom? Who or what has the right to define a religion or speak for a particular tradition? How does a religion as represented by leading

---

[1] In these comments about reifying religions as well as in earlier ones concerning the nature of religious boundaries, I want to acknowledge my debt to the still powerful discussion in the early chapters of Wilfred Cantwell Smith's classic study, *The Meaning and End of Religion* (San Francisco: Harper and Row, 1978).

figures, great historical events or sacred texts relate to that same tradition as practiced by ordinary people? Do we scholars study the former more than the latter because of something intrinsic to religion or something intrinsic to scholarship? In our attempt to study religions, have we also to some extent created them in our own image and for our own convenience?

Women

Power and authority questions build the bridge between the basic subject matter under discussion (African-American religions) and the specific thematic focus (women). Women have not often been the keepers of the texts or the leaders of the churches, synagogues, temples or shrines. So sacred texts rarely reflect women's experiences or their concerns, just as religious authorities rarely speak either for or about the realities of women's lives as women know them. Yet in many of the world's religions women do the majority of the maintenance work. They cook the food, sew the garments, and sing the songs from which the religious rituals (which they often attend in greater numbers than men) are composed. They also sustain, interpret, and pass on religious traditions through numerous acts of daily, often domestic, piety. Thus, focusing on the role of women quickly leads away from text and away from orthodoxy and authority toward what is frequently dismissed in the academy as "popular religion."

Moreover, women are natural religious *bricoleurs*. They are often motivated more by the demands of their role as family caretakers than by a search for abstract religious truth or purity. When there is a serious problem, they are likely to tap any and all spiritual resources available to deal with that problem, regardless of the theological contradictions implicit in their actions. This is as true in China, Japan, and Korea; in Sierra Leone, Nigeria and Ghana; as it is in Haiti, Cuba, Trinidad, and Brazil—or in feminist spirituality in North America, for that matter.[2] Women cross easily over the borders between religious traditions. In their spiritual kitchens they mix what is often derisively called "folklore" with the so-called higher religions, and the "higher religions" with one another.

There is some irony in including "women" in this volume as one theme among several that can profitably be traced through the world's

---

[2] One particularly interesting discussion of this phenomenon is found in Emiko Ohnuki-Tierney's "Health Care in Contemporary Japanese Religions," in *Healing and Restoring: Health and Medicine in the World's Religious Traditions*, ed., Lawrence E. Sullivan (New York: Macmillan, 1989), 59-87.

religions. Because attention to women leads to fundamental authority questions, this particular "theme" is more like a lens which dramatically changes our perspective on entire traditions as well as on our own academic discipline.

A course on almost any religious tradition that traces the path of women's religious lives tends to develop in the same directions as those dictated by the study of African-American religions. The common denominator, of course, is the relative lack of power characteristic of both women and blacks. But using the lens of women's lives to focus African-American religions in a particular way does not simply reinforce the critique of religious studies implicit in the larger subject matter. It adds a significant new dimension.

The slave system that brought large numbers of Africans to the New World produced cataclysmic changes in their lives, changes that provoked religious responses. One of the most interesting of these was a shift in gender roles within religious traditions, a shift that most likely began during slavery and then developed further in response to more recent social, political, and economic changes. In Cuban Santeria, Brazilian Candomble, and Haitian Vodou, to mention only the most obvious examples, there are a large number of women in leadership positions. Half or more of the urban Vodou temples are headed by women and, with only a few exceptions, all of the Candomble houses in northern Brazil are. In these religions women occupy a proportionately greater share of the leadership roles than they do in the African traditions out of which the New World forms came, and they certainly have more prominence than they would have in the Christian traditions picked up from the slaveholders. At present I can only speculate about the reasons for this, reasons which seem likely to be found somewhere in the mix of attitudes toward power and analyses of power that evolved among people who first experienced slavery and then a lingering, multi-faceted colonialism. A respect (perhaps even a need) for women's insights and for the distinctive styles of leadership they have developed is manifest in these religions.

Having women in leadership positions changes a religion in fundamental ways. Elsewhere I have argued at some length that the growing number of women leaders in Haitian Vodou has led directly to making women's lives and problems more visible (and thus more available for healing) within the religion as a whole.[3] Temple leaders are the ones who

[3] See chapter eight, "Ezili," in my *Mama Lola: A Vodou Priestess in Brooklyn* (Los Angeles and Berkeley: University of California Press, 1991).

go into trance most frequently and it is their possession-performances that bring the spirits, male and female, into the midst of the community. Since possession-performances are always a mixture of the traditional and the extemporaneous, it is natural that the spirits would undergo some changes when a significant number of the people embodying them are women. Several of the female spirits served in Vodou have shifted in obvious ways to reflect women's perspectives on the life arenas these spirits represent. For example, possession-performances of Ezili Freda, a Vodou spirit of love, are as likely today to comment on the dangers and constraints of sexually derived identity (as women actually experience them in contemporary Haiti) as they are to act out male projections of idealized female sexuality.

In many religions, female images of the divine are so heavily ideological, so thoroughly constructed out of male projections, that they provide only meager insight into the dynamics of women's lives. To some extent, African-American religions in the Caribbean and South America provide an alternative to this situation. I do not want to overplay the point, since the cultures in which these religions are embedded are in many ways still misogynist ones. But it is possible to learn a great deal about the lives of African-American women by analyzing female divinities or spirits and this is a rare experience in the study of the world's religions.

Power Issues in the Classroom

The analysis presented in the previous pages does not lead me to suggest that scholars of world religions stop reading the great religious texts. But we might find it both interesting and profitable to let go of our studied naivete about the power issues involved in texts. Texts lead to the creation of priestly and scholarly elites who are charged with keeping and interpreting those texts. Holding elite perspectives taken from sacred texts and great thinkers in tension with those of non-elites gleaned through study of popular religion provides both a more whole and a more dynamic view of a religious tradition. It also appears to be a necessary strategy if we want to include women.

Perhaps it is inevitable that scholars trained in Western academic traditions reify and intellectualize religions. It is easier to study a text than a performance and an ideal type than a lived religion. Ideal types hold still; they are relatively static and have fairly firm boundaries. The voices of authority are clear and easily identified. It might be argued that such abstraction is necessary to deal with a subject as complex as religion. But it is disturbing how much the habits of thought present in

Western academic contexts resemble the practices of colonialism. Drawing clear boundaries, establishing clean lines of authority and seeing that
things get written down were primary concerns of the colonial era. Many
of us who work in comparative religions pride ourselves on escaping an
earlier mode of scholarly work that, often unconsciously, supported
Christian hegemony. The question we now need to ask ourselves is
whether we in the academy render the world's religions in a way that
continues Western colonialism.

The fear of unwittingly reinforcing colonialistic attitudes is especially
poignant in relation to African-American religions for these are among
the most misunderstood and most often maligned in the world. When
Vodou is mentioned, images of zombis, pins stuck in dolls, and black
magic still spew from the racist psyche. Projections and fears still pass as
news in the popular media and academic books are often not much more
accurate. When I first began to teach out of my research in Haiti, I tried
to correct these stereotypes but I soon had to give up on that approach.
These days I simply offer as lively and convincing an alternative view of
the traditional religions of the Caribbean and South America as I can
manage. Oral histories and case studies are helpful, since it is more difficult to caricature three-dimensional people who speak for themselves
than abstractions such as "the Haitian people" which occupy center stage
in many anthropological texts.

It is impossible to explore gender issues in religions without analyzing
the social structures, politics, and economics of their locations. So attention to gender guides the teacher toward presenting religions in very
concrete terms, firmly rooting them in time and space. I have found that
such an approach has benefits beyond those related directly to women. A
relatively simple thing like keeping the technologies of a particular place
in mind when presenting the religion of that place is helpful. For example, when studying animal sacrifice, it helps a student to know that any
family in Jamaica, Cuba, or Haiti that enjoys a chicken dinner probably
had to kill the chicken first, and neither the killing nor the eating are
substantially different when they are done in the context of a ceremonial
meal. Knowing this recontextualizes religious sacrifice for North American students and moderates their sense of it as an act of primitive violence.

Starting from African-American subject matter or from a concern for
the visibility of women the teacher of religion is led toward a more
concrete, socially located view of religions than is common in most religious studies courses. Bringing such a view alive in the classroom is a

complex task. The challenges are great, but so are the potential benefits. The following syllabus, constructed for a course taught at Barnard College in the spring of 1988, is a partial response to these challenges.

Course Syllabus

Women in African-American Religions is a course that focuses, through the lens of gender questions, on religious systems that developed in the Caribbean and South America as a result of trans-Atlantic slavery. A central thesis of the course is that African religious retentions in the New World, like Christian borrowings, are neither random nor fragmentary, but systematic and thoroughly understandable in terms of history and circumstance.

A related point extends this thesis to the social arena and specifically to gender role constructs. The frequency with which women function as heads of households as well as heads of religious groups in African-American societies is not seen as aberrant or pathological. Rather it is understood as the product of long term social change and explained in terms of cultural heritage and history, as well as contemporary social, political, and economic conditions.

Theoretical concerns of the course include the function of religious imagery in describing and shaping the concrete life experience of women and the role of religion in situations of social change, particularly change that directly affects gender roles. These questions are pursued mainly through a study of the African-based religions of Brazil and Haiti because of their contrasting histories and because of the substantial amount of scholarly work about these two areas that is available in English.

INTRODUCTION TO THE COURSE

This is an historical lecture concerning West African religion and culture and women's roles in both. It also briefly recounts the history of trans-Atlantic slavery.

Unit I *Religion as an Attempt to Recreate Lost Families*: Religious Responses to Slavery, Colonialism, and Poverty

This unit explores the central role of family in several West African religions. It also theorizes about early slave religion, about which little is actually known, and its relation to the need to recreate lost families. The religious dimensions of New World family structures are analyzed, as well as the role of urban religious centers in creating fictive kinship networks.
Reading:

Bastide, *The African Religions of Brazil*, Introduction, chapters 1 and 2

Deren, *Divine Horsemen*, chapters 1, 2, and 4

K. Brown, *Mama Lola*, chapters 1 and 2

Laguerre, "Ticouloute and His Kinfolk: The Study of a Haitian Extended Family"

Unit II *The Historical Evolution of Religious Gender Imagery*

This unit analyzes changes in male and female spirits as they move from Africa to the New World
Reading:

Thompson, *Flash of the Spirit*, chapter 1

Larose, "The Meaning of Africa in Haitian Vodu"

Bastide, *The African Religions of Brazil*, chapters 10-14

Barnes, "Ogun: An Old God for a New Age"

K. Brown, "Systematic Remembering, Systematic Forgetting: Ogou in Haiti"

Gleason, *Oya*, parts 1 and 2

Brown, *Mama Lola*, chapter 8

Unit III *Women's Economic and Religious Leadership*

This unit explores women's role in Caribbean market economies as well as the financial and social responsibilities which fall to them as heads of households and religious leaders. Women's multi-generational social networks are explored as the context for creative survival strategies.
Reading:

Landes, *City of Women*, pp. 1-129

K. Brown, "Alourdes: A Case Study of Moral Leadership in Haitian Vodou"

K. Brown, *Mama Lola*, chapter 6

S. Brown, "Love Unites Them and Hunger Separates Them: Poor Women in the Dominican Republic"

Mintz, "Economic Role and Cultural Tradition"

Justus, "Women's Role in West Indian Society"

Henney, "Sex and Status: Women in St. Vincent"

Gussler, "Adaptive Strategies and Social Networks of Women in St. Kitts"

Unit IV   *Female Sexuality and Childrearing*: Religious Imagery that Describes Realities and Creates Possibilities

This unit examines women's sexuality and their childbearing and childrearing roles. These social data are placed in conversation with a variety of religious and folkloric images and stories which both interpret and shape women's experiences in these life arenas.

Reading:

Landes, pp. 129-248

K. Brown, "Olina and Erzulie: A Woman and a Goddess in Haitian Vodou"

Lowenthal, "Labor, Sexuality and the Conjugal Contract in Rural Haiti"

Simpson, "Sexual and Familial Institutions in Northern Haiti"

Farmer, "bad blood, spoiled milk"

Murray, "Women in Perdition: Ritual Fertility Control in Haiti"

Pressel, "Spirit Magic in the Social Relations between Men and Women (Sao Paulo, Brazil)"

Unit V   *Death, Sex, and Humor*: A Gendered View of Healing and the Whole Life

This unit examines the death and trickster spirits of African-based religions in Haiti and Brazil. It focuses on their exaggerated sexuality and overdetermined masculinity. Female counterparts to these spirits are investigated. The connection of this group of spirits with the healing arts is also explored. Consideration of healing also becomes the context for further study of the individual and communal functions of trance-possession, a central feature of these religions.

Reading:

K. Brown, "Afro-Caribbean Spirituality: A Haitian Case Study"

K. Brown, "The Power to Heal: Reflections on Women, Religion and Medicine"

K. Brown, *Mama Lola*, chapter 12

Deren, *Divine Horsemen*, chapters 5 and 6

Thompson, *Flash of the Spirit*, chapters 2 and 3

Pressel, "Umbanda Trance and Possession in Sao Paulo, Brazil"

Bourguignon, *Possession*

Conclusion to the course

Here an attempt is made to draw together various theoretical strands from the course as a whole. Roger Bastide's theory is used as focus and counterpoint for class discussions.

SELECTED BIBLIOGRAPHY

Barnes, Sandra T. "Ogun: An Old God for a New Age." Philadelphia: Institute for the Study of Human Issues, Occasional Papers in Social Change, 1980.

Bastide, Roger. *The African Religions of Brazil: Toward a Sociology of the Interpenetration of Civilizations.* Baltimore: Johns Hopkins University Press, 1980.

Bourguignon, Erika. *Possession.* San Francisco: Chandler and Sharp, 1976.

——————. ed., *Religion, Altered States of Consciousness and Social Change.* Columbus: Ohio State University Press, 1973.

Bramly, Serge. *Macumba: The Teachings of Marie-Jose, Mother of the Gods.* New York, 1979.

Brown, Karen McCarthy. "Afro-Caribbean Spirituality: A Haitian Case Study." In *Healing and Restoring: Health and Medicine in the World's Religious Traditions.* Edited by Lawrence E. Sullivan. New York: Macmillan, 1989.

——————. "Alourdes: A Case Study of Moral Leadership in Haitian Vodou." In *Saints and Virtues.* Edited by John S. Hawley. San Francisco and Berkeley: University of California Press, 1987.

——————. *Mama Lola: A Vodou Priestess in Brooklyn.* San Francisco and Berkeley: University of California Press, 1991.

——————. "The Power to Heal: Reflections on Women, Religion and Medicine." In *Shaping New Vision: Gender and Values in American Culture.* Edited by C. Atkinson, C. Buchanan, and M. Miles. Ann Arbor: U.M.I. Research Press, 1987.

——————. "Systematic Remembering, Systematic Forgetting: Ogou in Haiti." In *Africa's Ogun: Old World and New.* Edited by Sandra T. Barnes. Bloomington: University of Indiana Press, 1989.

Brown, Susan E. "Love Unites Them and Hunger Separates Them: Poor Women in the Dominican Republic." In *Toward an Anthropology of Women.* Edited by Rayna R. Reiter. New York: Monthly Review Press, 1975.

Chernoff, John Miller. *African Rhythms and African Sensibility: Aesthetics and Social Action in African Musical Idioms.* Chicago: The University of Chicago Press, 1979.

Deren, Maya. *Divine Horsemen: The Voodoo Gods of Haiti*. New York: Delta, Dell Publishing Company, 1970; reprint ed., New Paltz, New York: Documentext, McPherson and Company, 1983.

Farmer, Paul. "bad blood, spoiled milk: bodily fluids as moral barometers in rural Haiti." *American Ethnologist* 15:1 (February 1988): 62-83.

Gleason, Judith. *Oya: In Praise of the Goddess*. Boston: Shambala, 1987.

Gussler, Judith D. "Adaptive Strategies and Social Networks of Women in St. Kitts." In *A World of Women*. Edited by Erika Bourguignon. New York: Praeger, 1980.

Henney, Jeanette H. "Sex and Status: Women in St. Vincent." In *A World of Women*. Edited by Erika Bourguignon. New York: Praeger, 1980.

Justus, Joyce Bennett. "Women's Role in West Indian Society." In *The Black Woman Cross-Culturally*. Edited by Filomina Chioma Steady. Rochester, Vermont: Schenkman, 1981.

Laguerre, Michel S. "Ticouloute and His Kinfolk: The Study of a Haitian Extended Family." In *The Extended Family in Black Societies*. Edited by Demitri B. Shimkin, Edith M. Shimkin, and Dennis A. Frate. Paris: Mouton, 1978.

Landes, Ruth. *The City of Women*. New York: Macmillan, 1947.

Larose, Serge. "The Meaning of Africa in Haitian Vodu." In *Symbols and Sentiments: Cross-Cultural Studies in Symbolism*. Edited by I. Lewis. New York: Academic Press, 1977.

Leacock, Seth and Ruth Leacock. *Spirits of the Deep: A Study of an Afro-Brazilian Cult*. Garden City, New York: Doubleday, 1975.

Lowenthal, Ira. "Labor, Sexuality and the Conjugal Contract in Rural Haiti." In *Haiti—Today and Tomorrow: An Interdisciplinary Study*. Edited by C. Foster and A. Valdman. New York: University Press of America, 1984.

——————. "Marriage is 20, Children are 21: The Cultural Construction of Conjugality and Family in Rural Haiti." PhD dissertation. The Johns Hopkins University, 1987.

Metraux, Alfred. *Voodoo in Haiti*. New York: Schocken Books, 1972.

Mintz, Sidney W. "Economic Role and Cultural Tradition." In *The Black Woman Cross-Culturally*. Edited by Filomina Chioma Steady. Rochester, Vermont: Schenkman, 1981.

Murray, Gerald F. "Population Pressure, Land Tenure, and Voodoo: The Economics of Haitian Peasant Ritual." In *Beyond the Myths of Culture: Essays in Cultural Materialism*. Edited by Eric B. Ross. New York: Academic press, 1980.

——————. "Women in Perdition: Ritual Fertility Control in Haiti." In *Culture, Natality and Family Planning*. Edited by John F. Marshall and Steven Polgar. Chapel Hill: University of North Carolina Press, 1976.

Pressel, Esther. "Umbanda Trance and Possession in Sao Paulo, Brazil." In *Trance, Healing and Hallucination: Three Field Studies in Religious Experience*. Edited by F. Goodman, J. Henney, and E. Pressel. New York: John Wiley and Sons, 1974.

——————. "Spirit Magic in the Social Relations between Men and Women." In *A World of Women*. Edited by Erika Bourguignon. New York: Praeger, 1980.

Simpson, George E. "Sexual and Family Institutions in Northern Haiti." In *The American Anthropologist* 44 (1942): 655-74.

Thompson, Robert Farris. *Flash of the Spirit: African and Afro-American Art and Philosophy*. New York: Random House, 1983.

❧XVII❧

Teaching Comparative Religious Ethics

ROBIN W. LOVIN AND FRANK E. REYNOLDS

Over the past twenty-five years, Religious Studies has provided important leadership in the "globalizing" of liberal education. In the study of religious ethics, however, movement toward this global perspective has been slow. Perhaps this is because the normative dimension inherent in the study of ethics seems at odds with the methodological neutrality required in comparative studies. Perhaps it is because scholars and teachers in religious ethics have, unlike others in religious studies, developed their discipline chiefly in dialogue with philosophy, rather than with area studies, anthropology, and sociology. Whatever the reason may be, the fact is that little research and teaching in religious ethics has moved beyond the boundaries of the Western world. The ethical issues under consideration—war and peace, ecology, human rights, and scarce resources—certainly have global dimensions, but the critical perspectives brought to bear on them in religious ethics classes remain primarily Western and, indeed, Christian.

In the 1970s a number of ethicists, most of whom were teaching in religious studies programs, independently began to take steps toward the development of a new, more global approach to religious ethics. In 1971, James Smurl published a brief textbook titled *Religious Ethics: A Systems Approach* (Englewood Cliffs: Prentice-Hall, 1971). David Little and Sumner B. Twiss made more impact on scholarship in religious ethics with their *Comparative Religious Ethics: A New Method* (San Francisco: Harper and Row, 1975). Little and Twiss used a neo-Weberian understanding of rationality to develop a comparative interpretation of the ethics of the Gospel of Matthew, of Theravada Buddhism, and of the Navajo.

In 1978, Ronald Green presented a neo-Kantian theory of religious and moral rationality in *Religious Reason* (New York: Oxford University Press, 1978). This theory that religion provides the reasons for which a person may subordinate immediate personal desires to a universal moral law explains, according to Green, the rational basis for all systems of ethics, Western and non-Western, past and present. In a recent work, *Religion and Moral Reason* (New York: Oxford University Press, 1988), Green has sought to develop this thesis through studies of African, Hebrew, Hindu, and Chinese examples.

A further important methodological development among these early studies of comparative religious ethics was provided by Frederick Bird in his essay, "Paradigms and Parameters for the Comparative Study of Religious and Ideological Ethics," *Journal of Religious Ethics* 9 (Fall, 1981), 157-85. Bird provides an approach that is more oriented to an examination of the cultural contexts and class interests that shape religious expressions, and he contends that such a method applies to the comparative study of ethical systems generated by ideological movements as well as to religious ethics.

Finally, it is necessary to take seriously into account a work by John P. Reeder, *Source, Sanction, and Salvation* (Englewood Cliffs: Prentice-Hall, 1988). Although recently published and limited largely to a study of Christian and Jewish ethics, Reeder's work is based on scholarship which dates back to his participation in the earliest of the contemporary discussions of comparative ethics. His effort to develop a comprehensive framework for understanding religious and moral rationality offers important suggestions for comparative work across a wider range of religious traditions.

In the early 1980s, John Carman and Mark Juergensmeyer organized a multi-year project centered at Harvard Divinity School and the Graduate Theological Union at Berkeley. Their aim was to foster the development of this new field of comparative religious ethics by encouraging scholarly research and developing teaching materials for religious studies and liberal arts programs.

For anyone interested in the teaching of comparative religious ethics, the most important classroom resources will probably be collections of essays in which specialists in a variety of traditions or methods of study combine their efforts in a coordinated approach to the subject matter. Single-author works can develop and illustrate important theoretical and methodological points, but at this stage in the development of the discipline, only a joint effort can provide the depth and detail of knowledge required to give a vivid picture of the problems and possibilities inherent in cross-cultural and trans-historical comparative studies.

The Harvard-GTU comparative ethics project yielded three excellent collections of original essays, one edited by John S. Hawley, *Saints and Virtues* (Berkeley: University of California Press, 1988), one edited by Donald Swearer and Russell Sizemore, *Ethics, Wealth, and Salvation: A Study in Buddhist Social Ethics* (Columbia: University of South Carolina Press, 1990), and one edited by the authors of the present essay, *Cosmogony and Ethical Order: New Essays in Comparative Ethics* (Chicago: University of Chicago Press, 1985). In addition, John Carman and Mark Juergensmeyer have edited a series of extensive bibliographies dealing with the ethics of various traditions. This series is titled *A Bibliographic Guide to Comparative Ethics* (Cambridge: Cambridge University Press, 1991).

The scholarly collegiality and institutional cooperation that developed during this Harvard/GTU project led directly to the Harvard, Chicago, and the Graduate Theological Union sponsorship of a series of Summer Institutes and Workshops on the topic of "Religious Studies and Liberal Education: Towards a Global Perspective." Since the present volume is a result of these workshops that grew out of an effort to expand the comparative study of religious ethics, it is particularly appropriate that we offer some of our suggestions on the teaching of comparative religious ethics in this context.

In developing the conferences that led to *Cosmogony and Ethical Order: New Essays in Comparative Ethics*, the two authors of the present essay sought to generate a new kind of approach to comparative religious ethics that would draw upon the disciplines of both history of religions (Reynolds) and theological and philosophical ethics (Lovin). Both the book and a more recent "Focus on Cosmogony and Ethical Order," *Journal of Religious Ethics*, 14 (Spring, 1986) include introductions which articulate a version of "ethical naturalism" which is, we believe, a particularly apt theoretical starting point for comparative studies in religious ethics. Both also contain essays by other authors which describe the relationships between cosmogony and ethical order in a variety of traditions, ranging from ancient Israel and China to modern Europe and Latin America.

During the development of this work, we have jointly taught four courses at the University of Chicago in which we have experimented with various ways of introducing students to the study of comparative religious ethics through the study of cosmogony and ethical order. These courses, primarily for graduate students in ethics and the history of religions, have provided the classroom experience that informs the suggested course outlines that follow. However, these suggested course outlines also incorporate more recent insights that were stimulated by our own discussion of introductory courses for undergraduates, and was further developed in the course of conversations at the "Religious Studies and Liberal Education" Workshop held in Berkeley in June, 1989.

Three suggested course outlines are appended. Course IA and Course IB are presented as alternative possibilities for those interested in introducing comparative religious ethics through a course specifically focussed on Cosmogony and Ethical Order. Course II could serve (depending on how it is taught) *either* as a somewhat different kind of introductory course in comparative religious ethics, *or* as a more advanced course that builds on foundations established in one or the other version of Course I.

COURSE IA
COSMOGONY AND ETHICAL ORDER
AS AN INTRODUCTION TO COMPARATIVE RELIGIOUS ETHICS
(Focus on multiple cosmogonies)

The relationship between cosmogonies and ethics in different cultural systems provides a useful introduction to a comparative religious ethics. Most cultures and religious traditions have several accounts of cosmogony which are used for different occasions and circumstances. What is more, the differences between those cosmogonies often relate in significant ways to moral problems and tensions within the culture. For comparative purposes, the persistent patterns and significant variations in the way multiple cosmogonies are related to ethics provides opportunity to consider the possibilities and limitations of ethical generalizations across cultural and religious boundaries.

The course proceeds in six parts. The suggested class time for each part presupposes a 14-week semester. If the course is a 10-week quarter course (or if the teacher of a semester course wishes to treat the material in greater depth), part four can be dropped without disrupting the basic structure.

1. *Patterns of relationship between religion and ethics.* At the outset, we review some of the ways that religious believers and critical scholars

have attempted to understand the link between religious and moral beliefs. We suggest that no single, simple relationship (such as morality as divine command, or divine retribution for moral transgression) adequately structures these relationships for comparative purposes. We propose that an adequate framework for understanding must allow for complex, multi-faceted relationships between religion and ethics, and we use John P. Reeder's *Source, Sanction, and Salvation* to illustrate this sort of framework. Approximately one week of class time.

2.   *The Genesis cosmogony and ethical order.* The next four parts of the course treat the relationship between cosmogony and ethics as, in Reeder's terms, an inquiry into the *source* of ethical order. We begin with the familiar account of creation in Genesis 1-2, exploring the relationships between the two cosmogonies in this account, and their relationship to other cosmogonic ideas in the Hebrew tradition, and to the originary events of Sinai and Exodus. We also encourage an ethically sensitive treatment of the religious and cultural conflicts over the Genesis cosmogonies and the modern evolutionary cosmogony as a contemporary example of multiple cosmogonies. As an introduction to cosmogony and its ethical implications, we read Mircea Eliade, "Cosmogonic Myth and 'Sacred History'," in *The Quest: History and Meaning in Religion* (Chicago: University of Chicago Press, 1969), pp. 72-87. For treatment of the Genesis cosmogonies, we read Jon Levenson's *Creation and the Persistence of Evil* (San Francisco: Harper & Row, 1988). Further discussion can be found in Douglas Knight's essay on Hebrew cosmogonies in Lovin and Reynolds, *Cosmogony and Ethical Order.* The notes in both Levenson's book and Knight's essay provide additional useful bibliography. Approximately three weeks of class time.

3.   *Cosmogony and ethical order among the Trixano.* A more modern set of cosmogonies which aptly illustrates the transformation of cosmogonic ideas to encompass changing moral and cultural circumstances appears among the highland Indians of Guatemala. The Trixano are an indigenous people who combined their traditional cosmogonic myths with the Christianity of their Spanish conquerors to produce two quite different cosmogonies. One provides a moral order explicable and manageable on the Trixano's own terms; the other explains and provides guidance for their subordinate relationship to the now-dominant Spanish culture. Readings include Kay Warren's essay on the Trixano in *Cosmogony and Ethical Order*, which can be supplemented by all or part of her full-length book, *Symbolism of Subordination* (Austin: University of Texas Press, 1978). Though the full-length book is not presently available from the

publisher, efforts are underway to encourage the printing of a second edition. Both of Warren's treatments contain additional bibliographic references. Approximately two weeks of class time.

4.   *Cosmogony and ethical order in ancient China.* The example of ancient China shows that cosmogonies may provide ethical orientation by emphasizing the origins of a natural order, or by identifying the originary order with the beginnings of civilization. In the Chinese case, the former orientation was characteristic of Taoism, while the latter was associated primarily with the Confucian tradition. The working out of the tensions between the two orientations are traced both in controversies between the Taoist and Confucian schools, and, in the case of Mencius, in the attempt to incorporate both cosmogonies in a single, Confucian system of thought. Readings include Norman Girardot's essay on the Taoist tradition in *Cosmogony and Ethical Order,* which can be supplemented by all or part of his book, *Myth and Meaning in Early Taoism* (Berkeley: University of California Press, 1983); also Lee Yearley, "A Confucian Crisis: Mencius' Two Ethics and Their Cosmogonies," also in *Cosmogony and Ethical Order.* Other relevant books and articles are mentioned in the bibliographies included in these readings. Approximately three weeks of class time.

5.   *Cosmogony and ethical order in Theravada Buddhism.* Having introduced the idea of multiple cosmogonies in a number of cultural, religious, and philosophical circumstances, we proceed to consider one of the most developed systems of multiple cosmogonies supporting distinctive, yet related, patterns of moral reasoning and practice. We emphasize the way in which concepts of Buddhist ethics, including the earning of merit and the quest for Nibbanic cessation of struggle and suffering, can be systematically related to the cosmogonic myths which this tradition has developed and elaborated. This part of the course provides an opportunity to develop the analytical framework of parts one and two in relation to a second major tradition which is probably less familiar to the students than the Jewish and Christian moral ideas that dominate the first two parts of the course. Readings include Reynolds' essay in *Cosmogony and Ethical Order* and Winston King, *In the Hope of Nibbana* (LaSalle: Open Court, 1964). Other relevant books and articles are mentioned in the bibliographies included in the above readings. Approximately three weeks of class time.

6.   *Cosmogony and the Search for Moral Universality.* Having developed a concept of cosmogony as the source of moral ideas as an interpretative

framework for comparative ethics, we proceed to the question of whether it is possible to offer meaningful generalizations about morality across religious and cultural traditions. We briefly review the suggestions of Ronald Green and David Little and Sumner Twiss, and we suggest, by contrast, that the persistent relationship between cosmogony and ethical order across traditions supports an ethical naturalism, rather than a Kantian or Weberian rationalism, as the most appropriate theoretical starting point for comparative religious ethics. While it is difficult to identify universal moral principles, the generality of attempts to prescribe the form of a good human life within culturally understood constraints of nature allows us to relate moral systems which differ widely in their cultural settings and in their specific moral prescriptions. Readings include the introductory essay by Lovin and Reynolds in *Cosmogony and Ethical Order*. Supplementary books and articles are mentioned in the bibliography that is attached to that essay. Approximately two weeks of class time.

COURSE IB
COSMOGONY AND ETHICAL ORDER
AS AN INTRODUCTION TO COMPARATIVE RELIGIOUS ETHICS
(Focus on "normative" and "problematic" cosmogonies)

The relationship between cosmogonies and ethics in different cultural systems provides a useful introduction to comparative religious ethics. Most cultures and religious traditions have several accounts of cosmogony that are used for different occasions and circumstances. In some cases these cosmogonies establish a view of the natural and human world which provides normative ideals that serve as guides for ethical behavior. In other cases, the worldviews presented by the cosmogonies is more problematic, requiring the construction of ethical behavior that deals with these ambiguities and ambivalences. For comparative purposes, the persistent patterns and significant variations in the ways cosmogonies are related to ethics provides an opportunity to consider the possibilities and limitations of ethical generalizations across cultural and religious boundaries.

The course proceeds in seven parts. In a 14-week semester course, each part can be allocated approximately two weeks of class time. If the course is a 10-week quarter course (or if the teacher of a semester course wishes to treat the material in greater depth), part two and/or part five can be dropped without seriously disrupting the basic structure.

1. *Patterns of relationship between religion and ethics.* At the outset, we review some of the ways that religious believers and critical scholars have attempted to understand the link between religious and moral beliefs. We suggest that no single, simple relationship (such as morality as divine command, or divine retribution for moral transgression) adequately structures these relationships for comparative purposes. We propose that an adequate framework for understanding must allow for complex, multi-faceted relationships between religion and ethics, and we use John P. Reeder's *Source, Sanction, and Salvation* to illustrate this sort of framework.

2. *Cosmogony and ethical order in the Andes.* The next five parts of the course treat the relationship between cosmogony and ethics as, in Reeder's terms, an inquiry into the *source* of ethical order. We begin with a study of the primordial order of nature and society narrated in the cosmogonic myths of the Andean peoples, and an examination of the forms of ritual practice that are used to relate this order to the problems and choices of individuals and society. Moral action in this context emerges as a pattern of activity, often discerned by divination, that is required to maintain in the present the order set out in the cosmogonic myth. As an introduction to cosmogony and its ethical implications, we read Mircea Eliade, "Cosmogonic Myth and 'Sacred History'," in *The Quest: History and Meaning in Religion* (Chicago: University of Chicago Press, 1969), pp. 72-87. For the Andean traditions, we read Lawrence Sullivan's essay on Indian traditions of Peru in Lovin and Reynolds, *Cosmogony and Ethical Order.* The Sullivan essay may be supplemented by selections from his major work on South American religions, *Icanchu's Drum* (New York: Macmillan, 1988). Further references can be found in the Sullivan bibliographies.

3. *Cosmogony and ethical order in ancient Israel.* More familiar notions of cosmogony and the establishment and maintenance of a social and moral order are found in the Hebrew scriptures. We first explore the relationship between the two cosmogonies that are embedded in Genesis 1-2, then we trace their relationship to other cosmogonic ideas in the Hebrew tradition. We then focus attention on the stories of the Exodus and the Sinai covenant as continuations of the cosmogony of ancient Israel. Readings include Douglas Knight's essay in *Cosmogony and Ethical Order*, and Jon Levenson, *Creation and the Persistence of Evil* (San Francisco: Harper & Row, 1988). Note that if part two of the course is omitted, the Eliade article on "Cosmogonic Myth and 'Sacred History'" should be included in this part.

4. *Cosmogony and ethical order in Islam.* Islamic cosmogony develops many of the basic themes studied in the Hebrew scriptures, including the close connection between a created human and natural order and the requirements of moral behavior in everyday life. Qur'anic cosmogony, however, explicitly establishes the incompleteness of the original creation and thus connects the primordial order and its moral implications with the expectation of the Last Day. The role of prophecy in countering the degeneration of the created order, and the cosmogonic aspects of the social order established by Muhammad at Medina are also considered. Readings include Sheryl Burkhalter's "Completion in Continuity: Cosmogony and Ethics in Islam," in *Cosmogony and Ethical Order*, together with an article on "Islamic Law as Islamic Ethics" by Kevin Reinhart in *Jounral of Religious Ethics* 11 (Fall, 1983), 186-203. These articles may be supplemented with Fazlur Rahman, *Major Themes of the Qur'an* (Minneapolis: Bibliotheca Islamica, 1980), and Toshihiko Izutsu, *The Structure of Ethical Terms in the Koran* (Tokyo: Keio Institute of Philological Studies, 1959).

5. *Cosmogony and ethical order in ancient Greece.* In contrast to the Andean, Hebraic, and Islamic examples, in which cosmogony establishes a pattern which moral action sustains, the cosmogonic accounts of ancient Greece provided few clear directions for moral behavior and included elements which posed definite moral problems for the philosophy and religious practice of the classical age. The mythic emphasis on heroic virtues and apparent sanctions of the gods for deceitful and anti-social behavior required a transition to a form of civic or political morality conceived quite differently from the order of relationships that prevailed in the beginning. Readings for this part of the course include two essays by Arthur Adkins in *Cosmogony and Ethical Order*, which may be supplemented by his earlier book, *Merit and Responsibility* (Oxford: Clarendon Press, 1960). References to other relevant materials may be found in Adkins's bibliographies.

6. *Cosmogony and ethical order among the Aztecs.* The Aztec cosmogony, like the Andean, Hebraic, and Islamic cosmogonies, establishes a definite ordering of the natural and human worlds, but the ordering in this case makes severe demands on the people and the society called to sustain it. A cosmogony of five "ages" suggests that for those who live in the present, deteriorated age, the feebleness of the cosmic order is so extreme as to require the sacrifice of individual human lives in order to sustain the life of the cosmos. Human sacrifice thus becomes in this context a paradigmatic moral act. This introduces problems for the cross-cultural

assessment of violence and the relation of individual to social good which warrant significant discussion. In addition, the cosmogonic account and the sacrificial rituals which expressed it introduced very profound problems and tensions into the moral life of the Aztecs themselves. Readings include Kay Read, "The Fleeting Moment: Cosmogony, Eschatology and Ethics in Aztec Religion and Society," *Journal of Religious Ethics*, 14 (Spring, 1986), 113-38, and selections from Miguel Leon Portilla, *Native Mesoamerican Spirituality* (New York: Paulist Press, 1980). A strong criticism of Read's article is found in Charles Reynolds and Ronald Green, "Cosmogony and the 'Questions of Ethics'," *Journal of Religious Ethics*, 14 (Spring, 1986), 139-56. Read has responded to Reynolds and Green in *Journal of Religious Ethics*, 15 (Spring, 1987), 2-13.

7. *Cosmogony and the Search for Moral Universality*. Having developed a concept of cosmogony as an interpretative framework for comparative ethics, we proceed to the question of whether it is possible to offer meaningful generalizations about morality across religious and cultural traditions. We briefly review the suggestions of Ronald Green and David Little and Sumner Twiss, and we suggest, by contrast, that the persistent relationship between cosmogony and ethical order across traditions supports an ethical naturalism, rather than a Kantian or Weberian rationalism, as the most appropriate theoretical starting point for comparative religious ethics. While it is difficult to identify universal moral principles, the generality of attempts to prescribe the form of a good human life within culturally understood constraints of nature allows us to relate moral systems which differ widely in their cultural settings and in their specific moral prescriptions. Readings include the introductory essay by Lovin and Reynolds in *Cosmogony and Ethical Order*. Supplementary books and articles are mentioned in the bibliography that is attached to that essay.

COURSE II

MYTH, PHILOSOPHY, AND ETHICAL ORDER

AN EXPLORATION IN COMPARATIVE RELIGIOUS ETHICS

The relationships between myth, philosophy, and ethics has emerged as a central problem confronting those interested in comparative religious ethics. Increasingly, it is clear that myths which establish basic moral expectations and sanctions must be included in a comprehensive picture of the moral thought of a culture or a religious tradition. Mythic sources, however, raise in acute form problems of cross-cultural comparability and the cultural embeddedness of various modes of constructive and critical rationality. Both those interested in descriptive studies of the moral life of cultures and traditions and those whose principal concern is constructive normative thought thus have reasons for concern with the relations between myth and philosophy in religious ethics.

The course proceeds in six parts. The suggested class time for each part presupposes a 14-week semester. If the course is a 10-week quarter course (or if the teacher of a semester course wishes to treat the material in greater depth), part four can be dropped without disrupting the basic structure.

1. *Philosophy and ethics in the modern West.* The first part of the course provides a brief survey, or a useful review, of the development of autonomous, philosophical ethics, separated from mythical or religious sources and sanctions, and resting, presumably, on the requirements of reason alone. While providing an accurate and sympathetic historical treatment of this "Enlightenment project," this first part of the course must also make clear that the contemporary disillusionment with this ethical rationalism provides the starting point for a modern reassessment of the ethical importance of myth, ritual, and religious traditions. Selections from Kant's *Groundwork of the Metaphysics of Morals* and/or *Religion within the Limits of Reason Alone* provide paradigmatic statements of the Enlightenment project in ethics. Jeffrey Stout, *The Flight from Authority* (Notre Dame, Ind.: University of Notre Dame Press, 1981) or Alasdair MacIntyre, *After Virtue*, 2nd ed. (Notre Dame, Ind.: University of Notre Dame Press, 1984) provide historical review and critique of Enlightenment rationalism. Approximately two weeks of class time.

2. *Myth, philosophy, and ethics in ancient Greece.* While the Enlightenment era marked the emergence of the modern idea of an autonomous, philosophical ethics, modern thinkers have often treated Socrates, Plato, and Aristotle as forerunners in the establishment of philosophical ethics. Recent historical and philosophical studies call into question the notion of an ancient Greek ethics independent of mythical, ritual, and religious sources, and these contemporary authors provide material for an important reassessment of the relationship between myth and philosophy at the origins of Western thought. A central resource is the article by Arthur Adkins in Frank Reynolds and David Tracy, eds., *Myth and Philosophy* (Towards a Comparative Philosophy of Religions, No. 1; Albany: State University of New York Press, 1991). Additional readings could include two articles by Adkins in Lovin and Reynolds, *Cosmogony and Ethical Order*, and selections from Martha Nussbaum, *The Fragility of Goodness*

(Cambridge: Cambridge University Press, 1986). Approximately three weeks of class time.

3.   *Myth, philosophy, and ethics in ancient China.* In twentieth century thought, ancient China has been seen as another important locus for the transition from myth, ritual, and religion to independent philosophical thinking. As in the case of ancient Greece, more recent scholarship has called the reality of this transition into question. Both cosmogonic myth and philosophical speculation were important elements in shaping moral thought and practice in ancient China, and differences between philosophical schools prove to relate in important, systematic ways to the different myths of origin that played a central role in explaining the prevailing order of nature and society. Readings for this part of the course include Lee Yearley's "A Confucian Crisis: Mencius' Two Ethics and Their Cosmogonies," in *Cosmogony and Ethical Order*, and Norman Girardot, "Behaving Cosmogonically in Early Taoism," also in *Cosmogony and Ethical Order*. Additional resources include Norman Girardot, *Myth and Meaning in Early Taoism* (Berkeley: University of California Press, 1983), and Robert Campany, "Cosmogony and Self-Cultivation: The Demonic and the Ethical in Two Chinese Novels," *Journal of Religious Ethics* 14 (Spring, 1986), pp. 81-112. Approximately two weeks of class time.

4.   *Genesis, Enlightenment, and ethics.* While the Kantian paradigm of an autonomous, rational ethics became the ideal of Enlightenment thought, early modern ethics in the West showed considerable reliance on the ideas of divine creation as the foundation of moral and social order. The Genesis cosmogonies thus provide opportunity both for study of their ethical implications on their own terms and for an assessment of their impact on later moral thought. In the course, we highlight the relationship between the Genesis cosmogony and the image of the divine "watchmaker" and the mechanical universe of the eighteenth century, and we review the controversy between traditional "creationist" cosmogony and modern evolutionary theory in contemporary American society. Readings may include Jon Levenson, *Creation and the Persistence of Evil* (San Francisco: Harper and Row, 1988), Lovin's essay on, "Cosmogony, Contrivance, and Ethical Order," in *Cosmogony and Ethical Order*. Approximately three weeks of class time.

5.   *Myth, philosophy, and natural law.* Modern defenses of natural law have frequently included the notion that it is a pure form of autonomous, rational ethics, independent of mythical or religious presuppositions. Contemporary challenges to the autonomy of modern thought generally

have stimulated a re-examination of the religious roots of natural law, as well as a recognition of secularized forms of natural law thinking that have been important in modern moral and political philosophy. The development, decline, and revival of the idea of natural law provides an important case for descriptive studies in myth, philosophy, and ethics, and raises significant questions for the development of ethical realism, ethical naturalism, and other forms of contemporary normative theory. Readings in this area are numerous, but two studies by Winston Davis in Frank Reynolds and David Tracy, eds., *Myth and Philosophy* (Towards a Comparative Philosophy of Religions, No. 1; Albany: State University of New York Press, 1991) provide a statement of the historical developments that is particularly suited to the themes of this course. Useful treatments of the history of natural law are also found in Douglas Sturm's article "Natural Law," in the *Encyclopedia of Religion* (New York: Macmillan, 1987). John Finnis, *Natural Law and Natural Right* (Oxford: Clarendon Press, 1980) provides an important contemporary constructive statement of natural law thought, and includes a final chapter on the theological and religious implications of the concept. Approximately two weeks of class time.

6. *Myth, philosophy, and contemporary ethics.* The final part of the course provides opportunity for a return to the major issues of modern philosophical ethics raised in the first part of the course. At this point, students should be prepared to consider future possibilities for the development of normative thought in the context of a richer historical appreciation of the role of mythic, ritual, and religious elements in morality, as well as an awareness of the limitations of Enlightenment notions of the autonomy of reason. Further development of the previous discussion on natural law would be a possibility here, as would a discussion of the religious version of ethical naturalism presented in James Gustafson, *Ethics from a Theocentric Perspective*, 2 vols. (Chicago: University of Chicago Press, 1981), and the treatment of contemporary ethical theory in Jeffrey Stout, *Ethics After Babel* (Boston: Beacon Press, 1988). Alasdair MacIntyre, *Whose Justice? Which Rationality?* (Notre Dame, Ind.: University of Notre Dame Press, 1988) provides a further critique of the "Enlightenment project" with implications for the future prospects for constructive work in ethics. Approximately two weeks of class time.

XVIII

Comparative Ethics

MARK JUERGENSMEYER

This course, perhaps more than any other, confronts directly the issue of ethical relativism, a matter that is a personal as well as an intellectual concern. It is a dilemma faced by many in the modern world, including any international traveller who addresses the norms of other cultures, any thoughtful person concerned about social and economic policies on an international scale, and anyone who feels the tug of competing cultural loyalties in his or her own life. The point of this course is to take seriously the differences among ethical traditions without capitulating to an extreme relativism, by thinking sensitively about how these differences might be overcome.

There are many ways such a course can be taught. It can descriptively highlight the differences between traditions: "Ethics East and West," for instance, or *"Dharma* and Natural Law." It can focus on the current discussion about whether there is such a thing as a universal ethic or even a crosscultural framework for examining ethical norms. Or it can look at how issues of international importance, such as the rights of minorities, the status of women, the protection of the environment, and the limitations of violence, are handled in different traditions, and how international policies can be developed that take these points of view into account. The course to be described here attempts to follow all three of these ways, but that may be a bit much for one term: the course might be broken into a two-term sequence, one that covers ethical traditions the first term, and theory and issues the second.

Another way of doing the course is to focus on writers or ethical figures from different traditions. Lee Yearley at Stanford teaches a comparative ethics seminar focussing on Mencius and Aquinas, and I have for
years taught a seminar called "Jesus, Gandhi, Marx and Freud: Four
Models of Morality for the Modern World." My book, *Fighting with
Gandhi* (in paperback *Fighting Fair*), was a result of my thinking about
this course, and retains some of the flavor of the seminar. The course that
I will describe here is somewhat different: it attempts to cover more
comprehensively the major ethical traditions and some of the major issues that are involved in thinking about ethics crossculturally.

The ethical traditions

The course begins with Hindu ethics, focussing on the notion of
dharma as both a concept of social order and individual moral responsibility. A comparison is made with similar ideas in Buddhist ethics. While
lacking the social aspects of Hindu *dharma*, Buddhist concepts still have
the bases for forming a coherent social ethic; we look for those points of
reference in exploring the notion of the co-dependency of all forms of life
and in noting the compassionate example of the Buddha. We compare
Theravada and Mahayana traditions regarding ethical ideals and raise
the frequently-discussed issue of whether their ethical positions are essentially different.

A discussion of ethics in Native American, African and Caribbean-
African cultures involves the great variety of forms of ethical thought in
those cultures, as well as what appears to be common to all of them: an
emphasis on natural order, group concensus, and the embodiment of
personal virtues. We explore to what extent this appearance of similarity
is warranted, and compare the importance of these sorts of ethical standards and guides to the laws and moral codes that are thought to be
dominant in other traditions.

In Islam, for example, the idea of law is central (as it is, in somewhat
different ways, in Jewish and Christian traditions). We examine the notions of moral truth in Islamic law and the pragmatic ethics offered by
images of exemplary forms of behavior such as those described in the
Hadith as being characteristic of the Prophet, and those exhibited by
Muslim saints in many locales. In Jewish ethics, the familiar notions of
law and covenant are explored; and in the Christian tradition we look at
the tensions between law and grace, and between the particularity of
moral discipline required by the Christian community and the universal-

ity of ethical constraints expected of everyone in what many Christains understand as the natural moral order.

Secular ethical traditions are also considered. We explore the significance of post-Enlightenment notions of human rights and civic responsibility, which are central to modern thought and are sometimes at odds with traditional religious notions. We also look at such Marxist concepts as the idea of structural immorality and social obligation, which have an impact not only within socialist societies, but throughout the modern world. We also raise the question of whether traditional ethical theory, especially those forms of moral reasoning that are linked with the major religious traditions, have gender biases, and whether there is such a thing as feminist ethics.

In this overview of ethical traditions it is obvious that the class concentrates on commonly-accepted interpretations of such major ethical concepts such as *dharma* and law, and to some extent glosses over competing interpretations of those concepts and other ways of looking at ethics within traditions. Variations within traditions do not go completely unobserved, but the point of this course is not to exhume old ethical debates, but to trace the general characteristics of living ethical traditions (sometimes more clearly revealed in the behavior of its exemplary figures than in its concepts and codes) that color any discussion of crosscultural issues that impinge upon them.

Readings that describe these traditions' ethical characteristics are in abundance, but since they are also scattered I have found it convenient to prepare a single reader, photocopied and available for purchase, which compiles articles and chapters of books. Also useful are the introductions and annotated bibliographies prepared for the Berkeley-Harvard program on the comparative study of values, published by Cambridge University Press under the title *A Bibliographical Guide to the Comparative Study of Ethics*, edited by John Carman and myself. The price of the book makes it prohibitive for classroom use, but it can serve as a reference. Wadsworth Publishing Company has recently published two textbooks that make resources for comparative ethics more accessible: David Chidester's *Patterns of Action: Religion and Ethics in a Comparative Perspective*, and Denise and John Carmody's *How to Live Well: Ethics in the World Religions*. The essays in the volume edited by Cromwell Crawford, *World Religions and Global Ethics*, are also a valuable resource.

The search for a universal ethic

Is there a universal ethic? In raising this question the class turns to largely theoretical, rather than descriptive, studies of ethics. One set of theoretical writings begins with crosscultural comparative data, and then makes comparisons and comes to generalizations on the basis of this data. The pioneer in this way of proceeding is Max Weber; more recently Louis Dumont has taken up the Weberian task in comparing social values in India with those in the modern West.

Another group of writings relevant to the question of whether there is a universal ethic is more philosophical in orientation. Studies of this type look at patterns of moral reasoning and ask whether different ethical systems are tied together on a fundamental, formal level. Ronald Green has recently applied ideas first formulated by Kant to a variety of religious traditions and finds a common logic: the justification of moral actions—including those that might at first seem purely altruistic—on the basis of rewards granted by religion. Another recent work, authored by David Little and Sumner Twiss, provides a framework for the comparative analysis of ethical traditions. Critics of the latter approach, however, ask whether the categories of analysis that Little and Twiss employ are not themselves laden with modern Western philosophical values, and whether the analytic neutrality of their scheme is not, therefore, compromised at the outset.

The ventures of Green, Little, and Twiss are compared with linguists who search for deep structures beneath differing language systems. But just as there is a debate in linguistics over whether there are semantic deep structures as well as syntactic ones, there are also questions in the field of comparative ethics as to whether the search for intercultural ethics reveals areas of agreement that are substantive as well as formal. In this class we raise the question of whether there might be a biological ethic associated with the common facts of life and survival, and we look at various sides of the debate raised by sociobiologists in attempting to find the common genetic bases for all social values in animate—including human—behavior.

The last approach to intercultural ethics that we consider is perhaps the most basic one, looking at ideas or standards in one culture and seeing if there are analogues in another. We look at several specific examples: David Little's comparison of Islamic and Christian notions of religious tolerance, Frank Reynolds' comparison of Christian and Theravada Buddhist modes of action, and Ninian Smart's linkage of religious and moral styles in Islamic and Theravada Buddhist traditions. In each case the authors are looking less for agreement than complementarity, as Smart calls it: respect for what in another culture's moral position seems similar to one's own, even though profound theoretical differences persist.

Crosscultural topics in ethics

The final section of the course is an application of this last approach, the one in which complementary and analogical forms of ethical behavior are sought across cultural boundaries. Several issues of international importance are identified by the class and are viewed from multicultural ethical perspectives. The issues chosen for analysis will vary depending upon the interests of the class members. In the past these have included such topics as abortion, the status of women, animal rights, economic justice, environmental protection, the rights of minorities, issues of sexuality and sexual orientation, terrorism, war, and the limitations of violence. Teams of five to six class members are created for each topic. Each member of the team then chooses an ethical tradition and examines its attitude toward the topic. If, for example, a team's topic is abortion, one student in that team will explore Native American attitudes towards abortion, another will consider the attitude adopted in Marxist countries, and so forth. The paper that each student prepares constitutes his or her term paper, and each of the teams leads a classroom discussion on its topic. The point of the discussion is not only to allow each member of the team to summarize his or her research, but to determine to what extent the points of view being described are complementary. For the purpose of the discussion the whole class constitutes itself as a sort of parliament of ethical traditions, attempting to come up with global ethical solutions after taking the diversity of perspectives into consideration.

In doing research for their papers, students are expected to utilize both library resources and the expertise of faculty members specializing in various religious traditions. Some students may find helpful Chidester's *Patterns of Action*, which is organized around themes. The subject index to *A Bibliographical Guide to the Comparative Study of Ethics* may also be useful in directing students to the major primary and secondary literature related to the topic in each religious tradition.

BIBLIOGRAPHY

Caplan, A. ed., *The Sociobiology Debate*. New York and San Francisco: Harper and Row, 1978.

Carman, John, and Mark Juergensmeyer, eds. *A Bibliographic Guide to the Comparative Study of Ethics*. London and New York: Cambridge University Press, 1991.

Carmody, Denise Lardner and John Tully Carmody. *How to Live Well: Ethics in the World Religions*. Belmont, Cal.: Wadsworth Publishing Co., 1988.

Chidester, David. *Patterns of Action: Religion and Ethics in a Comparative Perspective*. Belmont, Cal.: Wadsworth Publishing Co., 1987.

Crawford, S. Cromwell. *The Evolution of Hindu Ethical Ideals*. Honolulu: The University of Hawaii Press, 1982.

Crawford, S. Cromwell, ed. *World Religions and Global Ethics*. New York: Paragon House, 1986.

Dumont, Louis. *Homo Hierarchicus: The Indian Caste System and its Implications*. Mark Sainsbury, trans. Chicago: University of Chicago Press, 1970.

Dumont, Louis. *From Mandeville to Marx: The Genesis and Triumph of Economic Ideology*. Chicago: University of Chicago Press, 1977.

Green, Ronald. *Religious Reason: The Rational and Moral Basis of Religious Belief*. Oxford: Oxford Unvieirsty Press, 1978.

Green, Ronald. "Review of Little and Twiss, *Comparative Religious Ethics*." *Journal of Religion*, 61:111-113.

Hawley, John Stratton, ed. *Saints and Virtues*. Berkeley: University of California Press, 1987.

Hindery, Roderick. *Comparative Ethics in Hindu and Buddhist Traditions*. Delhi: Motilal Banarsidass, 1978.

Juergensmeyer, Mark. "Doing Ethics in a Plural World." In Earl E. Shelp, ed., *Theology and Bioethics*. Dordrecht, Holland, and Boston: D. Reidel, 1985, pp. 187-201.

Juergensmeyer, Mark. *Fighting with Gandhi* (revised paperback version: *Fighting Fair*). New York and San Francisco: Harper and Row, 1984.

Little, David, and Sumner Twiss. *Comparative Religious Ethics: A New Method*. New York: Harper and Row, 1978.

Little, David. "The Present State of the Comparative Study of Religious Ethics." In *Journal of Religious Ethics* 9:210-227.

Lovin, Robin, and Frank Reynolds, eds. *Cosmogony and Ethical Order: New Studies in Comparative Ethics*. Chicago: University of Chicago Press, 1985.

Reynolds, Frank. "Contrasting Modes of Action: A Comparative Study of Buddhist and Christian Ethics." *History of Religions* 20:128-46.

Smart, Ninian. *Beyond Ideology: Religion and the Future of Western Civilization*, New York and San Francisco: Harper and Row, 1981.

Smart, Ninian. "Types of Religion and the Moral Strand." Unpublished paper prepared for the Berkeley-Harvard Program in the Comparative Study of Values, Berkeley, 1981.

Smith, Wilfred Cantwell. *Towards a World Theology: Faith and the Comparative History of Religion*. Philadelphia: Westminster Press, 1981.

Swearer, Donald. "Nirvana, No-Self, and Comparative Religious Studies." *Religious Studies Review* 6:301-3.

Weber, Max. *The Protestant Ethic and the Spirit of Capitalism*. Talcott Parsons, trans. New York: Charles Scribner's Sons, 1930.

Weber, Max. *The Religion of China*. H. Gerth, trans. Glencoe: The Free Press, 1951.

Weber, Max. *The Religion of India*. H. Gerth, trans. Glencoe: The Free Press, 1951.

Wilson, E. O. *Sociobiology: The New Synthesis*. Cambridge, Ma: Harvard University Press, 1975.

SYLLABUS FOR A COURSE ON GLOBAL ETHICS

PURPOSE: This is a seminar in comparative ethics, aimed at analyzing international moral issues from multi-cultural perspectives. There are three parts to the course: first a review of basic ethical concepts of some of the world's major religious and secular traditions; then an exploration of the controversial question of whether there is such a thing as a universal ethic; and finally an attempt to apply cross-cultural analyses to such issues as the care of the environment, the rights of women and minorities, medical ethics and international terrorism.

READINGS: Participants are expected to keep pace with the readings to be found in a Reader prepared especially for this class. Other readings are to be found in John Stratton Hawley, ed., *Saints and Virtues* (Berkeley: University of California Press, 1987), and in John Carman and Mark Juergensmeyer, eds., *A Bibliographic Guide to the Comparative Study of Ethics* (London: Cambridge University Press, 1991).

PROJECT TEAMS: Each member of the class participates in a small group (consisting of five or six members of the class). On Tuesdays the whole class meets in lecture-discussions; on Thursdays the teams meet to discuss their group projects. Each team focuses on a single ethical issue (e.g., abortion), and each member of the team prepares a paper on one tradition's ethical attitudes toward that issue (e.g., Native American attitudes toward abortion). The teams are responsible for giving an oral presentation to the class. The topic for the class discussion on that day is whether the various ethical perspectives are in any way compatible with one another.

READINGS

INTRODUCTORY: (Week #1)
Juergensmeyer, "Doing Ethics in a Plural World"
Hawley, "Introduction," to *Saints and Virtues*
Smart, "Religion and the Moral Strand"
Reynolds and Lovin, "Introduction," to *Cosmogony and Ethics*

Part One: ETHICAL TRADITIONS

HINDU ETHICS: (Week #2)
Crawford, from *The Evolution of Hindu Ethical Ideals*
Creel, "Dharma as an Ethical Category"
Embree, "Life's Duties," from *The Hindu Tradition*
Juergensmeyer, "Dharma and the Rights of Untouchables"

Hawley, "Morality Beyond Morality," in *Saints and Virtues*
Babb, "Satya Sai Baba," in *Saints and Virtues*

BUDDHIST ETHICS: (Week #3)
Macy, "Dependent Co-Arising: Distinctiveness of Buddhist Ethics"
Conze, "The Bodhisattva Ideal"
Tokuno, "Chinese Buddhist Ethics," from *Bibliographic Guide*
deBary, ed., "The Morals of a Monk," in *The Buddhist Tradition*
Tambiah, "The Buddhist Arahant," in *Saints and Virtues*
Tu, "The Confucian Sage," in *Saints and Virtues*

NATIVE AMERICAN ETHICS: (Week #4)
Gill, "Native American Religions"
Brandt, from *Hopi Ethics*

AFRICAN ETHICS: (Week #4)
Ray, "African Religions"
Brown, "Moral Leadership in Haitian Vodou," in *Saints and Virtues*
Sanneh, "Saints and Virtues in African Islam," in *Saints and Virtues*

ISLAMIC ETHICS: (Week #5)
Nasr, "The Shari'ah Divine Law: Social and Human Norm"
Arberry, trans, *The Holy Qur'an*, suras 107, 4
Jeffery, ed., "The Beatitudes and Maledictions of the Prophet"
Cragg & Speight, eds., introduction to *Islam from Within*
Brinner, "Prophet and Saint," in *Saints and Virtues*

JEWISH ETHICS: (Week #6)
Kellner, "The Structure of Jewish Ethics"
The Jerusalem Bible, The Deuteronomic Codes of Divine Law
Montefiore and Loewe, selections from *A Rabbinic Anthology*
Cohn, "Sainthood on the Periphery," in *Saints and Virtues*

CHRISTIAN ETHICS: (Week #6)
St. Augustine, selections from *The City of God*
Reinhold Niebuhr, selections from *Christian Ethics*
Lehmann, selections from *Ethics in a Christian Context*
Peter Brown, "Saint as Exemplar in Late Antiquity," and
Gelber, "The Exemplary World of St. Francis," in *Saints and Virtues*

MARXIST ETHICS: (Week #7)
Marx, selections from *A Critique of Hegel's Theory of Right*
Miller, "Replacing Morality," from *Analyzing Marx*

FEMINIST ETHICS: (Week #7)
Gilligan, selections from *In a Different Voice*; and "A Different Voice in Moral Decisions," in Eck, *Speaking of Faith*
Harrison, selections from *A Theology of Pro-Choice*

Part Two: QUEST FOR A UNIVERSAL ETHIC (Weeks 9-10)

Childress, "Issues in Comparative Religious Ethics"
Coleman, "After Sainthood?" in *Saints and Virtues*
Green, selections from *Religious Reason*
Juergensmeyer, *Fighting With Gandhi* (pb: *Fighting Fair*)
Kant, selections from *Metaphysics of Morals*
Rawls, selections from *A Theory of Justice*
Kilner and Sizemore, "Western Philosophical Ethics," from *A Bibliographic Guide*
Little & Twiss, selections from *Comparative Religious Ethics*
Reynolds and Lovin, "In the Beginning," *Cosmogony & Ethical Order*
Reynolds, "Contrasting Modes of Action"
Swearer, "Nirvana, No-Self, and Comparative Religious Ethics"

Part Three: GLOBAL ISSUES (Weeks 11-15)

Reading lists have been prepared for cross-cultural ethical perspectives on the following issues:
Abortion
Animal rights
Economic justice
Environmental protection
Human rights
Minority rights
Sexuality and sexual orientation
Terrorism
War and the sanction of violence
Women's rights

Other issues will be chosen and reading lists developed by the students

❧XIX❧

Creativity and Art: Artists, Shamans and Cosmology

THOMAS V. PETERSON

I

The painter Paul Cézanne wrote in his diary about his struggle to find some *"motif"* that would allow him to fashion a visual meaning of Mont Sainte Victoire. Having found this motif he would paint madly to the point where his rendering of the mountain was sufficiently developed to present his particular vision. While every such rendering presented a visual understanding of the whole, Cézanne repeatedly returned to his mountain to seek other motifs that would reveal the geological structure of the earth *or* the power of climatic forces *or* the interplay of nature's colors etc.[1] I would suggest that we might think of religious studies courses as analogous enterprises that have the same two distinct stages— squinting hard at the mountain of religious phenomena in order to find a motif for revealing what it means to be human and fleshing out that motif in the teaching process by building syllabi and conducting classes. What I am calling "motifs" here, others have been calling "themes."

So what can we say about the process of squinting hard at the "mountain" of religious phenomena to find appropriate motifs? There was considerable discussion in the Berkeley/Chicago/Harvard institutes about the values in teaching world religions to students in American colleges and universities. The two following justifications, summarizing the previous NEH institutes, came to prominence in discussions among participants in the summer of 1989: "To make the strange familiar and

[1] See Maurice Merleau-Ponty, "Cézanne's Doubt," *Sense and Non-Sense* (Evanston: Northwestern University Press, 1964), 9-25.

the familiar strange" and "To bring a truly global perspective to the issues that face people in the world today." An important mission among those of us teaching world religions, then, is to provide a forum where other people's voices may be heard as we address intellectual, economic, and aesthetic questions of an emerging global culture. Our discipline obligates us to insist that other people's perspectives be brought into the conversations that are taking place within the various disciplines of the university so that they may challenge our own western assumptions that increasingly impact upon other cultures.

To make the strange familiar and the familiar strange, we need to be very clear about our own intellectual agenda. If we do not initially clarify our most fundamental presuppositions, the insights and criticism of other peoples rarely end up challenging our basic western perspectives on reality. If a primary purpose in teaching the religions of the world to our students is to provide a counterpoint to our usually unquestioned assumptions, then we must allow people's religious beliefs and practices to challenge our most deeply held presuppositions. We must also, of course, continually revise our own intellectual agenda as we bring the Hindus' or Buddhists' fundamental concerns to bear on our questions. The very measure of the success of a thematic course may be the degree to which another people's religious experiences are allowed to broaden, challenge and eventually modify the very scope of the original theme.

Elsewhere in this volume Kendall Folkert has questioned the whole thematic approach because of its tendency to inject idiosyncratic personal, theological, and cultural biases into the study of other people's religious traditions. He is correct to warn us about the reductionism that can result when we arbitrarily organize the religious data of other people's traditions around some theme that happens to interest us. But the problem of subjectivity will not magically vanish by sleight of hand. We cannot simply bracket our own interpretations by taking some supposed objective stance.

When Folkert organizes his introductory course around rites of passage and uses Van Gennep's insightful observations about liminality, he is making the assumption that stages of transition present threatening situations across cultures. Even if this assumption is frequently born out by the study of other people's religious traditions, are we really free from bias when we organize our study of another people's religion around rites of passage? (I could easily agree that rites of passage are clearly delineated by the four stages of life in the *Laws of Manu*, but would argue that they are a somewhat arbitrary imposition on the ritual activity of the

Lakota people in North America.[2]) We cannot escape from the fact that we are bringing a western sociological category to bear in our study of another people's religion. Perhaps we wish to know how other people move from childhood to adulthood precisely because we handle it so poorly in our own culture.

There is, I think, no final solution to Folkert's concerns other than becoming more aware and honest about our reasons for examining the religious cultures of peoples throughout the world. But I believe that we must first acknowledge our own values and concerns in order to minimize them.[3] Implicit comparisons between another people's culture and our own are so often in the background of our courses in religious studies that it may be more honest to recognize them and to organize our courses explicitly around them, thereby subjecting our assumptions to scrutiny. But it is important that the theme we choose does not arbitrarily impose an alien structure on our "mountain" of religious phenomena. The theme should, rather, help us tease out some significant aspects of human life. Should the course reformulate the original theme or broaden its boundaries, then we have begun to make the familiar strange even as the strange becomes more familiar.

The course that I am presenting here went through a metamorphosis as the religious data began to challenge whether "creativity" was an appropriate category for the study of the religious traditions of non-literate peoples. I had originally entitled the course "Artists, Shamans and Creativity." Initially, I was content to allow the religious views of non-literate peoples to challenge modernist notions of creativity by suggesting that the creative process is more centrally involved in depth of meaning rather than novelty. Some of my conclusions dovetailed neatly with postmodern reflections by theorists in several disciplines.[4] When students in my class, however, began discussing the issue of creativity against the background of Marcel Griaule's *Conversations with Ogotem-*

---

[2] I begin to develop this argument in Thomas V. Peterson, "Initiation Rite as Riddle," *Journal of Ritual Studies* I, 1 (Winter, 1987): 73-84.

[3] Two anthropological works make a persuasive case for explicitly acknowledging Western assumptions when one encounters other peoples: Kennelm Burridge, *Encountering Aborigines: A Case Study: Anthropology and the Australian Aboriginal* (New York: Pergamon Press, 1973) and James W. Fernandez, "Edification through Puzzlement," in *Persuasions and Performances: The Play of Tropes in Culture* (Bloomington: Indiana University Press, 1986).

[4] Cf. John Gilmour, *Picturing the World* (Albany: SUNY Press, 1985) and Gilles Deleuze and Felix Guattari, *Anti-Oedipus: Capitalism and Schizophrenia* (Minneapolis: University of Minnesota Press, 1983). The latter work has an interesting interpretive section on the Dogon.

màli or Maya Deren's *The Divine Horsemen: The Living Gods of Haiti*, we began to seriously question whether "creativity" meaningfully addressed the Dogon or Haitian life. We finally chose the word "cosmologizing" to refer to the process through which humans weave together their worlds of meaning. As a result of these discussions with students, I finally changed the name of the course to "Artists, Shamans and Cosmology."

So far I have argued that there is nothing wrong with thematic courses as long as the theme itself is open to critique from the religious traditions that one is studying. In my experience, a theme helps clarify one's own presuppositions and more easily permits challenges to our most deeply-held values. But are there any clues about choosing a fruitful theme? In some sense the final value of a particular theme can only be discovered in the teaching process itself, just as one of Cézanne's motifs became clarified when it emerged in a specific painting. Teaching, like science and art, is experimental. It is difficult to give a rational defense for choosing one motif over another, because intuition is part and parcel of the interpretive process. It is easier to judge the success of a course as it unfolds and at its conclusion. But there are, I think, a couple of obvious observations that can be made about choosing appropriate themes.

First, the significance of the questions that one brings to bear on religious phenomena should not be underestimated. Religious studies is interdisciplinary, in large part, because our intellectual discourse emerges from conversations with historians, artists, philosophers, environmental scientists, anthropologists, and others. Paying lip service to our interdisciplinary stance without attending to its rigors has too frequently led us to raise idiosyncratic questions that bear little relationship to the major questions of academic discourse. Philosophical questions can become transmuted into arcane theological ones; historical issues can become narrow topics in church history. Then Folkert's criticism of our choice of themes returns to haunt us. If we are instrumental in bringing the perspectives of other peoples into an intellectual forum in our colleges and universities, we must make sure that we do not relegate them to the peripheries of intellectual discourse. Let us make sure that we are bringing other people's religious perspectives into the great conversations that are taking place within the various disciplines of the university. Professors of religious studies can accomplish this only if they themselves are seriously involved in the intellectual discourse of the academy.

Second, any given religious tradition will have a great deal to say about a particular range of human experiences. We have all encountered students who are excited about yogis because their miraculous powers to control bodily functions seem to offer new scientific possibilities. Yet, for the most part, professors of religious studies have bracketed such scientific questions because they seem less significant to our inquiries than those of values, importance, and meaning. With few exceptions, we will try to channel the students' concern to questioning *why* certain people will spend years in perfecting the discipline to enable themselves to walk on hot coals. Our discipline is first and foremost concerned with questions that concern the human imagination. We are drawn to Sikh poetry, Native American dances, and Dogon cosmologizing because they express the human act of endowing our world with importance and meaning. Themes or motifs that highlight human metaphorical activity are likely to yield impressive insights from human societies that otherwise seem peripheral to many other concerns of modern life.

There are many ways to organize a course around themes that involve the arts. The following course emphasizes the connection between traditional religious rituals and contemporary dramatic arts through the theme of cosmologizing. The central intellectual questions of the course center on how individuals and communities forge coherence in their world. Masking exercises have increasingly become more central to this course. They help students understand how personal identity merges with cultural mythology and how religious or artistic symbols focus ordinary human experiences. Accounts of traditional people's religions challenge modernist notions about individual autonomy, even while their myths and rituals suggest that the artistic process of forging meaningful worlds involves the interplay between the individual and his or her community. While the course is designed to challenge modernist notions that the creative process is entirely subjective and personal, it leaves the question of the individual's relationship with the community open-ended. The following is a slightly condensed and modified syllabus for the course.

II

HSR 308—ARTISTS, SHAMANS AND COSMOLOGY

This seminar, which meets for two hours twice weekly, focuses on how cultural worlds of meaning arise by examining artists and shamans as mediums in the creative process. Topics will include shamanic curing through ritual activity, the western artistic process of picturing the world, and the cosmogonic process of creating meaning through dreams, images, myths, metaphors, ritual activity, symbolic gesture, and language. Special emphasis on masking in this seminar will help focus on "image" at the point where ritual, myth, and the arts intersect.

As an upper division seminar, the course requires serious commitment and active engagement. Ideas will emerge from discussion; it is therefore essential that students come to class well-prepared to discuss the assignments. Generally, we will be exploring how cultural worlds of meaning are created. Since both artists and shamans are involved in creating worlds of meaning, we will explore the similarities and differences in the two enterprises with a goal to understanding the creative process itself.

REQUIRED BOOKS (Note: shorter selections, indicated in reading assignments, will be handed out before the class period.)

Barbara Myerhoff, *Peyote Hunt*, Cornell

Antonin Artaud, *The Theatre and Its Double*, Grove

Maya Deren, *Divine Horsemen: The Living Gods of Haiti*, McPherson

John (Fire) Lame Deer and Richard Erdoes, *Lame Deer: Seeker of Visions*, Washington Square Press

Alvaro Estrada, *Maria Sabina: Her Life and Chants*, Ross-Erickson

Marcel Griaule, *Conversations with Ogotemmàli: An Introduction to Dogon Religious Ideas*, Oxford

TOPICS AND READING ASSIGNMENTS: (Each class period is two hours. The course meets twice over fourteen and one-half weeks in the semester.)

A. "Introduction"
   Topics: 1. Who is the Cosmologizer?
   2. Reality, Imagination, and Transformation
   3. Poetic truth
   Day #1—Film: "My Dinner with André," Director, Louis Malle; Actors, André Gregory and Wallace Shawn **(Masking Exercise I)**
   Day #2—Handout: Wallace Stevens, "Man with a Blue Guitar," from *Collected Poems of Wallace Stevens* (New York: Knopf, 1955)

B. "The Shaman as Cosmologizer"
   Topics: 1. Characteristics of the Shaman
   2. Curing and Cosmology
   3. Cosmologizing through Ritual
   Day #3—Handout: Claude Levi-Strauss, "Effectiveness of Symbols" from *Structural Anthropology* (New York: Basic Books, 1976)
   Day #4—Myerhoff, pp. 29-111
   Day #5—Myerhoff, pp. 112-88
   Day #6—Myerhoff, pp. 189-264; Film "To Find Our Life"
   Day #7—Handout: Claude Levi-Strauss, "The Sorcerer and His Magic," from *Structural Anthropology* (New York: Basic Books, 1976)

C. "The Artist as Cosmologizer"
   Topics: 1. The Artist and Culture
   2. Art and Truth

3. Theatre of Cruelty

Day #8—Handout: M. Eliade, "Brancusi and Mythology," from *Symbolism, the Sacred and the Arts,* ed. Diane Apostolos-Cappadona, (New York: Crossroads, 1985)

Day #9—Artaud, pp. 7-52

Day #10—Artaud, pp. 53-83

Day #11—Handout: Peter Brook, "Lie and the Glorious Adjective," from *Parabola* VI, 3 (1981) and Peter Brook, "Leaning on the Moment," from *Parabola* IV, 2 (1979)

Day #12—Handout: Vassily Kandinsky, selection from *Concerning the Spiritual in Art* (New York: Dover, 1977)

D.   "The Cosmogonic Process"

1. "Masking, Possession, and Identity"

Topics: 1. Cultural Dimension and Images

2. Personal Identity and Cultural Symbols

3. Possession

Day #13—Deren, pp. 5-53

Day #14—Deren, pp. 54-150   **(Masking Exercise II)**

Day #15—Deren, pp. 151-224

Day #16—Deren, pp. 225-62

2. "Ritual Meaning and Symbolism"

Topics: 1. Ritual as a Cosmological Activity

2. Symbolism and Meaning

3. Dreams and Visions in the Cosmogonic Process

Day #17—Lame Deer, pp. 1-143 (optional 60-95, 129-43)

Day #18—Lame Deer, pp. 144-202

Day #19—Lame Deer, pp. 203-255

Day #20—Handout: R. Jenkins, "Two Way Mirrors," from *Parabola* VI, 3 (1981)   **(Masking Exercise III)**

Day #21—Discussion of Masking Exercise III

3. "Images, Language, and Metaphor"

Topics: 1. Language and the Metaphoric Process

2. Metaphor and Dreams

3. Healing and Meaning

Day #22—Estrada, pp. 1-62

Day #23—Estrada, pp. 63-125

Day #24—Handout: James Fernandez, "Edification through Puzzlement," from *Persuasions and Performances* (Bloomington: Indiana University Press, 1986)

Day #25—Handout: Benjamin Lee Whorf, "The Relationship of Habitual Thought and Behavior to Language," from *Language, Thought and Reality* (Cambridge, Ma.: MIT University Press, 1963)

E. "Conclusion: Cosmologizing and the Artistic Enterprise"

Topics: 1. Cosmologizing through Myth and Ritual

2. The Cosmogonic Process
3. Artists and Shamans as Cosmologizers
Day #26—Griaule, pp. 1-55
Day #27—Griaule, pp. 56-108
Day #28—Griaule, pp. 109-168, 186-91
Day #29—Repeat: Wallace Stevens, "Man with a Blue Guitar"

COURSE REQUIREMENTS

Seminar Participation—1/3 of grade

Regular attendance and participation are essential. All of us participating in the seminar must commit ourselves to reading the assignments and thinking about them before the class period when they will be discussed. Judgment on the grade will be made on the quality as well as the regularity of participation. The skill of listening to others and responding to their insights is very important.

Philosophical Journal and Masking Exercises—1/3 of grade

Each student will keep an up-to-date journal of reflections on the readings and on the class sessions. The journal must be kept in a loose leaf binder that will hold regular 9" X 12" sheets of paper. All entries are to have wide margins for my comments and dialogue with you about your ideas. You are to submit 8 entries throughout the semester (schedule and dates due on another sheet).

Each entry should be focused around a single theme or line of thought and be between 2-3 pages long. It should reflect readings and seminar sessions.

An entry in the journal is somewhere between a formal short paper and a diary-like, spontaneous thought. It is unlike a finished paper because issues may be left dangling and uncompleted—perhaps you will return to the issue in subsequent entries, relating it to new contexts. It is unlike a diary because it is careful reflection rather than short, spontaneous ideas. You are expected to work through an idea, turning it over, seeing its ramifications and limitations. It is both "unpacking" an idea and "fleshing it out." (A metaphor from painting that might be helpful is "the careful sketch" rather than the "completed picture.") In the first couple of entries, you should be concerned with *understanding* the major concerns of the course and with *developing your* questions that relate to the course. As the semester goes along, you may begin to play with some of the answers to your concerns and philosophical questions. But *remember* all answers that are profound will raise more questions than they will answer. The more you *understand* the limitations of your answers, the more interesting will be your journal.

Masking Exercises: On day #1 of class, each student will choose a mask from among those in my collection. (Or with permission, a student can decide to make his/her own mask.) On day #14, each student will bring a segment of a myth that he/she has written through the character of the mask. The segment should not exceed 5 minutes in reading time. It should be in narrative form rather than in analytical, expository style (we will discuss this in class). These brief stories will be read orally to the class, while someone else wears the mask. The class will then be divided into 5 groups of three to four students in each. They will work up a ritualized segment of approximately 15 minutes in length that reveal the masks through direct action by means of the interplay among the various masks in each group. Although sounds (grunts, marbles rolling etc.) are fine, there should be no excessive verbalizing. The characters should be conveyed by what they do and not by what they say. These enactments will be presented by the groups on day #20 and discussed on day #21.

An 8-12 Page Paper—1/3 of grade

Your paper should center on an artist, shaman, or other cosmologizer (e.g., some scientists, psychologists, historians, philosophers and others might fit this definition) that we have not read in class. There are two goals of this paper. First, you should explore *how* "your" cosmologizer does or does not fit into our emerging notions about the cosmogonic process. Second, the paper should provide a focus for some of the major ideas that you have been exploring in the journal throughout the semester and help you pull these ideas together.

This paper is not primarily a research paper. You need to do enough research to have a good understanding of the "cosmologizer's" work. I would discourage using secondary sources. You might be able to use one book (such as Carl Jung's *Memories, Dreams, and Reflections* or Leo Simmons, ed., *Sun Chief: The Autobiography of a Hopi Indian*) or a collection of short stories or poems or paintings or sculptures. The point is that you use these stories or poems or autobiographies or paintings to draw together the ideas that you have been exploring during the semester.

III

Although I have omitted dates and some of the details of the assignments in the course, I have condensed most of the written notes that I hand out to students about journals and the masking exercises. Let me comment briefly on both of them. Student journals are central to the course, because they allow each student to find a particular range of issues that are of personal importance. They encourage students to begin examining their deeply held values, personal experiences, and intellectual questions through the lens of another people's mythopoetic activities. In my experience the journals work very well for most of the students in this particular course. Through the journal students are engaged in the process of selecting their own intellectual themes for the course, though the syllabus necessitates that they have something to do with the connection between religion and the arts. Some themes will fizzle; others will be sustained throughout the semester. Students learn as much from their failures as from their successes. There is almost always a mixture of both in the journals. When they begin to understand why some themes work well and others do not, they gain important insights about the nature of people's religious lives and sometimes about their own.

Journals are central in this particular course, however, because students become engaged in the creative process as they reflect on their questions and write their entries. They are, to continue the metaphor from the beginning of this essay, squinting hard at the "mountain" of religion to find motifs and fleshing them out so that they can reveal insights about being human. When I started teaching thematic courses about creativity and the arts, I had little awareness that an intellectual journal might itself be a direct engagement in the creative process. I had initially assigned the journal for more mundane pedagogical reasons: to make sure students were engaging with the material, to facilitate their writing skills, and to allow me to have a more personal interaction with each individual student throughout the semester. One semester I assigned Marcel Griaule's *Conversations with Ogotemmàli* to my students at the end of the semester and we suddenly connected the process of our journal writing with the dialogue between the Dogon elder and the French anthropologist. We saw that Griaule's work was not simply *about* Dogon cosmogony, but it exemplified the cosmological process itself.[5] Similarly, our journals were not only about creativity, but exemplified the creative process. Both were concerned with how humans imaginatively construct their universe.

The creative process in the journal became so central to the students' experiences in the course that I reconstructed the syllabus to enhance the process. Griaule's work remains important in the concluding section of the course. I begin the course with Louis Malle's film, *My Dinner with André*. Although André is telling about his creative experiences, the meaning of those experiences is also being reconstituted as Wally raises his questions and objections. Why, after all, does André yearn for a dinner conversation with Wally? In part, there is a reorientation of the two worlds of discourse as they meet in that restaurant. Wallace Steven's "Man with a Blue Guitar" expresses poetically how the musician is an integral part of the world and yet transmutes and gathers the world together as the guitar is strummed. This poem both introduces students to the themes of the course and helps summarize them at the end.

There is not sufficient space to detail how other reading assignments might enhance and be enhanced by the journal. More important than justifying particular assignments is to suggest that themes of creativity and the arts allow teachers of world religions to introduce a meaningful ex-

---

[5] For a scholarly treatment of this issue see Thomas V. Peterson, "The Smith, the Teacher of Speech, and Creativity: A Postmodern Reflection on Cosmologizing through Myth," *Soundings: An Interdisciplinary Journal*, Summer 1991.

periential component into our courses without injecting overt religious beliefs and practices into the classroom. This implies, of course, that religion can be approached as a creative activity that relies on imaging the world through such art forms as poetry, music, painting, and dance. This claim frequently puzzles students in modern America because of our scientific (or perhaps better pseudo-scientific) mind set that does not allow poetry and truth to coexist in the same utterance. I am convinced that students have difficulty in understanding many people's religions (sometimes even their own), because they have not realized that the imagination is a valid way of creating meaning in the world.

In teaching my thematic courses around religion and the arts, I have been successful in using masks as a way to give students an experiential way to connect the two. I have a collection of high quality masks that I had an artist create. I asked her to draw her inspiration from a number of sources, but not to make any masks that replicated those used by people in their religious activities. A couple of students in the course invariably want to make their own masks; some of these have been donated to my collection. I actually prefer students to choose a mask that someone else has created, because I can then more easily raise questions about personal and cultural identity. The issue of cultural creativity is one that many students write about in their journals. But we have had useful class discussions about the creating of images out of pre-existent ones. Thus we raise questions about the cultural reservoir that artists and shamans use to create their own images.

There are two assignments throughout the semester (other than the first one of choosing a mask at the beginning of the course). I ask the students to refrain from wearing their masks until after they present their first assignment to the class. But they are to study it as a Balinese actor might contemplate his or her mask before donning it for a performance. They are to write a segment of a myth through the character that is produced by the image of their mask. They are not to worry about plot and should not use an expository style of expression. They might say, for example, "When Dongar saw the maiden, he hid behind the bushes," but not "Dongar was shy around women." Students are unusually anxious about this assignment, because instructors have so rarely asked them to write anything that is not analytical and expository. Yet these written assignments are uniformly among the best that I have ever received. This is true, even though the course frequently draws a number of students who have some difficulty with writing because their thinking is so often expressed through the visual arts.

After beginning to understand the process of thinking through images of masks by writing and sharing their mythic narratives, the students wear the masks and begin relating to each other through simple, non-verbal actions. The groups, comprised of three or four students, meet a few times to experiment with their personae that are conveyed through the masks. When the groups present their loosely choreographed movements in a class session on Day #20, emotions are powerfully and directly conveyed by the interchanges between the masked characters. For the participants the experience helps them understand the Haitian possession rites that they read about in Deren's *The Divine Horsemen*. There are also connections between Artaud's theatre of cruelty and the theme of metaphorical truth, here portrayed through bodily movement.

Let me clarify here (as I do in class) that participation in the masking exercises is not identical with participation in religious rites. I am not trying to create some pseudo-religious experience in these exercises. I am, however, trying to push a metaphorical understanding of truth to its limits and to suggest that we must take that notion very seriously if we are to begin to understand the nature of people's religious experience.

I shall not try to detail here the very complicated and open-ended discussion that occurs in journals and class discussions about the differences between traditional religious symbolization and the contemporary arts. But a concluding observation is in order. The course fundamentally challenges our notions about the relationship between individuals and their communities. Does meaning arise in the private worlds of individuals or within a communal context? Are the ideas and feelings of artists primary or do they take place within a process of cultural symbolization? By joining the issue of artistic creativity to religious symbolization through myths and rituals, students begin to question their unthinking commitment to the Cartesian enterprise of separating the self from the world. They do not so much deny their own creative forms of symbolic expression as they have an alternative way to understand them. Some even begin to entertain Maya Deren's notion of the "collective as artist." In the process of seeing alternative ways to view their own world, they also develop a deeper respect for the world views of traditional religious peoples.

Many scholars in religious studies use social scientific categories in their interpretation of religions. It is time, I claim, that scholars and teachers explicitly bring artistic categories to bear on the study of religion, because the issue of metaphorical truth is central to religious phenomena. And we must draw these categories directly from artistic practice (through dance, drama, music, sculpture, painting, drawing, etc.) rather than from aesthetic theories. Visual "thinking" through painting and bodily "thinking" through drama or dance can bring interpretive categories to bear on religious studies.[6]

---

[6] If one examines the readings in this course, one will find that many artists are allowed to speak: the painter Kandinsky, theatrical directors Artaud and Brook, poet Wallace Stevens, film director Louis Malle with "actors" André Gregory and Wallace Shawn. Less obvious from the syllabus is that John Erdoes, who edited Lame Deer's conversations, was an artist. Maya Deren was primarily a dancer and film-maker who interpreted Haitian religion from an artistic perspective.

Better Questions: "Introduction to the History of Religion and Art"

RICHARD M. CARP

Good teaching leads students (and teachers) to better questions; we do not so much answer our old questions as discard them. When students begin courses such as "Introduction to Religion," or "Pilgrimage," they are likely to believe that the central concepts around which the course is organized (eg., "religion" or "pilgrimage") have a clear and comprehensible meaning, even though they, as students, may not yet possess this meaning. A large part of teaching is to progressively disabuse students of this notion and introduce them to the problematic embodied by our organizing concepts, for it is this problematic that so engages us and leads us to devote our lives to its study.

Introducing the study of religion in the context of art facilitates encounters with a powerful set of problematics which applies not only to the study of religion but also to the conduct of life. We confront the semiotic problematic: the creation, maintenance, transformation, and transmission of meaning—in history, cross-culturally, and in our own lives.

PART ONE: GENERAL ISSUES IN THE STUDY OF RELIGION

We cannot study anything without data. "Religion" or "religiousness" or some such will have to be represented in class by evidence, even though by the end of the course the initial characterizations of this evidence may be called into question. Art and architecture are excellent media for presenting the facts of religion.

> Religion involves the whole person and the entire cultural landscape. It permeates the built environment, manifesting in art, music, architecture, ritual, ceremony, and pilgrimage as surely as in sacred books and other words. For many, if not most, people, religious experience is a matter of how the world feels and looks and sounds and smells, not of what they think about it. Many religious people do not use texts, whether they are non-literate or illiterate. Visual artifacts may appear to be illustrations of verbal concepts. The truth is often the other way around; texts may be explanations of concepts originally articulated visually, kinaesthetically or aurally.[1]

Material culture (the culture of "mater"—mother) is accessible to those on the margins of culture who have no access to official texts. Vernacular art and architecture give us an entree into the religious worlds of women, ethnic minorities, subjugated peoples, and others who are excluded from high culture. Non-literate cultures and culture-regions, too, have reflected profoundly on human experience, carrying out these reflections in sculpture, architecture, dance, music, and other media.

Art and architecture are evidence about the religious worlds of a broad range of individuals and cultures. This evidence provides starting grounds from which to develop our problematics (though the selection of evidence emerges from a prefiguring of the problematics).

"Religion" and "art" are, of course, our concepts, our problems: they belong to the Western tradition of thought and experience. Each has its own derivation, history, and tradition of use both in the culture and in the academy. Neither refers to any "thing." This is the first aspect of the problematic. A class in "religion" is going to study something that doesn't exist. Both religion and art are open concepts; it is impossible to give an unambiguous definition of either.

On the other side of the coin, our naive commonsense understanding of religion and an equally naive view of art might lead us to believe that religion and art are often deeply intertwined. We are familiar with great religious architecture from our own and other cultures, we know of the Western Christian traditions of folk and fine art, we have studied the anthropological evidence of the religions of the past (almost all from art and architecture), we know the thriving artistry of some contemporary

---

[1] Richard M. Carp, "Using Audio-Visual Resources to Teach About Religion," in Mark Juergensmeyer, ed. *Teaching the Introductory Course in Religious Studies* (Atlanta: Scholars Press, 1991).

new religions (eg., the African religions of the New World). Yet the arts do not occupy a prominent place in the academic study of religion.

This is another puzzling problematic. Why is the obvious so overlooked? Not only has the academy tended to think of religion in terms of texts and beliefs, the metaphor of "text" has become an overriding symbol for the process of meaning in late twentieth-century intellectual culture. Yet a close examination of many religious practices indicates otherwise. Lawrence E. Sullivan has shown that whole peoples sustain profound religious meditations through non-textual means: dance, song, or pottery can be as powerful as text in engendering meaning.[2] Karen McCarthy Brown has found that dance is used in some African religions in the new world as a method for thinking through and resolving real-world problems in relation with sacred beings or powers.[3] Our subject matter should compel the field beyond both texts and the metaphor of text. Yet by and large it has not.

This text-bias is an artifact of the Judeo-Christian, largely Protestant, roots of the academy in the United States and of the academic study of religion. It raises the problematic of knowledge, authority, tradition, and ambiguity in the construction of meaning. What counts as knowledge and why: in a religious tradition, in one's own economy of truth, in the university, in this specific classroom? What is "evidence"—according to whom?

In this way, investigating the thematic of art in religion poses important questions from the outset, not only about religion and art, but also about the academic study of religion. Art and architecture, because they have been marginalized in our field, provide an effective context in which to both practice and critique the academic study of religion. This critique, and the skill of affirming a position while critiquing it, should be woven into the fabric even of the introductory course.

The academic study of religion, honestly pursued, is an inherently deconstructive activity. We discover and show that religious symbols, acts, and communities are permeated by culture and history, class and gender, and repressed and unconscious desires. Ethically we must complete this deconstructive turn to acknowledge that the academic study of religion is equally deeply caught in the fissures of desire, history, culture, and context.

---

[2] Lawrence E. Sullivan, *Icanchu's Drum: An Orientation to Meaning in South American Religions* (NY: Macmillan Publishing Company, 1988).

[3] Personal communication.

To stop questioning at this point would threaten student and teacher with a world of radical relativism, but this, too, is an unstable position. Relativism itself is historical, situational, contextual, and constructed. It is not possible not to stand in a tradition, to take up no ethical stance in the world. "Cheap relativism" dissembles its own character as an ethical stance.

In our religious activities, people enact profound commitments about what is in fact the case with respect to human existence. These commitments cannot, in many cases, be reconciled. In the academic study of religion we study deeply these incompatible universes each claiming to be fundamentally valid (at least for some people). We study them from within a universe that makes its own claims to validity, veracity, and adequacy. Because of the profundity of the competing claims and commitments involved in our object of study, our students want to know how to evaluate what is in fact the case. Nor can we simply extol the commitments of the academy, although they do have precedence in the conduct of the class. Religion, even as we study it, calls into question the methods, motives and objectives with which we study it, and it is an intellectual virtue of the academy that our canons compel us to acknowledge that challenge. This fundamental existential problematic lies at the heart of the study of religion.

The tension is not to be resolved, but sustained, offering a dual potential for critique: of other's standpoints from one's own and of one's own standpoint from those of others.

Thought, knowledge, and understanding are mapping activities; through them we develop maps or guides for the conduct of experience. The study of religion intensifies our awareness of the human propensity to map and of the diversity of the maps we use. We are also constantly reminded of Korzybsky's famous dictum: the map is not the territory. The religions themselves admonish us that the names, pictures, stories, and rules of God are not God: mystery lies beyond all that. The tradition of the academy develops this theme in its own terms: from the sciences through the humanities we all acknowledge that our models are models, simplified symbolic representations of portions of our experience.

Maps, models, and symbol systems (like languages), gain their ability to signify from the internal relationships between elements that make them up. You have to be able to read a map before you can use the map to navigate the terrain. We have already seen that "religion" and "art" are elements in the developing and changing map called "Western thought." In fact they have developed in relation to one another and are implicated in each other's meaning.

> [Our understanding of] "art" and "artist" must be viewed in the context of their emergence contemporary with modernity in the West, beginning in romantic Germany of, say, 1840. The figure of the artist took on charismatic qualities formerly associated with religious or political leaders and became decisively associated with "creativity", heretofore a theological concept, and still a key metaphor in Judaic, Islamic, and Christian imagination. These developments were part of the Romantic revolt from reason that led to an affirmation of exaltation in Nature (a development of the concept of the sublime from Shaftesbury and Kant), of intense emotional experience, of imagination, of sexual ambiguity and fulfillment, and of intuition. Little wonder that creative artists are now thought to be wild, emotional, intuitive, sexually uncertain, and utterly fascinating (if not disgusting).[4]

Through the key concept of "creativity" art and artists in our culture are linked with fundamental sacred principles, while artists themselves live at the margins of our culture. Economically, politically, and in terms of the psycho-social traits commonly attributed to them, artists are "liminars" in our actual and symbolic economies.[5] Thus art and artists are involved in a metaphoric net that also includes religion and the sacred. There is a certain "charge" associated with art and artists that links them with the divine or the demonic.

Modern and contemporary practice of art is also often experienced as a spiritual activity. Many artists speak of their studio experience in terms of personal transformation and the obliteration of the subject/object dichotomy, language reminiscent of the mystical traditions. Robert Motherwell wrote "one's art is just one's effort to wed oneself to the universe, to unify oneself through union."[6] Max Beckman claimed, "Art is creative for the sake of realization, not for amusement; for transfiguration, not for the sake of play."[7]

The intended content of the work, too, is often explicitly religious. The early American modernists were once thought to have been purely secu-

---

[4] Richard M. Carp, "The Classroom Scene: Teaching, Material Culture, and Religion," in Mark Juergensmeyer, ed. *Teaching the Introductory Course in Religious Studies* (Atlanta: Scholars Press, 1991).

[5] See Victor Turner, *The Forest of Symbols: Aspects of Ndembu Ritual* (Ithaca, NY: Cornell Univ. Press, 1970), especially "Betwixt and Between: The Liminal Period in Rites of Passage" and *The Ritual Process: Structure and Anti-Structure* (Chicago: Aldine Publishing Co., 1969), especially Ch. 3: "Liminality and Communitas," p. 94 - 130.

[6] Herschel Chipp, ed., *Theories of Modern Art: A Source Book by Artists and Critics* (Berkeley: Univ. of Calif. Press, 1968), 563.

[7] Ibid., 189.

lar artists concerned with the formal properties of their materials. A major exhibition at the Los Angeles County Museum of Art in 1985 demonstrated that they were deeply involved in theosophy and other forms of religious investigation. They clearly thought that their paintings had religious significance. As the title of the exhibition shows, *The Spiritual in Art: Abstract Painting 1890-1985*, documents a vital dimension of the continued interplay between religion and art in American culture. The final and most important problematic opened by the study of religion in the context of art is the religious significance of the role of the arts in the construction of experience.

As John W. Dixon, Jr. put it (in "Art as Making the World," in the *Journal of the AAR*, March 1982):

> "World construction" is the construction of the world as it is for those who live within it. It is not a "world view," a way of seeing the world or an attitude toward it. It emerges from and in turn shapes the rhythmic ordering of the body's processes so there is no way of thinking of a person distinct from the world who has a view of that world and opinions about it. . . This constructed world is the world of those who have made it and live within it. It establishes the possibilities of their emotional life, the world of feeling. It creates the structures of the imagination that make possible the act of knowing. It defines purpose.[8]

Cultures differ in terms of their deep structures of perceptual experience, each having "its own characteristic manner of locomotion, sitting, standing, reclining, and gesturing."[9]

The process of ordering the body correlates with that of focusing the world. "External perception and the perception of one's own body vary in conjunction because they are two facets of one and the same act."[10]

> The developmental task of structuring body/world is accomplished within and in relation to the cultural landscape. The deep structures of the acculturated body correspond to those of the cultural landscape to which it acculturates.[11]

The cultural landscape is the accumulated sedimentation of what we now call the arts, architecture, and the design professions. Thus all

---

[8] John L. Dixon, Jr. "Art as the Making of the World," *Journal of the American Academy of Religion*, March 1982.

[9] Edward T. Hall, *Beyond Culture* (Garden City, NY: Doubleday, 1980).

[10] Maurice Merleau-Ponty, *The Phenomenology of Perception*, trans. C. Smith. (London: Routledge and Kegan Paul, 1962), 205.

[11] Richard M. Carp, "The Role of the Arts in the Liberal Arts Classroom," *Art and Academe*, Spring 1991.

meanings and systems of meaning are caught up in the context of the built environment—the world of material culture. Dixon goes so far as to claim:

> If the word "religion" is to have any use any longer, it should be applied to this structure. My "religion" is not my beliefs, my devotional feelings, my behavior. It is the totality of my world as I live it, within which I work out my character and my destiny.[12]

"Religion" narrowly defined as institutions, beliefs, rituals, practices and so forth, takes shape and gains its meaning within the total pattern of world experience within which it exists. The actual construction of the cultural landscape is a matter of religious concern. Although this notion seems new to the academic study of religion, it is not at all new to religion, which has always been profoundly generative of material culture. What is at stake is not only the expression of particular meanings but the processes by which meanings are structured and constructed.

PART TWO: AN EDITED SYLLABUS FROM "INTRODUCTION TO THE HISTORY OF RELIGION AND ART"

We will investigate the fundamental concerns of the academic study of religion: 1. the history of religious traditions, including the prehistoric origins of religion, Native American and African religious traditions, religions originating in the Near East (Judaism, Christianity, Islam), religions originating in India (Hinduism, Buddhism, Jainism), and religions originating in China (Confucianism, Taoism); 2. philosophical issues in the study of religion (eg., what is "religion" and what are its relationships to "art" and "science"?); 3. modern secularism and pluralism and their connections with religion.

Reading list:

Burckhardt, Titus. *Art of Islam: Language and Meaning*, London: World of Islam Festival Press, 1976.

Coomaraswamy, Ananda K. *Christian and Oriental Philosophy of Art*. (NY: Dover Publications, Inc., 1956)

DeLoria, Vine, Jr. *God Is Red*. (NY: Dell Publishing Co., 1973.)

Dillenberger, Jane. *Style and Content in Christian Art*. N Y: The Crossroad Publishing Co., 1988.

---

[12] John L. Dixon, Jr., "Art as the Making of the World," *Journal of the American Academy of Religion*, March 1982, p.22.

Dixon, John L., Jr. "Art as the Making of the World". *Journal of the American Academy of Religion*, March 1982.

Gold, Penny Schine. *The Lady and the Virgin: Image, Attitude and Experience in Twelfth Century France*. Chicago: University of Chicago Press, 1985.

Hopfe, Lewis M. *Religions of the World, 3d ed*. NY: Macmillan, 1983.

Los Angeles County Museum of Art. *The Spiritual in Art: Abstract Painting 1890-1985*. Los Angeles: Los Angeles County Museum of Art and Abbeville Press, 1986.

Martland, Thomas R. *Religion as Art: An Interpretation*. NY: State Univ. N.Y. Press, 1981.

Morris, Robert. "The Present Tense of Space," *Art In America*. Vol. 66, No. 1 (Jan/Feb 1978): 70-81.

Ringgren, Helmut and Strom, Ake Y. *Religions of Mankind: Yesterday and Today*. Philadelphia: Fortress Press, 1967.

Russell, John. *The Meanings of Modern Art*. NY: Harper & Row, Pub., 1981.

Suleiman, Susan Rubin, ed. *The Female Body in Western Culture: Contemporary Perspectives*. Cambridge, Mass: Harvard Univ. Press, 1986.

Sullivan, Lawrence E. *Icanchu's Drum: An Orientation to Meaning in South American Religions*. NY: Macmillan Publishing Company, 1988.

Thompson, Robert Farris. *The Flash of the Spirit: African and Afro-American Art and Philosophy*. NY: Vintage Books, 1984.

The course is a reading, lecture, and discussion class of about thirty-five students. It meets twice a week for one and a half hours each session for fifteen weeks. I show and we discuss slides of art and architecture as a regular part of most classes. I also leave slide sets on reserve in the slide library for student review.

Students are expected to attend class and participate, keep and turn in a journal every week, and take three exams during the semester. I read and comment in each journal and return them every week. Journals are to contain reflections on any topic whatsoever, so long as it has a bearing on the topics and issues of the class and the student makes those connections. It is not intended to be finished writing, but a sketchbook of ideas, insights and questions. Exceptional students can substitute a fifteen page paper for one exam.

We work from this outline:

Day One:	Introduction (Sullivan, Dixon)
Day Two:	Human Evolution, Religion and Art (Martland, Hopfe)

Day Three:	Paleolithic and Neolithic Religion and Art (Martland, Hopfe)
Day Four:	Egypt and Mesopotamia (Ringgren & Strom, Martland)
Day Five:	The Hebrews (Ringgren & Strom, Martland)
Day Six:	Greece (Ringgren & Strom, Martland)
Day Seven:	Rome (Ringgren & Strom, Martland)
Day Eight:	Early Christianity (Hopfe, Martland)
Day Nine:	Review. Take home portion of exam. (Exam will include brief in-class essays on slide images, short in-class essays identifying key terms, concepts, figures and events, and a take-home exam of two five- to seven-page essays.)
Day Ten:	Take-home exam due, in-class exam
Day Eleven:	Native America (Hopfe, deLoria)
Day Twelve:	Africa (Hopfe, Thompson)
Day Thirteen:	India (Hopfe, Martland)
Day Fourteen:	India (Hopfe, Coomaraswamy)
Day Fifteen:	China (Hopfe, Martland)
Day Sixteen:	China/Japan (Hopfe, Martland)
Day Seventeen:	Islam (Hopfe, Burckhardt)
Day Eighteen:	Islam (Hopfe, Burckhardt)
Day Nineteen:	Islam (Burckhardt, Martland)
Day Twenty:	Review and take-home exam
Day Twenty-one:	Exam (same format as first exam)
Day Twenty-two:	European Christianity and Judaism from the fall of Rome to the Renaissance (Hopfe, Gold, Miles)
Day Twenty-three:	The Renaissance: South and North (Dillenberger, Hopfe)
Day Twenty-four:	After the Renaissance: Reformation/Restoration// Mannerism/Baroque (Hopfe, Dillenberger, Martland)
Day Twenty-five:	The Baroque: Rembrandt and Reubens (Dillenberger, Martland)
Day Twenty-six:	Modern Art & Religion (Russell, LACMA)
Day Twenty-seven:	Contemporary Art and Religion (Morris, Thompson)
Day Twenty-eight:	Review (Sullivan)
Day Twenty-nine:	Exam (Same format as first two exams, but ten page essays.

PART THREE: DISCUSSION

The almost daily reading assignments from Hopfe's *Religions of the World, 3d ed.* and from Martland's *Religion as Art: An Interpretation* make up the spine of the course, while the other books are used intensively in sections, making up the remainder of the skeleton. They are fleshed out by the slide images I present in class, but the life-blood of the course is the student interaction that takes place in class and the individual dialogue I hold with each student in the journals.

Hopfe provides a lifeline for students. His book is a straightforward "Introduction to Religions" textbook, with the virtues and vices of the genre. It is organized regionally by area of origin. It provides the sort of simple, concept/text/philosophy approach to religion I have criticized above, but it also provides reasonably accurate information to which students can return when other aspects of the course are much more ambiguous. It offers useful information presented historically, it is readable, and in the context of the other course materials provides a needed balance in the direction of texts.

Martland, by contrast, has written a rhetorical philosophical treatise proposing to find a fundamental similarity between what we call religion and what we call art.

> [A]rt and religion [he says] provide the patterns of meaning, the frames of perception, by which society interprets its experiences and from which it makes conclusions about the nature of its world. They tell us what is; they do not respond to what is.[13]

Yet the artist and the religious person live with an intense awareness of the inadequacy of any expressive form to contain or communicate the fullness of reality. In his Overture, Martland addresses religion and art as "essentially contested concepts," citing Gallie and articulating one of the problematics of the class: "since . . . the concepts of art and religion are essentially open and contestable there is always more to be said."[14]

He works by example, attempting to make a convincing case by finding supporting data spread widely through what is already acknowledged as religion and art. Each chapter presents evidence from a broad cultural and historical range of both religion and art. He uses much of the data presented in Hopfe, but he presents it in different contexts and with a different internal ordering principal, so students see the same information used to support radically diverse thinking. Martland's intention is cumulative and persuasive, not sequential and conclusive. Students are brought to evaluate the quality of the evidence for their own conclusions and to estimate the degree of conclusiveness with which they can responsibly hold them.

Martland's thesis is sufficiently appealing and sufficiently powerful to keep students engaged in the book for an entire semester. It is suffi-

---

[13]   T. R. Martland, *Religion as Art: An Interpretation* (Albany, NY: SUNY Press, 1981), 12.

[14]   Ibid., 6.

ciently irritating and sufficiently dubious that students can energetically criticize and defend it, leading to heated in-class discussions of fundamental philosophical questions involved in the academic study of religion: What is transcendence? What is meaning and how is it generated, maintained, and transformed? Is "religion" a part of the human condition, like "economics" or are there people, or even cultures, without religion?

If Hopfe's matter-of-factness and Martland's semiotic musings provide two legs on which the class stands, the third is provided by art and architecture. They enter into the class in three ways: artifacts provide original evidence about religious activities, understandings and traditions; the activities we call art-making often are or can be paths of personal transformation and/or spiritual disciplines; the in-class encounter with art and architecture forces students to learn to think in physical media other than words and sensitizes them to the dimensions of meaning embedded in their own cultural landscapes.

The following are examples of the sorts of studies in which we might engage:

1. An investigation of the canonization of images in Christianity and Buddhism, resulting in both cases in widely used and clearly recognizable archetypes. Almost surely more of your students will know how the Buddha should look than will have read the Pali Canon; in all probability more will know how Jesus should look than have read the New Testament.

This is especially interesting because both processes emerged from Roman figure sculpture, especially from burial sarcophagi. Sacred images of the Buddha carried this figurative tradition across the Silk Road to China and then into Japan.

The Buddhist case also provides interesting comparisons between the ultimately victorious Mahayana sculptural tradition and the dramatic, gaunt Buddhas conjured by the Theravada tradition. The Christian case offers an opportunity to investigate the symbolic pulls at work in a figure asserted to be at once fully human and fully divine. The visual and plastic representation of this person brings this tension to a chrystalline focus.

2. Systematic comparisons of sacred spaces, eg., a cathedral, a mosque, and a Hindu temple. One might begin by noticing that mosques are oriented toward a central point: mosques share a common center. Cathedrals face east: churches share a common destination. Mosques and churches are places for communal worship, while the Hindu temple is a

place for individual devotions. Such comparisons can reveal much about the similarities and differences of the traditions whose spaces they are.

3. A comparison of the Northern and Southern Renaissance in Europe. Following Dillenberger, one might focus on a close comparison of the works of Matthias Grunewald in the North and Michaelangelo in the South.

> Northern art reflects an awareness of the unaccountable and chaotic elements in man and nature . . . [while] Mediterannean man stood more secure in a world that seemed to him benign . . .[15]

4. A recounting of the story of the Virgin of Guadalupe as an example of syncretic interaction between Christianity and indigenous religions in areas of Christian colonization. I often tell this story when we are studying medieval Christianity.

5. A discussion of the role of the arts in the African religions of the New World. These religions and their links with their African sources provide a wonderful example of the transmission of religious tradition largely through material, non-verbal culture. Contemporary African religions in the New World exist largely in the form of ritual and material culture.[16]

Introduction to the History of Religion and Art is, unabashedly, a survey class. Despite that, I make no claims, either here or in class, to cover "the whole of religion" (whatever that might be!). Rather I claim to offer a broad, historical and cross-cultural investigation into the interactions between "religion" and "art." This investigation introduces students to a set of problems that surround the study of religion. These problems center on the experience of meaning and its generation, maintenance, transmission, and transformation. They are relevant not only to religion and the study of religion, but to the academy and its ongoing task of self-definition and self-discovery, and to the conduct of personal life.

Text has become the overriding metaphor in the contemporary West for meaning of any kind. Yet religion demonstrates the human propensity for engaging in and articulating profound reflections in non-verbal media. Teaching about religion in the context of art introduces students to these worlds of meaning. It also sensitizes them to dimensions of meaning in our own cultural landscape and raises important questions

---

[15] Jane Dillenberger, *Style and Content in Christian Art* (NY: The Crossroad Publishing Co., 1988), 161.

[16] Robert Farris Thompson's groundbreaking *The Flash of the Spirit: African and Afro-American Art and Philosophy* (NY: Vintage Books, 1984) is an excellent study in exactly this process of religious and cultural transmission.

about the role of the cultural landscape in the deep structures of meaningful experience.

Students may find the encounter with other worlds of meaning, expressed in unfamiliar media, to be unsettling. When they realize that the facts about the construction of experience that apply to other people apply to themselves, they may be disturbed. When they understand that every sort of knowledge is a kind of map, and that no map is adequate to the territory, they may be troubled. These insights make us aware of the delicate, ambiguous character of human existence. It is these delicate, ambiguous, troubling, disturbing, and unsettling questions that I have come to love about the academic study of religion and that I hope to share with my students.

BIBLIOGRAPHY

Carp, Richard M. "The Role of the Arts in the Liberal Arts Classroom," *Art and Academe*, Nov. 1989.

Chipp, Herschel, ed. *Theories of Modern Art: A Source Book by Artists and Critics*. Berkeley: Univ. of Calif. Press, 1968.

Dillenberger, Jane. *Style and Content in Christian Art*. NY: Crossroad Publishing Co., 1988.

Dixon, John L., Jr. "Art as the Making of the World." *Journal of the American Academy of Religion*, March 1982.

Hall, Edward T. *Beyond Culture*. Garden NY: Doubleday, 1980.

Juergensmeyer, Mark, ed. *Teaching the Introductory Course in Religious Studies*. (Atlanta: Scholars Press, in press.)

Merleau-Ponty, Maurice. *The Phenomenology of Perception*, trans. C. Smith. London: Routledge and Kegan Paul, 1962.

Sullivan, Lawrence E. *Icanchu's Drum: An Orientation to Meaning in South American Religions*. NY: Macmillan Publishing Company, 1988.

Thompson, Robert Farris. *The Flash of the Spirit: African and Afro-American Art and Philosophy*. NY: Vintage Books, 1984.

Turner, Victor. *The Forest of Symbols: Aspects of Ndembu Ritual*. Ithaca, NY: Cornell University Press, 1970.

Turner, Victor. *The Ritual Process: Structure and Anti-Structure*. Chicago: Aldine Publishing Co., 1969.

1 of Comparison

KINS

> s an external fulcrum.
> mmanding a relatively
> :ures; comparison is the
> ate Sir Edward Evans-
> er.
> umont[1]

Critiques of Comparison *ion*

Both the phrase "comparative religion" and the approaches that ex-press the meaning of the concept have for most of this century been sub-ject to a variety of critiques. Some have been explicit, while others are implicit in the low esteem of comparative studies in certain quarters of the university. In an academic system in which so many disciplines keep expanding and often subdivide into still narrower specializations, the claim to span many continents or several millennia, or to synthesize di-verse disciplines, seems to many to bespeak a lack of academic serious-ness. It is so difficult to learn enough about any one subject that to claim to deal adequately with two or three seems both boastful and foolish. For this reason there are few comparative dissertations written even in the doctoral program in comparative religion at Harvard. The late Arthur Darby Nock is said to have expressed his criticism of comparative

---

[1] From Dumont's study of *homo aequalis, From Mandeville to Marx: The Genesis and Triumph of Economic Ideology* (Chicago: University of Chicago Press, 1977), 11.

religion in the following ironic comment: "To compare two religions, it is necessary to know at least one!"

There is also the criticism, at least as sharp but much more positive in its intent, from those who find the comparative approach to religion both possible in principle and full of potential, yet historically shoddy in its methods and disappointing in its results. Among such critics, none has been more thorough in his analysis and trenchant in his criticism than Jonathan Z. Smith, who quotes a line from Plato's Dialogue, the *Sophist*, spoken by the Stranger from Elea, "A cautious man should above all be on his guard against resemblances; they are a very slippery thing." [*Sophist*, 231a][2] Smith begins with a critical survey of previous comparative studies: ". . . [A]s practised by scholarship, *comparison has been chiefly an affair of the recollection of similarity. The chief explanation for the significance of comparison has been contiguity.*" [3]

For Smith the procedure is more like magic than science, more impressionistic than methodical. This criticism applies most sharply to the oldest comparative approach, which he calls the *ethnographic*, one that "is based essentially on travellers' impressions. Something 'other' has been encountered and perceived as surprising either in its similarity or dissimilarity to what is familiar 'back home.'"[4] The second approach, the *encyclopedic*, is more systematic, but its topical arrangement of material is not thought through. "The data are seldom either explicitly compared or explained."[5] In contrast, the third approach, the *morphological*, "allows the arrangement of individual items in a hierarchical series of increasing organization and complexity."[6] A major difficulty with this approach, that it has no place for historical change, would seem to be remedied by the fourth approach, the *evolutionary*. However, Smith maintains, as this approach was actually applied in its heyday at the end of the nineteenth century, when it virtually defined comparative religion, it illegitimately combined the ahistorical approach of morphology with "the new temporal framework of the evolutionist"[7] by forcing instances representing different value levels into a chronological scheme of supposed evolutionary developments. Although a true application of evolution to the comparative study of religion should be possible, Smith believes, it has

---

[2] See Jonathan Z. Smith *Imagining Religion: From Babylon to Jonestown* (Chicago and London: University of Chicago Press, 1982), 24.

[3] Ibid., 21.

[4] Ibid., 22.

[5] Ibid., 23.

[6] Ibid., 23.

[7] Ibid., 24.

not yet been worked out by any scholar. This leaves only the morphological approach, but two recent developments cannot be accepted by the many scholars who do not accept their presuppositions. These are Romantic and Neo-Platonic in the case of Mircea Eliade and Marxist in the case of the structuralists. Smith thus reaches an apparently negative conclusion. "We know better how to evaluate comparisons, but we have gained little over our predecessors in either the method for making comparisons or the reasons for its practice."[8]

Evolutionary Comparison and its Successors

Before turning to the positive side of Smith's analysis of comparison, we should look at the approach that was almost synonymous with comparative religion a hundred years ago, a comparison of religious phenomena that was accompanied by a ranking of religions in an evolutionary scheme. This scheme owes much to Hegel's philosophy of religion, in which Christianity is the highest form of religion, expressing the truth of Mind at the level of imaginative representation. The widespread acceptance of Darwin's theory of biological evolution encouraged belief in an evolutionary ranking of religions, worked out in detail by E. B. Tylor in England and C. P. Tiele in Holland. There were a few voices of caution, including that of Tiele's Dutch colleague, P. D. Chantepie de la Saussaye, who developed the first "phenomenology of religion" in an effort to provide preliminary comparison of religious phenomena that would not require a decision on the applicability of the theory of evolution to religion.

Tylor's influential work *Primitive Culture* spoke to the mood of Western Europeans at the end of the nineteenth century, when European scientific progress and colonial rule seemed to fit in with the superiority of European religion. Some readers were encouraged to take the further step of affirming European racial superiority. Edward A. Freeman, writing just a year after Tylor's book was published, applauded Tylor's discovery of the three ruling races in the development of civilization, the Greeks, the Romans, and the Teutons, commenting that "It is to the Comparative Method of research that we owe that greatest discovery of modern science which puts all these facts in their true order and their true relations to each other."[9] While the First World War did not end the

---

8 Ibid., 35.

9 See his *Comparative Politics: Six Lectures Read Before the Royal Institution in January and February 1873*, with *The Unity of History, the Rede Lecture Read Before the University of Cambridge, 1872* (London: Macmillan, 1896), 33.

development of "Aryan" racial theory, it did greatly weaken the European intellectual's confidence in European culture and religion as the culmination of civilization. The resultant disillusion with evolutionary theory certainly contributed to a rejection of the comparative method identified with that theory.

Some scholars, however, pursued comparative studies along different lines and protested the popular evolutionary theory. Wilhelm Schmidt and his students sought to remain historical but found regress rather than progress in the move from the "primitive monotheism" in the simplest (and presumed oldest!) human societies to the polytheism of technologically more advanced cultures. W. B. Kristensen, the Norwegian scholar who succeeded Tiele at Leiden, criticized both notions of historical development and ideal schemes ranking religions. Such schemes, he maintained, tell us something only about the scholar's own religion. Believers always give their own religion absolute value; they would never agree to put it on the lower rung of some evolutionary scheme. In the work of Kristensen's student Gerardus van der Leeuw, the "timeless" categories explored in the phenomenology of religion represent continuing elements of meaning even when they are transposed by later religions. For van der Leeuw, phenomenological comparison is a necessary connection between the historian's concern with the facts of religion and the theologian's concern with the truth of religion. Later phenomenologists of religion, including K. A. H. Hidding at Leiden, have tried to incorporate recognition of major historical changes affecting religions in much of the world. Some might argue that Mircea Eliade, whom Jonathan Smith criticizes for his lack of historical interest, also made such an attempt.

Wilfred Cantwell Smith has rejected both evolutionary schemes and timeless categories or archetypes in his effort to demonstrate the growing interconnection of the religious histories of the world. He insists that each religious phenomenon, anywhere in that history, be treated with respect as an expression of human faith. This approach gives impetus to a different kind of comparative focus that we shall return to below, on the interaction among religious traditions. With respect to thematic comparison, however, it encourages considerable caution and even skepticism. The religious meaning of all aspects of religious traditions, Wilfred Smith holds, lies only in their expression of the underlying faith of human beings.

We have briefly noted only a few of the various lines of scholarly development since the heyday of evolutionary comparison. We could also mention the largely ahistorical but quite hierarchical ranking of different common types of religion in the so-called "perennial philosophy," of which Huston Smith is an eloquent advocate. We certainly should mention the highly influential comparison of different societies by Max Weber, which concludes that certain important changes in religion and its social embodiement occurred only in Western civilization. Whether these unique developments are to be regarded as "progress" is not clear. To be imprisoned in what Weber calls the "iron cage" of instrumental rationality hardly seems to put the modern person, religious or secular, on the highest rung of human evolution!

In Defence of Comparison

The various and sometimes conflicting approaches to the comparative study of religion in the last hundred years have not helped to give such study credence in other parts of the university. It is important to recognize that despite external disdain and internal self-criticism, many scholars in the general history of religion recognize that comparison is fundamental, not just to the study of religion but to all understanding. Lawrence Sullivan states this succinctly: "All understanding passes through the travail of comparison, conscious or not."[10] In another publication Jonathan Smith puts this even more emphatically and applies it to all thinking: "The process of comparison is a fundamental characteristic of human intelligence . . . [and] is the omnipresent substructure of human thought. Without it, we could not speak, perceive, learn, or reason."[11]

Smith intends his critical analysis to set the stage for his own distinctive approach to comparative studies. He believes that the systematic study of religion necessarily involves comparison, but that this must be of a kind that takes differences as seriously as similarities and that seeks to ground comparison on some scientifically verifiable pattern rather than on impression or intuition. "We have yet to develop the responsible alternative," he concludes, "the integration of a complex notion of patterns and systems with an equally complex notion of history."[12]

We can accept this statement of the daunting task confronting comparative students of religion, and yet see our effort, not as a rejection, but

[10] See *Icanchu's Drum: An Orientation to Meaning in South American Religions* (New York: Macmillan, 1988), 19.

[11] From "Adde Parvum Parvo Magnus Acervus Erit," in *History of Religions 11* (1972): 67.

[12] Smith, *Imagining Religion*, 29.

as a further development of the less sophisticated comparisons of the past. Jonathan Smith's analysis suggests that previous scholars have begun with "the recollection of similarity" and that efforts of some later scholars to make their comparisons less arbitrary and more systematic have led them to ground their systems in some particular philosophical or theological position. Their approach is then bound to appear unscientific to those who do not share their philosophical or religious commitment. We think it would be better to acknowledge the traveler's impressionistic comparison of new observations with what is known back home as the beginning of an expansion in human understanding. "Scientific" comparison is not an alternative to this, but only a refinement of the comparison after closer scrutiny, with ongoing reflection concerning the basis of the perceived similarity or difference.

To the extent that one continues to think in one's own language, this understanding through comparison is an informal translation. If one is describing one's experience abroad to those back home, the translation must be more systematic. In fact, such letters and reports are the beginning of the modern comparative study of religion. Sometimes they have been supplemented by translations in the strict sense of stories, poems, laws, or other verbal materials from the foreign culture. Christian missionaries have often engaged in translation in the opposite direction, of Christian scriptures, catechisms, liturgies, or "lives of the saints." Most of the translation in both directions has been done without any explicit theory as to why such translation is possible between very different languages and very different cultures. To the extent that a theory was developed, it was an affirmation of certain universals in human culture. Thematic courses focus on one or another of such presumed universals, or, in the case of features shared by some religious traditions but not by all, certain striking commonalities. It is these less than universal similarities that are often most intriguing and have led to the most speculation concerning causes for the similarity, which is sometimes ascribed to historical influences, sometimes to similar developments of a common psychological potential, sometimes to Divine governance of all people or preparation of the "nations" for the Gospel.

Comparison is implicit in the modern study of religion because we use "religion" as a generic concept, assuming that religion in general is exemplified and articulated in specific "religions." Even the study of one religious tradition, by considering that tradition *religious*, presumes some comparability with other religious traditions. The concept implies a universal or potentially universal feature of human culture that we call *religion.* Whether or not religion really is universal, the idea of religion as universal is Western in its origin and development and relatively modern in its present connotations.

The appropriateness of religion as a defining category comes from its exemplification of an important feature of Western Christian language, which is filled with terms that point in two directions: to their pre-Christian usage in Greek or Latin and also to their newer Christian meaning. It was precisely this two-sidedness that made these terms so useful for the Roman Catholic missionaries in the sixteenth and seventeenth centuries as they attempted to describe for those in Europe the religious life of the vast range of people they were encountering in other parts of the world. Occasionally a non-Western term like *tabu* or *karma* has entered the general vocabulary of comparative religion, but on the whole it has been assumed that the basic categories of religious life and thought, including the category of religion itself, are rightly designated by their Western names. Wilfred Smith has shown in *The Meaning and End of Religion* how Western and how relatively recent our modern concept of religion is.[13] Once that is clear, however, we may be too easily inclined to regard our unconscious assumption as an unwarranted presumption and to treat the entire thematic comparison of religious categories as an exercise in futility.

Comparative research encounters the same kind of resistance wherever progress is deemed easier if research is limited to one area of similar data. There is greater difference between fields concerning the teaching of comparative courses, depending on whether those teaching in the field are confident that there is a genuinely common aspect of many or all cultures, for example, literature or economic activity, whose several manifestations can be compared. Even if there is such commonality, however, we need to ponder the question that Wilfred Smith has raised: whether our present conception of the field and way of studying it accords with the genuinely common element.

All such comparisons, moreover, involve the recognition of differences as well as similarities, and the comparison becomes interesting when both the similarities and the differences are shown to be important. We suggest that academically significant comparison is more likely to occur when it is not clear at the outset whether the similarities or the differences are more important; there is therefore something worth investi-

---

[13] Wilfred Cantwell Smith, *The Meaning and End of Religion: A New Approach to the Religious Traditions of Mankind* (New York: Macmillan, 1962). See especially Chapter 2, "'Religion' in the West," pp. 15-50, and the notes to Chapter 2, pp. 203-245.

gating. To investigate this question does not mean that it is easy to find an answer. Indeed, as one gets into a subject, one may discover differences where one had first seen only similarities, or one may discern some significant commonality beneath more obvious differences. To convey to students this sense of reversal or "doubletake" in the course of comparative investigation, is part of what it means for the teacher to "make the strange familiar and the familiar strange." Like any other investigation of human culture, we are seeking to understand ourselves as human beings, and thus we are personally involved in the study we undertake. We, as well as our readers, are engaged in what George E. Marcus and Michael M. J. Fischer have called a "prolonged, dialectic discourse about the open-ended nature of similarities and differences."[14] They go on to say:

> Difference in the world is no longer discovered, as in the age of exploration, or salvaged, as in the age of colonialism and high capitalism, but rather must be redeemed, or recovered as valid and significant, in an age of apparent homogenization and suspicion of authenticity, which, while recognizing cultural diversity, ignores its practical implications.[15]

There is no classroom answer to the question of whether similarity or difference is more important, for religious people define their own religious position by the stance they take about the relation of their religious traditions to other traditions. They may, for example, affirm the validity of only one specific kind of pilgrimage, or they may recognize the validity of certain practices or beliefs in other religious communities only if they share specific common elements. To the extent that teachers and students engaged in the comparative study of religion are themselves religious people, they are so in practice by their participation in particular religious communities and are thereby actively or passively involved in their communities' ongoing work of self-definition. Those teachers and students who do not consider themselves members of some specific religious community do not thereby gain some kind of scholarly objectivity, for they, too, have implicitly or explicitly taken a stand with respect to those most basic issues with which religious people are concerned: the ordering of their lives and the meaning of their death.

Later we shall return to the connection between academic comparison and theology (including theological ethics). Here we want rather to stress the distinction between them and the limitation of what can be achieved in academic comparison of religious phenomena. Academic students of

---

[14] See their seminal study *Anthropology as Cultural Critique: An Experimental Moment in the Human Sciences* (Chicago: University of Chicago Press, 1986), 161.
[15] Ibid., 167.

religion need to study closely things that may appear to theologians and philosophers of various religious communities to be only at the surface of the religious life. Many religious communities have set up elaborate qualifications of competence and restrictions on participation, believing that it is necessary to accept the tradition intellectually, and to undergo purification of what the tradition considers spiritually defiling. This is necessary if both ritual action within the community and knowledge of its traditions are not to be counter-productive and even dangerous. Some communities are apparently much more open than others, but in no case does either taking or teaching a class in comparative religion in a modern university meet the minimum requirements of religious participation and religious seriousness. To the religious people whose beliefs and actions we are discussing, our classroom procedure will look like treading on holy ground without removing our shoes!

We can and should exercise greater respect towards other people's sacred objects than has often been shown, and we may well develop an interest in a particular religious path that is personal as well as academic, but many of us have been asked difficult questions, such as "How can you understand this text if you do not commit yourself to its message?" or "How can you understand the path of purification if you continue to eat meat?" The definition of our comparative enterprise makes it necessary for us to seek to penetrate religious worlds to which we ourselves do not belong, and we therefore need to recognize that the kind of understanding we seek will be different from the faith or wisdom presumed or sought in every religious tradition. Traditional members of most of the religious communities we study more and more recognize that academic understanding does have its own legitimacy, one that does not depend on achieving religious wisdom. Not surprisingly, however, they consider such academic understanding very preliminary. We need not dispute that reaction now, for we have plenty of work ahead of us to reach even such preliminary understanding.

Even if the largest and most profound questions concerning the relative importance of similarities and differences cannot be answered, there are many smaller comparative questions that can and must be answered in order for intercultural understanding to take place.

All intercultural and interreligious translation has to weigh similarities and differences. Comparative religion can and should clarify a process of translation that we observe throughout human history, and in which we ourselves are engaged. This is a process in which one term is translated by another considered more similar than different, yet the differences are remembered in the subsequent interpretation and sometimes a better translation is proposed. Cultural "translation" (adaptation) is a similar ongoing process through which religious traditions maintain continuity while continuing to change.

All study of religion is at least minimally comparative because "religion" and the related cluster of concepts intend to be generic terms cutting across cultural and religious boundaries. It is also comparative as part of the total effort of inter-human understanding and communication. In both the listening and the speaking to one another we experience the connection between self and other but also the major and minor disruptions of that connection, sometimes so major as to appear an unbridgeable gulf between societies. Certainly the religious dimension of our common life is one in which barriers and misunderstandings are rife, and therefore the conscious effort to remove misunderstanding (the analysis of which we call hermeneutics) must address the questions of similarities and differences in the religious sphere. Where either the objective or the subjective pole of understanding is overemphasized this comparative aspect of understanding may be obscured. Much understanding, including much study of religion, purports to be a purely objective knowledge of the data unaffected by the subjects seeking to be understood. It is possible, however, to go to the other extreme and see the entire structure of knowledge as a vast cavern of solipsism, in which the most distant sounds prove to be only echoes of oneself. It is when the continuing interplay between self and other is recognized as fundamental to the problem of understanding that the comparative task in understanding becomes most evident.

The Range of Comparative Themes

Ken Folkert objected that we had chosen our initial "themes" without agreeing on a classification of religious phenomena. He considered "healing" an example of such arbitrary choice of "whatever turns you on and is momentarily relevant," and thought our original list was "a hodge-podge" of courses, a collection that seemed to represent the worst sort of outcome possible from hanging on to an outdated and empty rubric, viz., "comparative religion." While that initial decision did not include an attempt to rank "religions," he thought our choices showed that "we do a good deal of subjective or habitual selection of topics about which to be comparative, and these topics represent our own theological or cultural personal biases." To avoid these weaknesses Ken Folkert designed a course in which students are asked, to think not about "religion" or "religions," but to look for "religiousness" . . . [which] I leave as undefined as possible. Instead I ask them to try to see the world as if they were visitors from another planet, who do *not* know what "religion" is, know only that they are looking for certain patterns of human activity.

To define these patterns, he asked his students to look out for a special set of persons, special clothing, special language, special acts involving food, and utilization of special places. Doing so produces a range of subject matter, "from the eucharist to athletic events, and notably, rites of passage themselves." The course therefore does not deal with concepts, such as ideas of God or paths to salvation, which are "enormously complex translations of specific linguistically and culturally shaped terms into a generic term drawn from residential theology," a kind of comparison that he calls "a particularly vicious form of reductionism." The focus of his course on "rites of passage" in the life-cycle is intended to provide students with "a set of occasions that . . . represent as nearly as anything a pan-human experience" and that "range from events more directly associated in students' experience with formal religious institutions (e.g., marriage and funerals) to events whose major features are more outside of such institutions, e.g., childbirth." The course uses van Gennep's and Turner's concept of liminality to explicate the individual's or group's sense of "reality" or "identity." The course's basic theme is the relation between religiousness and "reality," understanding religiousness as the engagement in, or rejection of, ordering and structuring the raw fact(s) of existence." Life-cycle rituals and the calendar both illustrate this structuring process. Liminal states are those in which the structure is threatened and must be restored. The rituals for such purposes make much use of the boundary situation of the physical body: the openings between the body and the ouside world through which substances enter or leave the body. Ken Folkert wants us to distinguish "comparisons that are based on conceptual and reflective material . . . and comparison that is based as much as possible on observable activity," even though "these two are not finally separable."

We have pondered Ken Folkert's critique throughout the project. Tom Peterson discusses it explicitly in his essay. He approves of Ken's warning against the reductionism that can result from organizing material around some themes that happen to interest us, but he points out that Ken is accepting van Gennep's assumption of a cross-cultural constant: that points of transition between stages in the life cycle are in all cultures experienced as threatening.

Tom Peterson goes on to say that even if this assumption is frequently validated, organizing "our study of another people's religion around rites of passage" does not free us from bias. This central focus works better to interpret the Brahmanical stages of life than the ritual activity of the Lakotas. It is in any case a Western sociological category that we are utilizing, and we may have our own subjective reasons for emphasizing rites of passage. "Perhaps we wish to know how other people move from childhood to adulthood precisely because we handle it so poorly in our own culture." Tom Peterson concludes his response to Ken Folkert by suggesting that our own values and concerns can be minimized in comparative study, but not eliminated. Even to minimize them, however, we need first to acknowledge them. Indeed, it may be more honest to recognize implicit comparison and "to organize courses explicitly around them, thereby subjecting our assumptions to scrutiny." We should try to choose a theme that will not impose an alien structure but will "help us tease out some significant aspects of human life."

This final point reminds us of both aspects of Ken Folkert's essay: it challenges us to the self-scrutiny necessary to avoid imposing our own conceptions on other people's experience but also to the imaginative teaching that helps our students get beyond the bizarre to a genuine "pan-human experience." Ken Folkert left us with a strongly-felt and even harshly-worded warning, but has given us hope for new and greater insight, transcending our own cultural particularity, into our common human condition. This insight, he believed, could be developed systematically into a new anthropology for comparative study.

We believe that there is no limited set of themes that alone are appropriate for a comparative course. Each theme presents its own distinctive challenges as a focus for comparison. In using a theme we assume its cross-cultural nature, but it is suggested by some specific religious phenomenon of which other phenomena remind us. The themes that interest us—and our students—depend on the current state of scholarship, on the impingement of current cultural issues, as well as on personal interests. In previous generations certain forms of Western religion were easily assumed by Western scholars to be universal. It is also possible, however, to focus on a non-Western religious phenomenon whose Western analogy is not so clearly religious. To some extent this is true of Ken Folkert's choice of life-cycle ceremonies for a class of students with an American Protestant background, for whom the secular rite of passage in getting a driver's license may be more of a ritual event than any church ceremony. His course may well remind American students that what is of basic religious importance to so many people elsewhere in the world is for them in North America part of a non-religious dimension of their lives.

When we consider the theme of healing, we come to a similar realization, but with healing, what is now for most Westerners something quite secular has had profound religious significance for earlier generations of Christians and continues to be of religious significance for Christians elsewhere in the world, especially in cultures where healing is closely connected with transhuman powers who can bring curse or blessing. In recent centuries sacrifice and pilgrimage, too, have become more secular than religious; in most Protestant Christianity they have turned into metaphors, leaving the blood sacrifice of war and the pilgrimage of tourists on the edge of what is considered religious. In all these cases the effect of comparative study is to retrieve for current Westerners, at least in their scholarly imagination, something that is no longer central to Western religiosity, especially to those forms of Western religiousness that confine the religious to the spiritual, the moral, or the transcendent realm. Whether we proceed from the familiar to the strange, or from the strange to the familiar, we are engaged in a process of discovery, a journey of exploration, which ought to be a genuine intellectual experiment. Indeed, the excitement of this kind of course should be enhanced by some uncertainty about the outcome. Each new consideration of a theme should include the possibility of a real surprise, that familiar categories cannot be made to fit, or conversely, that something fits—like Cinderella's slipper—when least expected!

The themes included in this volume, as we noted in the Introduction, have in most cases been used in courses by our particular team of contributors. Other teachers might well have presented quite different courses. Even so, it should be obvious that the range of subject matter as well as our current manner of treatment is significantly different from that in the heyday of comparative religion almost a century ago. We may have learned something from the mistakes that gave such comparison a bad name, but to some extent the topics we avoid may simply reflect our unwillingness to deal with themes that seem to support a seventeenth century Christian orthodoxy, an eighteenth century rational theism, or a nineteenth century cultural evolutionism. Perhaps both comparative theology and comparative ethics can once again be the subject matter of thematic courses.

The feature that most distinguishes our comparative approaches from those of a century ago is our studious effort to avoid evaluative comparisons in the classroom. Lee Yearley's account of how he has revised his own successful course does raise some troubling questions about the relation between our theoretical intentions and the actual effect of our courses on the students who take them. We may even need to ask whether comparison is necessarily evaluative. If not, does our moral responsibility to our students require that we acknowledge or even encourage evaluative as well as non-evaluative comparison? The new version of Lee Yearley's course encourages students to moral and religious choices. Can such choices be made by a rational weighing of alternative worldviews, or are there non-rational factors affecting the students' view to such an extent as to make the appearance of rational choice in the classroom illusory?

These same issues ought to become explicit in courses on comparative religious ethics. There is a strong Enlightenment strain in our academic tradition that assumes that the choice of a particular religious faith is non-rational, but that the choice as well as the application of ethical values is completely rational. Is such a distinction between theological and ethical decisions justifiable? It may be more realistic to bring to light moral issues arising in a variety of cultures, some given a new form in the modern world, and to present the resources within different religious and philosophical traditions for dealing with these issues. Richard Carp takes the position, not only that different religious commitments cannot be reconciled, but that they are all opposed to the commitment claims of the academy. He believes that the mutual critique of these different commitments ought to be maintained in the classroom.

Comparative courses that attempt to be neutral need to be supplemented in our total curriculum by courses that openly proceed from a particular religious stance and try to develop its implications. At a time when all teaching assumed certain norms it was important to restrain normative judgments in the effort to understand another point of view or style of life. In certain circumstances that may still be the case, but Lee Yearley has vividly reminded us that a successful course presenting religious pluralism may reinforce the students' "bourgeois relativism," thus protecting our middle class American culture's "ethic" of success from any trenchant moral critique.

The dialogical spirit whose importance is increasingly recognized in our comparative scholarship requires both imaginative understanding of others and intelligible communication of one's own convictions. Normative approaches are needed, not to substitute for but to supplement our efforts at neutrality in the history and phenomenology of religions.

Cooperation in Comparison

Why has the phenomenal growth in the number of historians of religions and the improvement in their specialized training not led to comparable progress in the comparative study of religious themes? We might respond that our standards for viewing each religious phenomenon in its own cultural context have become so high that only a few intellectual giants in each generation can hope to know enough about even two subjects to compare them responsibly. That response, however, accepts as self-evident the individualistic notion of scholarly achievement that the study of religion shares with the rest of the humanities. From the first essay in grade school to the scholarly monograph, the emphasis is on "doing it by myself." Even the long footnotes and extensive bibliographies exposing our utter dependence on so many other scholars do not lead us to question the appropriateness of putting a single name under the title: our own. Here the humanities could well learn from the current practice of the natural sciences. Many scientific papers now list multiple authors because scientists have become convinced that worthwhile scholarship is too multifaceted for a single scholar to undertake, even with the assistance of giant computers. Why should we suppose that really worthwhile projects in the study of religion would be any less multifaceted or require the cooperation of a smaller company of scholars? Perhaps we have become more concerned with manageable projects in which it is possible to evaluate individual contributions than with working together on a grand design that, like some medieval cathedrals, quite dwarfs in space and time the individual participants.

Sometimes a thematic course can be taught collaboratively, and sometimes it may be possible to include a lecture by a colleague in a different field. More often the cooperation such a course requires can only be suggested by the reading list. Cooperation need not imply a lack of individual responsibility; it is motivated by a conviction that this is a project that no one person could carry out alone, a project that depends on the contribution of all. In these courses we are exploring our common humanity; we share our human diversity in recognizing the act of exploration as a collective enterprise.

Cooperation in comparison should not be limited to the relation among scholars; it should also characterize the relation between teachers and students. Students too, should be expected to contribute to the comparative project, for their range of relevant experience may complement that of their instructor. Not every piece of research or every course need be explicitly comparative, but in the study of religion there should always be a comparative question: why is this subject part of the study of religion? Thematic courses need to enable students to join with their teachers in feeling the force of that comparative question, as well as to join a vast company of inquirers stretching out beyond Western academia, back into the rich traditions of the past, and perhaps forward into the future as well.

A third dimension of scholarly cooperation should also not be forgotten. In the many translation projects that contributed so much to the development of comparative religion, and in so many research projects right down to the present day, those whom we seek to understand have become our teachers, a fact somewhat obscured when they are called "native informants"! Often that instruction is given with great patience and sometimes with considerable laughter at the outside inquirer's mistakes.[16] In a classroom at a great distance in time or space from the field of research it is easy to forget that most vital comparison is an exchange between living persons. Here the discovery of similarities and difference takes place on both sides, in a serious exchange that has a place for humor.

It is true that past cooperation in pursuit of understanding has often been onesided and exploitative. Usually both sides have a variety of motives, but whatever the motives, cooperation between people of different cultures is important even for determining kinship patterns or verb forms. It is indispensable as the translation process proceeds and the participants struggle over subtle shades of meaning. To bring the excitement of such cooperative learning through comparison to the classroom is a worthy goal of our teaching, which is also our cooperative learning as teachers and students.

Comparison in Historical Encounter

One of the objections to using a thematic approach in our teaching is that it seems to require us to separate one aspect of a religious or cultural complex from all that surrounds it and contributes to its meaning. That objection may have some force in an introductory course, especially when it is important for students to gain a sense of the unity of a tradition or a cultural whole. It is, however, just as necessary to focus the mind on a limited object when we follow the so-called historical approach, which in our survey courses has to be so sketchy that it is in fact a brief examination of the same cluster of themes in a variety of religious

---

[16] Lamin Sanneh has given many amusing examples in his *Translating the Message: The Missionary Impact on Culture* (Maryknoll, New York: Orbis, 1989).

traditions. One theme that could usefully be explored is each religious community's *concept* of history, not to try to show that history is only a concept, but to examine the lens with which we claim to work most fruitfully, since we call what we do the *history* of religion or religions.

In the actual process of scholarly discovery, to focus on a particular theme is not to ignore history. It is rather to recognize that two communities' histories, and possibly their diverse concepts of history as well, are intersecting in a new historical encounter, in which persons on both sides grope for some common categories to communicate and understand one another as human beings. Modern scholarship has produced growing stacks of monographs, surveys, and analyses, yet the situation in our classrooms, as in the world outside, has not progressed far beyond the awkwardness, the fascination, and sometimes the terror of the first moment of intercultural encounter. It is not yet clear whether we are beginning a common religious history, or whether our significant communal histories will insist on their continuing separateness. The understanding of one another's histories that we seek requires us to make distinctions, but it also gives us the opportunity to make connections. As we pursue particular themes in comparative study, we can extend to our classrooms this opportunity to participate in the vital task of understanding.

In the passage quoted at the beginning of this chapter, Louis Dumont uses the fulcrum as a metaphor for comparison. He suggests that modern civilization's knowledge of other cultures can provide the weight on the other side of the fulcrum to lift our understanding of modern civilization. Such comparison reverses the direction of the most naive comparison, which seeks to understand the alien by identifying similarities with what is more familiar to us. Certainly Dumont's more recent studies, emphasizing the contrast between traditional Hindu and modern Western ideals, focuses on understanding individualism and the ideal of equality in the modern West. In our present world, partly modern and partly traditional, where East and West increasingly overlap, both the "self" and the alien "other" need to be understood in their relation to one another.

The Institute at Harvard was given some insight into the complexities of such mutual understanding through an opening lecture by Dr. J. L. Mehta, emeritus Professor of Philosophy at Banaras Hindu University and for much of the decade up to 1979 Visiting Professor at the Harvard Center for the Study of World Religions. As it turned out, this was his last lecture, for he died less than a month later in Cambridge, after a heart attack. In his life and writings Dr. Mehta exemplified comparative reflection consciously situated in the midst of a specific historical encounter. He spoke of our "hermeneutic situation" as one full of new possibilities but also "a gnawing experience of vacuity and absence."[17] The dominant and affluent "West reaches back to its own religious past and out to more tradition-bound cultures" to meet "its own religious needs." India does the same, but in its own distinctive way. Dr. Mehta said that his own experience included "the double movement of understanding," seeking "to understand the West by attending to its philosophical tradition" and reaching for self-understanding "back again to the religious texts of my own tradition . . . reflectively appropriating it from the perspective of my participation in the 'world civilization' of the present."[18] Dr. Mehta used the Harvard Institute's themes of Pilgrimage and Scripture to challenge us to think of ourselves as fellow pilgrims with those whose pilgrimages and scriptures we seek to study. He asked us to imagine a group of Hindu pilgrims of diverse backgrounds setting out together on foot to a major shrine in the Himalayas:

> Their Scripture gives meaning to the pilgrimage and the latter in turn transforms a shadowy mass of words into a source of meaning in life, of which now the whole purpose may be seen to lie in discovering at last what that Scripture means in relation to the life to which it has given such fullness of meaning. Not until living itself is transformed into a pilgrimage, which is nothing if not living in the face of death, one's own, does Scripture disclose its sovereign majesty, become truly Scripture. We scholars play around with words, study them, maneuver them, and torture them, do things to them. But our pilgrimage through words is not pilgrimage until words begin to do things to us and to become the Word by which we live. *Then* Scripture begins to disclose its meaning, the meaning of *our* life and, with luck, the unity of these sorts of meaning as the end of our quest.[19]

---

[17] Mehta quoted in "Problems of Understanding," a public address delivered on June 13, 1988, printed in *Bulletin: Center for the Study of World Religions* 15:1 (1988-89): 5.

[18] Ibid., 6.

[19] Ibid., 12.